Early

KENTUCKY

Tax Records

Early

KENTUCKY

Tax Records

From The Register of the
Kentucky Historical Society

With an Index by Carol Lee Ford

CLEARFIELD

Reprinted for
Clearfield Company, Inc. by
Genealogical Publishing Co., Inc.
Baltimore, Maryland
1999, 2001

Excerpted and reprinted from *The Register
of the Kentucky Historical Society,*
with added Publisher's Note, Contents, and Index,
by Genealogical Publishing Co., Inc., Baltimore, 1984.
Copyright © 1984 by Genealogical Publishing Co., Inc.
Baltimore, Maryland. All Rights Reserved.
First printing 1984
Second printing 1987
Library of Congress Catalogue Card Number 83-82825
International Standard Book Number 0-8063-1067-7
Made in the United States of America

Note

———————=➤⟨❈⟩⟨❈⟩⟨❈⟩⬅=———————

A MONG THE MANY historic documents that were lost when the
British burned the Capitol in Washington during the War of
1812 were the first two censuses of Kentucky, the earliest one com-
piled while Kentucky was still a part of Virginia. Owing to the
destruction of these census records, genealogists doing research in
Kentucky have been obliged to reconstruct the lost data from a
number of related records, in particular, tax records. Indeed, of
the numerous records used as substitutes in reconstructing the
1790 and 1800 censuses, tax records are clearly the most important.
Like census records, they have the distinction of placing people in
a particular location at a definite time and identifying them in rela-
tion to their households and property. Those printed here represent
all the tax lists ever published in *The Register of the Kentucky
Historical Society* and are among the earliest Kentucky tax records
in existence.

In a few cases these tax records date from a period either imme-
diately before or after the 1790 and 1800 enumerations, and show,
by comparison with the *reconstructed* census records of 1790 and
1800, published by Charles B. Heinemann and G. Glenn Clift
respectively, the movement of early Kentuckians from one county
to another. In other cases the records serve both as an adjunct and
a corrective to the Heinemann and Clift works, though the vast
majority of the tax lists—giving the names of taxpayers, their
counties of residence, and the number of persons and chattels
attached to their households—do not appear in either work.

The consolidation and reprinting of these tax lists will not only
assure their continued survival but, owing to the scarcity of the
Register itself, will afford the researcher access to materials otherwise well out of his reach. As a matter of convenience the lists are
reproduced here without any changes but with an index to the
whole to assist the researcher in his quest for names.

Genealogical Publishing Company

Contents

Early
$\mathcal{K}$ENTUCKY
Tax Records

DEPARTMENT OF STATE ARCHIVES
Campbell County
(Copied from Original Parchment Enrolled Bill in State Archives)

An Act for forming a new county from the counties of Harrison, Scott and Mason.

Sec. I—*Be it enacted by the General Assembly* that from and after the tenth day of May next, all those parts of the Counties of Harrison, Scott and Mason within the following bounds, towit: beginning on the Ohio at the mouth of Locust creek on the lower side thereof; thence a straight line to the mouth of the north fork of licking; thence by a direct line to the mouth of Crooked creek, on the south fork of Licking; thence up said Crooked creek to the head of the main branch thereof; thence west to the dividing line between the counties of Scott and Woodford; thence along that line to the mouth of Big Bone lick creek, on the Ohio river; thence up the Ohio river to the beginning, shall be one distinct county, and be called and known by the name of Campbell.

Sec. 2—The Courts of quarter Session shall be held on the first Mondays of January, March, July and October in every year and the County Courts shall be held on the first Monday of every month in which the Court of Quarter Sessions is not by this Act directed to be held.

Sec. 3—The Justices to be named in the Commission of the Peace for the said County of Campbell shall meet at the house of John Grant in town of Wilmington in the said County upon the first Court day after the division shall take place and having taken the oaths prescribed by law and the Sheriff being legally qualified to act, the Justices shall proceed to fix upon a place to hold Courts in the said County at such place as shall be deemed most eligible and convenient and thenceforth the County Court shall proceed to erect the Public Buildings at such place, and until such Buildings are completed the Court of Quarter Sessions and County Court may adjourn to such place or places as they may severally think proper. And the Justices of the Court of quarter Sessions at their first Session and also the Justices of the County Court at their first Court shall proceed to appoint and qualify their Clerks. Provided always the appointment of a place to erect public buildings shall not be made unless the majority of the Justices of the County concur, nor of a Clerk unless a majority of the Justices of the Court for which the Clerk is to be appointed concur, but such appointments shall be postponed until such majority can be had. It shall be lawful for the Sheriffs of Harrison, Scott and Mason Counties to make distress for any public dues or officers fees unpaid by the inhabitants within their respective bounds at the time such division shall take place: and they shall be accountable in like manner as if this Act had not been made.

1

Sec. 4—The Courts of the Counties of Harrison, Scott and Mason, shall have jurisdiction in all Actions and Suits depending therein at the time of said division, and they shall try and determine the same, issue process and award execution in the same manner as if this Act had not been made.

Sec. 5—This Act shall commence from and after the tenth day of May next.

Ro. BRECKINRIDGE, Spea. H. Rep.

ALEXR. S. BULLITT, Spea. of the Senate

Approved December 17th 1794

ISAAC SHELBY, Governor
of Kentucky

FIRST COURTS OF CAMPBELL COUNTY
(Extracts from Executive Journal)

December 19, 1794

The Governor nominated and by and with the Advice and Consent of the Senate made the following appointments:
* * *
John Craig, Washington Berry and Charles Daniel, Justices of the Court of Quarter Sessions for Campbell County—

John Roberts, John Cook, Robert Benham, Phillip Bush, James Little, Thomas Kennedy and Samuel Bryant, Justices of Campbell County.

Squire Grant Surveyor, and Nathan Kelly Sheriff of Campbell County.

December 19, 1795—

The Governor nominated and by and with the Advice and Consent of the Senate made the following appointments:

John Bush, Henry Brashier, John Hall, James Miller, Squire Grant and John Ewing, Justices of Campbell County.

December 21st, 1795—

The Governor appointed Squire Grant Lieutenant-Colonel Commandant; James Little and John H. Craig; Majors of the 21st Regiment.

CAMPBELL COUNTY, ORDER BOOK No. 1

June 1, 1795—

"At the house of John Grant in the Town of Wilmington the Justices met agreeable to Act of Last Session of the General Assembly—

Justices: John Craig, Washington Berry, Charles Daniel, John Roberts, John Cook, Robert Benham, James Little, Thomas Kennedy, Samuel Bryan and Samuel Bush.

James Taylor, Clerk; Nathan Kelly, Sheriff; Squire Grant, Surveyor.

Ordered—that Newport at the Confluence of the Ohio & Licking Rivers be fixed on as the place for holding Court of this County in the future.

Letters of Administration granted Rebecca Campbell; widow of Colin Campbell, her late husband.

John P. Smith licensed to practice law.

Leave granted John Waller to build water-grist-mill & saw-mill in Town of Falmouth.''

DEED BOOK A—CAMPBELL COUNTY

Page 1½—

September 1, 1795—

James Taylor, Senior, of the County of Caroline, State of Virginia, to John Roberts, John Cook, Robert Benham, James Little, Thomas Kennedy, Samuel Bryan & John Bush, Gents., Justices of Campbell County Court * * * * a parcel of Ground in the County of

Campbell & Town of Newport, containing One Acre & 152 square poles * * * and known as the "Public Square" for use of Public Buildings * * * in consideration of fixing of the Seat of Justice * * * one Shilling, &c.

"Campbell County, the 19th in order of formation, was erected in 1794 (Dec. 19th) out of parts of Mason, Scott and Harrison; and embraced so much territory that Pendleton, Boone, Kenton and part of Grant County have since been erected from it. * * * *

Names Chargeable With Tax	Total Blacks	Horses	Cattle	Acres	Water Course (or Town)	Town Lots
Allin, Benj.		2				1
Allen, Hiram		2	4		Wilmington	1
Archer, Benj.		1	10	190	Bartle Big Run	
*Acklelender,? Math.		1	3			
Ayres, Thomas			1			
Ashbrook, John		4	7	300	Licking	
*Arnold, William	5	5	13			
Ashcraft, Jediah		1	4	100	S. of Licking	
Aygleton, Wm.						
Anderson, Henry		2	18			
Anderson, John		1	11		Falmouth	2
Ashby, Bailie						
Arnold, Elisha						
Arnold, John						
Anderson, Wm.					Wilmington	2
Brasher, John						
*Brasher, Henry			3			
Berry, Washington	17	4	2	1,000	Ohio River	
Bartle, John		1	19	886	Licking	
Belveal, Samuel			10			
Barrackman, Jacob		2	6			
Benham, Robert	2	3	10	18		
Benham, Peter		1	2			
Ball, Zopher		1	4			
Barber, John			1			
*Bally, Groomsbright (?)			5			
Beal, John			4			
Boner, William		2	3	130	Licking	
Bostick, Truman			2	60	Licking 3 mile	
Buel (or Benvel), Timothy		1	5	100	Licking	
Broadberry, David		1	9	100	Licking	
Bracken, Jesse		2			Wilmington	1
Bracken, Jesse				150	Grassy Creak	
Boyd, John	2	5	21	300	Grassy Creak	
Boyd, John					Wilmington	2
Boner, Charles		2	13			
Boner, Barnard		2	7			
Boner, John		2	7			
*Burnes (?), Arthur		2	9			
Bryan, Samuel		5	22		Falmouth	3
Bowman, John		1				
Bush, John	4	3	15			
Brown, John						
Boyd, Joseph		3				
Bryan, Mary	1	3	6			
B. Bullet, Clxr.				2,770	South Fk. Licking	
Bryan, Samuel				1,400	Davis Fk. Elkhorn	
Christy, Robert			2			
Coleman, Philip			1			
Camron, Daniel		1	6			
Craig, Robert			7			
Colwell, Robert			3			
Colman, Coonrod						
Campbell, Simon						

4

Names Chargeable With Tax	Total Blacks	Horses	Cattle	Acres	Water Course (or Town)	Town Lots
Crain, William				25	Licking	
C———, Willm., Junr.						
Corwin, Kezias		2	3	100	East Fk. Grassy Creak	
Corwin, Joseph		1	4	100	East Fk. Grassy Creak	
Corwin, Mathias		6	15	450	East Fk. Grassy Creak	
Corwin, Mathias					Wilmington	1
Cook, John	3	1	5	500	Licking	
Cook, John					Falmouth	3
Cook, John				333½	Hinkston	
Cook, Samuel	1	3	9	115	S. Fk. Licking	
Cook, Samuel					Falmouth	1
Crow, John					Wilmington	1
Cox, Daniel			3			
Croshon, Jeremiah		1	4		Wilmington	1
Croshon, Jacob		2	5	150	South Fk. Licking	
Croshon, Jacob				10	South Fk. Licking	
Crook, Jeremiah			2			
Childers, Robert			5			
Childen, (or Childers)		1	3			
Comines, William				50	Miller Run	
Crytigh (?), Francis		2	6			
Cleavlan, Levi						
Corn, George		4	18	100	Ohio River	
Cox, John		2	1			
Coner, John						
Camell, Thomas	7	3	2			
Clowd, William						
Courter, Mathew		1	5			
Courter, William		1	5			
Campben, Rubeck		3	6			
Clark, Thomas						
Chambers, John						
Colby, Charles						
Clansy, Mathew						
Cail, Thomas		2	4			
Carter, Charles				384¾	Cabbin Creek	
Curd, Edmund					Wilmington	2
Clark, Wm.					Falmouth	1
Cunningham, John					Falmouth	1
Chinowith, Wm.					Falmouth	1
Day, Aaron						
Dogby, William		2	4			
Dehart, John						
Dewitt, William		1				
Davis, James			5			
Decoursey, Wm.		4	10	200	Licking	
Daniel, Vivion		1			Wilmington	2
Daniel, Charles	2	2	8			
Daniel, Wm.	1	2	9		Wilmington	1
Dawson, Keziah		1	3			
Darringer, Jacob		2	6	95	Blank Creek	
Donavan, John			5			
Dewitt, Walter						
Dewitt, Lewis						
Ducker, John				150	Licking	

Names Chargeable With Tax	Total Blacks	Horses	Cattle	Acres	Water Course (or Town)	Town Lots
Davids, George						
Dykes, Wm.					Falmouth	1
Edward, Wm.				73	Four Mile Ck.	
Edward, Cade		2	9	100	Four Mile Ck.	
Eastin, Achilles	6	2	5			
Egbert, Nicholas		2	4			
Ewing, John	1	7	7	424	S. Fk. Licking	
Egnew, Samuel			7			
Edmondson, Wm.					Wilmington	1
Fowler, Jacob						
Fargason, Israel						
Foster, Jacob				10		
Fowler, Edward				6		
German, William	1		3		Wilmington	1
Griffin, Thomas		2	8	100	Licking	
Griffin, Thomas					Wilmington	1
Griffin, Ebenezer		2	18	200	Licking	
Glaves, Mathew	1	3	11		Falmouth	1
Glaves, Mathew					Falmouth	1
Glovien, James						
Gremsley, James			8			
Gausney, Wm.						
Grant, Squire	3	3	17	1,500	Elkhorn (Fayette)	
Grant, Squire				500	N. Fk. Lick. (Mason)	
Grant, Squire				300	Dick Riv. (Murser)	
Grant, Squire					Wilmington	5
Garrett, William						
Gayle, John				1,100	Johnson's Fk.	
Grant, John					Wilmington	33
Garrett, Elie					Wilmington	1
Green, James					Falmouth	1
Hester, Martin		1	9			
Hammersley, James		3			Falmouth	1
Hunter, John			2			
Humes, Elzaphan	1	1	4			
Humes, John		3	8	100	S. Fk. Licking	
Humes, John, Junr.					Wilmington	1
Humes, Joel		1				
Humes, George		6	11	100	S. Fk. Licking	
Howard, James		1	5	100	Licking	
Hawk, John			3			
Hyfield, Jeremiah		2	8			
Hold, Zachariah		3	7			
Hagan, Edmund						
Hall, John	1	2	7	120	Ohio	
Hosley, James			3			
Hardy, Elijah						
Hardester, Hezekiah			2			
Hardester, Uriah		2	2			
Harvey, John			19	120	Ohio	
Harrison, Henry						
Harwood, John					Wilmington	7

6

Names Chargeable With Tax	Total Blacks	Horses	Cattle	Acres	Water Course (or Town)	Town Lots
Harrison, Nicholas					Falmouth	2
Hatton, Henry					Falmouth	3
Hendrick, George					Falmouth	1
Huddle, George					Falmouth	4
Hemdrick, George					Falmouth	1
Johnston, Andrew Thomas		1	8	80	Riffle Creak	
Johnston, James		3	10	50	Riffle Creak	
Johnston, James		1	7	115	S. Fk. Licking	
*Jones, John	3	5	7	400	Ohio River	
Jones, John		1	5			
Johnston, John		4	3			
Jones, James		7	12			
Jones, John			6			
Johnston, Richard		1	2			
Kelly, Nathan		2	13			
Kelley, Joseph		1	13	100	Four Mile	
Kelly, George		2	5	150	Riffle Creak	
Kalglasen, David			11			
Kaster, Coonrod			2			
Keenan, Patrack			5			
Kilgore, John		4	10	200	West Fk. Grassy Creak	
Korger, Michell		2		150	Blanket Creak	
King, Edward		3	8	100	S. Fk. Licking	
King, Edward					Falmouth	2
Koil, Robert (Kyle)		2	10	100	Licking	
Kiger, George						
Kiger, John						
*Kendal, Anthony		3	3	100	Johnston's Branch	
Kendal, Anthony					Falmouth	1
Kilgore, John					Wilmington	1
Kee, John					Wilmington	1
Kemp, Reuben					Falmouth	1
Kindal, Steaven					Falmouth	1
*Lindsey, Thomas		4	10	320	Bartle's Big Run	
Lewis, David		1	2			
Laughoy, William						
Ligett, Alexr.		4	18			
Lewmus (Loomis), Reuben						
Leatherman, Jacob						
Lancaster, Thomas						
Lee, Christopher			4			
Lowrin, John		2	21			
Lee, James						
Lindley, Zenos						
†Little, James		1	9	250		
Laysun, Hite						
Lite, Jacob		2	22			
Linard, Jesse			2			
Leach, Keturah				5,250	Licking	
Lindsey, Olliver					Falmouth	1
Lumley, Wm.					Falmouth	1

7

Names Chargeable With Tax	Total Blacks	Horses	Cattle	Acres	Water Course (or Town)	Town Lots
McClure, James		3	5			
McKinney, Jos.		2	4			
Mills, Jacob			1			
Marnahan, John		1	3			
Miller, John, Junr.	1	2	5			
Miller, John		1	2			
Montgomery, Wm.			7			
Miller, James		1	5			
Messick, John		2	6		Wilmington	1
McMurtry, James		1				
Montjoy, Alvin	9	6	9	300	S. Fk. Licking	
Montjoy, Alvin				333½	Hinkston Ck.	
Montjoy, Alvin					Falmouth	7
Marshall, Geo.						
McLanahan, Elijah		3	3		Falmouth	6
Mathews, Guy			1			
McLain,, Alexr.		3	11	510	S. Fk. Licking	•
McLain, Daniel		1	7			
McCormack, John						
Mathew, William		2	12			
McCollom, John, Jr.						
McCollom, John						
Martin, John		2	3			
Morris, Isaac		1	2			
McCollom, James						
Monroe, William		1	4			
Mooney, Joseph			4			
Mooney, Sam'l			1			
McCoy, Robert		6	16	66	Pleasant Run	
Markland, Richard	1	1	4	100	Ohio River	
Markland, Thomas		1	7	85	Sand Run	
Markland, Jonathan	4	2	4	70	Sand Run	
McMahan, John		1	8	40	Ohio River	
Mosby, Thomas						
McDonley, Alexr.						
Mathews, Chitister	1	5	7	35	Ohio River	
More, Benjamin	1	1	2			
More, Samuel					Falmouth	2
McClaland, Jas.			5			
McLaughlin, Henry			3			
McLaughlin, John						
McLanahan, John		5	10			
Monroe, Alexr.		3	9	250	S. Fk. Licking	
Mize, Isaac						
Mitchell, William			1			
McVicker, Duncan		1	1	50	Miller Run	
Murphey, Peter			2	66	Ohio River	
McCandlis, James		3	21	102	S. Fk. Licking	
Muse, George				1,006	Brasher's Creak	
McDugle, Robert					Falmouth	1
McDugle, Robert					Falmouth	2
Marshall, David					Falmouth	1
McFox (?), Joseph					Falmouth	1
Marshall, Jonathan					Falmouth	1
Mothershead, Mary					Falmouth	1

8

Names Chargeable With Tax	Total Blacks	Horses	Cattle	Acres	Water Course (or Town)	Town Lots
Nelson, Robert			5			
Neel, William		2	13			
Neel, Makall (?)						
Orsburn, Usual (?)			1			
Ogg, Thomas						
O'Donally, Cornelius						
Pollock, James			2			
Poynts, John						
Perry, Samuel		3	8	1,000	Ohio River	
Packston, Samuel		1			Wilmington	1
Pettet, Amos		1	2	100	Licking	
Pickle, Henry			4			
Patterson, James			7			
Peak, Asa	1		7			
Peak, Presley		1	9			
Peak, Thomas			11			
Parker, Steven						
Parres, Ezekiel		2	7		Wilmington	1
Quick, Tunas		1	11	100	S. Fork Licking	
Quick, Tunas					Falmouth	5
Quick, Connelius		1	3			
Quigley, Marshall		2	3			
Redick, Joseph			10			
Redick, Thomas						
Riffle, Jacob			3			
Reed, William			5			
Reynold, Charles		1				
Reynold, Jonah		1	9			
Rardon, Ann			6			
Rardon, Timothy		1	4			
Ross, Jonathan			7			
Reas, Thomas	1		10	100	Four Mile	
Roberds, John		3	4	250	Licking	
Roberds, John				520	Licking	
Rout, William	1	7	3			
Rout, George					Falmouth	2
Robertson, Joseph		1	6			
Roberson, Andrew					Wilmington	2
Roxven (?), Francis		3	7			
Ryle, Joseph	2		6			
Reynold, Geo.		2	4			
Reed, Archble		2	9			
Reedenour, John		4				
Rush, John						
Riggs, Bethwell		2	22			
Robertson, Joel		9	1			
Riddle, George					Falmouth	2
Sergents, Thomas			2			
Sheen, John						
Spencer, William		2	3			
Smith, John						

9

Names Chargeable With Tax	Total Blacks	Horses	Cattle	Acres	Water Course (or Town)	Town Lots
Stewart, Wm.			4		Wilmington	1
Shoohoon, Darley (Shawhan)		2	7			
Spencer, James			5			
Spencer, William						
Spencer, John		2	5			
Smith, William						
*Smith, David		1	8			
Spurgeon, Isaac		1	6			
Spurgeon, Ezekiel		1	2			
Stephens, Elizabeth	4	4	17	2,000	Four-mile Creek	
Sharp, James					Wilmington	1
Sharp, John						
Sharp, Richd.						
Sinkes, Jacob		2	7		Falmouth	1
Sinkes, Charles			3		Falmouth	1
Sinkes, Charles				100	Licking	
Stewart, Charles		2	1			
Seward, Daniel			4			
Stewart, John						
Stewart, John			4			
Stewart, Jesse		2	5			
Springer, Benj.		2	5			
Smith, Wm.						
Scott, Obediah						
Shurd, Cornelius		1	2			
Steares (?), Hugh		1	4			
Smith, Joseph						
Smith, James						
Smith, James						
Standerford, Geo.						
Smith, Henry						
Sanders, John	8	4	25	490	S. Fk. Licking	
Sanders, Henry					Wilmington	4
Sanders, John					Falmouth	4
Senior, Bryan				(In the State since the 10th of March.)		
Sconey, Henry					Falmouth	2
Sconey, Thomas					Falmouth	1
Taylor, James, Sr.				500	Ohio-Licking	
Taylor, James, Sr.	2	2	8	900	Ohio (Ferry)	
Tryon, Noah						
Trussle, Solomon		2	9			
Tompson, Closs		3	4			
Thrasher, Stephen		1		145		
Thrasher, John, Junr.		3	7	100	E. Fk. Grassy Ck.	
Thrasher, John, Junr.					Wilmington	1
Thrasher, John	1	4	17	200	E. Fk. Grassy Ck.	
Thrasher, John					Wilmington	2
Thrasher, Josiah		3	10	100	E. Fk. Grassy Ck.	
Thrasher, Josiah					Wilmington	1
Thatcher, Daniel		4	12	100	E. Fk. Grassy Ck.	
Thatcher, Daniel					Wilmington	1
Thatcher, Amos		1	3		Wilmington	1
Tebbs, James	6	7	9			
Turbet, William						
Turbet, Wm.					Falmouth	1

10

Names Chargeable With Tax	Total Blacks	Horses	Cattle	Acres	Water Course (or Town)	Town Lots
Turner, John						
Terry, Robert		1	6			
Tetrack, Jacob		2	6			
Taylor, John				2,000	Woolperts Ck. Bourbon Co.	
Tryon, Jeremiah						
Tendal, William		3	8			
Vance, Joseph						
Vanhook, Sam'l		1	5			
Vants, John				100	S. Fk. Licking	
Vants, John					Falmouth	1
Vanhorn, Ezekiel				216	Licking	
Vance, Samuel					Falmouth	2
Vooden, Henry						
Vooden, William						
Wilscn, James		1	6			
Wilson, Hill		1	4	150	Licking	
Wilson, Hill					Wilmington	2
Willson, William		2	3			
Willison, Richd.		3	4			
Welch, Edward			2			
White, Jacob		1	9			
Waller, John	1	2	8		Falmouth	12
Waller, John				450	Cabbin Ck.	
Waller, John				300	Licking	
Waller, John				333½	Hinkston	
Waller, John				9,090	Big Sandy	
Waller, John				5,000	Big Sandy	
Walls (or Watts), Thomas						
Walker, Andrew		4	6			
Williams, Ellison		2	5			
Williams, John		1	12			
Williams, James		1				
Williams, Alfred				50	McConnel's Run	
Winsor, Christopher			9			
Winsor, Thomas						
Weaver, Peter		4	8			
Welch, William		3	5			
Werrell, William	2	1	5			
Werrell, William, Junr.		1				
Wells, Thomas	1	1	2			
Weathers, Margaret				1,554	Big Sandy	
Wiley, John					Wilmington	4
Williams, Obediah					Falmouth	1
Washburn, Lewis					Falmouth	2
Zelent, Ezekiel						

*2 white males over 21.
†4 white males over 21.

Campbell County 15th of October 1795.

I do certify that this Book has been examined by the Original Vouchers as the Law directs and find they agreè.

Teste—

James Taylor, C. C. Ck.

DEPARTMENT OF STATE ARCHIVES — CHRISTIAN COUNTY TAX LISTS—1800.

Note by the Editor:—

Christian County was formed from Logan in 1796, and named in honor of Col. William Christian.

In 1798 the counties of Livingston and Henderson were formed from part of its territory. With this issue we publish the Tax List of Christian for 1800, and that for Livingston for 1799, which was returned with the books of the Commissioner of Christian County. The act creating the new county had provided that it was not to go into effect until there was a certain proportion of population to the extent of the territory.

It is the intention of the Editor to publish the earliest tax lists of Henderson County in the next issue of the Register, thus covering the territory originally included in Christian, except the part included in Muhlenberg. Subdivisions of all four counties have been made since 1800, but these can be easily traced by reference to Collins' History.

Auditor of Public Accounts, 1800.

John Campbell, Commissioner of Christian.

Persons Names Chargeable with the Tax	Acres Land	Water Course	Blacks	Horses
A				
Adams, Robert				
Alman, Thomas				5
Adams, Eliz'th				1
Adams, Drury	184	Little R.		2
Adams, James				1
Anderson, Charles	200	Spring Crk		4
Armstrong, Wm.	175	Little R.		4
Arthur, Thomas	200	Pond R.		3
Adams, Robert	200	Red R.		1
Atkinson, Joseph				3
Armstrong, Alex'r	200	Little R.	1	1
Adams, James	100	Red R.	3	2
Adams, Matt'w	200	Red R.	2	3
B				
Bradley, Sam'l	200	Little R.		
Bradley, Sam'l	200	Little R.		2
Bradley, Sam'l	200	Little R.		
Broom, William	200	Henderson Co., Pond R.		1
Butler, Edward				1
Barnett, Thomas	134	Pond R.		1
Blackburn, Wm.	200	Little R.	2	6
Black, David	200	Little R.		2

Persons Names Chargeable with the Tax	Acres Land	Water Course	Blacks	Horses
Black, David	200	Pond R.		
Barton, John				1
Bratcher, John	183	Pond R.		5
Bozorth, Abner	100	Little R.		3
Brown, Jeheue	200	Little R.		2
Brooks, Jessee	200	Red R.	5	6
Brooks, Jessee	200	Little R.		
Bowles, James	200	Little R.	1	4
Bowles, James	100	Little R.		
Black, Thomas	200	Little R.		2
Brandon, Charles	200	Little R.		4
Brandon, Charles	200	Little R.		
Bell, John				
Brown, Robert	200	Little R.	2	4
Burns, Peter	150	Little R.		1
Bosheers, Isaac				
Birdsong, Wm.			3	2
Birdsong, Shedruck	117	Little R.		3
Bullard, Joseph	150	Hays Crk.	3	4
Bax (or Box), Joseph	200	Little R.		1
Barnett, William, Jr.	200	Pond R.		
Barnett, James	200	Pond R.		
Burns, Equiller	200	Pond R.		1
Barnett, William, Sr.	200	Pond R.		2
Blaylock, Lewis				
Bredges, Waller	200	Pond R.		1
Bolinger, John				4
Betts, William	1,777⅔	Little R.		
C				
Campbell, John	200	Red R.		8
Cannan, James	200	Red R.	1	2
Campbell, James	150	Pond R.	5	1
Cheek, James	150	Pond R.		2
Clark, Benj'a	200	Little R.	6	2
Cain, Bailey				3
Cannon, William	100	Little R.	1	2
Campbell, Dan'l	200	Pond R.		8
Cemmons, Joseph				
Cortney, William				1
Castleberry, Paul				1
Campbell, Dan'l				
Caruthers, Wm.	100	Little R.		1
Campbell, Angus				
Caruthers, John, Jr.				1
Cortney, Wm.				1
Chapman, Willis	100	Pond R.		1
Clark, John	200	Pond R.		1
Campbell, Caty			1	
Caits, Joshua	200	Pond R.	2	3
Caits, Joshua	200	Red R.		
Caits, Joshua	200	Henderson Co., Deer Crk.		
Caits, Joshua	150	(Ch'n.) Red R.		
Caits, Joshua	200	(Hend'n) Deer Crk.		
Caits, Joshua	200	(Hend'n) Deer Crk.		
Cravens, Mary	200	Little R.	2	3

Persons Names Chargeable with the Tax	Acres Land	Water Course	Blacks	Horses
Cotton, Young				
Caits, Isaac				
Clark, Isaac	150	Red R.	1	6
Clark, Isaac	125	Warren Co., Big Barren		
Craig, John	200	Dollisons Crk.		2
Cawley, William				1
Colyer, David	200	Spring Crk.	1	5
Cook, James	200	Little R.		2
Cook, James	200	Little R.		
Cook, John	200	Little R.		
Cook, Reuben	175	Little R.	3	4
Cawley, Andrew, Jr.	200	Little R.		1
Cawley, Andrew, Jr.	200	Little R.		
Cawley, Jacob	200	Little R.		3
Coon, Benjamin	200	Little R.		
Clark, Jesse	100	Red R.		3
Campbell, James	200	Livingston Co., Cooks Crk		1
Cook, Silas	200	Little R.		1
Cornelius, Levy				2
Cravens, Jeremiah	200	Little R.	3	4
Caruthers, Sam'l				3
Costlow, John				
Cavanaugh, Wm.				
Cavanaugh, Chars.	200	Pond R.	1	3
Cup (or Cus), Henry	140	Little R.		2
Cravens, Robert	200	Little R.	1	5
Cravens, Robert	200	Little R.		
Cravens, Robert	100	Little R.		
Castley, William	100	Pond R.		1
Carpenter, Peter				
Colvan, John	200	Little R.		1
Cravens, Wm.	200	Little R.	2	3
Carpenter, Christian				1
Colvan, Job	200	Little R.		3
Cotton, John				
Cornelius, Jesse	100	Little R.		5
Caruthers, John	150	Little R.		2
Carpenter, Henry	135	Red R.		4
Coon, George	175	Little R.		1
Codry, John	200	Red R.	7	1
Codry, John	150	Red R.		
Clark, Henry, Jr.	200	Red R.	8	3
D				
Davidson, John	200	Red R.	5	12
Davidson, John	200	Red R.		
Dillingham, Vachel			4	3
Davis, Edwards	133	Little R.		7
Dillingham, Jas.	200	Little R.	1	1
Dupuy, James	100	Little R.		1
Dillingham, Michael	200	Little R.	2	3
Dillingham, Michael	175	Little R.		
Dupuy, David	100	Little R.		1
Doughlass, William	200	Pond R.		1
Deeson, John				2
Dawney, William	200	Pond R.		1

Persons Names Chargeable with the Tax	Acres Land	Water Course	Blacks	Horses
Davis, Jamis	1,120	Red R.	3	8
Davis, Jamis	120	Red R.		
Dryden, William	200	Little R.	3	7
Deeson, Samuel	150	Little R.	3	4
Deeson, Samuel	200	Little R.		
Dempsey, John	200	Hay's Crk.		1
Dempsey, John	200	Dollison's Crk.		
Davis, Hananiah				1
Davis, Josiah				1
Dempsey, Jeptha				1
Dickson, James	200	Dollison's Crk.		5
Davis, Jeremiah				
Davis, Isaac			1	1
Dyar, John	200	Little R.	2	6
Dempsey, William				4
Dickson, James				1
Davis, David				2
Davis, James				3
Deesan, John	200	Little R.		2
Davis, Azariah				2
Dillingham, Vachel, Sr.	200	Little R.	3	1
Davis, Clement	100	Pond R.		
Davis, Sam'l	200	Red R.	2	2
Downey, Josiah	120			3
Davis, Joseph	200	Hend'n, Tradewater	8	12
Davis, Joseph	200	Pond R.		
Davis, Joseph	200	Pond R.		
Dunlap, James				1
Dunlap, Moses	100	Pond Crk.		2
Dunlap, Benj'a	100	Pond Crk.		1
Dunlap, Wm.				2
Downey, Job.				3
Dupuy, Joseph	100	Little R.		1
E				
Ewing, Young	200	Red R.	7	5
Ewing, Young	200	Red R.		
Elkins, Joshua	200	Pond R.		3
Earl, Sam'l	200	Little R.	5	6
Earl, Sam'l	100	Little R.		
Evrett, William	200	Little R.	4	4
Estes, Asa	200	Little R.		4
Ewen, Sally	200	Red R.	4	2
Elliott, Thomas				1
F				
Fristoe, Daniel	200	Red R.		2
Fristoe, Daniel	200	Horse Creek		
Ferguson, Peter	495	Red R.	6	3
Ferguson, Peter	105	Tradewater		
Ferguson, Peter	200	Red R., Livingston Co. (?)		
Fort, Jesse			1	1
French, Simon	125	B. Barren, Warren Co.	1	3
French, Simon	180	Red R.		
Fewel, Henry				
Flemming, Wm.				

Persons Names Chargeable with the Tax	Acres Land	Water Course	Blacks	Horses
Fort, Micajah				1
Frame, John			1	5
Fryatt, Rob't	200	Little R.		1
Flemming, James	200	Little R.		1
G				
Griffith, Wells	200	Little R.	5	3
Griffith, Wells	122	Little R.		
Garretson, James				1
Gibbs, Sam'l	200	Logan Co., Muddy R.	1	2
Gibbs, Sam'l	200	(Ch'n) Red R.		
Gibbs, Sam'l	172	Red R.		
Gray, John	150	Little R.		2
Gray, John	200	Little R.		
Gray, John	100	Little R.		
Gray, John	100	Little R.		
Gillihan, Wm.	200	Little R.		4
Gray, Rob't	100	Little R.		2
Garretson, Arthur				1
Gulliher, Patrick				1
Guthrie, Matt'w	200	Pond R.		2
Grace, Henry				
Gray, Margret	100	Little R.		1
Gibson, Henry	200	Spring Crk.	5	4
Gibson, Henry	200	Spring Crk.		
Goodwin, Sam'l	200	Little R.		6
Greer, Robert				
Grant, Charley	200	Little R.		1
Goodwin, Robert	200	Little R.		
Goodwin, Jesse	200	Little R.		4
Goodwin, Jesse	200	Little R.		
Goodwin, Robert, Sr.	200	Little R.		1
Green, William				1
Griffith, Eli	200	Little R.		1
Gullett, Andrew				1
Griffen, Wilson				1
Garretson, James				1
Garretson, Joseph				
Grayson, Thomas	200	Pond R.	1	10
Gorden, William	200	Tradewater, Hend'n Co.		2
Griffin, Owens				1
Grayson, William	200	Deer Crk., Hend'n Co.	1	1
Grayson, William	100	Pond R., Ch'n Co.		
Gilkey, James	100	Tradewater, Ch'n (?) Co.		1
H				
Huk (?), Absalom	200	Red R.		5
Hogan, Walter				
Husk, William	150	Little R.		3
Hardin, Sam'l	100	Little R.		3
Hogan, Thomas				2
Higgins, Jesse	100	Pond R.		1
Hudgens, Jacob				1
Hicks, James				2
Hodge, Sam'l	150	Pond R.	1	6
Hodge, Sam'l	200	Pond R.		

Persons Names Chargeable with the Tax	Acres Land	Water Course	Blacks	Horses
Hodge, Sam'l	122½	Little R.		
Hodge, Sam'l	200	Pond R.		
Hodge, Sam'l	150	Pond R.		
Hogan, James				
Hicks, Henry				2
Huks, Willis	200	Little R.		
Huks, Willis	100	Little R.	1	5
Huks, Willis	200	Beech Crk., Liv'n Co.		
Hide, Ezekiel				1
Hunter, Doroty	100	Red R.		2
Hicks, Richard				
Horton, Robert				
Hammonds, Peter				
Hightower, Oldham				1
Hammocks, Wm.			1	2
Hughes, Charles	180	Little R.	1	1
Hawkins, Thos.	200	Cumberland R.	2	3
Henry, William	200	Pond R.		
Henry, William	200	Pond R.		
Henry, William	200	Pond R.		
Hall, Andrew				
Hall, William				
Henry, John				1
Harbour, Joseph	200	Little R.		2
Howard, William	200	Little R.		
Hall, William	200	Pond R.		1
Henry, Thomas				1
Hern, William				1
J				
Jones, Cade				8
Jones, Thomas	200	Pond R.		3
Johnson, John				1
Jones, Thomas				2
Jeeter, Henry				2
Jones, Eliz'th	150	Little R.		2
Jinkins, Shedrick				
Jurdin, John				1
Johnson, Hugh	165	Little R.		2
Johnson, Hugh	200	Tradewater, Liv'n Co.		
Isball, Thomas				3
Jameson, Samuel	200	Red R.		3
K				
Keenar, Abraham	200	Red R.		
Keenar, Abraham	200	Red R.		4
King, James				1
Kuydendall, Joseph	200	Pond R.	4	7
Kuydendall, Joseph	200	Pond R.		
Kenedy, William				1
Knight, Thos.				1
Knight, John				2
Kerr, James	100	Little R.		4

Persons Names Chargeable with the Tax	Acres Land	Water Course	Blacks	Horses
L				
Loyallass, Reuben	200	Little R.		1
Lindsay, Caleb	200	Dollerson Crk.		5
Lacy, Benjamin	200	Pond R.	1	4
Leer, Coonrod				1
Lewis, Alex'r	200	Pond R.		3
Logan, Elliston	175	Red R.	1	3
Linn, Adam	200	Ramsey's Crk.	2	3
Logan, Matt'w	200	Red R.	10	8
Logan, Matt'w	100	Red R.		
Logan, Hugh				1
Luster, Thos.				1
Linley, Sarah				2
Linley, Thos.	200	Little R.		1
Linley, John	200			1
Lutterel, John	200	Mat.y (?) Creek		3
Linley, William				3
Lewis, Samuel				6
Logan, Charles	150	Red R.	3	3
Logan, Jonathan	135	Red R.	4	6
Logan, Jonathan	107	Red R.		
Lockheart, James	200	Pond R.	1	9
Lockheart, James	200	Tradewater		
Logan, David	228	Red R.	6	4
Logan, David	16	Red R.		
M				
Mann, George	200	Red R.		4
May, Ambrose				1
May, Chisham				1
McLean, Ephraim			2	3
McCowen, George, Jr.	100	Pond R.		1
McWilliams, Hugh				2
McLean, James			1	5
McCowen, Sam'l				2
McCowan, Geo., Sr.	160	Pond R.		1
McCown, Wm.				
Merry, Colvan	200	Pond R.		3
Merry, Colvan	200	Pond R.		
Moore, William	200	Pond R.		3
McCollester, Dan				2
Mcfarlin, Walter	200	Pond R.		1
McClenden, Benja.			2	2
Merryfield, John				2
McCullough, Jas.				3
Mannaz, Richd.				
McWaters, Moses	150	Little R.		1
McWaters, Aaron	200	Little R.		1
Morris, Thomas	200	Little R.		2
Means, William, Sr.	170	Little R.		3
M'faddin, John	131¼	Red R.		2
M'Clenden, Fred'k				1
Mann, And'w	200	Red R.		4
M'Dannel, Jas.	200	Little R.		3
Means, Robert				1
Marky, David	120	Little R.		2

18

Persons Names Chargeable with the Tax	Acres Land	Water Course	Blacks	Horses
Mayberry, John	200	Little R.	2	1
M'Waters, James	200	Little R.	3	1
M'Waters, Benja.			2	1
Morris, Thomas	200	Little R.		1
Morris, Thomas	150	Little R.		
Morris, Thomas	105	Little R.		
Morris, Thomas	150	Little R.		
Morris, Thomas	200	Little R.		
McDannel, John				2
McAdow, David	192½	Pond R.		1
Moore, Adam	100			3
Miller, Martin				6
Means, Sam'l	150	Little R.		2
Means, Sam'l	150	Little R.		
M'Waters, Hugh				1
Mcfaddin, Jacob			2	1
Means, William, Jr.	100	Little R.		1
Means, William, Jr.	150	Little R.		
McElmurry, David	100	Little R.		2
McNight, James	150	Little R.		2
Menser, Dan'l	150	Little R.		6
Mcfaddin, Sam'l	100	Red R.		7
Mann, Jacob	200	Red R.		5
Miller, George	112½	Red R.		3
Morrow, William	200	Little R.		3
M'faddin, Shepherd	200	Red R.		2

N

Neelly, John				
Neelly, Andw.	200	Red R.		6

O

Owens, Mordekiah				1

P

Parks, Sam'l	200	Pond R.		
Pool, Ephaim	107	Little R.		2
Patterson, Alexr.				
Poe, Terry				1
Pots, Mary	150	Little R.	1	5
Pirkins, John	200	Red R.		1
Pyles, William				1
Pyle, John				1
Pratt, Zepheniah	100	Pond R.		3
Peasley, William	200	Pond R.		3
Pennington, Isaac	200	Pond R.	3	6
Pennington, Isaac	200	Pond R.		
Padfield, William	200	Little R.		3
Padfield, William	50	Little R.		
Pennington, Jacob	150	Pond River		1
Pyle, Nicholas	200	Little R.		8
Pyle, Nicholas	200	Little R.		
Pyle, William	200	Little R.		3

Persons Names Chargeable with the Tax	Acres Land	Water Course	Blacks	Horses
R				
Robertson, James	200	Pond R.		1
Roberts, Thomas	200	Little R.		
Reeves, James	200	Little R.		1
Rodger, Jean	200	Saleen Crk.		2
Reeves, William				1
Reeves, William, Jr.				
Rodgers, John	200	Little R.		3
Rodgers, John	200	Little R.		
Rodgers, Edwd.				
Rodgers, Larkin	100	Elk Fk. R. R.		3
Rasco, William			6	2
Roberts, John	200	Red R.		4
Roberts, John	100			
Roberts, Joseph	200	Red R.		4
Roberts, James	200	Red R.		3
Roberts, Obediah	200	W. F. R. River, Spring Crk.		3
Roberts, Joshua	150	W. F. R. River		3
Robertson, Jas.				2
Reeves, John	150	Little R.		2
Reeves, Martha	300	Red R.	3	2
Reeves, Martha	50	Red R. Tennessee (?)		
Riggs, Dan'l	200	Red R.		3
Robertson, Abner				3
Rachels, Vanentine	150	Pond R.		2
Reece, David	200	Red R.		1
Robertson, John	200	Pond R.		7
S				
Stevens, William				1
Scott, Thomas				2
Scoggins, Ethelred	200	Little R.		1
Stagner, Henry	100	Little R.		
Shelley, David				1
Stanford, John	200	Red R.		4
Stuart, John				1
Saunders, Jeffery	200	Pond R.		1
Sullivan, Dennis				2
Smith, John				
Smelser, Paulser	200	Pond R.	2	3
Spencer, John	200	Pond R.		4
Scott, Richard				3
Stuart, James	200	Pond R.	5	6
Stuart, James	100	Pond R.		
Stuart, James	100	Long Crk., Muhlenberg Co.		
Stuart, James	200	Pond R., Muhlenberg Co.		
Stuart, David				1
Stroud, William	200	Pond R.	3	3
Steele, Sam'l				
Stuart, Abraham	200	Pond R.	3	20
Stephenson, Jonathan				*
Stroud, Isaac	150	Pond R.	2	3
Saunders, Martin				
Stroud, William				2
Scott, John	100	Saleen Crk.		2
Scott, Sam'l	200	Little River		3

*1 store.

Persons Names Chargeable with the Tax	Acres Land	Water Course	Blacks	Horses
Scott, Sam'l	100	Little R.		
Shelley, Absalom				1
Shelley, John	100	Long Crk.		4
Shelley, Reuben				3
Shelley, William				
Smith, David	200	Drakes Pond	12	3
Smith, David	200	Drakes Pond		
Smith, David	200	Drakes Pond		
Smith, David	200	Elk Fork		
Smith, David	200	Pond R.		
T				
Teague, Van, Jr.				1
Teague, Van, Sr.	200	Pond R.		2
Teague, Abel				1
Thompson, John	160	Pond R.	2	4
Thompson, John	150	Pond R.		
Turpin, Jesse	100	Little R.		3
Thompson, Peter	150	Red R.		5
Thompson, Joel	200	Little R.		1
Thompson, James	120	Pond R.		7
Taylor, Edward	200	Pond R.		7
Taylor, Edward	200	Little R.		
V				
Vaughan, Ann				2
Vaughan, Eliz'th	200	Little R.		1
Vaughan, Thos.	200	Little R.		3
Vaughan, James	200	Little R.		2
W				
Wort, Henry				4
Wadlington, Thos.	200	Little R.	14	10
Wadlington, Thos.	200	Little R.		
Wilson, James	200	Pond R.	1	18
Wilson, James	200	Pond R.		
Williams, James	200	Pond R.		2
Ward, William	200	Pond R.		1
Ward, William	200	Henderson Co.		
Ward, William	200	Tradewater, Hend'n Co.		
Ward, William	100	Canoe Crk., Hend'n		
Woolsey, Thomas				1
White, John				1
Wallace, Timothy				1
Wilson, John	200	Dollerson's Crk.		2
Wilson, John	100	Dollerson's Crk.		
Weldon, John	187	Little R.		3
Weldon, John	112	Little R.		
Weldon, John	200	Dollerson's Crk.		
Wyatt, William	200	Little R.		5
Walker, Rich'd				1
Wilson, Rich'd				1
Wilson, Thos.				1
Woolf, Henry, Sr.	200	Little R.	5	11
Woolf, Henry, Jr.		Little R.		2
Woolf, Fielding	200	Little R.		2

Persons Names Chargeable with the Tax	Acres Land	Water Course	Blacks	Horses
White, John	200	Little R.	2	6
White, John	200	Little R.		
Wilson, John	125	Red R.		1
Wilson, John	150	Red R.		
Wallace, Wm.	100	Red R.		5
White, Sam'l				3
Wood, David	175	Little R.		2
Williams, Dan'l	120	Little R.		1
Williams, Stephen	200	Little R.		1
Wortman, Henry	120	Little R.		2
Wilson, Matt'w	200	Pond R.		3
Williams, John	200	Little R.		2
Williams, John	100	Little R.		
Waller, Pleasant				1
Wallace, Jacob	200	Little R.		3
Woods, Barth'w	200	Little R.		4†
Woods, Barth'w	200	Little R.		
Woods, Barth'w	200	Little R.		
Y				
Young, Adam	200	Dollerson's Crk.		3
Young, Adam	128	Muddy R., Logan Co.		
Young, David	100	Little R.		2

†Town lot $200.

W. M. ab'v 21—421, acres 64,088. Black 257, horses, etc., 1,013.

Christian County, Sct.

I John Clark Clerk for said County do Certify that the within Alphabetical Book that hath been taken by John Campbell Commissioner for the Tax for Christian County for the year 1800 is a True Copy taken from the Original Lists thats now filed in my office. Witness my hand this 22nd day of July, 1800.

(Signed) Jn. Clark, C. C. C.

CHRISTIAN COUNTY TAX LISTS—1799.

To the Auditor, George Madison Esqr.

Christian County, Sct.

I John Clark, Clerk for said County do certify that the foregoing alphabetical Book of Taxable Property hath been duly Examined and Compared with the original lists taken by the within named Jacob Dooms, Commissioner as the Law Directs Given from under my hand at Office this 19th day of August, 1799.

(Signed) John Clark, C. C. C.

No. 1.

List of Taxable property within the District of Jacob Doom, Commissioner in the County of Christian for the year 1799, which includes the (now) County of Livingston.

Note by Editor.—The County of Livingston was formed from Christian in 1798, but evidently not organized until after the return made in 1799.

Persons Names Chargeable with the Tax	Blacks	Horses	Acres Land
A			
Mary Atchison		1	
William Ashley		1	
James Armstrong		2	200
Charles Arrington			
John Atchison		2	
Adam Alexander			
B			
James Buckhanen			200
Moses Burnet			
Thomas Belew	6	3	400
Charles Belew			
William Bogard			
William Brown			
Larkin Bennett		2	100
William Burdon		2	
Edward Burdon			
Benjamin Briant			200
William Brown		6	200
William Brown		6	200
Joseph Barnes		4	200
William Bonds	4	8	600
James Berry	1	2	400
William Baldwin		5	200
Elisha Baldwin		2	200
William Baldwin		2	
Daniel Brown	4	5	200
John Bridges			200
Delley Baird			
James Berry			
Lewis Barker		5	200
Isaac Buller	8	9	200
Daniel Briant			
William Brown	1	2	400
C			
Alexander Capshaw		1	
John Campbell			
William S. Cox			
Robert Cook		1	

Persons Names Chargeable with the Tax	Blacks	Horses	Acres Land
James Conners		2	200
George Cowhorn		1	200
John Chisholm		6	200
Isham Chisholm		2	200
Elisha Chisholm		1	200
Justinian Cartwright		1	1,000
Zachariah Cox		(Military)	4,000
John Caldwell	9	4	400
David Caldwell	12	12	400
Hugh Crawhorn	1	1	100
Henry Croghan	1	5	
John Connaway			120
John Camack		4	200
John Cole		2	200
Gideon Clarke			
Grayson Cowfield	16	5	800
Eli Crow		1	
James Curren	2	4	200
D			
James Deacon	1	4	200
William Dean			
John Davidson		6	400
Frances Dodds		2	200
James Dobbins		2	200
Joseph Downs			
Hyram Downs			
Wiley Davis	2	1	200
William Downs, by his att'y in Joshua Downs..	11		
William Dodds		1	
Mary Dodds		1	200
Jacob Davis			
William Daniel			
Benjamin Davis			
Robert Dobbins		3	200
George Davidson			200
Samuel Duvall		1	200
Arthur Davis			
Aquila Dolahide		5	200
William Dobbins			
Benjamin Deliplane			
Joshua Deleplane			200
E			
George Elmore			
William Edwards			
Alexander Elder	1	4	200
William Elder	1	3	200
Leonard Evans		1	200
John Edes		4	200
John Elder			
Robert Elder			
F			
Phillip Ford			200
David Fort	2	3	200
Spear Fort	2	4	200

Persons Names Chargeable with the Tax	Blacks	Horses	Acres Land
Isaac Flonrey		7	
George Flin		1	200
Moses French		1	200
Levi French		1	100
Peter Fletcher	2	3	
John French			
James Furgason	2	1	200
Thomas Furgason			200
Richard Furgason	2	1	200
Hamlet Furgason	1		200
John Ford		1	400
William French			
Leonard Francis			
William Flin		2	
Samuel French		2	200
Jesse Ford		1	600
Josiah French		5	
John Ferrell (or Terrell)		1	200
John Fagan			
G			
Thomas Gist	5	1	
James George		3	200
Matt'w M. Gooch		1	
James Grier		3	200
William Grier			200
John F. George		2	200
William Greenstreet			
James Greenstreet			
John Givens	3	1	200
Joseph Givens		1	200
James Grier			
William Gilkey		2	200
John Gary		2	200
George Gordon	3	2	200
Dudley Glass			100
William Glass		1	200
John Gaskins		3	200
Jonathan Grier		2	200
Josiah Grier		3	
Frederick Groves		4	
Joseph Green			
Jesse Grier		1	
H			
Andrew Hamilton			
Edward Hamilton			
Zebulon Hubbard			200
George Hardin		4	200
Benjamin Hardin			
John Hamilton	2	3	316
Loudy Hall		1	200
John Hutchings			
George Hubbard			
William Huff			
Jeremiah Harrison		2	200
Ephraim Hill			200

Persons Names Chargeable with the Tax	Blacks	Horses	Acres Land
David Hill			200
Robert Hill			200
Robert Hodges	6	2	200
James Henderson			200
Ezekiel Henry		2	
Joab Hardin		2	200
Absolam Hardin		2	200
Daniel Hazle			
Jacob Herald		2	200
Peter Huffman	(Henderson Co. Military)		1,000
John Hunter		1	
Isaac Huffman		(Military)	666⅔
Christian Huffman		(Military)	1,000
Israel Harman		4	
Christopher Hammond		2	200
John Holiday		2	
Enoch Hooper	4	1	
Thomas Henry		3	200
John Harrington	6	5	
Joseph Hill		1	
Abram Harden		1	200
I			
James Ivey		4	200
J			
Joseph Jenkins		2	200
Andrew Jones	1	3	200
Benjamin Jones		5	200
Alexander Johnson		7	200
William Johnson		1	200
Jesse Jones		1	
John Jones		1	100
John Johnson			
James Johnson		1	200
Comfort Joy		1	150
James James			
Isaac Jobe		1	
Jacob Johnson			
John Johnson		4	200
Richard Jones		2	200
K			
Joseph Kenedy	1		200
Samuel Kincade		3	200
George Kincade		1	
William Kilgore	1	1	200
Jesse Kirkendall		1	
Jane Kirkendall			200
John Kelham	1	1	
David Kilgore		1	150
Benjamin Kivell	2	5	378
L			
Hugh Lewis		2	100
Lenard Lacy			200
William Low	6	3	400
John Low			200

26

Persons Names Chargeable with the Tax	Blacks	Horses	Acres Land
Joshua Low			200
John Lewis		4	200
Hugh Lewis			
Earl Lewis		1	200
James Luske (or Lushe)		3	
Robert Luske (or Lushe)	1		200
Edward Lacy	3	1	100
Thomas Lewis		1	
Daniel Lerue			
Samuel Lamkin		3	150
Mary Lowry		5	200
William Leach		2	200
William Lemar		4	
James Lewis			
George V. Luske (or Lushe)		1	400
William Lancaster		1	
Jesse Lamb	1	5	150
Mary Lacy		1	
Peter Lerue		1	
M			
James McNale (?)		2	200
George Murphy		1	200
Richard Miles	9	2	200
Thomas McCoy			
John McClerey			
Matt'w McCormack			
Cornelieus Merry		1	200
Edward Maxwell	1	5	400
John Moneste		3	200
William McKee			
Robert Montgomery			
Joseph Miller		1	100
Andrew Mayes		1	
John McKlemurrey		3	200
John Montgomery		1	
William Mercer		1	200
James Miller			400
George Marchbanks		1	200
Johnston Marchbanks		1	160
William Miles	7	2	200
Ephariam Manning			
Hugh McMullen		2	200
Mary Miller	1	5	520
Arthur Murphy		3	
Josiah Moore		1	
Reuben Martin		3	200
John Mercer		1	200
John Maxwell			200
Edward Mitcheson	6	4	200
George Mayes		1	200
Robert McMullen		1	
William Mitcheson	8	4	200
Coyranes (?) Miller		2	200
Jones Menser (?)		2	200
Alexander Moore			
Zachariah Medlock	3	3	200

Persons Names Chargeable with the Tax	Blacks	Horses	Acres Land
Joseph McMurtrie			200
Edward Medcap			200
Andrew Mathis			
Thomas McCabe		2	
N			
Ezekiel Norris	1	1	200
James Neely		4	300
John Newman			
O			
William Owens	1	3	200
John Owens			200
Robert Orr			
Alexander Orr		1	200
William Orr		1	200
P			
Michael Purtle	4	2	200
Peter Purtle		2	200
Martha Purtle		2	200
Samuel Purtle			200
William Perkins	4	3	200
Richard Perkins		1	200
John Pounds		1	100
William Perkins, Jr.	1	3	300
Thomas Perkins		1	200
William Perkins		1	
Michael Purtle			200
John Phelps		1	200
Ephraim Pratt		1	200
Soloman Perkins		2	200
William Prince	9	7	400
Thomas Peale		5	200
John Peale			200
John Prince	1		
Enoch Prince	1	3	300
Isaac Parker		2	100
Joseph Perkins		1	200
James Page			
Josiah Prickett		1	200
Q			
Charles Quigley			
R			
James Russell	1	3	200
John Russell		3	200
William C. Rodgers		2	200
Olive Renfrow	2	2	
Joshua Renfrow			
Jonathan Ramsey	4	5	200
John Russell		1	200
Francis Roach		3	200
Amos Robinson		4	200
Maximilly Rutor	1	1	200
Josiah Rousaville		4	200

Persons Names Chargeable with the Tax	Blacks	Horses	Acres Land
John Roach		2	100
Elisha Reece	1	2	200
John Ritchey		3	
Henry Rose		1	
James Ritchey	3	9	600
William Rudy			
George Robertson		1	
John Ritchey	1	2	200
Micajah Reeder		1	200
Reuben Rolling		3	200
Robert Ritchey		1	200
Joseph Reed		7	
Obediah Russell		1	
S			
Samuel Saxton			
Abram Son		4	200
James Satterfield		1	200
Mathew Seller	6	8	200
Adam Sharp		1	200
William Story		1	150
Jno. Scarlett			
Benj'n R. Smith			
Moses Shelby	7	10	400
William Shaw			
Robert Smith			
Joseph N. Sams			200
Charles Staten		5	
John Story		4	150
William Stinson		1	
John Stapleton		6	200
William Simpson	1	4	200
William Simpson		1	200
Thomas Simpson		2	256
Benjamin Simpson			
Julias Sanders			
Alexander Stinson		4	200
Alexander Scott			
James Smart		2	200
Elijah Stevens		1	200
Adam Sharp		1	200
Isaac Sutton			200
Absolam Stokes		3	
Stephen Sullivant		5	200
George Saddlers	3	3	200
John Scott		3	400
T			
Joseph Thompson		4	200
John Thompson		1	
John Tice (?)		2	
George Taylor			
John Tolly	1	1	200
Elisha Thurman			1,000
Isaac Taylor		1	
Isaac Tetsworth	3	2	200
Benjamin Tetsworth		2	200

Persons Names Chargeable with the Tax	Blacks	Horses	Acres Land
Abram Tetsworth			200
John Thomas		1	
James Thompson			200
John Tannyhill		1	
Obediah Terrell	1	2	200
James Taylor		2	200
Robert Thompson			
V			
Thomas Vaughn			200
John Vaughn			200
Benj'n Vaughn		1	200
W			
William Woten		1	150
John Wyatt		1	200
Hugh G. Wiley		1	200
John Wadlington		1	200
Septimus Williams			
Thomas Wadlington		1	200
James Wadlington	1	5	200
James T. White		1	520
Joseph Wiley		1	200
James Wadlington		2	200
George Walling		1	400
John Wheeler	7	6	200
Robert Woods	1	9	
Jesse Williams			200
Arthur Williams	1	1	
Jessee Williams, Jr	1	1	200
John Williams	1	1	200
Robert Woodsides		1	
Josiah Watson		1	
Richard Williamson	1	1	200
Shemi (?) Watson		1	
Bartholemew Williams		1	
Archabald Woods			
Y			
Josiah Young		4	200
White males over 21—386	242	660	60,226

I do certify that the foregoing Sheets contain the whole of the Taxable property that came within my knowledge within my District subject to Taxation the Tenth day of March last; and that the whole of the land herein listed is held by Certificate granted by the Commissioners in November last, except such as are marked "Military" and the persons who have listed the said Lands are settlers in the County and generally reside on the Lands; therefore no notice is taken of the water courses on which the Lands lie.

(Signed) Jacob Doom, Commr.

Editor's Note.

The Act of the Kentucky Legislature approved Dec. 13, 1798, creating Livingston County from Christian, provided that the new County should not have separate representation "until the number of free white males over 21 should entitle them to representation equal to Ratio that shall be established by Law." See Original Enrolled Bill No. 32, 1798.

It was provided that the first Court to organize the County government should be held at the house of Michael Purtle.

FAYETTE COUNTY TAX LIST FOR YEAR OF 1788.

The Historical Society has come into possession of the manuscript tax list of Fayette county for 1788. As this list was made years before Kentucky became a state, it is a very valuable historical document. Fayette county at that time included a large part of the territory lying north and east of the Kentucky river. We publish it in the exact form it appears in the little book in which it was written, one hundred and thirty-three years ago, showing the classes of property then liable for taxes.

A List of Taxables Taken
For the Year 1788.

Persons' Names	No. Tithables.	Negroes over 12.	Horses	Carriage Wheels	Stud Horses and Rate.
A					
Arnold, Nicholas	5	3	3		
Arnold, John	1		2		
Adkins, James	1		3		
Aryes, Samuel	1		1		
Arnold, James	1		4		
Admire, George	3	2	2		
Admire, George, Junr.	1		4		
Akers, Thomas	1		3		
Allin, Elisha	1		1		
Akers, Joseph	1		2		
Ashhurst, Robert	2	1	4		
Anderson, Henry	1		2		
Allison, John	2	1	2		
Allin, Joseph	1		2		
Allin, Richard	7	6	8		
Allin, William	2	1	6		
Anderson, Joseph	1		1		
Anderson, Theop's	1		1		
Adams, Alexander	1		2		
Armstrong, Robt.	1	1	2		
Allison, Jno., Jun'r	1		5		

Persons' Names	No. Tithables.	Negroes over 12.	Horses	Carriage Wheels	Stud Horses and Rate.
Ammons, Thomas	4	4	6		
Arnett, James	1		2		
Allison, Robert	1		1		
Allison, Elizabeth			3		
Ashley, Joel	1		3		
Allin, Sylvanus	1		1		
Allison, Wm.	1		2		
	45	19	78		
B					
Blackburn, George	6	7	13		
Berry, Samuel	1		2		
Berry, Benjamin	2	1	5		
Burton, John	4	2	2		
Burton, John	2		2		
Blanton, Thomas	4	2	3		
Black, John	4	2	10		
Boyd, John	1		2		
Burbridge, Thomas	2	1	2		
Beak, John	1		2		
Boyd, John, Jun'r	1		1		
Black, James	3	2	5		
Black, John, Jun'r	1		1		
Black, James, Jun'r	1		4		
Black, Alexander	2	1	5		
Bowman, Abraham	4	3	15		
Boyd, Samuel	1		3		
Bennitt, Matthew	1		2		
Brooke, Ebinezer	1		1		
Bradley, Edward	1		2		
Bradley, Edward, Jun'r	1		2		
Berry, Wm.	1		4		
Boyles, John	1		1		
Bell, Thomas	1		1		
Black, Joseph	1		5		
Bartley, Matthew	1		5		
Berry, Reuben	2	1	3		
Baldin, John	1		1		
Baites, Ephraim	1		2		
Bledsoe, William	5	5	2		
Brock, Henry	1		1		

Persons' Names	No. Tithables.	Negroes over 12.	Horses	Carriage Wheels	Stud Horses and Rate.
Bradshaw, Benj.	6	5	6		
Bradshaw, Wm.	6	5	3		
Bartlet, James	2	2	4		
Bartlet, Anthony	1		1		
Barrett, M. Andrew	1		1		
Boston, Benj.	1		1		
	76	39	124		
B					
Brookey, John	2		3		
Byres, Joseph	1				
Baxter, Samuel	1		2		
Bradford, John	1	1			
Boyd, Hugh	1				
Blair, Samuel	1		2		
Black, Samuel	1		4		
Black, Robert	2		3		
Bennit, Thomas	1		1		
Bradley, James	1		2		
Baker, John	1		20		
Bell, John	2		2		
Burk, Elihu	1		1		
Bryant, Daniel	3	2	4		
Bags, Andrew	2		1		
C					
Campbel, George	1		1		
Carathers, Thomas	1		3		
Conner, John	2	1	5		
Collier, John	1		4		
Craig, John	14	13	13		
Craig, Lewis	8	7	7		
Craig, Joseph	5	4	5		
Craig, M. John	1	1	2		
Cole, Rich'd	1		2		
Carlyle, George	1		4		
Cothron, Hugh	1		3		
Collins, Elisha	1		3		
Crosswait, Jacob	4	2	4		
Crosswait, Samuel	1		2		
Campbell, Robert	1		2		
Campbell, William	2	1	4		
Campbell, James	1		5		

Persons' Names	No. Tithables.	Negroes over 12.	Horses	Carriage Wheels	Stud Horses and Rate.
Cunningham, Hugh	1		3		
Collins, Joel	2	1	4		
C	70	33	121		
Collins, Joseph	2	2	5		
Creed, Elijah	1		1		
Clifford, Michel	1		3		
Cash, Warrin	1		1		
Carathers, James	1		3		
Castleman, Lewis	4	2	3		
Coms, George	1		2		
Creel, Chas.	1		3		
Cavins, Robert	1		2		
Cherry, Moses	1		10		
Cook, Hosea	1		2		
Cook, Jesse	1		1		
Chancellor, David	1		1		
Cave, Richard	4	4	6		
Clay, Mastin	4	3	4		1-20
Carr, Joseph	1		2		
Curd, John	12	11	6		
Curd, James	1		3		
Crittendon, John	5	4	5	4	
Carneal, Thomas	3	2	4		1-12
Conelly, Arthur	1		2		
Carathers, Benj.	1		2		
Colson, Wm.	1				
Campbell, John	1		2		
Cathers, Edward	1		31		
Crocket, Joseph	4	3	4		
Coger, Michael	3	2	5		
Carlane, Thomas	3	2	8		
Connelly, Wm.	1		1		
Connelly, John	2		3		
Cloyd, Robert	1		4		
Coyle, James	1		3		
Coleman, Page	2	1	3		
Chance, Joseph	1		1		
Collins, John	1		1		
Cox, S. Benj.	1		1		1-29
	71	35	106	4	3-52

32

Persons' Names	No. Tithables.	Negroes over 12.	Horses	Carriage Wheels	Stud Horses and Rate.
C					
Clark, Frances	1		6		
Coyle, Joseph &					
William Scott	2		3		
Collins, Joseph	1	1	3		
Clark, James	1		6		1-20
Church, Thomas	1		2		
Campbell, John	1		3		
Conner, Wm.	1		1		
Crow, John	1		1		
Casey, John	1		1		
Carter, John	1		2		
Cravin, Harmin	1		2		
Cobourn, John	3	2	1		
D					
Dun, James	1		2		
Dale, George	1		2		
Dale, George, Jun'r	1		1		
Dale, Robert	1		1		
Dale, William	1		2		
Dale, William, Jun'r	1		1		
Dale, Isaac	1		2		
Dale, Abram	1		2		
Decouse, William	1		2		
Davis, Partrick	2	1	4		
Davis, William	1		3		
Davis, Joseph	1		3		
Delaney, Joseph	3	2	4		
Dohorty, James	1		5		
Dohorty, Joseph	4	3	1		
Dohorty, George	1		1		
Dedman, Samuel	1		5		
Dedmond, Richmond	2	1	1		
Dupey, John	5	4	5		
Dupey, James	6	5	7		
Dupey, Bartholomew	12	8	8		
Dean, James	1		2		
Duglas, Samuel	1		6		
	64	26	98		1-20

Persons' Names	No. Tithables.	Negroes over 12.	Horses	Carriage Wheels	Stud Horses and Rate.
D					
Denison, Daniel	3		6		
Downey, John	2		1		
Devenport, James	1		1		
Douglas, Nathaniel	2	1	3		
Denhit, Peter	1		1		
Durst, David	1		2		
Doyle, Martin	1		1		
Denney, Aron	2		2		
Dickey, Samuel	1		3		
Dawson, Christilon	4	1	5		
Dondon, Nathiniel	1		2		
Duncan, Charles	1		2		
Drake, Samuel	2	1	8		
Drake, Ephram	1		15		
Drake, Samuel, Jun'r	1		8		
Dearengar, John	1		1		
Dryden, David	1		3		
Donnell, Thomas	1		2		
Davis, John	2	1	5		
Dryden, Nathaniel	1		3		
Dunlap, Alex	2		21		
Davis, Richard	2		3		
Davis, William	1		2		
Dale, Rawley	2	2	4		
Dann, Jeremiah	1		1		
Davis, John	1		1		
Drake, John	3		11		
Delham, Frances	3	2	3		
Dickinson, Archey	1		3		
Davison, Thomas	1		1		
Davis, Hannaniah	2		2		
Dun, Zephaniah	2		2		
	46	6	127		
E					
Eaton, Joseph	1		4		
Eaton, George	1		3		
Egbird, David	1		1		
Elam, Josiah	1		2		
Ellison, Robert	3	1	3		

Persons' Names	No. Tithables.	Negroes over 12.	Horses	Carriage Wheels	Stud Horses and Rate.
Ellison, Thomas	1		2		
Elliott, Robert	3	1	2		
Elliott, Wm.	1		5		
Ethington, John	2		3		
Evans, Nathaniel	5	3	7		
Evans, David	1		3		
Esley, Stephen	1		3		
Evans, William	1		7		
Elder, Andrew	1		5		
East, Joseph	1		1		
Eastin, Philip	1		1		
Ellison, Peter	2		4		
F					
Fisher, Daniel	1		1		
Franklin, John	2	1	5		
Fisher, James	2		2		
Forker, Robert	3	1	4		
Fitzgerald, Daniel	1		4		
Finnea, John	3	3	4		
Finnee, James	2	1	3		
Franklin, James	1		2		
Finley, John	1		1		
Fields, Henry	3	2	3		
Farmer, Abner	1		1		
Ficklin, John	1		4		
Forkner, Joseph	2	1	3		1-24
Frund, John	1		1		
Fox, Richard	1		1		
	53	13	95		1-24
F					
Forkner, John	4	3	2		
Fergason, Larkin	2		1		
Fitzgarald. Bartlet	1		2		
Finch, John	1		1		
Finch, James	1		1		
Fitch, Daniel	1				
Finia, William	2	1	2		
Foster, Samuel	1		1		
Floyd, Thomas, Doct	1		3		
Forkner, John	3	2	2		

Persons' Names	No. Tithables.	Negroes over 12.	Horses	Carriage Wheels	Stud Horses and Rate.
Forester, Gressum	1		1		
Frazer, James	1		4		
Frazer, Wm.	1		2		
Frazer, David	1		1		
Fuller, Henry	1		3		
Fulton, Hugh	2	1	4		
Frazer, Joseph	3	2	1		
Frazer, George	2	2	3		
Foley, Peter	1		2		
G					
Garnet, John	2	1	2		
Gatewood, Andrew	6	6	7		
Gatewood, Augustus	3	2	3		
Garrett, William	1		5		
Greathouse, John	1		10		
Greathouse, Wm.	1		2		
Greathouse, John, Jr.	1		2		
Goron, John	1		5		
Gwin, Robert	1		5		
Gatewood, Peter	7	5	7		
Gatewood. John	2	1	2		
Gray. Johnathan	1		4		
Grinstead, Wm.	1		1		
Guttrey, Benj.	2	1	3		
	59	27	92		
G					
Garton, Uriah	1		1		
Grimsley, James	1		1		
Glass, Thomas	2	1	2		
Gale, Joseph	1		1		
Gay, John	1		12		
Gay, James	1	1	5		
Greer, Stephen	1		4		
Griffen, Ralph	1		1		
Griffen, Gordon	1		1		
Griffen, Ebenezer	1		4		
Graves, David	2		2		
Gregory, Samuel	1		3		
Gray, George	1		3		
Gray, Rich'd	1		2		
Graham, Arthur	1		3		

Persons' Names	No. Tithables.	Negroes over 12.	Horses	Carriage Wheels	Stud Horses and Rate.
Graham, Ferguson	1		2		
Gibbens, John	1		3		
Goodlow, Bivin	1		6		
Garnet, Thomas	7	4	4		
Galey, Samuel	2		4		
Griffin, Wm.	1		3		
Graves, Edmond	1		7		
Givens, John	1		3		
Griffen, John	1		2		
H	33	6	69		
Hamilton, Samuel	2	1	4		
Hutson, Tanley	1		1		
Howard, Allen	1		1		
Haydon, John	5	6	5		
Haydon, Wm.	1		1		
Haydon, Ezekiel	3	2	3		
Haydon, Wm., Jun'r	1		1		
Haydon, Abner	1		1		
Hanks, George	1		1		
Hazzard, John	2	1	3		
Hazzard, Martin	1		1		
Hiler, James	2		2		
Holeman, Henry	1		3		
Holeman, Edward	1		3		
Holeman, Edward, Jun'r	1		4		
Holeman, Daniel	1		5		1-12
Holeman, George	1		2		
Holeman, Nicholas	1				
Humphrey, Merry	1		1		
Hill, Wm.	1		1		
Hampton, Andrew	2	1	10		
Harmon, Thomas	1		2		
Hedden, Jacob	1		2		
Hedden, Abram	1		3		
Hughs, Joseph	1		6		
Hughs, Wm.	1		5		
Hynes, Richard	1		2		
Henderson, Samuel	2	1	4		
Henderson, Alex.	1		7		
Hutton, James	1		4		
Hensley, Richerson	2		3		

Persons' Names	No. Tithables.	Negroes over 12.	Horses	Carriage Wheels	Stud Horses and Rate.
Henderson, John	1		3		
Halloway, James	3	2	4		
Hestings, William	1		1		
Haydon, James	1		1		
Haydon, Benj.	1		1		
	49	14	100		1-12
H					
Hutton, Hendrick	1		2		
Hammond, John	1		1		
House, Andrew	1		2		
Haff, Paul	1		4		
Harper, Mary	1		2		
Henderson, Joseph	1		2		
Huson, Jane	1		4		
Hensley, George	2		1		
Howard, Leroy	2	1	2		
Henderson, John	1		2		
Hickey, Simon	1				
Harmon, William	1		2		
I					
Indecut, Joseph	1		3		
Indecut, Moses	1		3		
Indecut, Aron	1		1		
Indecut, Barzella	1		1		
Ireland John	1		2		
J					
Johnson, Joseph	1		1		
Johnson, Andrew	1		2		
Johnson, Cave	4	3	10		
James, Daniel	3		2		
Jameson, George	1		7		
Jenkins, Matthew	1		1		
Jack, Frances	1	1	1		
Jack, John	1		1		
January, Ephraim	1		2		
Jameson, John	2	1	2		
Jones, John	1		8		
Jones, John, Jun'r	1		2		
	37	6	73		

Persons' Names	No. Tithables.	Negroes over 12.	Horses	Carriage Wheels	Ordinary License	Billiard Tables	Stud Horses and Rate.
J							
Jamason, William ..	1	....	7				
Jamison, Samuel	1	....	2				
Jackson, Philip	1						
January, Thomas	1	....	1				
Jones, James	2	1	3				
Jamison, John, Jr.....	1	....	4				
Jamison, Samuel	1	....	5				
January, John	1	....	2				
January, James	1	....	3				
Johns, John	1	....	2				
Johnson, Wm.	5	5	5				
K							
Knight, James	1	1	3				
King, John	3	2	9				
King, Abram	1	....	1				
Kay, John	4	3	3				
Kincade, David	1	....	1				
Kincade, John	1	....	2				
Kizer, Christopher ..	4	2	8		1	1	
Kellar, Isaac	1	....	3				
Kinkade, John	2	....	3				
Kincade, Andrew	1	....	4				
Kelly, Samuel	1	....	8				
Kirkham, Sam'l	1	....	6				
Kirkpatrick, Alex....	1	....	2				
Kincade, Hapson	1	....	4				
Keen, Frances	2	3	1				
Kirkham, Robert.....	1	....	12				1-20
Kincade, Archibald..	1	....	1				
Kincade, Wm.	1	....	1				
Keldar, John	2	....	5				
Kinder, Peter	1	....	1				
	49	19	123		1	1	1-20

Persons' Names	No. Tithables.	Negroes over 12.	Horses	Carriage Wheels	Stud Horses and Rate.
L					
Lips, Jacob	1	......	1		
Lewis, William	1	......	1		
Linsey, Theodones	1	......	1		
Long, John	3	2	4		
Ligget, James	1	......	3		
Lea, W. Frances	3	2	4		
Locket, James	6	5	6		
Lesenby, William	1	......	1		
Lee, James	1	......	4		
Lewis, William	13	11	8		
Lewis, Nicholas	2	1	2		
Lowry John	1	......	3		1-12
Lamb, Samuel	2	1	6		
Lusk, Hugh	1	......	3		
Lewis, John	6	4	6		
Lucas, John	2	......	2		
Linsey, John	1	......	1		
Lewis, Thomas	1	......	1		
Lot, William	2	1	2		
Lamb, Wm.	2	1	10		
Lowry, Stephen	1	......	5		
Lewis, Thomas	9	8	11		
Brought forward H					
Hadden, Wm.	1	......	2		1-12
Huckstep, John	2	1	2		
Hogan, James	3	2	3		
Hollingshead, Frances....	1	......	2		
Hill, John	1	......	3		
Harmon, Robert	1	......	2		
Hall, Thomas	1	......	2		
Harbert, Elisha	1	......	3		
Hunt, Wilson	1	......	2		
Harget, Peter	1	......	2		
His, Elisha	1	......	1		
Hargester, Thomas	1	......	3		
Heat, Benjamin	1	......	3		
Hawkins, James	4	3	3		
Hadden, William	2	......	1		
	84	42	119		2-24

Persons' Names	No. Tithables.	Negroes over 12.	Horses	Carriage Wheels	Stud Horses and Rate.
M					
McCumsey, John	1		5		
Munson, Samuel	1		4		
Munson, Samuel, Jun'r.	1		4		
McLanane, John	1		3		
Munson Isaac	1		1		
Moss, Frederick	2	1	4		
Moss, Wm.	1		1		
Martin, Benj.	2	1	6		
McMurtry, Wm.	1		2		
McClure, John	1		2		
McClure, Samuel	1		2		
McCommon, Matt	1		3		
McGuire, James	1		6		
McCrackin, Cyrus	2	1	6		
Moore, Joseph	1		4		
Marten, John	3	1	4		
Martin, Jerimiah	1		3		
Marten, Wm.	1		1		
Marten, Henry	2		1		
Martin, Thomas	1		1		
McThomas, Quady	1		1		
McQuady, Wm.	2				
McQuady, John	1		2		
McGill, Alex.	1		3		
McHuron, Silas	1		2		
Masten, John	2		4		
McNeal, Thomas	2	1	4		
McNeal, Jonathan	1		4		
McConnell, James	1		2		
Mitchel, Robert	3		7		
Montgomery, Samuel	3		5		
Montgomery, Robt.	1		2		
Milburn, Dudley	3	3	3		
Marshal, Humphrey	5	4	10		
Marshall, John	3	1	3		
	56	13	113		
M					
Marshall, Thomas	8	7	11		
Marshall, Thos., Jun'r.	4	3	2		
Middleton, H. John	1		10		

Persons' Names	No. Tithables.	Negroes over 12.	Horses	Carriage Wheels	Stud Horses and Rate.
Martiny, Earnest	1		2		
Mitchell, Rosanna	2		5		
Miles, Eve	2				
Mitchell, John	1		1		
Montague, Thos.	4	3	2		
McBride, Sam'l	1		2		
McBride, James	2	1	1		
McCrackin, John	1		1		
Martin, Alexr.	1				
Moore, Shadrack	4	3	3		
Musselman, Chrisly	1		2		
Miles, Samuel	1		1		
McConnell, Will'm	3	2	3		
McConnell, Wm., Jur.	1		8		
McConnell, Mary	2		1		
Martin, John	3	2	2		
Morfet, Robert	2		11		
McIlvain, Moses	1		3		
McClary, John	2	1	5		
McClary, Sam'l	2	1	3		
Madison, George	2	2	3		
Moore, John	1		5		
McDaniel, Wm.	1		4		
Meek, James	1		6		
McIlvain, Samuel	1		4		
Martin, Will'm	2				
Meek, William	2	1	6		
Meek, John	1		2		
	61	26	109		
M					
McClure, Thomas	1		3		
Miller, Henry	1				
Mooney, John	1		1		
Mooney, Patrick	1		1		
McConnel, John	1		4		
McConnel, Alex.	1		2		
Moore, Benj.	1		1		
McClary, Samuel	1	1	3		
McCorkle, Elizabeth	1		4		
Moore, Quinten	1		1		
McClure, Nathaniel	1		2		

Persons' Names	No. Tithables.	Negroes over 12.	Horses	Carriage Wheels	Stud Horses and Rate.
McWilliams, Hugh	2	......	2	......	......
McLane, James	1	......	3	......	......
McClure, Moses	1	......	2	......	......
McClure, Thomas	1	......	3	......	......
McIlvain, John	1	......	1	......	......
McIlvain, James	1	......	1	......	......
Martin, Alex.	1	......	1	......	......
Mutre, George	4	3	3	......	......
McCune, Andrew	1	......	2	......	......
Muldery, Hugh	1	......	3	......	......
McCanley, Andrew	2	2	4	......	......
Martin, James	3	2	4	......	......
McHuron, Sam'l	1	......	2	......	......
Mayfield, John	1	......	3	......	......
Morris, Evans	1	......	2	......	......
Mickin, Mark	1	......	2	......	......
	34	8	59	......	......
N					
Neal, John	2	1	3	......	......
Neal, Charles	1	1	2	......	......
Neal, George	1	......	7	......	......
Nevell, William	1	......	7	......	......
Nixon, Henry	1	......	2	......	......
Nuttle, Elijah	4	3	4	......	......
Napper, John	1	......	5	......	......
Nicholson, Thomas	1	......	3	......	......
Nelson, Benjamin	1	......	......	......	......
O					
Oneal, Robert	2	1	3	......	......
Oneal, William	1	......	4	......	......
Oliver, John	2	1	3	......	......
P					
Powel, William	2	......	3	......	1-20
Price, John	4	2	6	......	......
Price, John, Jun'r	1	......	7	......	......
Prait, Joseph	1	......	3	......	......
Pattie, John	4	3	6	......	......
Parker, Alex & James	2	......	2	......	......
Patterson, Robert	3	2	4	......	......
Payne, Edward	18	16	10	......	......

Persons' Names	No. Tithables.	Negroes over 12.	Horses	Carriage Wheels	Stud Horses and Rate.
Payne, Henry	5	4	5	......	......
Payne, William	4	3	6	......	......
Payne, Edward, Jun'r	3	3	3	......	......
Parker, John	4	3	3	......	......
Parker, James	3	1	3	......	......
Paterson, Joseph	1	......	2	......	......
Proctor, John	2	1	3	......	......
Proctor, Thomas	1	......	2	......	......
Philip, William	1	......	1	......	......
Philips, Robert	1	......	1	......	......
Peoples, Robert	1	......	3	......	......
	79	45	116	......	1-20
P					
Payne, Sanford	5	4	2	......	......
Price, William	1	1	8	......	......
Phillips, Joel	1	......	......	......	......
Poe, Benjamin	1	......	1	......	......
Poe, John	1	......	......	......	......
Pritcher, Isaac	1	......	2	......	......
Perry, Lewis	2	1	3	......	......
Perry, Benj.	1	......	2	......	......
Proctor, Wm.	1	...	1	......	......
Proctor, John	2	......	2	......	......
Patterson, Moses	2	......	......	......	......
Piles, Conradus	3	2	3	......	......
Pruit, Joseph	1	......	2	......	......
Pruit, Elisha	2	1	3	......	......
Polly, Peter	2	......	2	......	......
Piercen, James	1	......	4	......	......
Piercen, Benj.	1	...	1	......	......
Pelham, Charles	2	......	3	......	......
Q					
Quesenberry, James	2	1	5	......	......
Quesenberry, John	1	......	......	......	......
R					
Roberts, William	5	4	4	......	......
Richerson, William	1	......	2	......	......
Rue, Richard	1	......	2	......	......
Rucker, James	4	2	4	......	......
Reding, Isaac	1	......	1	......	......

Persons' Names	No. Tithables.	Negroes over 12.	Horses	Carriage Wheels	Stud Horses and Rate.
Rice, William	1		1		
Rentfro, James	1		2		
Rice, Richard	2	1	3		
Rice, Benjamin	1		1		
Richie, James	1		4		
Richie, Samuel	1		4		
Rankins, David	4	2	8		
Rankins, David, Jun'r.	1		4		
	57	19	84		
R					
Rankins, Thomas	1		2		
Roberts, John	1		3		
Roberts, Thomas	1		2		
Rear, Alex.	2	1	6		
Robertson, Jeremiah	1		1		
Ramsey, George	1	1	6		
Rickets, Archie	1				
Rhodes, Frederick	1				
Rigs, John	1		1		
Reynolds, James	1		5		
Rowland, David	3	1	3		
Rankins, William	1		2		
Rowland, John	1		1		
Ramsey, Alex.	1	1	4		
Rud, Thomas	1		2		
Richards, William	1		2		
Raley, James	1				
Rankins, Adam	3	2	2		
Rankins, Jeremiah	1		2		
Rees, David	1				
S					
Steel, Wm. Maj'r	1		1		
Scott, Gabriel	1		5		
Scott, David	1		3		
Scotter, George	1		5		
Scott, Robert	1		2		
Scott, James	1		2		
Scott, William	2		9		
Scott, Thomas	1		4		

Persons' Names	No. Tithables.	Negroes over 12.	Horses	Carriage Wheels	Stud Horses and Rate.
Scot, Samuell	1		2		
Scott, George	1		4		
Scott, Charles	18	14	6		
	54	20	88		
S					
Scace, James	2		2		
Singleton, Jeconiah	1		1		
Stucker, Michael	1		3		
Sample, Samuel	2		2	•	
Sample, Benjamin	1		1		
Sample, John	1		2		
Smith, Elijah	2	1	2		
Stevenson, Samuel	1		9		
Stevenson, John	2		5		
Stevenson, John, Jun'r.	1		4		
Stevenson, Wm.	1		4		
Stevenson, Benjamin	6	5	2		
Sullivan, William	2	1	1		
Sublet, Lewis	3	2	3		
Sanders, Katharine	5	5	5		
Steel, Robert	1		2		
Simpson, John	1		2		
Snap, George	1		1		
Singleton, Manoah	1		3		1-12
Singleton, Edmond	5	5	30		1-20
Smithey, Wm.	1		3		
Sanders, John	12	11	4		
Shouse, Henry	1		2		
Shouse, Christian	1		3		
Siercey, John	1		1		
Stoggell, Abram	1		2		
Stott, Ranley	4	3	3		
Saduskie, Jacob	1		3		
Saduskie, James	1		2		
Stone, Wm.	5	4	4		
Stone, William, Jun'r	1		2		
Stone, John	1		2		
Smith, S. George	3	2	4		
	74	40	126		2-32

Persons' Names	No. Tithables.	Negroes over 12.	Horses	Carriage Wheels	Stud Horses and Rate.
S					
Scot, John	7	7	4		
Sidebottom, Jos	1		2		
See, Coonrod	1		1		
See, John	1		4		
Stewart, Wm.	1		1		
Sinnett, John	1				
Springer, Edw.	1		6		1-12
Steels, Andrew	3	2	6		
Step, Thomas	1		5		
Step, James	2	1	1		
Step, Joshua	3	1	5		
Stevenson, James	1	1	8		
Smith, James	1	2	3		
Scott, William	2		5		
Stevenson, Sarah	1		2		
Shaw, Samuel	1				
Sheriden, Martin	1		1		
Scott, George	1		9		
Scott, Levi	1		4		
Scott, Elisha	1		8		
Scott, Elijah	1		3		
Scott, Wm.	1		1		
Sanders, James	1		1		
Steel, Wm.	1		4		
Searcy, Bartlet	1		3		
Searcy, Richard	2		3		
Searcy, Edmond	1		2		
Smith, Elizabeth	2	2	1		
Sumneers, John	1		1		
Stogdel, Jedidah	1		1		
Stocker, John	1		1		
Spawlden, Wm.	1		1		
Smith, Joseph	1		3		
Sappington, Sylvens	1		3		
Stewart, Richard	1		1		
	46	15	99		1-12
S					
Smithey, Wm., Sen'r	2	2	2		
Smithey, Thomas	1		1		

Persons' Names	No. Tithables.	Negroes over 12.	Horses	Carriage Wheels	Stud Horses and Rate.
Steel, Robert	2	1	5		
Stevens, John	1		2		
Steurman, Thos.	2	1	2		
Snell, John	1		1		
Short, John	1		1		
T					
Taylor, John	3	3	3		
Tillery, Wm.	2	1	1		
Trabue, Daniel	3	2	4	2	
Trabue, Edward	3	2	2		
Trabue, Olamph	2	2	2		
Thomas, Wm.	2	1	3		
Thomas, William	1				
Todd, John	1		3		
Thomas, John	2	1	3		
Thomas, Thilemon	3	2	3		
Thompson, Closs	1		3		
Thompson, Laurence	1		1		
Thompson, Closs, Jun'r.	1		5		
Trimble, John	1		3		
Trimble, James	3	2	11		1-12
Trimble, Robert	1		5		
Tronsdel, John	1		3		
Torbet, James	1		4		
Taylor, Richard	1		1		
Turner, Wm.	1		2		
Twiman, Reuben	2	1	2		
Twiman, Wm.	1		1		
Thatcher, Amos	1				
Turner, Ebzey Lewis	5	4	5		
Turpin, Horatio	10	9	9		
Trotter, David	3	2	4		
	66	36	101	2	1-12
T					
Tate, Thomas	1		3		
Tracey, Samuel	1		3		
Tompson, Robert	2		8		
Tyra, John	1				
Thurman, Philip	4	3	2		

Persons' Names	No. Tithables.	Negroes over 12.	Horses	Carriage Wheels	Stud Horses and Rate.
Thirman, Richard	1		1		
Travis, Charles	1		2		
Tompson, Jediah	1				
Tompson, John	1		1		
U					
Utterback, Benj.	1		2		
Usselton, John	1		1		
Usselton, Robert	1		1		
V					
Vaughn, John	1	1	4		
Verbal, Philip	1		3		
Vanlandingham, Jas.	1		1		
Vance, David	1		1		
Verbal, Henry	1		1		
Veach, William	1		2		
Vance, Andrew	3	1	5		
Vance, John	1		2		
W					
Ward, Joseph	3		6		
Whiteacre, Henry	1		2		
White, John	2		8		
Walker, Wm.	1		3		
White, William	1				
Walker, Samuel	1		3		
Wallace, John	1		2		
Wood, James	1		0		
Walker, David	4	3	4		
	41	8	71		
W					
Walker, George	1		1		
Whitesides, Wm.	2	1	3		
Watkins, John	13	14	9		1-10
Westerman, Charles	1		2		
Woolfork, Lonyell	6	5	5		
Woolfork, Richard	6	5	5		
Woolfork, Augustin	4	3	4		
West, Charles	4	5	4		
Woolmore, John	1		2		

Persons' Names	No. Tithables.	Negroes over 12.	Horses	Carriage Wheels	Stud Horses and Rate.
Williams, John, Sen'r	1		3		
Williams, John	2	1	1		
Williams, John	2		3		
Williams, John	1		6		
Williams, Alford	1		3		
Weekley, Thomas	1		3		
Whiteacre, Thomas	1		1		
Whiteacre, John	1		4		
Whiteacre, Mark	1		3		
Wood, Elijah	1		10		1-20
Wats, John	3	2	3		
Walker, Randal	3	1	2		
Walker, John	1		1		
Walker, Henry	1		3		
Ware, Isaac	5	4	4		
Wooldridge, Josiah	2	1	4		
Wooldridge, Edmond	4	4	5	4	
Wooldridge, Robert	3	2	1		
Wooldridge, Elisha	2	1	3		
Wilcoxson, Daniel	1	1	3		
Wilcoxson, Aron	1		2		
White, Wm.	1		1		
Wharton, Richard	1		1		
Wallace, Joseph	1		3		
Wilson, Thomas	1		6		
Wallace, Caleb	6	5	9		
Worley, Caleb	4	3	5		
	90	58	128	4	2-30
W					
Williams, Mary	2	3	4		
Williams, James	1		1		
Wilson, Marget			3		
Wilson, James	1		4		
Wilson, Mary			3		
Wilson, James	1		3		
Willhite, John	1		4		
Ward, John	1		3		
White, James	1		2		
Wood, Thomas	1		2		
Woolmore, Jacob	1		2		
Welch, George	1		3		

Persons' Names	No. Tithables.	Negroes over 12.	Horses	Carriage Wheels	Stud Horses and Rate.	No. of the Page	No. Tithables	Negroes Over 12	No. Horses	Carriage Wheels	Ordinary License	Billiard Tables	Studhorses	And Rate the Season
Walden, Williams	1	......	2	......	......	1	45	19	78	......	......	......	......	......
Wiat, John	1	......	2	......	......	2	76	39	124	......	......	......	......	......
Wisdom, Thos.	1	......	2	......	......	3	70	33	121	......	......	......	......	......
Wright, James	1	......	2	......	......	4	71	35	106	4	......	......	3	54
						5	64	26	98	......	......	......	1	20
Y						6	46	6	127	......	......	......	......	......
Young, William	1	......	4	......	......	7	53	13	95	......	......	......	1	24
Young, Leonard	1	......	1	......	......	8	59	27	92	......	......	......	......	......
Young, Reuben	2	......	4	......	......	9	33	6	69	......	......	......	......	......
Young, John	1	......	1	......	.	10	49	14	100	......	......	......	1	12
Young, John, Jun'r	1	......	1	......	......	11	37	6	73	......	......	......	......	......
Young, Laurence	1	......	1	......	. ... .	12	49	17	119	......	1	1	2	24
Young, Rich'd	6	6	10	......	. .....	13	84	42	123	......	......	......	1	20
						14	56	13	113	......	......	......	......	......
Z						15	61	27	109	......	......	......	......	......
Zachary, Charles	2	1	3	......	......	16	34	8	59	......	......	......	......	......
						17	79	45	116	......	......	......	1	20
	30	10	67	......	. .....	18	57	19	84	......	......	......	......	......
						19	54	20	88	......	......	......	......	......
						20	74	40	126	......	......	......	2	32
						21	46	15	99	......	......	......	1	12
						22	66	36	101	2	......	......	1	12
						23	41	8	71	......	......	......	......	......
						24	90	58	128	4	......	......	2	30
						25	30	10	67	......	......	......	......	......
							1424	611	2480	10	1	1	16	1218

RICHARD YOUNG,
Comm'r for the year 1788.

Fayette County, Virginia, to wit:

I, Levi Todd, clerk of the county aforesaid, do certify that this book is a true copy from a list of vouchers returned to me by Richard Young Gent, one of the Commissioners of the tax for the county aforesaid for the year 1788.

LEVI TODD.

DEPARTMENT OF STATE ARCHIVES, FLOYD COUNTY.

Editor's Note—

The following list of "Tithables" for 1790 is copied from the returns made by George Stockton, Commissioner of the Tax for District No. 3, Mason County.

As will be seen by reference to the abstract copied from the records of the Mason County Court, August 26, 1789, at the time that Mason County was divided into districts, George Stocktons territory included all that part of the County to the south of North Fork of Licking and east to the Big Sandy, which territory included the district cut off in 1799 from Mason, Fleming and a small portion of Montgomery to form the large county of Floyd. In the absence of an original tax list of Floyd County earlier than 1835 it has been considered proper to publish this list of District No. 3 of Mason County for 1790, as being the one which would correspond most closely with what was afterwards Floyd County, altho it contains some names which were outside its bounds proper, and some names are omitted which we might expect to find as early settlers in the Big Sandy country.

In addition to the excerpt taken from the records of the Mason County Court which we publish below we also publish the Act of the General Assembly creating the County of Floyd, and follow this with the tax lists.

At a Court held in the town of Washington, Aug. 26, 1789,

Ordered that this County be laid off in 3 districts as follows, to wit:

District No. 1 to begin at and include Charlestown, thence along the way proposed for a road through Washington so as to include all the westward of the main street, thence along the main road to the North Fork, thence down the same to the river.

District No. 2 to begin at Charlestown and run the same lines as No. 1 to the North Fork so as to include all the inhabitants east of said division.

District No. 3 is to contain all south of the North Fork to the County line, and Miles W. Conway is appointed Commissioner of District No. 1, Arthur Fox of No. 2, and George Stockton of No. 3.

AN ACT FORMING A NEW COUNTY OUT OF THE COUNTIES OF FLEMING, MASON AND MONTGOMERY—APPROVED DECEMBER 13, 1799—

Section 1—

Be it enacted by the General Assembly of the Commonwealth of Kentucky—

That from and after the first day of June, 1800, all that part of the county of Fleming, Montgomery and Mason, included in the following boundary, towit: Beginning at the mouth of Beaver creek, near the narrows of Licking; thence north thirty degrees east to the Mason line; thence with the said line to a point opposite the head of Little Sandy; thence a straight direction to the forks of Great Sandy; thence along the division line between this state and the state of Virginia to the head waters of the Main branch of the Kentucky; thence down the same to the mouth of Quicksand; thence a straight line to the fifty mile tree on the state road; thence along said road in a direction to Mountsterling, to Blackwater; thence down the same to the mouth thereof; thence down the Licking to the beginning, shall be one distinct county, and called and known by the name of Floyd. But the said county of Floyd shall not be entitled to a separate representation, until the number of free male inhabitants therein contained, above the age of twenty-one years shall entitle them to one representative, agreeable to the ratio that shall hereafter be established by law.

Section 2—A court for the said county shall be held by the Justices thereof, on the first Monday in every month, except the months in which the courts of Quarter Sessions are held &c. &c.

Section 3—The justices to be named in the commission of the peace for the said county of Floyd, shall meet at the house of James Brown, in the said county, on the first court day after the said division shall have taken place * * * and fix on a place for holding courts in said county; then the court shall proceed to erect the public buildings in such place; and until such buildings are completed, shall appoint such place for holding courts as they may think proper &c. &c.

On December 21, 1799 Governor James Garrard nominated "by and with the consent of the Senate John McIntire, James Young and Jesse Spurlock Justices of the Floyd County Court of Quarter Sessions, and James Harris, Neely McGuire, Henry Stratton, Goodwin Lejeans (?), James Evington and Barnet Wooding, Justices of the Peace.

A LIST OF TAXABLE PROPERTY IN 1790, TAKEN IN THE THIRD DISTRICT OF THE COUNTY OF MASON (AFTERWARDS FLOYD COUNTY)

By Geo. Stockton, Commissioner

Persons Chargeable with the Tax.	Horses
Allen, Adam	
Arms, William	1
Buchannan, James	3
Bruce, Alexander	1
Baker, Francis	1
Bescom, Henry	1
Barnes, Joshua	2

Persons Chargeable with the Tax.	Horses
Brown, Presley	1
Berry, Joseph	1
Berry, Withern	
Badley (or Bodley), Andrew	
Beeson, Mejor (?)	
Black, Thomas Bell	
Cornwell, Thomas	2
Cornwell, John	1
Chinith, William	1
Carr, Hanah	1
Cassity, Michael	3
Clifford, John	2
Chinith, Richard	2
Cox, John	
*Colvin, Joseph Vance	
Camble, John	2
Crusan, Benjamin	1
Cole, Joseph	4
Culbeson, John	
Dougherty, Roger	2
Davis, Samuel	
Dickson, Griffy	3
Drake, Isaac	
*Drake, Abraham	2
Drake, Cornelius	2
Davy, Thomas	2
Dancy, Laken	2
†Dilliplain, Ben	
†Davy, Owen	4
Elrod, Thomas	1
*Edwards, Isaac	1
Early, William	
*Early, Thomas	2
Early, Joseph	
Estill, William	1
Floro, Robert	2
Floro, John	2
Floro, James	1
*Fitsgerl, Bartholemew	2
†Ferren, Isaac	3
Fitzgerl, Wm.	
Ferren, Bethersel (?)	
Fitzgerl, Eliza	2
Finch, John	3
Furlow, John	

Persons Chargeable with the Tax.	Horses	Persons Chargeable with the Tax.	Horses
Fitch, Elisha		Oliver, Peter	1
Furlow, Robert	2		
		Parks, Thomas	1
Gray, Mathew	1	Purdum, John	2
Gray, John	1	Peck, Joseph	
Gray, Isaac	2	Pettit, Thomas	
		*Parrish, Joseph	3
Hester, Jacob	1	Powel, Joseph	2
Hedly, George	2	Pursley, Francis	
Henderson, Robert	1	Plumer, Benj'n	1
Heins, Joseph	2	*Plumer, George	1
Heath, John	1		
*Hance, William	2	Rigs, John	
Hull, Isaac	2	Richards, Rheuben	1
Haven, John	3	Richards, John	2
Heath, Joseph	2	‡Ross, John	3
Hill, Joseph	1	Rolston, George	
Heath, Samuel	2	Rickets, Robert	1
Hester, Johnson	1	Russor, Joseph	1
		Rice, Bevel	
Johnston, John	1	Rous, Wilson	2
Jones, Samuel		*Reed, James	2
Jones, Benjamin		Reeves, Asea	1
		Reed, Samuel	
*Kiger, George	3	Reeves, William	1
Kenen, William		Reeves, Eley	
Kiger, John	2	*Roden, William	2
		Rolph, James	2
Logan, John		Reed, Hambleton	8
Lawrence, Isaac	1		
Lee, Alexander	2		
Long, Benjamin		Scot, William	1
Losson, James	1	Stout, Obadiah	4
Longly, Thomas	1	Stout, John	
		Smith, Samuel	2
McKee, Guion	1	Suters, George	1
Mickey, Daniel	2	Storrum, Henry	1
Marshal, John		Secret, William	1
Martin, Esael	1	*Stockton, George	3
Mills, Edward	2	Sweet, Thomas	1
Mills, Thomas	3	Stockham, William	
†Mahan, James	6	Shiveley, John	
Mills, Thomas	2	Smith, James	1
Mills, Jacob	2	Stansbury, Jeremiah	
Marshal, Thomas	2	Stags, Joseph	
*Markwell, William		Sumers, William	1
Morris, David	2	Sumers, John	3
Miller, Thomas		Sweet, Joshua	
		Slow, Thomas	2
Northcut, William		Shotwell, John	2

Persons Chargeable with the Tax.	Horses
†Sweet, Benjamin	4
Smith, Henry	1
Thomson, Andrew	1
Truet, George	1
Tapley, James	2
Tenant, Richard	2
Talor, John	3
Vanburcolo, Wm.	3
Wood, John	
Williams, John	
Wood, Andrew	2
*Wood, William	2
Wilkies, Josept	1
Wilson, Amis	1
Wilson, Thomas	1
**Williams, Thomas	1
Williams, Laurence	1

Persons Chargeable with the Tax.	Horses
Wallons, Thomas	2
Walton, Jabe	
Wilson, George	2
Wilson, Samuel	8
Welch, John	2
Web, John	2
Wood, Abraham	
††Williams, Thomas	1
Warner, John	2

This list of tithes and taxable property is for the year 1790.

(Signed) T. Marshall, Jr.

"Stockton's list 203.

"I have examined the foregoing list.

(Signed) T. Marshall, Jr., C. M. C."

*2 white males over 21.
†3 white males over 21.
‡4 white males over 21.
**At Flore's Station.
††At Fleming's Station.

DEPARTMENT OF STATE ARCHIVES — FRANKLIN COUNTY TAX LISTS, 1795.

A List of the Taxable Property Within the District of Thomas Lillard, Commissioner for the County of Franklin for 1795.

Persons Named Chargeable With the Tax	White Males Above 21	White Males Between 16 and 21	Total Blacks	Horses, Mares, Colts, and Mules	Cattle	Water Course	Acres
A							
Armstrong, Robt.	1		1	5	23		6,250
Arbuckle, Jno.	1			1	3	Ohio	1,682
Arnold, Jane					5		500
Arnold, Jno.	1		2	9	34		1,500
Abbott, Wm.	1			1			
Arnold, Jno., Jr.	1			3	8	Kentucky	140
Arnold, Jas.	1		3	5	22	Benson	460
Armstrong, Jno.	1	1		2	4		
Arnold, Stephen	1			2		Benson	400
B							
Berryman, Thos.	1			1	30		200
Boyd, Wm.	1			4	8		100
Bimson, Jos.	1			2	5		
Buntin, Andw.	1	1	4	6	22		42
Baker, Robt.	1		5	3	28		400
Byrne, Jno.	1		2	2	16		
Bennett, Benj.	2	1	3	4	15		200
Batey, Geo.	1						130
Brown, Jas.	1		1	2	4		
Bourner, Benj.	1			1			
Baker, Reuben	1			1			
Baker, Thos.	1			1			
Bell, Thos.	1			1	7		
Baker, Jas.	1			1			
Bane, Leroy	1			2	6		100
Bratten, Geo.	1			1			
Berry, Searcy	1			3	10		50
Bohannon, Austn.	1			4	5		
Bratten, Robt.	0	1					
Bennett, Timy.	1			1	4		
Brown, Scott	1		2	2			67
Berryman, Jno.	1						

Persons Named Chargeable With the Tax	White Males Above 21	White Males Between 16 and 21	Total Blacks	Horses, Mares, Colts, and Mules	Cattle	Water Course	Acres
C							
Crockett, Hamn.	1			1	8		119
Coffman, Elean.				3	8		1,300
Crockett, Antoy.	1		5	5	53		150
Crockett, Wm.	1			2	10		
D							
Driskill, David	1			3	11		120½
David, Charles	1			2	8		
Douthit, Silas	1			4	21		231
E							
Emmerson, Jesse	1		1	6	8		142
G							
Gibson, Henry	1	1		4	16		145
Gullion, Robt.	1			3	18		50
Grimes, Stephen	1		1	1		3 acres in an outlot in Harrodsburg	
H							
Hughe, Ephm.	1			1	2		
Hamilton, Andy	1			5	15		1,400
Howley, Dennis				5	17		150
Hutton, Saml.	1			1	13		100
Hutton, Jas.	1			4	14		136
Hoblet, Boston	1			1	1		
Hutton, Saml.	1			2	2		
Hutton, Jos.	1		1	1	8		50
J							
Jones, Jos.	1			5	16		
Jett, James	1		1	5	7		
Jack, Saml.	1			1	8		
Johnson, Jno.	1			4	5		
L							
Logan, Thos.	1			3	25		50
Ledgerwood. Jas.	1		3	6	17		550
Lillard, Jno., Jr.	1		3	4	13		270
Lightfoot, Jno.	1		14	12	41		292
Lillard, Thos.	1		6	7	22	Waters of	372
Lillard, Thos.						Glenn's	500
Lillard, Thos.						Creek	200
Lillard, Thos.						Caml. Co.	700
Lillard, Thos.						Licking	1,000
M							
McCampbell, Jno.	1	2		1	10		152
McGuire, Jas.	1			1	23		211
McClure, Staley	1			1	2		
McBrayer, Hugh	1			2	2		
McBrayer, Jno.				1			
Moore, Jos.	1			1	10		50
McMichael, Jas.	1			2	13		

Persons Named Chargeable With the Tax	White Males Above 21	White Males Between 16 and 21	Total Blacks	Horses, Mares, Colts, and Mules	Cattle	Water Course	Acres
Moore, Chas.	1			5	24		
Miller, Henry	1			7	13		685
Mitchell, Joe F.	1	1		3	8		
Moland, Jesse	1			1	3		
Mayhall, Timy.	1			2	3		
McBrayer, Jas.	1			3	3		300
P							
Paxton, Thos.	1		1	2	7		500
Petty, Rodham	1		1	2	5		130
R							
Robinson, Jno.	2	1		4	9		250
Robinson, Heny.	1			2	9		
Richmons, Wm.	1						
Robinson, Wm.	1	1	4	6	20		300
Righthous, Thos.	1			3	2		
Robinson, Wm.	1	2		6	37		150
S							
Simmons, Thos.	1						121
Shouse, Chas.	1			2	7		
Shouse, Jacob	1			2	1		
Sammons, Jno.	1			3	5		
Satterley, Jno.	1			1			
Sammones, Nathan	1			1			
Smith, Thomn.	1			2	1		50
Satterley, Saml.	1	1	3	1	6		60
T							
Trasey, Wm. (Exempt)				2			
Trasey, Jno.	1			1			
Trasey, Saml. (Exempt)				1	6		50
W							
Wilson, Thos.	1			5	24		605
Warren, Peter	1			3	5		92
Wilcockson, Aron	1		1	3	18		
White, Wm.	1			3			
White, Jas.	1			4	18		100
White, Jas.	2			2	2		½
Wayd, Jno.	2			5	15		200
	97	13	69	280	922		18,760½

FRANKLIN: Sct.

I do hereby Certify that the within Book contains a True Copy of Persons and Property as Certified by the Clerk of Mercer County.*

Given under my hand this 17th day of February, 1796.

Daniel Weisiger, C. F. C.

*Note:—Evidently the names contained in this list were of persons who were residents of the part of the new county of Franklin which had been taken from Mercer in 1794.—Ed.

Persons Named Chargeable With the Tax	White Males Above 21	White Males Between 16 and 21	Total Blacks	Horses, Mares, Colts, and Mules	Cattle	Water Course	Acres
A							
Applegate, Daniel	1			1	10		53
Apperson, Richd.	1		10	1	27		847
Ailen, David	1			4			
Adams, Andrew	1				3		
Anderson, Joseph	1	1			2	Hammons C. ..	200
Andrews, Alexan.	1						
Anderson, Joseph	1			2	13		634
Anderson, Reuben	1		1		1		
Anderson, Amos	1		2	1	6		125
Astor, Samuel	1			2			
Anderson, Andw.	1				3		
B							
Bledsoe, Jacob	1		1	1	5		
Bledsoe, Elizabeth			3	2	6		116
Bullard, William	1			1			
Brandenburg, Henry	1			2	14		
Bledsoe, William	1		1	3	11		
Branham, Thomas	1			1			
Bartlett, John	1		6	5	13		50
Blanton, Carter	1		7	5	8	Dry Run	116
Blanton, William	1		3	1	7		47
Brown, John	1	1	9	6	20		405
Bunham, John	1		1		6		
Bullard, R.	1		5	1	6		
Byby, Neal	1			1			
Branham, Gaydon	1			2			
Beard, Samuel	1		2	2	9		
Byby, John	1			2	4		
Bell, William	1			2			
Bledsoe, Abraham	1		2	5			
Bell, Thomas	1			1	2		
Branham, William	1		1	3	6		
Bryan, John	1			2			
Bulavare, Esther		2	6	5	25		150
Burchfield, Robert	1			1	10		
Blanton, James	1		3				
Byrn, James	1			1			100
Burham, James	1			1			
Baker, George	1				5		
Brown, Jesse	1		2	3	7		188
Brown, George	1	1	4	5	16	S. Fork Benson, Shelby Co.	321
Boyd, John	1			3	8		50
Burbridge, Rowland	1			6	34		150
Brydon, Robert	1		3	1	6		48
Bledsoe, Joseph	1		5	13	101		470
Badgley, Robert	1				4		
Bledsoe, James	1		1	5	3		50
Branham, Turner	1		4	2	1		

Persons Named Chargeable With the Tax	White Males Above 21	White Males Between 16 and 21	Total Blacks	Horses, Mares, Colts, and Mules	Cattle	Water Course	Acres
Bartlet, Henry	1		5	5	14		108
Briggs, Andrew	1			3	6		
Bradly, Thomas	1			2	16		100
C							
Cook, William	1			5	2		80
Church, Robert, Sr.	1		3	3	19		400
Church, Richard	1			2			
Colston, John	1			6	3		
Curtner, Cristopher	1			1			
Curtner, John	1						
Cox, Thomas	1			10	7		200
Copling, Samuel	1		4	3	10		112
Clark, James	1			3	8		
Chandler, Ranter	1				1		
Coachman, Jonathan	1			1			
Caril, John	1						
Cosby, Garland	1		1	2	4		
Craig, Jeremiah	1		5		6	Clark Co.	650
Church, Thomas	1			1	2		
Cook, Margaret			4	6	8		70
Cammick, Cristoph	1		1	2			
Church, Robert	1			4	9		
Cook, Seth	1			5	6	Maddison Co., Silver C.	80
Church, William	1			1			
Crutcher, John	1		1	3	8		
Cristean, Gilbert	1		4	4	8		
Carson, Elisabeth				1	10		
Craig, Joseph	1		2			Ohio Co.	466
Church, Henderson	1			2			
Cox, Agnes		2	1	7	17		685
Carson, David	1						
Corteet, Sarah			2	1	2		
Cook, Abraham		1		2	3		
Chandler, John Jack	1	1	1	2	10		80
Clemont, Barnet	1				5		
Craig, Benjamin	1		3	9	17	Several counties	7,157
D							
Demint, John	1			2	7		76
Duff, Samuel	1						
Davis, Samuel	1		1	1	4		
Devine, Roger	1		1	1	2		50
Demint, Joreab ?	1			7	26		50
Dunn, William	1				5		
E							
Ewing, Baker	1		9	7	11	Lincoln Co.	3,000
Edwards, Simeon	1				8		
English, Elisha	1			4	10		
Ewin, Thomas	1			1			
Edwards, John	1	2	4	1	9		81
Edrington, Joseph	1			2	15	Madison Co.	120
Easterday, Lewis	1			1	7		100

Persons Named Chargeable With the Tax	White Males Above 21	White Males Between 16 and 21	Total Blacks	Horses, Mares, Colts, and Mules	Cattle	Water Course	Acres
Elliot, Eleazor	1				7		
Edwards, Benjamin	1		1	1	6		33
Elis, Joseph	1						
Ellis, Obediah	1			2	9		
Edrington, Benjamin	1			1	11		
Edrington, John	1		1	4	11	Shelby Co.	507
Edwards, Uriah	2	2	7	6	23		75
Ellis, Jesse	1						
Edwards, Mildred		1	10	2	3		
Ellis, William	1			1			
Ellis, Eleazor	1			1	7		
F							
Fester, John	1				2		
Faris, William	1				4		
Fenwick, William	1		17	8	19		317
Fenwick, Robert	1		10	3	5		35
Faught, Joseper	1				3		
Farmer, Joel	1			1	3		
Farmer, John, Jr	1			1			
Farmer, Elisha	1			3			
Fewel, Rhoddy	1			1			
Fenwick, Enoch	1			1			
Frought, Powel	1	1	4	3	15		
Floyd, Gideon	1			1	1		
Farmer, John, Sr.	1	2		2	11		
Fowler, John	1		8	2	2		
G							
Graham, William	1			2			
Gest, Thomas	1		6	14	20		
Garnet, Benjamin	1		8	5	7		100
Garnet, George	1			1			
Gano, Isaac E.	1		2		2		
Griffith, Thomas	1			13			
Garnet, Sarah				1	1		
Gullion, Henry	1		1	1	1		
Griffin, Ninian	1			2			
Gale, James	1			1	6		
Goare, Isaac	1				4		32
Grimes, James	2		2	2	7		90
Gano, John	1		1	4	6		200
‡Gano, Daniel	1				1		
Gore, William	1		5	2	29		100
Gullion, Jeremiah	1		1	1	12		
Gibson, Sarah		1	2	2	9		35
Gains, William	1			2	6		50
Gano, Richard	1			1			
Grimes, John	1		1	1	1		
H							
Handcock, Simon	1			9	3	9	120
Hubble, William	1			2	3	5	130
Hall, William	2				2	13	130

Persons Named Chargeable With the Tax	White Males Above 21	White Males Between 16 and 21	Total Blacks	Horses, Mares, Colts, and Mules	Cattle	Water Course	Acres
Hutten, Robert	1		14	3	14		163
Hay, Cristopher	1	2	1	5	8		500
Hayden, William	1			4	6		140
Haydon, James	1		10	4	20		156
Hickman, Thos.	1		3	1	12		
Haydon, James	1		3	1	11		
Holt, Daniel	1				1		
Hatten, Elizabeth					5		4
Head, Benjamin	1			1	8		40
Hawthorn, James	1					Green Co.	200
How, John	1						
Holloway, Robt.	1			3	9		50
Hickman, Will	1	1		3	12		2,172
Hawkins, Elisha	1			1	7		63
Hicklin, Thomas	1			7	24		82
Hampton, James	1			4	9		200
Hawkins, Will	1	1	6	5	24		
Hickman, Willm., Jr.	1		1	2	10		51
Hatton, Dempsey	1						
I							
Innes, Harry	2		15	16	50		10,265
J							
Jackson, John	1			1	3		
Johnston, David	1			2	7		50
James, Daniel	1	4	3	1	16		198
Jones, Joshua	1						
K							
Katon, Hezekiah	1			2	2		
Kinada, Benjn.	2		1	1	1		
L							
Lindsey, Nicholas	1			3	2		
Lewis, Jesse	1			5	11		
Lloyd, Thomas	1		3	3	15		100
Long, John	1			3	3		
Lindsey, Vachal	1		1	3	2		
Lee, John	1			2	4		
Long, John	1		3	3	13		
Logan, John	1	1	15	11	43		3,900
Logan, John, Jr.	1				1		
Lafon, Nicholas	1			1			
Letcher, Stephen G.	2		13	3	6		
Lindsey, Anthony	1			2	7		50
Lee, Gersham	1			1	3		
M							
Murray, William	1		1	2			544
Major, John, Sr.	1		13	5	19		705
Marshall, William	1		1	1	2		
Montgomery, Saml.	1			1	6		
Murphy, John	1	1		5	8		

Persons Named Chargeable With the Tax	White Males Above 21	White Males Between 16 and 21	Total Blacks	Horses, Mares, Colts, and Mules	Cattle	Water Course	Acres
Montgomery, Joseph	2		2	5	9		226
McKinley, Hanna			1		1		
McCall, William	1						
Muster, John	1			1	3		7
Moore, Eleanathen	1			1			
Montgomery, John	1			1	3		
Michel, John	1			3	17		
Miles, John	1			6	18		29
Majors, James	1			1			
Montgomery, Robert	1		3	9	20		200
Manning, William	1		4	2	6		180
Mason, James	1						
McCracken, Senica	1	1	3	4	15	Franklin and Shelby	1,980
Martin, Elijah	1				3		
Montague, Thomas	1	1	4	5	18		245
Mershon, Titus	1			2			
McAndrew, Buneon	1			4	10		
Major, Thomas	1		4	3	12		
Mershon, Benj.	1						
Moxley, Samuel	2		14	7	32		205
Major, John, Sr.	1		4	5	12		100
McCreary, Andw.	1						
Martin, Thomas	2			6	13		100
Marstan, John	1			3	14		27
Montgomery, Wm.	1		4	5	17		201
N							
New, Jethra	1			3	3		
Newberry, Henry	1						
Noel, Caleb	1			4			
Nash, John	1	1		3	12		110
Neal, William	1		6	5	11		150
O							
Owen, William	1		5	3	13		
Oliver, Thomas						Mercer	1,500
P							
Powel, Owen	1			1			
Poe, Benjamin	1			2	2		
Parmer, Thomas	1	1		2	6		25
‡Payne, McDaniel	1			1			
Peak, Thomas	1			2	10		50
Peak, Daniel	1		2	2	5		100
Piper, Ase	1			1	7		
Pemberton, Richard	1		7	4	4		
Perry, John	1			1			
Phillip, Joel	1			1	3		
Porter, James	1		2	3	5		97
Patterson, Robert	1		7	10	2		430
Pemberton, Burnet	1		12	7	20		200
Pemberton, Henry	1		2	1	2		
Pulliam, Benjamin	1				2		

Persons Named Chargeable With the Tax	White Males Above 21	White Males Between 16 and 21	Total Blacks	Horses, Mares, Colts, and Mules	Cattle	Water Course	Acres
Poe, Virgil	1			1			
Poly, John	1						
Porter, William	1	1		2	2		10
Poindexter, Thomas	1		8	1	5		
Price, John	1		8	7	12		872
Patterson, Alexander	1			1	10		
R							
*Roberts, James	1		6		7		979
Robertson, Owen	1			1			
Roberts, William	1		2	4	7		150
Rennicks, John	1		1	1	5		
Richards, Philomen	1		3	5	3		
Rowlet, William	1			3			
Ross, Zachariah	1			2	13		
Robertsen, Samuel	1			1			
Robertson, Mills	1	1		2	11		69
Richards, William	1			3	9		100
Renifro, James	1			2	8		710
Rowland, George	1	2	3	3	6	Green Co., Sinking Cr.	600
Rayburn, James	1			2	5		
Richardson, Nathl.	4		14	5	34	Franklin and Green	500
Reynolds, Thomas	1			1			
Roberts, John	1		1	5	15		
Reyon, John	1		3	1	9		
Robinson, George	1			1			
S							
Samuel, Reuben	1	1	4	1	1	Elkhorn	322
Samuel, Jiles	1	1	12	4	12		165
Sullinger, Robert	1		2	1	2		
Scanland, Robert	1	1	3	2	10		62
Stevins, John	1			6	5		100
Saunders, Nathaniel	1		17	7	17		4,132
Stout, David	1		2	1	1		
Slaughter, George	1		3	1	6	Jefferson	550
Straughen, John	1			1	8		
See, George	1						100
Sullinger, Larkin	1			1			
Sheets, William	1			7	13		
Smith, John	1		6	10	9		1,000
Samuel, William	1		5	3	17	Shelby, Ky.	274
Settle, Thomas	1		1	2	7		4,998
Samuel, Peter	1	2	7	5	19		966
Short, John	1			1			
Surmones, William	2		1	4	4		
Saunders, Nathl., Jr.	1		2	2	4		150
Smithers, William	1	1		5	12		150
Sacre, James	1		1	4	7		50
Saunders, John	1	1	15	11	25		1,100
Smither, Robert	2		1	5	10		1,404
Scott, Benjamin	1			4			

Persons Named Chargeable With the Tax	White Males Above 21	White Males Between 16 and 21	Total Blacks	Horses, Mares, Colts, and Mules	Cattle	Water Course	Acres
Sullinger, James	1		3	2	2		41
Stapp, Benjamin	1			1			
Scrogen, William	1			1	3		
Scanland, Edmond	1			1			
Sheets, Henry	1			2	3		
Slater, John Toms	1			3			
Swift, Thomas	1		3	3	11		
Saunders, James	1		2	3	7		
Samuel, William	1						200
T							
Taylor, Joshua	1		6	2	3		168
Todd, Thomas	1	2	7	3	10		12,390
Tunstell, William	1		3				
Tunstell, Thomas	1		9				105
Thompson, William	1						
Trigg, William	1		13	7	12		300
Tinsley, Jonathan	1			1	7		
Tate, James	1			5	15		100
Tureman, William	1		4	2	8		75
Tinsley Archd.	1						
Travis, John S.	1		2	2	5		500
U							
Underwood, Jonathan	1			2	2		
V							
Vaughan, Edmund	1		9	3	13		150
Voorhees, Peter G.	1			1			125
Vawter, Jesse	1			3	9		100
Vanpelt, John	1			1	5		
W							
White, William	1		1	2	3		60
William, Andrew	1			2	7		109
Widner, George	1			2			
Ware, Edmond	2		7	3	10		200
Wilson, Joshua	1			2	3		
White, Ambrose	1			1	8		78
**Weysiger, Daniel	1		2	2	9		18½
Wylie, Henry	1			1			
Wyant, Jacob	1				9	Maddison	204
Wilson, John	1			1	8		
Wilson, Finelon	1		8	7	11		175
Weir, David	1						
Wooldridge, Robert	1		6	2	10		50
†Worthington, Edward	1		1	1	1		146
Ware, William	1		8	2	15		
Y							
Yates, Jacob	1						
Young, Nimrod	1		1	1	7		
	321	44	637	798	2,180		79,980

*Ordinary license.   †Billard table.
**Ordinary license and retail store.   ‡Retail store.

NON RESIDENTS LAND ENTERED.

August 6th, 1795, Samuel Shannon Enters The following Tracts of Land for the payment of Taxes With The Commissioner of Franlin (Franklin?) County.

2000 Acres	1st Rate	Bourbon	County	Stoners fork
2000 Acres	2nd Do	Clark	Do	
5600 Do	2nd Do	Do	Do	Slate Creek
560 Do	2nd Do	Do	Do	Do Do
560 Do	1st Do	Fayette	County	Cane Run
560 Do	1st Do	Scott	Do	Elk Horn
560 Do	2nd Do	Do	Do	Do Do
560 Do	2nd Do	Do	Do	Do Do
560 Do	2nd Do	Woodford	Do	Kentucky Waters
560 Do	2nd Do	Do	Do	Do Do
560 Do	2nd Do	Scott	Do	Elk Horn

Saml. Shannon

William Thompson Enters for Ephriam Jackson of Philadelphia 3000 Acres 2nd Rate Land Lying in Kentucky for the paymt of Taxes for the years 1792 1793 & 1794.

William Thompson.

Sepr. 25th 1795 David Coplin Enters for Agness White 526 Acres 2nd Rate Land Lying in Green County Caseys Creek

David Coplin.

Sepr. 25th 1795 David Coplin Enters for Philips and Young of Philadelphia 100,000 Acres 3rd rate land lying in Franklin County on Eagle Creek payment of taxes 1795.

David Coplin.

Samuel Handcock enters for Isaac Thompson Louden County Virga land in Kentucky as followeth To-wit:

375 Acres	¾ of 500	on Kentucky	Opposite Drennens lick C Shelby County.
2250 Do	¾ of 3000	Do	on the forks of Mill Creek Shelby County.
59½ Do	½ of 119	Do	on cany fork Rough Creek Hardin County
940½ Do	½ of 1881	Do	Do Do Do Do Do Do Do
730½ Do	½ of 1461	Do	on Drennens lick Creek Shelby County.
500 Do	½ of 1000		on cany fork Rough Creek Hardin County.

775 Acres ¾ of 1000 Nancy Thompson on Kenty Shel Co.
775 Acres ¾ 1000 Samuel Thompson on Kentucky Do.

Samuel Handcock
Atty in fact for said
Thompson.

Aug. 13th 1795 Thomas Posey enters for Charles T. Mortimer of Fredericksburg, Virginia 4125 Acres of land Lying in Shelby County waters of Patens Creek Second rate also enters for himself 1200 Acres of Land Suryed for John Thornton lying in Bourbon County licking waters Second rate also 800 Acres in Logan County Trade waters Second rate also 2000 Acres on Muddy River Logan County Second rate.

T. Posey.

57

Joseph Donephan enters for John Heath 1000 acres of Land on Brush Creek Neilson County second rate Aug. 20th 1795.

Joseph Donephan.

Thomas Posy Enters 18 Aug. 1795 One thousand Acres of Land lying on the waters of Llyods fork Second rate also 1000 Acres on cedar Creek both in Jefferson County.

T. Posey.

John Smith Enters for the Heirs of William Strother Maddison Deceased for the following tracts of Land to the Commissioner of Franklin County Aug. 13, 95 1000 Acres of land in Jefferson County on the trace from the falls to Bullits lick Fern Creek patent bearing date the 15 May 1784. Also 2000 Acres in Jefferson County on the Waters of Bullskin patent bearing date the 23 Apl. 1793.

Also 1000 Acres in Jefferson County about 10 Miles below the falls of Ohio on the Same patent bearing date the 17 May 1790.

John Smith.

Leedwell Grimes Enters for John Steep and Jno. Tucker of the State of Virginia Supposed to be lying in the County of Logan 1280 Acres of Second rate land this 2nd July 1795.

Leedwell Grimes.

John Arthurs Enters for thomas Harris 10,000 Acres of Land on the Salt fork of licking of the Second rate this 30 June 1795.

John Arthurs

Elias Hedger enters July 29th 1795 500 acres of Land Second rate in Shelby County on the waters of drennings lick Creek for the payment of Taxes 1795.

Elias Hedger.

William Marshall of Henrico County and State of Virginia enters for Bowler Cock of the County and State aforesaid 3946 acres of land on the headwaters of brush Creek a branch of Cumberland Supposed to be in the County of   Second rate also 3804 Acres on Dicks river in the County of Lincoln Second rate also 2250 adjoining the last mentioned Survey Second rate also Enters for Andru Reynald and James Brown Ass'ee of William Reynold 11,294½ Acres in 10 Surveys Military land Second rate also 3 Surveys in the name of James Williams of Baltimore containing 1331 Acres the waters of the Kentucky river Second rate Woodford County also for Geo. Picket of the City of Richmond Virginia ass'ee of Martin Sheriman one Thousand Acres Military land the Same ass' of Nathaniel Savage 900 Acres Military land also for Richard Adams 2000 on the waters of Licking County of Bourbon Second rate also 4000 four hundred thirty seven and one half Acres Land located in the names of Charles Marshal Simon Morgan William Marshal on the waters of Cabin Creek in the County of Mason also 3000 acres in the name of William Marshall Junior, Mouth of Sandy Mason County Second rate 2750 in the names of Simon Morgan Charles Marshall and William Marshall on the waters of the Ohio and Cabin Creek Mason County also Enters for Charles Johnston 5145½ Acres lying on the South Side of the north fork of the Kentucky granted by John McCall third rate

58

also for William Fenwick 2000 Acres granted to William Thomas Hays Ass'n of Benjamin Murray lying when patented in Fayette Co. Second rate which was in 1786 this 6th July.   Sige William Marshal.

William Marshall also enters for Elias Longham 1166⅔ Acres Ohio River Mason County Second rate.   William Marshall.

John Brown Henrico County State of Virginia enters 1168 Acres of land on Clear Creek County of Woodford patented in the name of Charles Marshall also 586 patented in the name of Willm Marshall on the Same Creek and in the Same County both of which are of the Second rate or Quality also an undivided Moity of 736 Acres And 754 Granted to the Executors of George Meriweather also One Other undivided moity of 2972 Acres granted to Nicholas Meriweather all lying on Clever Creek Hardin County Second rate or quality this 6th day of July 1795 for 1792 1793 1794 & 1795.
                                          John Brown.

Benjamin Craig Enters for his Father Toliver Craig 500 Acres land first rate.
                                          Benjamin Craig.

Octr. 24th 1795 Allen Womack from Pittsylvania County and State of Virginia Enters 5000 Acres land lying on each side of Little Sandy Mason County third rate.
                                          Alen Womack.

William Murray Returns for William Murray not an Inhabitant of this State but of the Natchez District in province of West Florida.

200 Acres land in the County of Shelby part of an undivided 1000 Acres Tract in the said County William Murrays name first Rate on fox Run a Branch of Brashears Creek.
                                          William Murray.

October 24th 1795 George Matterson Enters for James Curray 1000 Acres of land on trade Water Logan County 2nd Rate.
                                          George Matterson.

October 10th 1795 Samuel Price Enters for Benjamin Stephens 1000 Acres land lying on mill Creek Harrison County second Rate sd. Stephen living in the County and State of   Samuel Price.

Octr 16th 1795 Moses Cherry & Hugh Emmison Enters 200 Acres The half of an Undivided Tract of 400 Acres Land in the County of Shelby between the Waters of Little Kentucky & Drinnons Creek second Rate Entered in the name of Peter Crawford.
                                          Moses Cherry.
                                          Hugh Emmison.

Octr 9th 1795 Archibald Beard Enters for Joseph Dunlap of the County of Franklin & State of Pennsylvania 696 Acres land lying on the Kentucky River In the County of Franklin second Rate.   Archd Beard.

Octr. 24th 1795 Thomas Watson Enters for John Watson of the County of Prince Edward & State of Virginia 1968 Acres of land lying between and on the waters of the main

59

& south Fork of the licking below Indian Creek and Adjoining the lands of Daniel Brodhead Harrison County heretofore entered as 3rd Rate Land.

Thos. Watson.

Septr 29th 1795 James Herd Enters for Genl Daniel Morgan of Frederick County State of Virginia the following Tracts of land (Viz.)

2666⅔ Acres Waters of lost Creek Branch of the Ohio Green County Second Rate.

1000 Acres in the name of Drury Ragsdale Assignd To Genl Morgan On the Waters of the Ohio Near Hendersons line County   Second Rate 1000 Acres in the last mentioned name Assigned to Genl Morgan on Trade Water River County of Logan 2nd Rate.

1256 Acres in the name of John Earl Assigned to Genl Morgan on the Waters of a Creek which Empties in Hingstons fork Of Licking on the North side between the Upper & lower Blue lick Traces Harrison County Second Rate.

2000 Acres on the Waters of Stoners & Hingston forks Of Licking County of Bourbourn second Rate 1532 Acres on the Waters of Stoners fork North East Side Bourbourn County second Rate.   James Herd.

Octr 9th 1795 Archibald Beard Enters for himself 500 Acres the half of an Undivided Tract of 1000 Acres land in Nelson County on the waters of the Beach fork of Salt River second Rate also for Daniel Beard of Franklin County and State of Pennsylvania The half of an Undivided Tract of 1000 Acres land On which Beardstown is Established In Nelson County first Rate Also for himself of the County and State Aforesaid 300 Acres in Nelson Cty second Rate Also for Richard Beard of the County and State Aforesd 150 Acres on Buffaloe Creek in Nelson County Second Rate.

Archd Beard.

Oct. 28th 1795 Daniel Weiseger Enters for John Roberts of the County of Prince George and State of Virginia 1200 Acres of Military Land Waters of Green River supposed to be in the County of Logan second Rate for the payment of Taxes.

Also for John Murchie of Chesterfield County and State of Virginia 2987 Acres of land on salt River Nearly opposit the County of Jefferson On the Register Books second rate for the payment of Taxes.   Daniel Weisiger.

Octr 29th 1795 Gabriel Lewis Enters for John Lewis of Spotsilvania County & State of Virginia.

25000 Acres of Land on Green River Hardin County 2nd Rate The half of an Undivided Tract of 50000 11000 acres The half of an Undivided Tract of 22000 Acres on Floyds Fork Jefferson County 2nd Rate 12000 Acres on Rockcastle Lincoln County 2nd Rate 10000 Acres on Sandy Creek Mason County 3rd Rate 6847½ Acres on Elk Horn Franklin County 3rd Rate 2233¼ Acres the Half of an Undivided Tract of 4466½ Acres on the Waters of Millers Creek Clark County 3rd Rate 1672 Acres in 2 Surveys Adjoining on the Waters of Floyds Fork Jefferson County 3rd Rate.

6000 Acres Lying on Licking Creek supposed to be in Harrison County 2nd Rate 1000 North fork of Bear Grass Jefferson county 2nd Rate.

1800 Acres the 6th part of an entry made in The name of the Exors. of Fielding Lewis decd. on Kentucky River Shelby Cty. 2nd Rate patented in the name of Lewis & May on Hardin Creek & Rowling fork of Waters Supposed To be in Washington County 2nd Rate.

55542 Acres on Richland Creek Lincoln County 3rd Rate.

2000 Acres on Hardens Creek Hardin County 2nd Rate.

1000 Acres Springers Military Claim On The Ohio Jefferson Cty. 2nd Rate Also for John Minor Jr. of Spotsylvania County & State of Virginia 2433 Acres on the Waters of Little Kentucky Shelby County 2nd Rate.

Also for John Brownlow of the County & State Aforsd 1000 Acres on the Ohio Franklin County 2nd Rate.   Gabriel Lewis.

Oct 29th 1795 Robert Paterson enters for Charles Patterson of Buckingham County & State of Virginia 5625 Acres of Land Lying on The Waters of The North fork of Licking & Salt Lick Creek Mason County 3rd Rate.

Also 4000 Acres on the first Large Creek Emptying into the Ohio Above Big Bone Creek Campbell County 2nd Rate.   Robert Paterson.

Octr 30th 1795 James Farquher Enters 500 Acres of Land Lying on the Waters of Drinnons Lick Creek County of Shelby For the Paymt of Taxes 2nd Rate.
                                                             James Farquher.

Novr 2nd 1795 James Brown Enters for John Mitchel Of Philadelphia Pensylvania 5000 Acres of land lying as Follows (i. e.) on the North side of a fork On Kentucky Adjoining lands Entered by Robert Lewason when patented in Fayett County Which Was in may 1786 Now Clark or madison, Part Of A tract Of 126574 Acres Granted to James Reynalds 3rd Rate Also 3037 Acres part of a Tract of 16142 acres Granted to Sd Reynalds on the 7th day June 1787 then in Lincoln County On Warrant 18,026 16,418 18,043 18,044 18121-18025. 15301-19967. 19962 3rd Rate.

                                           James Brown
                                           for John Mitchel.

Novr. 2nd 1795 John West Enters 90 Acres of land lying On the Dividing Ridge between the little Kentucky & Ohio River Shelby County 2nd Rate.
                                                             John West.

Novr. 2nd Daniel Gano Enters 12,653⅛ Acres of land a part of A Tract of 50,612½ Acres lying on Red River a fork of Kentucky Clark County 3rd Rate for payment Of Taxes.   Daniel Gano.

October 31st 1795 Robert Kirk Enters 666⅔ Acres land At the Mouth Of Parekeet On the Ohio. County of Logan Also 134½ Acres Adjoining the Above third Rate for the Payment Of Taxes.   Robert Kirk.

Novr 3rd 1795 John S. Wills Enters 56534 Acres Of land for Thomas Pierce liveing in the County Of Isle of Wight And State Of Virginia lying on the head Of the Main Branch Of Licking Creek supposed to be in   County 3rd Rate part Of A tract Of 61,435½ Acres Granted To William Hardie Heir to Samuel Hardie Decd Wm Davis Francis Boykin Robert Marshall & John Laurence 20th Apl 1792.
                                           John S. Wills
                                           for Thomas Pierce.

Nov. 3rd 1795 Charles Toliver Enters for himself & Mary Peyton heirs Of Alexander Dick Of Carolina and Mathews Counties And State Of Virginia 3110⅔ Acres Of land lying on the Main fork Of the West fork Of Wolf Creek a branch Of Cumberland River Granted to James Mercer Esqr. Devisee of Sd Dick the 14th Of Octr. 1785 2nd Rate Also 5000 Acres lying on the little Kentucky Granted to sd Mercer aforesaid 19th Apl. 1792 then in Jefferson County now supposed to be Shelby 3rd Rate Also 2000 lying on the Main West fork Of Glenns Creek when patented in the District set apart for the Officers Of Virginia State line Which Was in October 1785 2nd Rate Also 1000 Acres on a ridge between two small Drains at the head of an Eastern branch Of the Main fork Of Lynns Camp Creek when patented In Nelson County Which Was in Novr 1787 Granted to George May 2nd Rate.   Charles C. Tallafereo.

A list of lands Returned by John Brown to the Commissioners Of the land Tax for Franklin County State Of Kentucky 2000 Acres 1st Rate Woodford County Waters of South Elkhorn.

1000 Acres Shelby County 2nd Rate Guests Creek.

5000 Acres 2nd Rate Shelby County Fox Run 3 years Tax paid by Aquilla Whittaker.

862 Acres 2nd Rate Shelby County On a branch of brashiers Creek.

4000 Acres 3rd Rate Shelby County Ohio River.

1400 Acres 3rd Rate Franklin County Kentucky River Clay Lick.

1000 Acres 2nd Rate Franklin County Kentucky River above Clay Lick.

1000 Acres 3rd Rate Jefferson County Chenowith River.

500 Acres 3rd Rate Jefferson County Ohio River.

70 Acres 2nd Rate Jefferson County 18 Mile Island.

200 Acres 2nd Rate Jefferson County Ohio River.

400 Acres 2nd Rate Jefferson County Pond Creek.

2400 Acres 3rd Rate Hardin County Indian Camp Creek.

3833⅓ Acres 3rd Rate part Of 15000 Acres Hardin County Rough Creek.

1000 Acres 3rd Rate Hardin County Green River.

300 Acres 3nd Rate Washington County Pleasant Run.

1000 Acres 3rd Rate Logan County Little River.

1000 Acres 3rd Rate Logan County West fork Red River 3 years Tax paid by
                                                            Wm. Croghan.

1000 Acres 3rd Rate Logan County Flinns fork Tradewater 3 years Tax paid by
                                                            Richd Taylor.

6800 Acres 3rd Rate part of 8000 Acres Lincoln County Frazers Creek.

Also Enters for Anthony Walton White Of Brunswick state of New Jersey 10,000 Acres Of Land lying on Rough Creek Hardin County 3d Rate.

Also for James Swan Of Philadephia state of Pennsylvania 50,000 acres Lying On Ottor Creek Harden County 3rd Rate 5000 Acres Lying on Big Sandy Mason County 3rd Rate Also for the Rev. John Hart of Philadelphia & state Aforesd 1400 Acres Logan County North fork Of Trade Water 3rd Rate 540 same County East fork Of Muddy River 3rd Rate 1000 same County Green River 3rd Rate 500 Acres same County Muddy River 3rd Rate 200 Acres same County East Branch Pond River 3d Rate 171 same County Green River 3rd Rate Also for Richard Gernon of Philadelphia and state last mentioned 1000 acres lying in logan county Joining William Drineands Survey 2nd Rate also for Samuel Meridith & George Clymer Of Place aforesaid 666⅔ Acres part of 2000 Campbell County landing Creek 3rd Rate 333⅓ Acres part of 1000 Mason County Joining Mays lick 1st Rate 666⅔ Acres part of 2000 Campbell Cty Bank Lick Creek 3rd Rate Also for Samuel Meridith of the same Place 6644 Acres part of 19,934 Clark County Slate Creek 3d Rate 66⅔ Acres part of 200 Franklin County Kentucky River 2nd Rate 333⅓ Acres on a branch Of Licking above Hington bourbourn or Harrison Cty. 3rd Rate Also 133⅓ Acres Campbell Cty. forks of licking 2nd Rate 133⅓ Acres part of 400 Branch Of Licking above hington Harrison County 2d Rate Also for George Clymer of Philadelphia 3666⅔ Acres part of 14000 Acres Waters of Harrods Creek Jefferson County 2nd Rate.

Jno. Brown.

Novr. 5th 1795 Gabriel I. Johnston Enters 250 Acres of Land part of an Entry made in the name of Edward Arskins for 600 Acres Jefferson County Waters of Fern Creek 3d Rate. Gabriel I. Johnston.

June 7th
Andrew Kinnacannon Enters 1157 Acres of land on Elkhorn 2nd Rate Franklin County.

Andrew Kinnacannon.

Edmond Vaughan Enters for the heirs of John Mitchel Decd. 833½ acres land lying in the County of Woodford on the Waters of the North fork Of Elk Horn 3rd Rate this 9th Novr 1795. Edmond Vaughan.

Novr. 9th 1795 Robt. Todd Enters 666⅔ Acres Land the ⅓ Part of a 2000 Acre Entry lying on Robinsons Creek a branch Of Green River in the County Of Green 3d Rate also the residue Of Sd Tract of 2000 for James Brown and Adam Guthrie.

Robt. Todd.

Octr 13th 1795 John Chilton Enters for the Estate of Charles Chilton Decd. 1666⅔ Acres land lying on Panthers Creek the South side thereof when patented in Jefferson County which was in 1779 & 1783 for the payment of Taxes 2d Rate.

John Chilton.

Novr 11th 1795 Price Curd Enters for John Curd 1000 Acres Land lying on Licking on the south side Indian Creek bourbourn cty 2d Rate Also 1000 Acres in Shelby County waters Of Brashers Creek 2d Rate Also for William Curd Of buckingham County & state Of Virginia 1000 Acres on the Waters Of Elkhorn supposed to be in Scott County 2d Rate.

Price Curd.

HART COUNTY, KENTUCKY

The destruction by fire of the Court House of Hart County with practically all its contents in 1928, has reduced to a minimum the authentic records of that county. For this reason it seems proper to publish at this time some original data of the county which is on file in the Kentucky State Historical Society "Archives Department," and which may prove of interest and service in the future.

The county was formed from portions of Hardin and Barren in 1819, under an Act which reads in part as follows:

"An Act for the erection of the county of Hart, out of the Counties of Barren and Hardin, Approved January 28, 1819.

"Section 1

"Be it enacted by the General Assembly of the Commonwealth of Kentucky:

"That from and after the first day of April next, so much of the counties of Barren and Hardin as is included within the following boundary, to-wit: Beginning at the mouth of Little Barren river, running thence up the same to Elk Lick;

thence with the Green county line four miles and a half; thence a straight line to a point ten miles and one-half due north of Barren court-house; thence a due west line to the Warren county line; thence with the same to Green river; thence down Green river to the mouth of Nolin creek; thence up the same to the mouth of Jacob Miller's spring branch; thence a straight line to Benjamin Martin's old place, where —— Raglin now lives, leaving the same in the new county, and the same course continued to Green county line; thence with the same to Green river; thence up the same to the beginning; shall be one distinct county, to be called and known by the name of Hart.

"Section 2.

"The justices of the peace for the county of Hart shall meet at the house of *Thomas Woodson*, on the second Monday in April next and after taking the necessary oaths of office, and qualifying their sheriff according to law, they shall proceed to elect a clerk, &c. * * * *

"Section 3.

" * * * The county of Hart shall form a part of the 8th judicial district; and the circuit judge assigned to that district shall attend and hold the court for Hart county. And the circuit court for Hart county shall be held at the house of *Elijah Creel* until a court-house is provided by the county court.

* * * * *

"Section 7.

"All the inhabitants of the county of Hart, residing on the opposite side of Green river from that on which the court-house is fixed, shall cross the said river, at any ferry within the county free of any charge therefor, in going to and returning from their several county and circuit courts, elections, and general and regimental musters.

* * * * *

"Section 8.

"The surveyor of Barren county shall run and mark the boundary of the county of Hart, on the south side of Green river, and the surveyor of Hardin county shall run and mark the boundary of the county of Hart on the north side of Green river; for which services the said surveyors and their chain-carriers shall be paid, out of the first levy of the said county of Hart.

"And whereas it is represented * * that considerable sums of money and property would be subscribed by individuals, for the purpose of erecting the public buildings for said county, and thereby lessen, if not wholly relieve the county from an expence, if authorized for that purpose: Therefore,

"Section 9.

"Be it enacted, That the clerk of the county court of said county is authorized and empowered to open subscription papers, for the purpose of proposals or subscriptions, in money or property, to any amount *not exceeding eight thousand dollars*, from any person or persons, for the erecting the public buildings * * * * and all sums so subscribed and received, or so much thereof as the county court shall deem nceessary for that purpose, shall be applied by them to the erecting of the public buildings, and the residue if any, to be paid over to the person or persons subscribing the same.

"Section 10.

"Be it further enacted,

"That *James Ray, of Mercer, Anthony Butler* and *Thomas S. Slaughter, of Logan, William Buckner, of Green,* and *Martin H. Wickliffe, of Nelson,* or a majority of them, be, and they are hereby [appointed] commissioners to fix on a place for the seat of justice for said county, who shall meet at the house of Elijah Creel, on the third Monday of April next or as soon thereafter as practicable, and each having taken the oath before some justice of the peace for said county, to discharge the duty of a commissioner in fixing the place for the permanent seat of justice of said county of Hart, without favor, affection, partiality or prejudice, according to the best of his skill and ability, shall proceed to select the most proper place for the seat of justice for said county, having due regard to population, territory, public convenience and situation, and the capacity

65

of the land in said county for sustaining future population, and also such subscriptions or proposals as shall be made by any person or persons for erecting the public buildings for said county. * * * And as soon thereafter as practicable, the county court shall cause to be erected, on the place so designated by said commissioners for that purpose, the necessary public buildings."

February 6, 1819, Governor Slaughter appointed "with the consent of the Senate" the following gentlemen to be Magistrates of Hart county: William Kasinger, Richard Munford, Isham Hardy, Arthur McGaughey, George McLean, Benj. I. McCall, Philip Maxey, Robert Ferguson, Jacob Holderman, Ephriam Maxey, Thomas B. Holt, Thomas B. Munford, Dudley Rountree, William Whitman and Jesse Wood.

Jacob Holderman declined to serve, and Aylette H. Buckner, (father of Gen. Simon Bolivar Buckner) was commissioned in his place, Nov. 12, 1819.

Joshua Crump was appointed Sheriff, Robert S. Thompson, Surveyor, and Roland Miller, Coroner.

George T. Wood, (father of Major-General Thomas J. Wood, U. S. Army 1865) was the first Clerk of Hart County, and served in that capacity for many years.

Richard I. Munford, for whom the county-seat was named, was the first Member of the Legislature from Hart County, and was elected in 1820.

HART COUNTY TAX LIST—1819

The following names appear as Taxpayers on the first list taken in Hart

County. The name of the Commissioner is not given. The record shows names of parties making original entries, where names differ from those appearing in the tax lists. To conserve space these are omitted in this publication, but information concerning them may be obtained from the State Historical Society.

A

Allen, Luke P.—½ acre lot, Munfordville.
Allgood, Joseph R.—
Allgood, Samuel—
Atterberry, Michael—
Atterberry, Solomon—
Atterberry, Thomas—385 acres, Bacon Cr.
Atterberry, Elijah—140 acres, Nolin.
Atterberry, J.—
Alexander, David—
Atterberry, Michall—10 acres, Bacon Cr.
Atterberry, Elisha—150 acres, Bacon Cr.
Atterberry, Simeon—
Atwell, Richard—
Ashworth, John—100 acres, G. River.
Ashworth, Samuel—
Alderson, Aaron Jr.—150 acres, Barren.
Angel, Martin B.—100 acres, L. Barren.
Allen, David—400 acres, Barren.
Amos, Erasmus—110 acres, Barren.
Amos, James—50 acres, G. River.
Amos, Benj'n—1 lot, Woodsonville.
Amos, Francis—
Amos, William—70 acres, G. River.
Amos, Johnson—
Amos, Mordeca—
Allen, Maryan estate—1 lot Woodsonville.*
Amos, Charles—200 acres, Barren.
Amos, J. Bailey—
Alderson, Aaron Sr.—†100 acres, Cumberland R.
Alderson, Aaron Sr.—100 acres, Cumberland R.
Alderson, Aaron Sr.—127½ acres, Barren R.
Alderson, Aaron Sr.—144½ acres, Barren R.
Alderson, Aaron Sr.—200 acres, Barren R.

---

* The property of Nancy W. Williams.
†Cumberland County.

Alderson, Aaron Sr.—200 acres, Barren R.
Alderson, Aaron Sr.—130 acres, Barren R.
Alderson, Aaron Sr.—150 acres, Barren R.
Alderson, Aaron Sr.—100 acres, Barren R.
Alderson, Aaron Sr.— 50 acres, Barren R.
Alderson, Aaron Sr.— 65 acres, Barren R.
Alderson, Aaron Sr.— 45 acres, Barren R.
Alderson, Aaron Sr.—150 acres, Barren R.
Alderson, Aaron Sr.—150 acres, L. Barren.

B

Bush, Thomas—250 acres, G. River.
Buckner, Aylett Exr.—976 acres, Bacon Cr.
Bolling, John—100 acres, G. River.
Bumgardner, Jacob—1500 acres, G. River.
Brown, William M.—¼ acre lot, Munfordsville.
Buckner, Henry W.—
Bell, George—
Bumbaugh, Thomas—
Burner, Abraham—102 acres, Lincamp.
Butler, Enoch—550 acres, Nolin.
Brook, William—900 acres, G. River.
Bell, Jacob—
Butler, James—
Butler, Simon—150 acres.
Bernett, William—
Blissett, George—325 acres, Nolin.
Butler, James—70 acres, Nolin.
Butler, Joel—
Butler, William—
Brown, Isaac—
Brown, Lewis—325 acres, Roundstone.
Bradshaw, Thomas—347 acres, Bacon Cr.
Bomer, John—207 acres, Bacon Cr.
Bush, Henry—
Black, James—
Butler, Shubel—
Bartlett, Elijah—
Balley, John—
Blair, James—
Black, Moses—
Bush, John—
Blackwell, Robert—381 acres.
Brunk, Jacob—
Bumgardner, Christian—
Bolling, Susannah Exr.—100 acres, G. River.
Bolling, W. W.—124¾ acres, G. River.
Bell, Jacob—
Burnett, Wm.—

Bartlett, Elijah—
Biggs, Stephen—477 acres, Barren.
Biggs, Stephen—213 acres, Barren.
Biggs, Stephen—150 acres, Barren.
Biggs, Francis—
Bain, Matthew R.—
Bates, James—24½ acres.
Bates, James—25 acres.
Bates, James—50 acres.
Bates, Thomas—200 acres.
Bunnell, Jeremiah—100 acres, L. Barren.
Bunnell, Jeremiah— 70 acres, L. Barren.
Bunnell, Jeremiah—200 acres, Barren.
Bunnell, Jeremiah—191 acres.
Bunnell, Jeremiah—2 lots Nos. 134 & 135 Monroe.
Bogartin, John—
Bell, Henry—100 acres, G. River.
Blair, Andrew—
Blair, Alexander—100 acres, Barren.
Burris, Robert—1 lot, Woodsonville.
Brooks, Miles—316 acres, G. River.
Brumfield, Joel—50 acres, G. River.
Brooks, John—100 acres, G. River.
Brook, George—82½ acres, G. River.
Bird, Robin H.—100 acres, G. River.
Bird, Robin H.— 70 acres, G. River.
Bird, Robin H.—150 acres, G. River.
Bird, Robin H.—1 lot in Woodsonville.
Bird, Wm.—150 acres, G. River.
Bird, Matthew—200 acres, G. River.
Brooks, Jas.—100 acres, G. River.
Brooks, Jas.—50 acres, G. River.

C

Clark, Moses—500 acres, Cub Run.
Clopton, John—
Cann, James—
Clopton, John—
Caswell, John—688 acres.
Collins, Adam—
Caswell, John—
Clopton, David—
Cann, John—
Cradic, John—
Copland, John—162 acres, Roundstone.
Constant, William—100 acres, B. Creek.
Clemmons, Isaac—
Clemmons, William—100 acres, Lincamp.
Clemmons, William—216 acres, Lincamp.

Cotrell, Henry—150 acres, Dog Cr.
Cotrell, John—120 acres, Dog Cr.
Craddick, John—
Cox, Beverly—
Caswell, Elijah—50 acres, Cub Run.
Coonrod, Thomas—
Cotrell, Joshua—
Cally, James—1000 acres, Bacon Cr.
Creel, Elijah—100 acres, G. River.
Creel, Elijah—1 acre, G. River.
Creel, Elijah—2 acres, G. River.
Creel, Elijah—6 acres, G. River.
Carter, Mainfield—400 acres, G. River.
Carter, Mainfield—1 acre, G. River.
Cogdell, Joseph—
Cogdell, Wm.—
Cogdell, Thomas—
Conner, Livingston—
Cogdell, John—
Carlisle, John—
Chastine, Peter—75 acres, G. River.
Cox, James—
Clark, George—
Conyears, William—200 acres, Barren.
Conyears, William—100 acres, Barren.
Chandoin, Andrew—2 lots in the Town of
    Somerville, Nos. 67 & 68.
Chandoin, David—
Chandler, Martin—50 acres, G. River.
Clark, Merril—
Clymer, Jesse—
Clymer, James—450 acres, Barren.
Clark, John—
Cook, Wm.—150 acres, Barren.
Carter, Daniel—150 acres, G. River.
Carter, Daniel—30 acres, G. River.
Carter, Daniel—10½ acres, G. River.
Carter, Daniel—6½ acres, G. River.
Carter, Robert, Sen.—100 acres, Barren.
Carter, Robert—50 acres, Barren.
Carter, Robt. Jr.—
Carter, Brittain—
Coats, Thos.—239 acres, Barren.
Craddock, Wm.—
Crump, Joshua—100 acres, G. River.
Crump, Joshua—40 acres, G. River.
Coats, George—200 acres, G. River.
Crump, Romeo—1 lot in the Town of Wood-
    sonville.
Chamberlain, Young—

Crain, George—81 acres, G. River.
Chandler, Jas.—100 acres, G. River.
Chandler, Jas.—1 Lot in Woodsonville.
Coonrod, John—
Close, John W.—
Craddock, Willis—
Crain, Anderson—
Close, Henry—1 Lot, Woodsonville, No. 17.
Crump, Archer—
Clark, George—100 acres, G. River.
Clark, George—100 acres, G. River.
Clark, George—45 acres, G. River.
Clark, George—75 acres, G. River.
Clark, George—23 acres, G. River.
Clark, George—1 lot, Woodsonville.
Conlee, William—156¾ acres, G. River.

D

Dawson, John—300 acres, G. River.
Dilles, Henry—260 acres, Lincamp Cr.
Dunavan, Peter—
Davis, John—
Drewry, Michael—
Duley, William—
Dunwoodaci (?) Wm.—
Dale, Wm.—
Davis, Elihu—399 acres, Lincamp Cr.
Davis, Israel—
Doyle, Richd.—150 acres, G. River.
Dorsey, Robert W.—1000 acres, Bacon Cr.
Dawson, Thomas—306 acres.
Davore, John—
Davis, George—124 acres, G. River.
Dennison, Isaac—
Defever, John—150 acres, G. River.
Dorsay, James—260 acres, G. River.
Dorsay, James—250 acres, G. River.
Dennison, Zacheriah—
Dawsey, John—
Dennison, Zadock—
Dennison, Benj'n Jr.—
Dennison, Ben Sr.—240 acres, G. River.
Davidson, Hezekiah—200 acres, Barren.
Davidson, Hezekiah—150 acres, Barren.
Dunagan, Alex—2 lots Woodsonville, No. 6.
Dyers, John—25 acres, Barren.
Dodson, Jas.—
Donan, David C.—170 acres, Barren.
Donan, David C.—100 acres, Barren.

Donan, David C.—One lot in Greenburgh.
Donan, David C.—4 lots in Munroe, No. 121, 132.
Durham, John—

E

Edgar, John Jr.—200 acres, Barren.
Edgar, John Jr.—87½ acres, Barren.
Edgar, John Jr.—200 acres, Barren.
Edgar, John Jr.—120 acres, Barren.
Edgar, Johnston—
Ennis, James—50 acres, Barren.
Ennis, James—14 acres, Barren.
Ennis, Archibald—
Ennis, Wm. Senr.—200 acres, Barren.
Edgar, John Senr.—
Edgar, James—250 acres, Barren.
Edgar, James—100 acres, Barren.
Edgar, James—50 acres, Barren.
Edgar, James—50 acres, Barren.
Ennis, Wm. Jr.—
Edgar, Isiah—113 acres, Barren.
Edgar, Samuel—
Epperson, Richard—
Elmore, Thornton—
Emmon, Drewry—
Edsill, Benjamin—

F

Fowler, Matthew D.—
Fowler, Edward—
Fuqueay, Joseph—400 acres, G. River.
Furguson, John—300 acres, Bacon Cr.
Furguson, David—301 acres, Bacon Cr
Flatt (?) Aaron—
Ford, William—
Findley, Isaac—164 acres, Bacon Cr.
Findley, Samuel—600 acres, Bacon Cr.
Furguson, James—200 acres, Bacon Cr
Ford, George—50 acres, Barrens.
Forbis, Robert—130 acres, Barrens.
Forbis, Robert—224 acres, Barrens.
Forbis, Robert—100 acres, Barrens.
Forbis, Robert—25 acres, Barrens.
Furguson, Robert—400 acres, Barrens.
Furguson, Robert—200 acres, Barrens.
Furguson, Robert—200 acres, Barrens.
Furguson, Robert—200 acres, Barrens.
Furguson, Robert—100 acres, Barrens.
The above lands were not entered with the Commissioner for taxation.

Forbis, James—
Farris, Jesse—200 acres, G. River.
Freeman, Thomas—
Flatt, John—100 acres, G. River.

G

Garvin, Valentine—150 acres, Barren R.
Goff, Wm. Jr.—150 acres, Barren R.
Goff, Wm. Senr.—150 acres, G. River.
Garvin, David—125 acres, Barren.
Garvin, David—1 lot Munroe, No. 35.
Grinstead, Jesse—250 acres, Barren.
Giddings, George—
Gardner, Alexr.—200 acres, G. River.
Garrison, Jas.—100 acres, G. River.
Garrison, Benj'n—60 acres, G. River.
Garrison, Benj'n—50 acres, G. River.
Garrison, Benj'n—100 acres, G. River.
Garrison, George—100 acres, G. River.
Gill, Wm.—100 acres, G. River.
Gardner, Elisha—97 acres, G. River.
Gaddie, Jesse—
Gardner, John—150 acres, Bacon Cr.
Gaddie, John—300 acres, Bacon Cr.
Gaddie, Silas—
Gaddie, Wm.—750 acres, Bacon Cr.
Gaddie, Wm.—70 acres, Bacon Cr.
Gibson, Thomas—
Greenstreet, Peter—52 acres, Green Co.
Gibson, Daniel—
Gardner, Wm.—50 acres, Little.
Goodman, Amos—75 acres, G. River.
Godfrey, Jas.—
Gum, Jacob—5 acres, Lincamp.
Gray, Reuben—
Gardner, Edmund—
Garrison, Matthew—50 acres, G. River.
Gaddy, Tolbert—
Goodman, Stephen—100 acres, Bacon Cr.
Gardner, Wm. 990 acres, Bacon Cr.
Gibson, Thomas—200 acres, G. River.
Gibson, John—50 acres, G. River.
Gum, Jesse—101 acres, Lincamp.
Grayham, Wm.—100 acres, Lincamp.
Gum, Elijah—175 acres, G. River.

H

Harris & Maury—4 lots.
Hodgens, John—113 acres, Lincamp.
Hawkins, Jas.—

Holt, Thomas B.—
Hardin, Solomon—
Hazel, Caleb—
Hawley, David—250 acres, Bacon Cr.
Haskins, James C.—
Hill, Ephraim—80 acres, Bacon Cr.
Hensley, Samuel—
Happer, Robert—
Hall, John—
Happer, Stephen—
Harper, Jonathan—
Houchins, Charles—
Holloday, James—
Harris, John—
Highbaugh, Henry—
Highbaugh, Jno.—
Highbaugh, Geo.—42 acres, Nolin.
Huston, Isaac—160 acres, Bacon Cr.
Hawlin, Samuel—
Hawkins, John—
Holderman & Wilkins—1060 acres, Lin-camp.
Holderman & Wilkins—5575 acres, Lin-camp.
Holderman, Jacob—
Houchins, Benj'n—
Huston, Jesse—
Hays, Wm.—
Huston, Wm.—150 acres, Bacon Cr.
Huston, Wm.—50 acres, Bacon Cr.
Holland, Wm.—100 acres, L. Barren.
*Harness, Hezekiah—62 acres.
Harnis (?) Thomas—50 acres, Barren.
Hyzer, Jacob—75 acres, Barren.
Hyzer, Jacob—50 acres, Barren.
Hind, Elizabeth—100 acres, Barren.
Hind, Samuel—200 acres, Barrens.
Hind, Samuel—76 acres, Barrens.
Hind, Lewis—150 acres, Mud Lick.
Hind, John—
Hind, William—73 acres, Barrens.
Houk, George—
Hardin, Thomas—
Harlow, Lewis—
Hardy, George—125 acres, Barrens.
Hardy, George—150 acres, Barrens.
Hardy, George—100 acres, Barrens.
Hall, Michael—150 acres, Barrens.
Harlow, Randal—400 acres.

* Billiard Table.

Harlow, Randal—400 acres, Barrens.
Humphries, John—
Harper, Isaac—
Hindman, Matthew—50 acres, Barrens.
Hill, James—100 acres, Barrens.
Hill, James—100 acres, Barrens.
*Harper, Matthew—200 acres, G. River.
Harper, Matthew—100 acres, G. River.
Harper, Matthew—2 lots Woodsonville.
Harper, James—250 acres, G. River.
Hill, Nelson—100 acres, G. River.
Hardin, John—
Hardy, Ishom—100 acres, Blue Sp.
Hardy, Ishom—75 acres, Barrens.
Harper, Hanse—75 acres, G. River.
Harper, Hanse—200 acres, G. River.
Harper, Hanse—85 acres, G. River.
Harper, Hanse—100 acres, G. River.
Harper, Hanse—60 acres, G. River.
Harper, Hanse—200 acres, G. River.
Harper, Hanse—10 acres, G. River.
Harper, Hanse—1 Lot Woodsonville.
Harper, Samuel Jr.—
Hazlip, Robert—
Heatherly, Nathan—
Harper, Samuel Sr.—
Harper, Silas—
Highbaugh, Henry—
Hodge, Fred—

I and J

Ines, Alexander—65 acres, Barrens.
Ines, Alexander—25 acres, Barrens.

Johns, Elihu—
Jones, Robert—
Jones, Wm.—
Jones, George M.—80 acres, G. River.
Jones, Barnabas—75 acres, G. River.
Jones, Thomas—
Johnston, James—
Johnston, Jonah—
Jaggers, Levi—
Jaggers, Wm.—200 acres, Bacon Cr.
Jones, Wm.—150 acres, Nolin.
Jones, Rodger—
Jones, George—75 acres, G. River.
Jones, Philip—

*Wholesale and retail store.

70

Ireland, Peter—500 acres, Nolin.
Ireland, Wm.—500 acres, Nolin.
Jaggers, Nathan—100 acres, Bacon Cr.
Isaac, Jehu—
Isaacs, Samuel—305 acres, G. River.
Isaacs, Samuel—150 acres, G. River.

K

King, Arthur—50 acres, Bacon Cr.
Kesinger, Solomon—140 acres, Bacon Cr.
*Kesinger, Wm.—120 acres, Bacon Cr.
Kesinger, Solomon—200 acres, Bacon Cr.
Kesinger, Joseph—113 acres, Bacon Cr.
Kesinger, Peter—
Kesinger, Isaac—
Keeling, James—
Keeling, Richd.—
King, Hiram—
Kelly, Robert—200 acres, G. River.

L

Lard, Joseph—673 acres, Barrens, 4 lots,
  Munfordsville.
Logsdon, Wm.—352 acres, G. River.
Logsdon, Elisha
Logsdon, John K. Jr.—
Logsdon, James.—
Logsdon, Samuel—50 acres, G. River.
Logsdon, Joseph—
Light, Jacob—
Lewis, Mary—
Lively, Mark—200 acres, G. River.
Lard, Hezkh.—
Lard, Jesse—
Lively, Canon—32 acres, G. River.
Lively, Canon—200 acres, G. River.
Lively, Canon—58 acres, G. River.
Lively, Canon—2 lots Woodsonville.
Lard, John—1 lot, Woodsonville.
Leech, John—52 acres, G. River.
Leech, Henry—
Leech, Joseph—
Logsdon, John Sr.—100 acres, G. River.
Logsdon, John—32 acres, G. River.
Lindsy, Lewis—
Lamberton, Wm.—
Lee, Henry—
Logsdon, Wm.—170 acres, Roundstone.
Lamkin, David—300 acres, Roundstone.
Lamkin, David—½ acre, Roundstone.

* Wholesale and retail store.

Leza, Henry—200 acres, Dog Cr.
Logsdon, Hiram—
Logsdon, John—
Logsdon, James—
Logsdon, Thomas—200 acres, G. River.
Lamkins, Jeremiah—85 acres, Bacon Cr.
Lamkins, Jeremiah—138 acres, Bacon Cr.
Lamkins, Jeremiah—200 acres, Bacon Cr.
Lemmons, Abraham—
Logsdon, Wm.—
Logsdon, John—
Lobb, Reuben—

M

Martine, J. W.—½ acre, G. River.
Martine, J. W.—2 acres, G. River.
McCubbin, Zacheriah—
McGuire, Jesse—
Mellon, James—
Murphy, John—
McDaniel, Charity—
Middleton, Handley—173 acres, Bacon Cr.
Meeks, Perdy—450 acres, Nolin.
Miller, James—
Mardon, Jacob—
McCubbin, James—100 acres, G. River.
McCary, John—
Moore, David—
McGhaughey, Arthur—
McClain, John—
Moore, Archild—272 acres, Bacon Cr.
Moore, Archibald—150 acres, Bacon Cr.
McGhaughey, A.—297 acres, Bacon Cr.
McGhaughey, A.—703 acres, Bacon Cr.
Munford, Thomas—605 acres, Lincamp.
Munford, Thomas—1 lot in Munfordsville.
  fordsville.
McCandler, Wm.—
Merrit, Thomas—
McCubbin, Joseph—
McCubbin, John—
Munford, Richd.—2151 acres, G. River.
Munford, Richd.—163 acres, G. River.
Munford, Richd.—200 acres, G. River.
Munford, Richd.—34 acres, G. River.
Munford, Richd.—32 acres, G. River.
Munford, Richd.—15¼ acres, G. River.
Munford, Richd.—9 acres, G. River.
Munford, Richd.—¼ acre, G. River.
Munford, Richd.—4 acres, Munfordville.
Murray, Charles—1 lot Munfordville.

Miller, Robert—
McClain, George—350 acres, Bacon Cr.
McClain, George—63 acres, Bacon Cr.
McClain, George—5 acres, Bacon Cr.
McClain, George—400† acres.
McClain, George—55† acres, Bacon Cr.
McClain, George—300 acres, Bacon Cr.
Mayfield, George—100 acres, G. River.
Maxey, Ephraim—200 acres, Barrens.
Maxey, Ephraim—200 acres, Barrens.
Maxey, Ephraim—30 acres, Barrens.
Maxey, Ephraim—22 acres, Barrens.
Maxey, Ephraim—102 acres, Barrens.
‡Maxey, Ephriam—838 acres, Ohio R.
McCaul, Benj'n J.—200 acres, Barrens.
Merry, Owen T.—400 acres, Barrens.
Munford, Richd.—100 acres, Barrens.
Munford, Richd.—4 lots in Munfordville.
Moore, George—100 acres, G. River.
Moore, Isham—100 acres, G. River.
Melton, Joel—
Macy, Clement—
Maxey, Philip—236 acres, G. River.
Maxey, Philip—200 acres, G. River.
Maxey, Philip—7 acres, G. River.
†Maxey, Philip—835 acres, Ohio R.
Maxey, Philip—3 acres, Woodsonville.
Maury, Eli—120 acres, L. Barren.
Maury, Eli—77 acres, Barrens.
Maury, Eli—3 lots, Monroe.

N

Nut, Robert A.—
Norton, Wm.—
Newton, John—

O

Oldham, John—225 acres, Roundstone.
Oldham, John—500 acres, Buff (?) Cr.
  (Grayson Co.)
Oaks, John—
Orol (?) Wm.—160 acres, Lincamp.
Osbourn, Daniel—95 acres, Lincamp.
Owen, Charles B.—
Owen, Joseph—125 acres, Barren.
Owen, Peter—
Orchard, James—100 acres, G. River.
Orchard, Wm.—165 acres, G. River.

---

‡ Henderson Co.
† Warren Co.

Ooley, Peter—200 acres, G. River.
Ooley, Peter—26 acres, G. River.

P

Prewitt, Sally—145 acres, G. River.
Pointer, John—100 acres, G. River.
Pointer, John—50 acres, G. River.
Pease, Wm.—186 acres, G. River.
Phillips, James—
Pulliam, Gideon—200 acres, G. River.
Pulliam, Charles—70 acres, G. River.
Pulliam, Charles—400 acres, G. River.
Pulliam, Lucy—150 acres, G. River.
Pulliam, Lucy—50 acres, G. River.
Pulliam, Lucy—124 acres, G. River.
Pulliam, James—
Pearman, Wm.—
Puckett, Polly—200 acres, G. River.
Puckett, Polly—300 acres, G. River.
Posey, Wm.—50 acres, G. River.
Posey, Wm.—50 acres, G. River.
Posey, Wm.—10 acres, G. River.
Puckett, Thomas—
Perkins, Wm.—100 acres, L. Barren.
Perkins, Wm.—100 acres, L. Barren.
Perkins, Wm.—1 lot in Munroe.
Perry, Barthl.—
Parrish, Little Berry—100 acres, Bacon Cr.
Parrish, Little Berry—100 acres, G. River.
Parmer, Legrand—249 acres, Bacon Cr.
Penny, James—
Peoples, Abraham—100 acres, Bacon Cr.
Powell, Stephen—125 acres, Lincamp.
Peaterson, Francis—
Pegg, Martin—90 acres, Bacon Cr.
Peoples, Jesse—100 acres, Bacon Cr.
Peoples, John—
Peoples, Bird—100 acres, Bacon Cr.
Portwood, Loyd—
Pulliam, Ann, Adm.—272 acres, G. River.
Pindle, Hanay—
Palmer, James—110 acres, Bacon Cr.
Pepper, Daniel—
Pepper, Jos.—150 acres, Lincamp.
Pepper, Jos.—160 acres, Lincamp.
Pepper, Jos.—360 acres, Lincamp.
Pepper, Jos.—100 acres, Lincamp.
Pepper, Jos.—
Patterson, J.—½ lot in Munfordville.
Patterson, J.—1 lot in Munfordville.

R

Reams, Robert—150 acres, Cain Run.
Rowlett, Peter—250 acres, G. River.
Romans, Jacob—
Romans, Isaac—
Reace, David—
Rhoades, John—
Ragland, Joel—200 acres, Bacon Cr.
Reynolds, Nathan—100 acres, G. River.
Rowe, John—
Rountree, Dudley—122 acres, G. River.
Rountree, Dudley—500 acres, G. River.
Rountree, Dudley—200 acres, G. River.
Rountree, Dudley—1700 acres, G. River.
Rountree, Dudley—220 acres, Rolling Fk.
Rountree, Dudley—200 acres, G. River.
Rountree, Dudley—334 acres, Barren.
Rountree, Dudley—80 acres, G. River.
Rountree, Dudley—130 acres, G. River.
Rountree, Dudley—200 acres, G. River.
Rountree, Dudley—50 acres, G. River.
Rountree, Dudley—20 acres, G. River.
Rountree, Dudley—178 acres, G. River.
Rountree, Dudley—50 acres, G. River.
Rountree, Dudley—20 acres, G. River.
Rountree, Dudley—200* acres, Paint Lick.
Rountree, Dudley—69 acres, B. Barren.
Rountree, Dudley—15 acres, Brush.
Rountree, Dudley—4 acres, Barren R.
Rountree, Dudley—½ lot in Glasgow.
Rountree, Dudley—2 acres, G. River.
Rountree, Dudley—16 acres, G. River.
Reams, Neddy—
Ragland, Gid. Jr.—
Runnals, Wm.—
Runnals, Bartlett—180 acres, G. River.
Roe, Robert—
Reynolds, Edward—250 acres, G. River.
Reynolds, Edward—150 acres, G. River.
Ranny, John—
Robeson, Eleanor—
Robeson, John—
Robson, Allen—170 acres, Barrens.
Robson, Allen—1 lot in Munroe.
Robertson, Wm.—382 acres, Barrens.
Robertson, Wm.—25 acres, Barrens.
Reaves, Thomas C.—
Rountree, Turner R.—2 lots in Munroe.
Reed, George—

*Garrard County.

Rowlett, Phil—400 acres, G. River.
Richardson, Isham—400 acres, Barrens.
Rowlett, Littleberry—50 acres, G. River.
Richardson, Wm.—
Rolston, Wm.—120 acres, G. River.
Richardson, Wm.—359 acres, G. River.
Archibald, Murphy—500† acres, Goose Cr.
Richardson, John—
Reynolds, David—50 acres, G. River.
Riche, Tabitha—
Reynolds, Matthias—200 acres, G. River.
Reynolds, Chs.—

S

Skaggs, Sarah—
Skaggs, Matthew—
Smith, Henry—
Stute (?) George—
Shadoin, John—
Stewart, Wm.—
Smith, Wm.—
Skaggs, James—
Smoot, John—
Sims, John—110 acres, Bacon Cr.
Smoot, John—80 acres, Roundstone.
Strange, Bird—
Skaggs, Nancy—150 acres, Lincamp.
Skaggs, Nancy—150 acres, Lincamp.
‡Skaggs, Nancy—234 acres, Little Brush Cr.
Stewart, Richard—75 acres, G. River.
Salling, Wm.—
Stone, John—
Sanders, Edward—
Self, John—
Self, Sally—100 acres, Dog Cr.
Smith, Benj.—
Sanders, Joseph—
Sanders, John—
Stall, Joel—
Sanders, Samuel—
Skaggs, Richard—100 acres, Barrens.
Skaggs, Richard—35 acres, Barrens.
Skaggs, John—
Shirley, Daniel—200 acres, Barrens.
Shirley, Samuel—
Short, Moses—170 acres, G. River.
Short, Moses—170 acres, G. River.
Short, Moses—50 acres, G. River.

†Clay County non-resident and W. Richardson is to pay his tax.
‡Green County.

Smith, Daniel—35¾ acres, G. River.
Smith, Daniel—100 acres, G. River.
Sturgeon, James—50 acres, G. River.
Sturgeon, John Jr.—
Sturgeon, James—100 acres, G. River.
Sturgeon, James—115 acres, G. River.
Sturgeon, James—50 acres, G. River.
Sturgeon, Squire—
Simpson, George H.—1 lot Woodsonville.
Stewart, Thomas—
Sullivan, Rachel—
Smelcer, Jacob—
Smith, John—100 acres, G. River.
Smith, Nancy—100 acres, G. River.

T

Trowbridge, Sally—100 acres, Barren.
Thompson, John—200 acres, Barren.
Trump, Frederick—110 acres, Barren.
Trent, Alexander—
Trobridge, Job Senr.—269 acres, G. River.
Trobridge, Job Senr.—50 acres, G. River.
Trobridge, Job Senr.—30 acres, G. River.
Trobridge, Job Jr.—
Thompson, William—200 acres, L. Barren.
Thompson, William—100 acres, L. Barren.
Thompson, William—56 acres, L. Barren.
Thompson, William—50 acres, L. Barren.
Thompson, William—50 acres, L. Barren.
Thompson, William—158 acres, L. Barren.
*Thompson, William—100 acres, Ohio R.
Thompson, William—1 lot in Munroe.
Tevas, Thomas—
Thompson, Robert S.—200 acres, G. River.
Thompson, Robert S.—200 acres, L. Barren.
Thompson, Robert S.—400 acres, Barrens.
Thompson, Robert S.—150 acres, Barrens.
Thompson, Robert S.—92 acres, Barrens.
Thompson, Robert S.—50 acres, Barrens.
Thompson, Robert S.—150 acres, Barrens.
Thompson, Robert S.—50 acres, Barrens.
Thompson, Robert S.—240 acres, Barrens.
Thompson, Robert S.—240 acres, Barrens.
Thompson, Robert S.—2 lots in Munroe.
     Said Thompson pays Taxes on the fol-
lowing tracts of land:
          —400 acres, Barrens.
          —200 acres, Barrens.
          —90 acres, Barrens.

*Livingston County.

—29 acres, Barrens.
—11 acres, Barrens.
—100 acres, Barrens.
—37 acres, Barrens.
—160 acres, Barrens.
—320 acres, Barrens.
—2 acres, L. Barren.
—550 acres, L. Barren.
—550 acres, L. Barren.
—400 acres, L. Barren.
—37 acres, L. Barren.
Taylor, Simeon—50 acres, G. River.
Turpin, Nathan—60 acres, G. River.
Turpin, Nathan—86 acres, G. River.
Taylor, Isaac—82 acres, G. River.
Tharp, Thomas—
Taylor, Joseph—
Taylor, John—
Taylor, Andrew—
Thompson, Daniel—
Trotter, Charles—50 acres, G. River.
Trotter, Wm.—
Taylor, Ninian—150 acres, Bacon Cr.
Tharp, Greenberry—150 acres, Bacon Cr.
Tharp, Rutha—100 acres, Bacon Cr.
Tharp, Rutha—176 acres, Bacon Cr.
Taylor, James—150 acres, Bacon Cr.

V

Vinciner, George—
Vanmeter, Nathan—

W

Wright, Wm.—100 acres, G. River.
Williams, James—
Wood, William J.—250 acres, G. River.
Wood, William J.—100 acres, G. River.
Wood, William J.—50 acres, G. River.
Wood, William J.—1200 acres, Blue Springs.
Wood, William J.—32 acres, G. River.
Wilson, Jeremiah—1000 acres, Barrens.
Winlock, Wm.—
Willson, Jno.—
Willson, James—1 lot, Woodsonville.
Wiltberger, J. W.—90 acres, G. River.
Wiltberger, J. W.—3 lots Woodsonville.
Wardrope, Wiatt—
Woodson, Robert S.—
Wardrope, Younger—200 acres, G. River.
Wardrope, Younger—80 acres, G. River.
Wardrope, Younger—200 acres, G. River.

Wilson, Jas.—4½ acres, G. River.
Wilson, Jas.—9 lots Woodsonville.
Woodson, Thomas—436 acres, G. River.
Woodson, Thomas—350 acres, G. River.
Woodson, Thomas—200 acres, G. River.
Woodson, Thomas—5 lots Woodsonville.
Williams, John D.—200 acres, L. Barren.
Woosley, Joseph—75 acres, G. River.
Woosley, Joseph—1 lot, Woodsonville.
Walton, Larkin C.—100 acres, G. River.
Walton, Larkin C.—44 acres, G. River.
Wells, Phil—
Wells, Wm.—
Willson, John—
Whitman, Wm.—200 acres, Lincamp.
Whitman, Wm.—½ acre, G. River.
Whitman, Wm.—30 feet in Woodsonville.
West, John—
Wells, Thomas—
Wright, Tabitha—160 acres, Lincamp.
Wright, John—
West, James—100 acres, Nolin.
Whitman, Dan'l—
Wilson, John—178 acres, Bacon Cr.
Winn, John——
Warfield, Caleb—119 acres, Lincamp.
Wright, Levi—
Wyett, Isaac—150 acres, Lincamp.
Wyett, John M.—
Wyett, James—274 acres, Lincamp.
Warsing, Jacob—
Willson, Christy—
Wells, John—50 acres, Roundstone.
Wilson, William—150 acres, Bacon Cr.
West, James—
Wright, Allen—180 acres, Bacon Cr.
Walters, Jadiah—
Wright, John—173 acres, Bacon Cr.
Wright, John—309 acres, Bacon Cr.
Wright, Carter—125 acres, Bacon Cr.
Wells, Lewis—370 acres.
Wood, Isaac W.—

Wood, Jesse—100 acres, G. River.
Waller, John—
Webb, John—
Wright, Vincent—150 acres, Bacon Cr.
Watkins, Samuel—453 acres, Lincamp.
Webb, Martin—100 acres, G. River
Watkins, Elijah—
West, Thomas—
Whitman, John—
Watkins, John—310 acres, Lincamp.
Whitman, Richd.—
Watkins, James—216 acres, Lincamp.
Whitman, Thomas—230 acres, Lincamp.
Whitman, Thomas—250 acres, Lincamp.
Whitman, Chris.—270 acres, Knoxes Cr.
Willson, John, Jr.—1 lot in Munfordville.
Whitman, Wm.—
Wood, George T.—1 lot in Munfordville.
Willson, Wm.—150 acres, G. River.

Y

Yates, John H.—
Yates, Wm. G.—

There are 16 white Males over 21 years for 1819 in Woodsonville.

There are 2 white Males over 21 years for 1819 in Munroe.

Hart County, Sct.

I, George T. Wood, Clerk of the County Court of the aforesaid County, certify that I have compared the within and foregoing with the original lists of taxable property for the year 1819 and find a true copy.

(Signed) G. T. WOOD, C. H. C. C.

Total Voters 598
Tavern Licenses 2
Billiard Table 1
Stud Horses 3
Valuation Land &c $528,355

DEPARTMENT OF STATE ARCHIVES
HENDERSON COUNTY

Henderson County was formed under an Act of the Kentucky Legislature approved Dec. 21, 1798, as follows:

"An Act for dividing the County of Christian:

Section 1. Be it enacted by the General Assembly: That all that part of the county of Christian, from and after the fifteenth day of May next, included in the following bounds, to-wit: Beginning on Tradewater, opposite the mouth of Montgomery's fork; thence to the head of Drake's creek; thence down Drake's creek to Pond river, and down the same to Green river, and down the same to the Ohio, and down the same to the mouth of Tradewater, and up the same to the beginning, shall be one distinct county, and called and known by the name of Henderson. But the said county of Henderson shall not be entitled to a separate representation, until the number of free white inhabitants therein contained, above the age of twenty-one years, shall entitle them to one representative, agreeable to the ratio that shall be hereinafter established by law.

* * * * *

Section 3. The justices of the court of quarter-session and county court named in the commission for said county of Henderson, shall meet at Samuel Bradley's tavern, in the town of Henderson, in the same county, on the first court day after said division takes place; and having taken the oath prescribed by law, and a sheriff being duly qualified to act, the justices shall proceed to appoint a clerk, separately, to their respective courts, as they may severally choose to do, and to fix on a place to erect the public building in said county, where the courts for said county thereafter shall be held. . . ."

Note.—While the town of Henderson was not incorporated under the laws of Kentucky until 1810, a village or settlement known as "Red Banks" was established there as early as 1784. (See History of Henderson County, by E. L. Starling, p. 254.) A list of the inhabitants of Red Banks in November, 1792, was published in the Register, May, 1927, having been found enclosed in a petition for relief and a request for the appointment of a magistrate for the community, addressed to Governor Shelby, in File Box No. 1, Archives Department, Historical Society.

The "Ordinance of the Transylvania Company, commonly called Richard Henderson & Co.," authorizing Gen. Samuel Hopkins, as agent and attorney in fact of the company, to lay off the town of Henderson, and dispose of the lots therein, was drawn up, signed and sealed by the "Proprietors" August 9, 1797, in Granville, North Carolina, and recorded in the County Clerk's office in Henderson County, Kentucky, October 29, 1799. (See History of Henderson County, pp. 255-258.)

A LIST OF THE TAXABLE PROPERTY IN THE COUNTY OF HENDERSON

Ancas McAllister, Commissioner, 1799.

A

Anthony, Jonathan—Ohio River, Town of Henderson.

Agnew, Robert—Canue Creek.

Andrew, James—

Ashby, John—620 a. Auter Crk.*

Ashby, Stephen—620 a. Auter Crk.

Ashby, Enoes—620 a. Auter Crk.

Ashby, Daniel—620 a. Auter Crk.

Ashby, Absolom—620 a. Auter Crk.

Adams, Charles—Trade watter, Wagoners Settlement.

Auston, Nathaniel—Mouth of Highland Creeke, Koxes land.

B

Bennet, Evans—Ohio R Town of Henderson.

Brooner, George—Ohio R. Town of Henderson.

Burk, Andrew—Ohio R. Town of Henderson.

Barnett, Jacob—Ohio R., Hendersons Grant.

Barnett, Mary—Ohio R., Mouth of Lost Creeke.

Buttler, Joseph—Ohio R., Town of Henderson.

Buck, Wardner—Ohio R., Town of Henderson.

Black, Andrew—Highland Cr., Near the Lick.

Branson, Hannah—Auter Creek, Ashbys Settlement.

Berry, William—Auter Cr., Ashbys Settlement.

Berry, Ruben—Auter Creek, Ashbys Settlement.

Berry, Enoch—Norris Creek, Ashbys Settlement.

Browder, Isham—Elke Cr., Ashbys Settlement.

Black, William—Highland Cr., Near the Lick.

Barnett, William—Ohio R., Dimond Island.

Barnet, Humphry—Ohio R., Dimond Island.

Beard, Robert—2000 a. Bluff Creek, Ohio County. Walker Daniel & Joseph Barnet & Robert Berd.

C

Christian, John & Company—Highland cr., Robertson Lick.

Christian, Mathew—Highland Cr., Robertsons Lick.

Combs, John—Elke Creek, Ashbys Settlement.

Calhoun, John—Trade watter, Joneseas Settlement.

D

Dunn, Hannah—Town of Henderson.

Duncan, Samuel—Town of Henderson.

Davis, Charles—368½ a. Green River, Hendersons Grant.

Davis, James, Junr.—Flat Creek, Davisses Settlemnet.

Davis, James, Snr.—Flat Creek, Davises Settlement.

Davis, Robert & Benjman—Flat Creek.

Davis, Richard—Flat Creeke.

Davis, Harison—Drakes Creek.

Davis, John—Drakes Creeke.

Davis, Thomas—Drakes Creek.

Dodge, Richard—Flat Creek, Ner the Mouth.

Dodge, John—Flat Creek Nere the Mouth.

Dodge, William—Flat Creek Nere the Mouth.

Dorning, Thomas—Canue Creek, Came since the 11 of March.

Duggan, John & James—Canue Creek, Cam sinc the 11 of March.

E

Eastwood, Abner—Grave Creek, Near Harmans ferry.

F

Fullerton, William—Dear Creek, Kob Lick.

Fill, Mathias—Town of Henderson.

Fleehart, Joshua—Ohio R., Hendersons Grant.

Franceway, Norrod—Race Creek, Hendersons Grant.

Friel, Thomas—Green R., Hendersons Grant.

Folley, James—Elk Cr., Ashbys Settlement.

Folley, Richard—Elke Creek, Ashbys Settlement.

Fletcher, Thomas—Ohio R., Duffes Settlement.

Fewgate, George—Elke Creeke, Ashbys Settlement.

G

Gates, William—Ohio R., Dimond Island.

Griffeth, Elias—Race Creeke Hendersons Grant.

Grisson, John & William—Deer Creek, McBays Settlement.

Griffeth, Able—Trade watter, Jonesses Settlement.

Graham, Samuel—Jonesses Settlement.

Gillgore, John—Green River, Wininghoms Settlement.

Green, Massey—Highland Cr., Nere the white Lick.

H

Husband, John—Ohio R., Henderson Town.

Housley, Thomas—Ohio R., Town of Henderson.

Huges, Roland—Canue Creek, Hendersons Grant.

Hay, Adam—Mouth of Racecreek Grant.

Hay, Michal—Mouth of Race Creeke.

Halmark, William—Race Creeke Grant.

Huges, James—Dear Creeke, Neare the Lick.

Harman, Isack—Green R., Harman's Ferry.

Herring, Ruben—Deer Creeke, Harmans Ferry Grant.

Harman, Abraham—Dear Creek.

Harden, Newless—Elke Creek, Ashbys Settlement.

Howel, Jelson—Elk Creek, Ashbys Settlement.

Hopkins, Edmond—Canue Creek, Hendersons Grant.

Hopkins, James—Canue Creek, Hendersons Grant.

†Holloway, George--Town of Henderson, Grant.

Houseman, John D.—Town of Henderson, Grant.

Hukes, Sherwood—Ohio R., Hendersons Grant.

‡Hopkins, Samuel—15582a. Ohigo R., Hendersons Grant.

Hopkins, Samuel—3267a. Ohio R.

Same for Richd Hendersons Heirs, 4600 & 989a. Henderson County & Grant.

Same for Bulocks Heirs—4600a. Henderson County & Grant, 989a. Ohio County & Grant.

Simpson, John—Ohio R., Dimond Island

Same for Unsted—6950a. Henderson County & Grant, 989a. Ohio County & Grant.

Same for Alvez—9200½a. Henderson County & Grant 197a. ⅓ Ohio County & Grant.

Same for Hogg—4402½ a. Henderson County & Grant, 989½a. Ohio County & Grant.

I

Ingleman, Joseph—Ohio R., Town of Henderson.

J

Johson, David—Ohio R., Henderson Town.

James, William—50a. Ohio R., Hendersons Grant.

Jefreson, John—Trade watter, Joneses Settlement.

Jonese, Felden—Tradwatter, Joneses Settlement.

K

Knox, Hugh—1000a. Ohio R., Mouth of Highland.

Kuykendell, Amos—Deer Creek, Nere the white Lick.

Knight, John—Green R., Hendersons Grant.

Kimbell, Jesse—Race Creek, Hendersons Grant.

Knight, Isack—Race Creek, Hendersons Grant.

Kukendell, Adam—Highland Cr., Nere the white Lick.

Kuykendall, Abner—Highland Cr., Nere the white Lick.

Kuykendall, John—Drakes Creek.

Kuydendell, Simon—Wears Creek.

L

Landers, Abraham—Canue Cr., Hendersons Grant.

Lauerance William—200a. Canue Cr., Hendersons Grant.

Lauerane, John—Race Creek, Hendersons Grant.

Landers, Jacob—Canue Creek, Hendersons Grant.

Luzader, Isack—Race Creek, Hendersons Grant.

Lauerane, Adam—200a. Race Crk., Hendersons Grant.

Landers, John—Canue Crk., Hendersons Grant.

Lindsey, Neviel—Highland Cr., Robertsons Lick.

Lock, John—Dear creek.

Linn, William—Norrids Creek.

Logan, James—Norrids Creeke.

Leeper, John—Highland Creek, Nere Robertsons Lick.

M

Mathis, Morton & Daniel—Lost Cr., Walkers Settlement.

McComb, John—Canue Creeke, Stovers Settlement.

McAllister, Eneas—Canue Creeke.

McCoy, James—Highland Creeke.

McGerah, Robert—Cainey fork trad watter.

Mcbey, Silase—Clear Creeke, Trad watter.

McComb, William—Canue Creek.

Morison, James—Trade watter, Jonesses Settlement.

Madox, Thomas—Ohio R., Nere the Mouth of trad watter.
Manham, Ephram—Ohio R., Dimond Island.

N

Newman, Jacob—Highland Cr., Nere Robertsons Lick.

O

Owens, Ezirah—Ohio R., Dimond Island.
Owens, Ruben—Ohio R., Dimond Island.
Odel, John—Drakes Kreeke.
Owens, William—Clear Creeke.
Otto, John—Town of Henderson.

P

Perce, James—Ohio R., Town of Henderson.
Patterson, Thomas—Ohio R., Dimond Island.
Preather, Thomas—320a. Auter Cr.
Patton, James—Trade watter, Jonesses Settlement.
Patterson, William—Pond Creeks, Came since the 10 of March.

R

Rutgess, Aarond—200a. Canue Creek, Hendersons Grant.
Rolison, Lauerance junr.—Race Creek, Hendersons Grant.
Rolison, Laurence Senr. & William—Race Creeke, Hendersons Grant.
Rowan, Andrew—Ohio R., Town of Henderson.
Ryburn, John Jur.—Highland Cr., Nere Robertsons Lick.
Ryburn, John Senr.—Highland Cr., Nere Robertsons Lick.
Richards, Philimon—Deer Creeke, Nere the Lick.
Rubey, Petter—Deer Creek.
Row, Marton—Deer Creek, Knob Lick.
Rankin, Adam—408½a. Ohio R., Hendersons Grant.

S

Sutton, Jehu—Ohio R., Henderson Tow.
Sholls, Henery—Ohio R., Town of Henderson.
Sprinkle, Michal Jr.—Ohio R., Town of Henderson.
Sprinkle, Michal Sr.—Ohio R., Town of Henderson.

Sprinkle, Jacob—Ohio R., Town of Henderson.
Sprinkle, John—Ohio R., Town of Henderson.
Smith, Elias G.—Ohio R., Town of Henderson.
Smith, Thomas—Ohio R., Henderson Grant.
Sellars, Isham—Canue Creek.
Slover, John—200a. Canue Creek.
Settles, John—Highland Creeke.
Stepheson, Joseph—Deer Creeke.
Stull, Jaurard—Trad watter, Fare Run.
Sutterfield, Jesse—Trad watter, Fare Run.
Stuart, William—Clear Creeke, trade watter.
Stegall, Moses—Deer Creek.
Sibley, John—Jonesses Settlement.
Simpson, John—Ohio R., Town of Henderson.
Stanley, John—Ohio R., Town of Henderson.

T

Thompson, Joseph—Ohio R., Town of Henderson.
Tucker, William—Ohio R., Town of Henderson.
Thorn, Daniel—Ohio R., Town of Henderson.
Timmons, George—320a. Auter Cr.
Tolbert, Edmond—Cane Run of trade watter.
Thomkens, James—Clear Creeke.
Tingley, Benjeman—trade wa, Johenses Settlement.
Terrel, Robert—trade watter, Near Duffes.

U

Up, Jacob—Ohio R., Town of Henderson.

V

Vankerke, Jacob—Race Creeke, Hendersons Grant.
Veatch, James—Highland Cr., Nere the white Lick.
Vance, Pattrick—Ohio R., Dimond-Hendersons Grant.

W

Wagenon, John, Jr.—Ohio R., Town of Henderson.
Wagenon, John, Sr. & Burell—Ohio R., Town of Henderson.
Walker, John—Ohio R., Mouth of Lost Creek.

Worthington, James—Canue Creeke, Hendersons Grant.

Worthinton, Joseph—Canue Creeke, Hendersons Grant.

Winningham, Ishom—Green River, Hendersons Grant.

Winemillar, Jacob—Canue Creeke, Slovers Settlement.

Wallace, David—Highland Cr., Neare Robertsons Lick.

Welb, Esse—Highland Cr., Nere Robertsons Lick.

Ward, William—Drakes Creek.

Winingham, Thomas—Green River, Hendersons Grant.

Wagoner, John—Trade watter, Nere the Logue? Pond.

Wells, William—Dimond Island.

Wilkins, John—Pond Creeke, Came since the 10 of March.

Wallace, Widow—Drakes Creeke.

Y

Yong, Nathan—Race Creek, Hendersons Grant.

---

*Otter Creek.
†Retale Store.
‡4 coch & chariot whels.

A LIST OF LOTS WITHIN THE TOWN OF HENDERSON, AENEAS McCALLISTER COMMISSIONER

	No.	Lots of 10 accor	No.
George Sprinkle	1		
Jonathan Anthony	3	24-23-50	1	8
John & Michal Sprinkle	3	21-15-20	1	7
David Jonson	2	33-34	1	2
Michal Sprinkle, Seinor	1	19	1	10
Wardner Buck			1	31
Abraham Landons	1	88		
Joseph Worthington	1	5		
Henery Purviance	10	93-94-135-136-7-67-6-30-134-68	2	4-5

	No.	Lots of 10 accor	No.
Daneal Hughes	1	133	1	32
Eaneas McAllister	3	3-4-22		
John Husband	4	13-14-58-59		
Anney Husband widow	1	60	1	13
William Wells	3	6-9-12		
Jacob Sprinkle	1	118	1	23
Jacob Up	1	16		
Hannah Dunn	1	....		
George Holoway	1	65	1	6
Robert Berd	1	45		
Thomas Housley	1	176		
Propritors of the Town of Henderson		139		
Evens Bennet	3	138-139-140		

Valluation of the lots in the Town of Henderson agreeable as they are Rated first Rate 25 Second 12½ Third-Rate 6¼ out lots of 10 accors Rated the same.

Aeneas McCallister Commissioner
Henderson county, to wit,

I do hereby certify that the foregoing is a true copy of the list of taxable property lodged in my office by Aeneas McCallister Esq. commissioner of the tax in this county, having examined the same as the law directs. Given under my hand this 11th day of October 1799.

Jno. D. Haussman—C. H. C.

HENDERSON COUNTY 1799
(Summary)

207 Slaves at 6¼ Cents	12.93¾
412 Horses at 1½ do.	6.18
1 Licence at 10 $	10.00
1 Stud rate Covering	25.
200 Acres 1st rate Land	.34
668 " 2d ditto	.66
131.592 3d ditto	82.24
	112.60¾

STATE ARCHIVES
TAX LISTS OF JEFFERSON COUNTY—1789

The four Tax Lists of Jefferson County which follow were among those which have been removed from the basement of the old Administration Building at Frankfort, and are part of the official records of the auditor's office. These lists were made up from vouchers returned from the commissioners of the tax from the various districts of the county to the County Clerk.

The lists of this date give no returns for lands, and among those so far discovered, no returns for lands are given until 1792, the year that Kentucky became a separate state. Comparison with lists after that period indicates that those herewith presented cover a comparatively small area of the country as it was at that time bounded. It must be remembered that Nelson County had been formed in 1784, thus eliminating the territory of the present counties of Washington, Hardin, part of Green, part of Bullitt, Ohio, Breckinridge, Grayson, part of Butler, Daviess, part of Hart, Meade, part of Spencer, part of Edmonson, part of Anderson, Hancock, Marion, Larue, Taylor and part of McLean, but otherwise the county was as originally laid out.

A list for 1796 (which gives location of lands) indicates that the greater number of those recorded lived in Brashears, Pond Creek, Floyd's Fork Six Mile, Beargrass Creek (outside of Louisville) etc. It is unfortunate that the earlier lists which have been preserved do not include the town of Louisville nor the settlements on Harrod's Creek, but they are included in the lists for 1796 and '99, and these we hope to publish at a later date.

It is interesting to note that in the list of John Churchill, Gen. George Rogers Clark was recorded as being a member of the household of his father, John Clark. The list of 1796 gives their returns separately, recording the homeplace of John Clark as "318 acres on Beargrass in Jefferson County," with "24 blacks, 6 horses and 33 cattle," and four other tracts of land in Shelby, Franklin and Logan Counties, amounting to 6,400 acres. Seven tracts belonging to Geo. R. Clark, and amounting to about 10,000 acres are listed without any personal property, which was probably because of his residence at that time, at Clarksville, on the Indiana side of the river.

List of taxable property within the district of Jenkin Phillips, Commissioner in the County of Jefferson for the year 1789.

Persons' Names Chargeable with the Tax	Number of White Males Above 21	White Males Between 16 and 21	Blacks Above 16	Blacks Above 12	Horses and Cattle
A					
William Adams	1	1			3
Samuel Applegate	1				1
Richard Applegate	1				
Stacey Applegate	1				
Joshua Archer	1				
B					
Runyan Bowman	1	1			2
Edmund Basey	1	1			
James Blackwell	1	1	2		2
Thomas Blake	1		1		1
Jehu Baldwin	1				
John Burkes	1				2
William Bell	1				3
Joseph Brookes	1			1	6
C					
Jacob Clover	1	1			2
Richard Carsen	1				
Elisha Caturmus	1				1
James Callahan	1				
Jonathan Cooper	1				1
Nathan Curry	1				3
Wm. Croghan	1		1		2
George Cat	1				4
James Caturmus	1				4
Wm. Chapman	2				2
John Churchill	1		4	1	2
Armstd. Churchill	2	1	16	2	6
John Campbell	1	1	13	2	8
John Cox	1				1
John Clarke	2	1	11	3	6
James Cox	1				4

82

Persons' Names Chargeable with the Tax	Number of White Males Above 21	White Males Between 16 and 21	Blacks Above 16	Blacks Above 12	Horses and Cattle
D					
Michael Dillon	2				1
Henry Ditto	1		1		4
Thomas Downs	1				
Joseph Donnahoo	1				2
E-F					
Archibald Frame	2				1
James Ferrill	1				2
John Felty	1				4
G					
Charles Grigsby	1				4
John Gobin	1				1
Hugh Grimes	2				2
Edward Goodwin	2				
William Goodwin	1				1
H					
[1] E. L. Hall	1				
William Hollis	1				1
Joseph Hunter	2				2
Fredk. Hucklebury	1				3
David Hartman	2				2
Robert Homes	1	1			4
John Hughes	1		11		2
Matthw. Hineman	1				2
James Higgins	1				
Jnt. Harrison	1		1		2
I-J					
Patrick Joyes	1		1		2
Benjamin Johnston	1	1	3		8
Benjn Johnston, Junr.	1		3	1	1
Wm. Johnston	1				

[1] Practicing physician.

Persons' Names Chargeable with the Tax	Number of White Males Above 21	White Males Between 16 and 21	Blacks Above 16	Blacks Above 12	Horses and Cattle
K					
Augustus Kaye	1				
James Kerlin	1				1
John Kennison	1	1			3
Sam'l Kirby	1		1		4
Absalom Kennison	1				3
Joseph Kinney	1	2			4
L					
William Linn	1		1		4
George Leech	1				
James Lambert	1				
Isaac Leap	1				
Ml. Lacassagne	1	1			1
Peter Leatherman	1				1
Christian Leatherman	2		1		3
M					
Isaac Marshall	1				2
Moses Moore	1		5		9
Jas. Francis Moore	1				6
James Macauley	1			1	1
David Morgan	1	2			
Daniel McCleland	1				5
David Meriwether	1		4	1	4
¹ Wm. Meriwether, Senr.	1		9	1	4
N					
Elias Neale	1	2			2
O					
John Oliver	1				1
Wm. Oldham	1		4		6
Saml. Oldham	1		8	1	7

¹ 4 Carriage wheels.

Persons' Names Chargeable with the Tax	White Males Number of Above 21	White Males Between 16 and 21	Blacks Above 16	Blacks Above 12	Horses and Cattle
P					
George Pearce	2				4
Wm. Peak	1				2
Wm. Payne	1				
John Perkins	3				2
Andw. Parks	3				
James Patten	1			1	1
Wm. Peyton	1		2	1	4
Wm. Pope	1	1	2	1	5
Silvanus Prince	2	1	7	1	3
Basil Prather	1		6	1	4
R					
Thomas Richie	1				1
Ezekl. Rawlins	1				1
George Rees	1				
Heny. Reed	1				
James Rob	1	2			8
Edmund Rice	1		1		6
Stepn. Richardson	1				1
William Rhodes	1				
Elizabeth Regar					
S					
James Sullivan	2	2	6		14
James Sneade	1		1		2
Davd. Staniford	1				1
Michl. Sprinkle	2	1			
Wm. Smith	1				
Silv. Stotts	1				2
Christian Shively	1				3
James Steward	3	1			
Peter Stacey	1				4
James Stephenson	1	1			2
Jacob Shiveley	1				1
Henry Shiveley	1				2
John Scott	1				1
James Sturgus, Junr.	14		5	2	23
John Spruce	1				1
Christ. Sanders	2			1	1

Persons' Names Chargeable with the Tax	Number of White Males Above 21	White Males Between 16 and 21	Blacks Above 16	Blacks Above 12	Horses and Cattle
T					
Edward Thomas	1		2		1
Mark Thomas	1				2
George Thompson	1				
U					
Jacob Up	1				
V					
John Vaughan	1				
Geo. Ventioner	1				
W					
Saml. Welch	1				2
Saml. Wells	1	1	4	1	8
Danl. Wentzell	1	1			
Joseph Winkley	1				
Rd. Jones Waters	1	1	1		2
Samuel Watkins	1				
Geo. Wilson	2	1	4		13
Robt. Wilson	1				1
Y					
Isaac Yates	1				
Total amounts	164	33	143	23	316
Errors excepted Jenkin Philips.					
Returned on separate list, Jenkin Phillips	2	1	6	4	9

A List of the Taxable Property Within the District of John Churchill, Com. in the County of Jefferson for the Year 1789.

Persons' Names Chargeable with the Tax	Number of White Males Above 21	White Males Between 16 and 21	Blacks Above 16	Blacks Above 12	Horses and Cattle
A					
Applegate, Richard					
Applegate, Saml.					1
Archer, Joshua					1
Armstrong, Willm.					
Anderson, Richard C.			5		7
Asturgus, John					3
Asturgus, James				2	11
B					
Blackwell, James	1			2	1
' Brookes, Joseph			1		7
Burks, John					
Bartlet, Mary	2		1	1	3
Baldwin, James					
Beatty, Cornelius					2
C					
Coldwater, John					1
Calloway, Saml.					1
Coones, Felix	1				1
Crown, Robert					
Croghan, Willm.			1		1
Campbell, John			13		6
Clark, John, Geo. R. Clark	1		10	2	6
Churchill, Armt., Wm. and John Churchill	1		17	3	6
Cocks, James					2
Cat, George					2
Clover, Jacob					1
D					
Downs, Thos.					1
Ditto, Henry			1		3
Davis, John					
Davis, Jesse					1
Dillon, Michl.					
Davis, John					

³ Listed as members of Brookes household, Js. Ferrel, Joel Farmar and Chas. Patterson.

Persons' Names Chargeable with the Tax	Number of White Males Above 21	White Males Between 16 and 21	Blacks Above 16	Blacks Above 12	Horses and Cattle
E					
Elms, Williams					2
F					
Field, Lewis					1
French, David					1
Frame, William					3
Frain, Archibald				1	3
Finley, James					
Felty, John					4
Foster, Luke					
Thomas Fillips for Jenkin (Fillips, Saml. Fillips, Will) Calough	1		5	2	7
G					
Goodwin, William					
Goodwin, Edward	1				3
Grymes, Hugh					1
Grigsby, Charles					5
Gregg, John	1				2
H					
Harris, Willm.			1		3
Hartman, David					2
Hunter, Joseph and Joseph Hunter					1
Holmes, Robert, Thomas Beatty	1				4
Hutchison, Saml.					1
Huckleberry, Fredk.	1				2
Hall, Elisha L. (Apothecary)			1		1
Hughes, John			10		3
J					
Johnston, William					
Joyes, Patrick				1	1
'Johnston, Benjn.			2		1
Johnston, Ga. Jones			2	1	1
Johnston, Benjamin, Jr.					1

'1 h., 2 m., 1 colt.

Persons' Names Chargeable with the Tax	Number of White Males Above 21	White Males Between 16 and 21	Blacks Above 16	Blacks Above 12	Horses and Cattle
K					
Kendall, Thomas, Danl. Kendall and Jas McKinley	1				1
Kenny, Joseph	1				3
Kennison, Absalm.					2
Kurolin (?), James					1
Kay, Aug.					
Kirby, Saml.	2		1		2
Kennison, John	1				3
L					
Leatherman Xn, and Silvester Stotes	2		1		4
Leatherman, Jacob					
Lynn, William			2		4
Leach, George					
Lard, Hezekiah	1				
Lambert, James					1
Lacassagne, Michl.			1		
Letherman, Peter					
M					
Moore, Fr. Jas.					
McCauley, Jas.					2
Morgan, David	1				
Martin, George, Jos. Bland & Jno. Errevine(?)					
McClellan, Danl.					2
⁵ Merrimether, Wm.			8	3	4
Merriwether, W. D.			4	1	2
N					
Neale, Elias	3		2		2
Neil, Nico.					
Nolain, Phil.					
O					
Owens, George					
Obannon, Jno.					
Oliver, Jno.					
Oldham, Saml., and Jas. Callahan			7	1	7
Ops, Jacob					1
Oldham, William			3		5

⁵ 4 carriage wheels.

Persons' Names Chargeable with the Tax	Number of White Males Above 21	White Males Between 16 and 21	Blacks Above 16	Blacks Above 12	Horses and Cattle
P					
Pope, William			2	1	3
Perril, Jerh.					2
Pryor, John					
Peyton, Wm.			2		2
Payne, William					
Perkins, John, Wm. and Jno. Perkins	2				3
Purviance, John			1		3
Prather, Basil			5	1	4
Q					
Quartermous, Jas., Elijh. Quartermous					4
R					
Rounder, Joseph, Peter Rounder	1				3
Robb, James					3
Ralph, Morris					
Reece, George					
Reager, Jacob, Geo. Kinder			1		2
Rittenhouse, Jesse					
Reid, Henry				1	
Rhodes, William					
Reager, Burk					3
Ross, Lawrence, Shapley Ross			6		13
Rice, Edward			1		4
S					
Slaughter, George, Abm. Field			3	3	1
Stewart, James, Jno. Stewart	2				3
Shively, Henry					1
Shively, Jacob					1
Smith, David					1
Saunders, C. Jas.					3
Standeford, David					1
Stevenson, Jas.					
Sullivan, Jas.			6		12
Springle, Michl., Henry Springle					3

Persons' Names Chargeable with the Tax	Number of White Males Above 21	White Males Between 16 and 21	Blacks Above 16	Blacks Above 12	Horses and Cattle
S					
Smith, John					
Shively, Christr.					3
Shackelford, Jno.					
Scott, John					4
Shrade, John					
Stacy, Peter					4
T					
Tuell, John					
Thruston, Buck			1		1
Thomas, Mark					1
V					
Venshioner, Geo.					
Vaughan, Jno.					2
W					
Wright, Eliza.					3
Wilson, George			5		15
Ward, Richard					
Winlock, Jo.				1	5
Wade, Joseph					
Waters, J. Richd.			1		
Watkins, Saml., Wm. Peaque					2
Wentzell, Daniel					
Wells, Saml.			3	2	5
Wood, Robert					1
William, Evan					1
Total 139	26	28	135	25	288
			25		
			(?)150		

NOTE.—It will be seen that many names appear on the list of both Jenkin Phillips and John Churchill, indicating that the territory assigned to these two commissioners over-lapped to a considerable extent.

Persons' Names Chargeable with the Tax	Number of White Males Above 21	White Males Between 16 and 21	Blacks Above 16	Blacks Above 12	Horses and Cattle
A					
Adams, Hugh	1				2
Adams, William	1				1
B					
Burian (?), Jesse	1				1
Boon, Moses and Moses Boon, between 16 and 21	1				1
Buskirk, John	1				2
Boon, Jonathan, and Isaah Boon, between 16 and 21	1				2
Bennett, Stanford	1				2
Brenton, Robert	1				2
Brenton, James	1				2
Bella, Peter, and Peter White, Jun., between 16 and 21	1				1
Brenton, James	1				2
Bogard, Cornelius	1				1
Bogard, Ann Mary					2
Brashearse, Marsham	1			1	3
Boon, Samuel, and John Boon, between 16 and 21	1				2
Bailey, Robert	1				1
Brenton, Henry and Joseph Brenton, between 16 and 21	1				3
Bowling, George	1				1
Ballard, James	1				2
Brackett, John	1			2	3
Ballard, Bland	1				4
C					
Calbert, Daniel	1				1
Cooper, William	1				3
Conway, Hugh	1				1
Cook, Moses	1				1
Cooper, Jonathan	1				1
Cooper, Evan	1				1

Persons' Names Chargeable with the Tax	Number of White Males Above 21	White Males Between 16 and 21	Blacks Above 16	Blacks Above 12	Horses and Cattle
C					
Carman, Joseph, and Caleb Carman, between 16 and 21	1				2
Cooper, Samuel	1				2
Clynes, Joseph	1				1
Clynes, Nicholas, and Nicholas Clynes, between 16 and 21	1				1
Crim, Peter	1				3
Clynes, John	1				
Clynes, Peter	1				2
D					
Daniel, Martin	1			1	2
Daniel, John	1			1	1
Dunker, Benjamin	1				2
Drake, Jesse	1				4
Devour, Daniel	1				2
Demmere, Peter	1				1
Demmere, Samuel	1				2
Dunkin, Nimrod	1				3
Denbo, Solomon	1				
E					
Eastes, William	1				1
Eaton, Joseph	1				2
Evans, Joseph	1				1
Evans, Margratt, and Robert Evans, between 16 and 21					3
F					
Fullengwider, Peter	1				3
Fullengwider, Henry, and Jacob Fullengwider	2				2
Fleming, Thomas	1				1
Fleming, James, and James Fleming, between 16 and 21					

Persons' Names Chargeable with the Tax	White Males Number of Above 21	White Males Between 16 and 21	Blacks Above 16	Blacks Above 12	Horses and Cattle
G					
Garrett, Nathan	1				1
Greenwood, Philip	1				1
Gasway, John	1				1
Gasway, Richard	1				
Garrett, John, Maurice Garrett and William Garrett, between 16 and 21	2				
Garrett, Isaac	1				
Grigory, Andrew, and John Grigory, between 16 and 21	1				1
Grigory, Richard	1				2
Guinn, Jones Thomas	1		6	1	6
Garshim, Thomas	1				
Glenn, William	1				
H					
Holbrook, George	1				5
How, John	1				2
Higgins, Jonathan, and Jonathan Higgins, between 16 and 21	1				
Humes, John	1				2
Hughes, Benjamin, and Morgan Hughes	2				5
Hughes Jesse	1				1
Hogland, Richard	1				2
Hogland, James	1				1
Hogland, Jamima, and Henry Hogland, between 16 and 21					1
Hunter, Henry	1				4
Hunter, Samuel, and Samuel Hunter, between 16 and 21	1				
K					
Katchum, Daniel	1				2
Kaneda Samuel	1				
L					
Lemaster, Richard	1				1
Lunsford, George	1				1
Lemaster, James	1				2
Long, Anderson, and Caleb Faver	2			1	2
Lowden, Robert	1				4

Persons' Names Chargeable with the Tax	Number of White Males Above 21	White Males Between 16 and 21	Above 16 Blacks	Blacks Above 12	Horses and Cattle
L					
Lock, Rebeccah					1
Lemmon, Robert	1				2
M					
Metcalf, John	1				1
Meriwether, Nicholas	1		3		1
McDoogle, Charles	1				3
Mckentire, Archibald	1				2
McManness, John, Sen., and James Mc-Manness, between 16 and 21	1				3
McManness, George	1				
McManness, John, Junr.	1				1
Matthews, Edward	1				2
Markswell, George	1				1
Merifield, Alexander	1				2
McKindley, Samuel	1				1
Montgomery, Allexander	1				3
McWaid, Henry	1				1
McWaid, James	1				1
Midcalf, William, Thos. and James Midcalf, between 16 and 21	1				3
Merifield, John	1				1
N					
Neeld, William	1				1
Newkirk, Elias	1				1
Nickolas, Thomas	1				1
Newland, Jacob	1			1	3
O					
Owen, Brackett, and John Owen and Abraham, David and Joseph Owen, between 16 and 21	2			6	8

Persons' Names Chargeable with the Tax	Number of White Males Above 21	White Males Between 16 and 21	Blacks Above 16	Blacks Above 12	Horses and Cattle
P					
Prestley, William Bowling	1				2
Patterson, John	1				1
Pritchet, Richard	1				1
Pannell, Moses	1				
Passmore, Augustean	1				1
Pryor, William, and Benjamin Pryor, between 16 and 21	1				6
Q					
Quirk, Thomas	1				1
R					
Ryker, John	1				1
Ryker, Jorardus	1				1
Ryker, Samuel, and Samuel Ryker, between 16 and 21	1				1
Rice, William, and William Rice, Junr., between 16 and 21	1				3
Read, John	1				1
Ray, William	1				2
Robert, John	1				
Risley, John, and Davy Risley and John Risley, between 16 and 21	2				5
Russell, Nicholas	1				1
Reed, John	1				
Rose, Martin	1				4
Rose, Godbre (?), and Matthew Rose	2				9
Roben, Vincent					1
Robens, Isaac, and Isaac Robens, between 16 and 21					
Roberts, Benjamin	1				1
Roberts, William	1				2
S					
Shannon, Samuel	1				2
Sturgeon, Thomas					1
Shannon, William	1			3	2
Standiburn, Thomas	1			2	6
Stinson, Charles	1				1
Sparks, James	1				1

Persons' Names Chargeable with the Tax	Number of White Males Above 21	Between Between 16 and 21	Blacks Above 16	Blacks Above 12	Horses and Cattle
S					
Sulevan, Daniel	1				
Smith, Nicholas	1				1
Smith, Jacob	1				1
Sinclear, Nelly					1
Standly, Joseph	1				1
T					
Thom, Elizabeth					1
Tucker, John	1			1	1
Tyler, Robert	1				9
V					
Vancleave, Ralph	1				1
Vancleave, Benjamin, and Aaron Vancleave..	2				2
Vancleave, John, and Aaron and Benjamin Vancleave, between 16 and 21	1				4
W					
Watson, William	1				3
Whitaker, Martha, and & Elisha Whitaker, between 16 and 21			1		1
Whitaker, Acquilla	1				3
Whitaker, Abraham	1				
Wheeler, Benjamin	1				3
Williams, John, and Theophelas Williams, between 16 and 21	1				2
Williams, Basil	1				1
Workman, Joseph	1				
Williams, James, and Martin and Peter Williams, between 16 and 21	2				2
Willson, George	1				
White, Elizabeth					1
Wheeler, Joseph	1				
Y					
Young, John	1				6
	157		27	4	289

Brashears Creek, 1789.

A List of Taxable Property in the District of Frs. R. Slaughter, Com., in the County of Jefferson for the Year 1789.

Persons' Names Chargeable with the Tax	White Male Tithables Above 21	White Males Above 16 and Under 21	Blacks Above 16	Blacks Above 12 and Under 16	Horses, Colts Mares, Mules
A					
Applegate, Thomas	2				4
Applegate, John					
Abbott, John					2
Asher, Barlett for David White	1				4
Asturgus, James, Senr.					4
Abbott, Richard					
Adams, William					3
Ashby, David, and Fielding Ashby			1		7
Amos, Thomas					1
Arnold, Josiah					1
Agun, William			1		4
Adams, Francis					
B					
Brendley, Jacob					3
Bruner, Michael, and Jacob Bruner					
Bruner, George					3
Bruner, Leonard					1
Bishop, George					1
Brown, Hugh					2
Batman, Thomas					1
Batman, John					2
Bacey, William					2
Breeden, Richd.					2
Bullett, Alexander			21	2	6
Bartlett, John					1
Breckenridge, Alexr.			5		13
' Buckner, Nicholas, for Philip Buckner			6		3
Bemson, Joseph	1				
Breasheare, Nicholas	2				2
Belt, Josiah					2
C					
Curry, Daniel					2
Coons, Nicholas	1				

⁵ William Daniel, member Buckner household.

Persons' Names Chargeable with the Tax	White Male Tithables Above 21	White Males Above 16 and Under 21	Blacks Above 16	Blacks Above 12 and Under 16	Horses, Mares, Colts and Mules
C					
Chinowith, Richd., and John Rose and John Chinowith	1				3
Calloway, Rachael					2
Colman, Jacob, Senr.					1
Crawford, Joseph					1
Crawford, Robert	1				2
Curry, Thomas			2		2
Clark, William					
Colman, Jacob, Senr.					
Colgin, Daniel, and Lawrence Mooney					6
Cornelius, William					1
Chinowith, Arthur					3
Cayriss, Mary	1				1
Cayriss, Simeon					1
Cummins, William	2				4
Condict, Timothy					
Cravenson, George					2
Clark, Philip					
Cunningham, James					2
Copper, Nathaniel					
Chambers, James					2
Clover, Henry					
Cooper, Lewis (or Levin)					2
Choon, Andrew					1
D					
Dailey, Charles					
Dailey, Philip					2
Dailey, John					
Daniel, Peter					1
Dukar, Abraham (or Deckar)					3
Denny, James					4
Davis, Evin					1
Danolson, Robert, and Charles Mezeek					
Doherty, John					
Day, John					
Daniel, Mary	1		1		2
Dement, Benona					2

Persons' Names Chargeable with the Tax	White Male Tithables Above 21	White Males Above 16 and Under 21	Blacks Above 16	Blacks Above 12 and Under 16	Horses, Mares, Colts and Mules
D					
Done, James, and Elijah Collard for J. Dunn..					3
Davis, John					1
Decker, Nicholas (or Dukar)					1
Dunbar, James					1
E					
Eillis, Isaac					6
Eastin, Richard			4	4	7
Edwards, Fredk.			2		6
Eaken, Robert					4
' Earukson, Benjamin, and Stepn. Richardson			3	3	2
F					
F— (name illegible)					
Farnsley, James					2
Forguson, William		1			1
Ford, Hezakiah					2
Finley, John					1
Floyd, Robert, and Thomas Potter			2		4
Fowler, Joshua					1
Falls, Jane					4
Floyd, Charles					3
Fenley, Richard, and Charles Fenley			5	1	5
Freeman, Thomas			2		2
Finley, Isaac			3	2	3
Freeman, Elisha					
Floyd, William					3
G					
Gray, Robert					1
Goban (?), Joseph					1
Gray, James					
Gilmore, Robert					5
Garner, Thomas					2
Gray, William					1
Grissom, James		1			
Guthrie, James					2
Grimes, Elias					1
Garrenhart, Michl.					2

⁷ 2 carriage wheels.

Persons' Names Chargeable with the Tax	White Male Tithables Above 21	White Males Above 16 and Under 21	Blacks Above 16	Blacks Above 12 and Under 16	Horses, Mares, Colts and Mules
H					
Huckleberry, George			2		3
Hawks, John					2
Hill, Hardy					2
Holt, John					1
Hubbs, Samuel					2
Hubbs, Jacob					1
Hooke, Henry					1
Hooke, George					2
Hooke, Andrew					3
Hite, Isaac			7		12
Hite, Abraham, Senr.			6		22
Hite, Joseph			3		1
Hughes, Abijah					1
Hornback, Isaac, and Saml., Abm. and Corns.					
Hornback			2		4
I-J					
Jones, Christopher					2
Jones, George					2
Inman, William					3
Johnston, Thomas					3
Jackson, William					5
Johnson, William					1
Junkin, Anthony					3
Junkin, Lancelott					5
Irmin, John					2
Johnston, William	1		3		6
K					
Keykendall, Jacob					3
Keisar, Fredk., and Fredk. Koisar					3
Kennady, William					4
Keykendall, Moses			1		6
Kendall, William					2
L					
Lucas, William					2
Litherland (?), John					
Laferty, Barnabas					1
Lenin, Charles					
Leviston, George					2

Persons' Names Chargeable with the Tax	White Male Tithables Above 21	White Males Above 16 and Under 21	Blacks Above 16	Blacks Above 12 and Under 16	Horses, Colts Mares, Mares and Mules
M					
McKeown, Robert					3
McDaniel, Peter					1
Mong, Adam					1
Murphy, James					2
Minter, Thomas					4
McClain, Thomas					1
Mayfield, Micajah					4
McMickle, Daniel					
Mariwether, Jas.			4	2	1
Millar, William					1
McClure, George					6
McClintic, John					2
McClure, Daniel					6
McClure, Mary					2
McClure, William					1
McClure, John					6
McCormic, Peter					
McKegg, James					
Mooney, Jacob					2
Meriwether, William, Jr.			4	1	3
Melown, John					
McClintic, Samuel					2
Moore, John G.					2
Milhollin, Jonathan					2
McDowl, Alexr.					1
Millar, Saml.					1
Murray, William	2				7
McCarty, Thomas					
Mundle, John	1				2
McCastling, James					1
N					
Nixon, Jonathan					
Neal, Thomas					1
Newkirk, Tobias					3
Newkirk, Elias					
Newkirk, Peter	2				1
Newkirk, Benja.					2
Nicholson, Daniel					3
Noland, Ephraim					1

Persons' Names Chargeable with the Tax	White Male Tithables Above 21	White Males Above 16 and Under 21	Blacks Above 16	Blacks Above 12 and Under 16	Horses, Mares, Colts and Mules
O					
Owen, Jacob	1		4		1
Osburn, William			1	1	3
P					
Pomroy, George					2
Patterson, James					2
Postleright, John					1
Parks, Joseph					1
Pope, John					1
Purcell, Thomas					
Potts, John					3
Phelps, Thomas	2		1		4
Phelps, Anthy.					
Q					
Quirk, Thomas (or Quick)					
Quinn, John					2
Quirk, Denis (or Quick)					3
Quirk, Jacob (or Quick)	1				3
R					
Rose, Benja.					1
Ramley, John					
Rogers, John					
Reid, John, Senr.					2
Rowan, Andrew					3
Reed, John					1
Richardson, James			1		3
Reid, John					1
Ramsey, Thomas					
Rollings, Assahel					1
Robertson, James					1
Romine, John			1		3
S					
Steward, Rachael					1
Spears, Robert					1
Shake, Christo.					1
Smith, Peter					3
Smith, Henry					1

Persons' Names Chargeable with the Tax	White Male Tithables Above 21	White Males Above 16 and Under 21	Blacks Above 16	Blacks Above 12 and Under 16	Horses, Mares, Colts and Mules
S					
Smith, Philip					2
Spears, Paul					2
Simon, John					2
Scott, James					5
Scott, Andrew					1
Spears, Moses					1
Steward, James					
Shaw, John					2
Sharp, John					2
Smith, Adam					4
Smith, Henry					2
Safford, Thomas					2
Smith, John					3
Slaughter, John					3
Stafford, Benja.					2
Sale, Anthy.			7		2
Scott, Robert					2
Sparks, Daniel					2
Seaton, Flenor (?)					2
Seaton, Rodham					1
Shanklin, Richd.					2
Sebastian, Benjamin, Wm. Robinson and Waidright (?)			4	2	6
Stanoder, Frances		1	1		5
Standeford, James					2
Slaughter, Cadw., Frans. R. Slaughter and James Stone		1	11	2	4
Shake, George					3
Shrayder, Jacob					1
T					
Thompson, William					1
Tyler, Edward, Jr.					1
Tuley, John, and Charles Tuley		1	5		4
Tyler, Robert					1
Terrill, Richd.			2		3
Tyler, Edward, Senr.					2

Persons' Names Chargeable with the Tax	White Male Tithables Above 21	White Males Above 16 and Under 21	Blacks Above 16	Blacks Above 12 and Under 21	Horses, Mares, Colts and Mules
T					
*Taylor, Richard			5	2	9
Tyler, Moses					3
Tylor, William					1
Tullis, Griffin					1
Taylor, William			10	2	4
Tullus, John					1
Thixton, John, and William Thixton					6
V					
Veech, John					4
Veech, George					3
Vanbuskirk, Michl.					1
W					
Waters, John					2
Wothington, James					
White, William					2
Warford, John, and David Warford		1			2
Welch, Samuel					2
Williamson, Ann		1			1
Welch, William					3
Wheat, Jacob					3
Wheat, Coonrad					2
Woolfolk, Richard					1
Winchester, William					4
Wagle, Jacob					
Woodin, Robert					4
Williams, John					2
Wallace, Jas.		1			2
Westfall, Henry					
Wilkinson, Benja.					
Winkley, Joseph					
Total, 264	*22	33	144	24	579

* Probably Lieut. Col.
* Living in household of other persons listed.

KNOX COUNTY, KENTUCKY

Knox County was formed under an Act of the Legislature approved December 19, 1799 as follows:

Section 1—

Be it enacted by the General Assembly, That from and after the first Monday in June next, all that part of the county of Lincoln included in the following bounds, to wit: Beginning where the Pulaski line strikes the Tennessee line east to the top of Cumberland mountain; thence along the said mountain to the line of Madison county, and with the same to a point due east of the mouth of the branch of Kentucky river that the wilderness road goes down; thence up the said branch to the said road; thence with the said road to the aforesaid Madison line, and with the same to the head of Rockcastle river, and down the said river to the Pulaski line, and with the Pulaski line to the beginning, shall be one distinct county and called and known by the name of Knox.

Section 2—

The Justices to be named in the commission of the peace for the said county of Knox, shall meet at the house of John Logan, in the said county, on the first court day after the said division shall take place, and having taken the oaths prescribed by law, and a sheriff being legally qualified to act the justices shall proceed to appoint and qualify a clerk, and fix on a place for holding courts in said county, at or as near the centre thereof as situation and convenience will admit; and thenceforth the courts shall proceed to erect the necessary public buildings at such place; and until such buildings be completed to appoint such place for holding courts as they shall think proper. etc. etc.

KNOX COUNTY TAX LIST—1800

Names
Arthur, Thos.
Arthur, Ambrose
*Aulsup, John
Aulsup, Joseph
Arnet, Stephen
Ausbon, Edmund
Asher, Dill
Asher, John
Akman, John
Aulverson, Wm.
Baggley. Thomas
*Ballenger, John
Barnard, Gilbert
Bundy, Reuben
*Ballenger, Richard
Brewer, John
Brown, John
Bunch, James
Britain, James

Names
Britain, George
Britain, Parks
Blanton, John
Boling, Benj.
Brown, Joseph
Brown, Moses
Bunch, George
*Brinlee, Stephen
Britain, Levy
Baley. James
Baker, Bris
Black, John
Branham, John
Belue, Stephen
**Collins, Joel
Collins, Joseph
Cullon, James
Coffey, John
Cox, Jacob

Names
Cash, James
*Cox, Fredarach
Colsten, Henry
*Cummons, John
*Cox, Jess
Curtes, Nathaniel
*Comstock, Isaac
Cox, Wm.
Cox, Solomon
Cox, Thomas
Cox, Christopher
Commons, Wm.
Commons, Hugh
Cox, Solomon
*Cox, John
*Curtes, Samuel
*Cumstock, Wm.
Daniel, Wm.
Daniel, James

Names	Names	Names
Daniel, Terry	Hawkins, Ezekiel	Martin, Wm.
Daniel, Spencer	Hawkins, Thos.	Milner, Daniel
*Davis, Richard	*Hord, Samuel	Nicholson, Richd.
Dunking, Benj.	Hobs, James	Nichols, Wm.
Dunking, Jas.	Hord, Thomas	Payne, Joseph
Deweese, Thomas	Hord, James Sr.	*Payne, Obediah
*Deweese, David	Hord, James Jr.	Pircieafield, Jeremiah
Dean, John	Hobs, Wm.	Plat, Ralf
*Dixon, Nathan	Hobs, Christopher	*Pearl, Wm.
Eaton, John	Hobs, Vincen	Peterson, Wm.
Farris, John J.	Hutson, John	Runnels, Daniels
Farris, Elisha	Hukum, Wm.	*Ruddick, John
Farris, Lewis	Haynes, Andrew	*Reace, Joshew
Farris, Nimrod	Hughet, Goldsmith White	Rose, George
Farris, George	Johnston, Thos.	*Sneed, Wm.
Farris, Wm.	Jones, Edmund	*Stewart, Alex.
Farris, John Sr.	Jones, John	Stewart, John
Freeman, Aaron	Jones, Stephen	Stewart, Charles
*Grisham, Uriah	Jones, Waymon	Salyears, Isaiah
*Gooding, Thomas	Johnston, James	*Smith, Gadian
Gooding, John	*Johnston, David	Stephens. Richd.
Green, Lewis	*Johnston, Daniel	Stinson, Jos.
Gerdan, John (Jordan?)	*Johnston, Jos.	Sellers, Thos.
*Gayston, Hugh	Johnston, Wm.	*Slaughter, John
*Gibson, Wm.	*Juram, Abraham	*Shewmaker, Lenard
Grinstaff, Jacob	Killems, Gilbert	Spurlock, Wm.
Goan, Claborne	King, Henry	Shotwell, Daniel
Goan, Isiah	Loe, James	*Sloe, Joel
Gooding, Alexander	Loe, John	Smith, Elijah
*Gatliff, Charles	*Logan, John	Turner, Wm.
*Gatliff, Reace	*Laughlin, John	Taylor, Stephen
*Gatliff, Cornelius	Laughlin, Thos.	*Thomas, John
*Gatliff, James	*McWheater, Robt.	Tacket, Thos.
Grisham, Wm.	*McNeal, Jonathan	*Wade, Pleasant
Hale, (or Hall) James	*Mahan, James	White, Wm.
*Hodges, James	McNight, Jas.	Wilder, Jos. Jr.
Hogan, Wm.	Moseley, Samuel	Wilder, Jos. Sr.
Hawkins, Jess	Moss, Andrew	Welbourn. Edward
*Hawkins, John Sr.	McMorn, Wm.	*Wood, John
Hawkins, John Jr.	*Mahan, Thos.	Walkers, Joel

First Rate Land	825 acres	Blacks over 16	26	
Second Rate Land	9,609	Total Blacks	53	
Third Rate Land	17,774	Horses	363	
White males over 21	180	Stud Horse	1	
Between 16 & 21	19	Value Town Lotts		£30

I do certify that the within contained List a true Copy.
Teste—Richard Ballinger—C. K. C. C. P. T.
Sept. 4th, 1800.

*Land owners.
**Town lots.

DEPARTMENT OF STATE ARCHIVES—LINCOLN COUNTY TAX LISTS, 1789

A LIST OF TAXABLE PROPERTY WITHIN THE DISTRICT OF JOS. BLEDSOE, COMMISSIONER IN THE COUNTY OF LINCOLN FOR THE YEAR A. D. 1789

Persons' Names Chargeable With the Tax	White Males Above 21	Above 16 and Under 21	Blacks Above 16	Blacks Under 16	Horses, Colts and Mules
Atkinson, Joel	1		1	1	2
Allen, William	1		1		5
Allen, John	1				4
Allen, William	1				1
Alford, John	1				1
Arnett, David	1	1	2		3
Butcher, Samuel	1	2			2
Baker, Richard	1				3
Barkster, James	1				1
Black, Paterick	1				2
Breeding, George	1				3
Breeding, John	1				1
Black, James	1				12
Blase, Alexander	1				1
Breeding, Peter	1				1
Brown, John	1				1
Blanks, Shadrack	1				5
Balderidge, Robt.	1				2
Bailey, John	1	1	2		4
Bowdery, James	1				3
Purt, Benjamin	1				
Burton, Mary					5
Black, Hugh	1	1			7
Burt, Moses	1	2			4
Berrimon, Thomas	1				4
Buckhannon, William	1	1			2
Baunty, Albert	1	1			9
Ball, Elizabeth			1		2
Ball, William	1		2		3
Bailey, James	1		1		3
Ball, James	1				1
Boon, Jeremiah	1				2
Brownlee, Alexander	1				4
Byrd, John	1				3
Baylor, Walter	1		13	2	11
Bledsoe, Jos.	1				2

108

Persons' Names Chargeable With the Tax	White Males Above 21	Above 16 and Under 21	Blacks Above 16	Blacks Under 16	Horses, Colts and Mules
Cavanaugh, Wm.	1	1			9
Cloyd, James	1	1			5
Chapman, Daniel	1	1			2
Cook, Henry	1				4
Churchwell, Richard	1	1			9
Churchwell, Ephraim	1				5
Chapman, William	1				3
Cloyd, James	1				8
Chapman, Richard	1				4
Casey, James	1				1
Casity, William	1				3
Crautch, Jonathan	1				3
Commens, Gabriel	1				2
Colyer, Moses	1				4
Campbell, Michael	1				3
Cutting, Francis	1				4
Cook, Henry	1	1			6
Chapman, Sarah					4
Cook, John	1				5
Cook, David	1				14
Coghill, James	1	1			3
Crage, James	1				6
Christill, George	1				7
Cottinton, Benj.	1				4
Clark, Christopher	1				1
Crage, John	1		2	1	5
Colson, John	1				2
Davison, George	1	2	1		6
Davis, John	1				1
Davis, Samuel	1	1			14
Davis, James	1	2			5
Davis, Jesse	1				1
Devin, William	1				5
Devin, James	1				2
Emberson, Samuel	1		3	2	4
Elmore, Matthew	1				3
Evens, Edward	1				4
Evens, John	1				1
Emberson, Jesse	1				4
Embree, John	1	3	3	1	9
English, Stephen	1				3
English Charles	1				2
English, Fannie					1
Faris, James	1		2	1	5
Faris, John	1	1			3
Forbis, James	1		1		6
Flint, John	1				1
Fullin, William	1				2
Forbis, James	1	1	2	2	13

Persons' Names Chargeable With the Tax	White Males Above 21	Above 16 and Under 21	Blacks Above 16	Blacks Under 16	Horses, Colts and Mules
Forbis, Jonathan	1				11
Faris, Johnson	1				1
Faris, Isaac	1		1		3
Faris, Isum	1				3
Faris, James	1				1
Feland, Caty		1			6
Faris, Nathan	1		3		2
Gatliff, Charles	1				3
Gelispie, William	1		1	4	5
Galbreth, Hugh	1				3
Gill, John	1				1
Glover, William	1		1		4
Glover, Jos.	1		1		6
Grissum, Laurence	1				2
Grissum, Tobe	1		1		4
Gill, Richard	1	1			2
Graves, Benj.	1				8
Goggins, William	1				4
Hall, John	1	1			6
Hudgens, Daniel	1	1			3
Henry, Watson	1				4
Harmon, Voluntine	1	1			3
Harmon, Jacob	1				2
Huston, Archable	1				3
Hutcherson, Thos.	1			1	4
Hannah, Alexander	1	1			3
Hall, Joseph	1				4
Hunt, Richard	1				2
Hartgrove, John	1				3
Higgins, Peter	1				3
Hogan, Joseph	1				1
Hamilton, Thos.	1	2			7
Hounsley, Charles	1				
Hudgens, Anne			2		4
Howdeshel, Jacob	1	2			6
Haner, Christopher	1	1			7
Helm, Joseph	1		1		7
Hines, Samuel	1				3
Huffman, Frederick	1				3
Hays, Hugh	1				6
Hays, James	1				6
Jones, John	1		8	1	16
Jackson, John	1	1			5
Jackson, Joseph	1	1	4		6
Johnson, John	1	1			3
Jenkins, Samuel	1				1
James, John	1		7		10
James, George	1				3
Jackmon, Richard	1	1	3	1	5

Persons' Names Chargeable With the Tax	White Males Above 21	Above 16 and Under 21	Blacks Above 16	Blacks Under 16	Horses, Colts and Mules
Kimberlin, Jacob	1	1			7
King, John	1			1	8
Kissinger, John	1				2
Karr, John	1	2			2
Knox, James	1		1		3
Kinley, James	1				2
Kilburn, Henry	1				2
Levi, Solomon	1				5
Logan, David	1				9
Lumpkins. Philip	1		1		4
Leeper, Hugh	1		1		8
Lyn, Joseph	1				6
Leeper, Andrew	1				3
Logan, John	1		4		7
Lumpkins, John	1	1			4
Langford, Mary			2		3
Langford, Benjamin	1				4
Laurence, Mary			1		4
Logan, Thos.	1		1		4
Langford, Stephen	1		2		4
Lewis, Joseph	1				7
Logan, William	1		4		5
Lare, Andrew	1				9
Lare, Matthias	1				1
Logan, Benjamin	1		5	2	13
Martin, John	1				2
Montgomery, Wm.	1		4		6
McClure, Wm.	1				
Montgomery, Thos.	1		1		4
McCarley, James	1	2	1		9
McClavel (?) Jane					5
Montgomery, Jane		2			5
McHenry, John	1				1
McHenry, Jos.	1				1
McClure, James	1				3
Montgomery, Wm.	1		5		6
McClure, Robt.	1				4
McClure, Thomas	1				2
McClure, John	1				6
McKinney, Daniel	1	3			8
McGuire, Joseph	1				
McGuire, Laurence	1				2
McMichael, James	1				4
McColester, George	1				3
Moore, Robt.	1				17
McClure, Nathan	1				7
McKinney, John	1				4
Motesed (?), Nathaniel	1		1		3
Milner, John	1	1			4
McKinley, Andrew	1			2	6

Persons' Names Chargeable With the Tax	White Males Above 21	Above 16 and Under 21	Blacks Above 16	Blacks Under 16	Horses, Colts and Mules
Martial, William	1	1	3		5
May, Jacob	1	1			1
Mann, Jacob	1				4
Mann, Charles	1	3			9
Mckinney, Denes	1				3
Morrison, John	1				3
Mckinney, Archable	1				4
Mathis, Brister	1				2
McMerry, John	1				5
Nash, Marrill	1				4
Noah, George Sr.,	1				
Noah, George Jr.,	1				1
Neel, William	1				6
Nezbit, James	1				1
Nevill, James	1	1			4
Oneel, Bryant	1				2
Penicks, William	1				4
Perren, Josephus	1	1	2	2	2
Pettett, Benj.	1		1		6
Price, Moses	1				2
Powel, Thomas	1	1	1		3
Porter, William	1				3
Ping, John, Sr.,	1				2
Ping, John, Jr.,	1				2
Purnal, William	1		1		2
Penington, Timothy	1				3
Pigg, William	1		5		8
Pointer, William	1				2
Penicks, James	1				3
Perrel, William	1	1	2		8
Pierce, Jeremiah	1		1		7
Pipe, Silvenus	1	2			3
Potter, Lewis	1				1
Robinson, Oso	1				2
Roberts, Jesse	1		1		3
Rufner, Ruben	1				5
Ridgel, Anne					4
Robinson, John	1		2		3
Reatherford, Caty					4
Reatherford, John	1				1
Russel, Joseph	1				4
Stevinston, Thos.	1				4
Short, John	1	2	1		5
Shaw, Thos.	1				3
Short, Joel	1				1
Shaver, Peter	1				
Slade, Anne			3		2

112

Persons' Names Chargeable With the Tax	White Males Above 21	Above 16 and Under 21	Blacks Above 16	Blacks Under 16	Horses, Colts and Mules
Sidebottom, Peter	1				1
Sidebottom, Charles	1				1
Sparks, Thomas	1		1		2
Swope, George	1				1
Stevinston, David	1				1
Scott, John	1				
Stone, William	1				3
Swan, James	1				1
Stevinston, Robt.	1				1
Stoll, Solomon	1	1			2
Spoonemer, Philip	1	1			3
Smith, William	1	1	1		2
Smith, Ruben	1				5
Stevens, Abraham	1				1
Hayton, James	1				2
Shannon, Hugh	1				2
Smith, Thomas	1				1
Stapp, James	1	1	1	1	2
Stapp, William	1				1
Sutton, Christopher	1	1	3		1
Stone, Thos.	1	1			3
Sutton, William	1				2
Shipmon, Stephen	1				2
Shipman, Nicholas	1				
Shakelford, Zachariah	1		1		5
Truby, Christopher	1				1
Vaughn, John	1	1			3
Vardemon, John	1				1
Vardemon, John, Jr.,	1	1			3
Vardemon, Anziah	1				1
Vaughn, Thomas	1				3
Ventress, William	1				1
Wyatt, John	1				1
Ward, Denny	1	1			7
Warren, Charles	1	1			7
Whitley, James	1				1
Walker, Alexander	1				3
Wright, William	1				2
Weas, Philip	1				2
Wilkerson, John	1		1	1	9
Whitley, William	1		1		18
Wright, James	1				2
Warren, John	1				2
Wolf, Jacob	1				
Wood, John	1				2
Wood, Thomas	1				7
Wood, Edward	1				
Wilson, Matthew	1	1			1
Whitting, Charles	1				4

Persons' Names Chargeable With the Tax	White Males Above 21	Above 16 and Under 21	Blacks Above 16	Blacks Under 16	Horses, Colts and Mules
Wilson, George	1				2
Weathers, John	1				4
Young, John	1				8
Yarberer, James	1				
Yarberer, Randel	1				1
	20	2	2	1	64
	27	9	6	1	57
	22	5	11	6	68
	30	8	13	4	102
	25	9	17	2	129
	23	6	26	2	121
	27	12	16	2	121
	23	4	13	4	99
	24	9	9	5	,110
	28	7	17	2	121
	23	7	5	1	63
Total Amount	272	78	135	24	1055

Joseph Bledsoe, Comr.,

Lincoln County, 1789.

I certify that I have examined the foregoing list of Taxable property, and find it as corrected to be a true copy. Given under my hand this 26th day of August, 1789.

WILLIS GREEN. C. L. C.

Commissioners Book Within the District of Charles Campbell for the year 1789

Persons' Names Chargeable With the Tax	White Males Above 21	Above 16 and Under 21	Blacks Above 16	Blacks Under 16	Horses, Colts and Mules
Alexander, William	1				
Arnold, Reuben	1		1		2
Arnold, Humphrey	1		2		5
Anderson, John	1				8
Atkins, William	1				
Armstrong, John	1				1
Alexander, James	1				4
Anderson, James	1			1	6
Adams, Matthews	1				6
Bryant, John G.	1				2
Brydon, Robert	1				1
Brown, Garfield	1				1
Burton, Ambrose	1		3		3
Brown, Joseph	1	1			3
Bright, Henry	1				4
Bailey, Robert	1				
Bright, Jacob	1				2
Bright, John	1				2
Bowles, Riche	1		1		5
Barnet, Robert	1	1			7
Bledsoe, Joseph	1	1	5	2	11
Buford, John	1		4		7
Bailey, William	1				8
Bryant, John	1		3		4
Burdit, Joshua	1				3
Burdit, Joseph	1				1
Barnet, Edward	1	1	1		6
Butler, James	1				3
Banks, William	1				2
Ball, Benjamin	1	2			3
Banks, Reubin	1				
Banks, Linn	1	1	1		2
Blackwood, Sam'l	1				2
Boyd, Charles	1				1
Brydon, Barbara	1		2		1
Boyd, George	1				1
Blythe, David	1				3
Bias, Jeremiah	1			1	3
Baker, Elijah	1				2
Chilton, Thomas	1		1		5
Cooley, Daniel	1				1
Cartwright, Wm.	1				2
Campbell, Wm.	1				5
Campbell, Charles	1		1		2
Clinton, Archiable	1				1
Calverd, John	1				2
Certain, Isaac	1				2
Carson, John	1		2		3

Persons' Names Chargeable With the Tax	White Males Above 21	Above 16 and Under 21	Blacks Above 16	Blacks Under 16	Horses, Colts and Mules
Crawford, Rebecca		1			6
Collier, Alexander	1	2			6
Campbell, Wm. S. C.	1				1
Collier, Robert	1				1
Collier, John	1				1
Cain, George	1				5
Camden, William	1				1
Chambers, John	1				5
Cain, John	1	1			2
Caldwell, John	1				3
Caldwell, Robert	1				2
Clury, John	1				7
Cotner, Frederick	1				6
Collier, Anthony	1				4
Couts, Henry	1				1
Copeland, Jacob	1		1		7
Cosbey, Charles	1				1
Daniel, Aaron	1				1
Duncan, Samuel	1	1	2	1	4
Dryden, William	1		4		5
Douglas, George	1	1			4
Downing, John	1				6
Dewitt, Walter	1	1			2
Downing, James	1		5		2
Downing, Andrew	1				3
Dow, Francis	1				9
Denton, Thomas	1				4
Downing, Ezekiel	1				2
Davis, Asel	1				4
Edwards, Milley			2	1	2
Edwards, John	1		2		2
Elliot, Alexander	1		1		4
Forbis, Robert	1				2
Freeland, Garret	1				3
Ferrel, John	1				3
Fresh, Frances	1				1
Floyd, John	1		2		6
Floyd, Benjamin	1		2		4
Floyd, George	1		2	1	2
Floyd, David	1		1		1
Freeman, Elisha	1				2
Gill, Samuel	1		1		3
Gibbs, Jeremiah	1				1
Graham, John	1				5
Gibbs, Ezekiel	1				
Green, Robert	1				1
Garrison, Abraham	1				
Hyette, Joseph	1				1

Persons' Names Chargeable With the Tax	White Males Above 21	Above 16 and Under 21	Blacks Above 16	Blacks Under 16	Horses, Colts and Mules
Hay, William	1				3
Hambleton, Wm.	1	1			10
Hyette, William	1				2
Hind, James	1		1		6
Hambleton, John	1				5
Hay, John	1				
Hart, Israel	1		1	1	7
Hopkins, William	1	1			7
Harber, Amos	1				2
Hall, Leonard	1			1	3
Hopkins, Francis	1				3
Huffman, Frederick	1	1			3
Harber, Elijah	1				7
Haggard, Benjamin	1				2
Harmon, Jacob, Jr.	1	1			4
Hawkins, John	1	1	2		3
Johnston, William	1			1	1
Jackman, John	1		1		13
Innis, John	1	1			5
Jones, John	1		3	1	2
Johnston, John	1				4
Jones, William	1				
Kee, William	1				1
Kamper, John	1			1	2
Kidd, James	1				1
Lampton, William	1	1			1
Lampton, John	1				2
Lawson, David	1		1		2
Long, William	1	1			4
Lampton, William	1				2
Lasefield, Ezekiel	1				1
Lamm, Nathan	1				7
Lynim, Andrew	1				1
Linkey, Robert	1				
Love, Robert	1				2
Linkey, James	1(a white servant)				1
Lapesley, John	1		2		5
Murphy, Zephamiah	1				4
Mann, William	1				4
McEwen, David	1	1			5
McNeely, John	1				3
Miller, Abraham	1				5
McEwan, William	1				4
Mobley, Benjamin	1				1
McCarmack, Hugh	1				4
Murren, Michael	1				

Persons' Names Chargeable With the Tax	White Males Above 21	Above 16 and Under 21	Blacks Above 16	Blacks Under 16	Horses, Colts and Mules
Marshal, Sarah					4
Mobley, Edward	1				7
McQuinney, Wm.	1				4
McQuinney, Sam'l	1				1
McQuinney, John	1				3
Mattock, Ralph	1				1
Montgomery, Samuel	1			1	3
Maxberry, Samuel	1		1	2	1
Montgomery, Thos.	1		1		7
Montgomery, Wm.	1		2		13
Mayfield, George	1	1			5
Montgomery, Robt.	1				4
McMullen, John	1				2
Murphey, John	1				2
Miller, George	1	2			4
Mayfield, Isaac	1				4
Maxberry, John	1				1
Maxberry, Sam'l	1				1
Manifee, Wm.	1				3
Manifee, Nimrod	1				2
Mitchel, John	1				3
Morris, Jesse	1				3
Mobley, James	1				2
McDowell, Alexander	1				2
Musker, Nowell	1				1
Nelson, Samuel	1				1
Nelson, William	1				3
Noble, William	1				1
Noble, Darrell	1				1
Nowell, Garrett	1				
Noble, John	1		2		1
Noble, Mark	1				3
Newton, Peter	1				2
Nickolson, James	1				4
Nowell, Drusilla		1	2	1	2
Odam, Willis	1	1			4
Owsley, Thomas, Sr.,	1				15
Owsley, Daniel	1		6	2	1
Owsley, Thomas, Jr.,	1				1
Owsley, Henry	1		4	1	6
Owsley, William	1		2	1	13
Owsley, Anthony	1		2		5
Provin, John	1		1		12
Pawling, Henry	1		4		6
Pope, Humphrey	1				2
Pope, Alexander	1		1		2
Perkins, Christian	1				3
Pope, Thomas	1	1	3	1	3
Pollard, James	1				1

Persons' Names Chargeable With the Tax	White Males Above 21	Above 16 and Under 21	Blacks Above 16	Blacks Under 16	Horses, Colts and Mules
Parks, William	1				10
Pollard, Abraham	1				2
Parker, Thomas	1				5
Price, Abraham	1				6
Price, Isaac	1				2
Preston, John	1	2			7
Pointer, William	1				3
Reed, James	1				1
Reed, John	1				4
Ramsey, Seth	1				1
Richardson, Wm.	1	1			6
Rutherford, Joseph	1	2			3
Rutherford, Joseph	1	1			5
Ratliff, Richard	1				6
Rolls, Marmaduke	1				3
Rowls, Hardy	1	1	1		9
Richardson, Jesse	1		1	2	4
Rice, Charles	1				2
Sutton, Benjamin	1				5
Sutton, John	1				6
Shepherd, John	1				2
Sleet, John	1		4		7
Silvers, Joseph	1				4
Smith, Thomas	1				2
Southren, William	1				1
Singleton, Robt.	1			2	4
Sunn, Abraham	1				2
Summers, John	1				6
Summers, Thos.	1				1
Sellers, Nathaniel	1	1			3
Seller, James	1				2
Sellers, Joseph	1				1
Slade, William	1				2
Sellers, John	1				5
Stein, William	1				3
Shadrock, John	1				1
Smith, Elijah	1				1
Stringer, Limeledge	1				1
Stringer, Wm.	1				2
Simpson, Wm.	1				2
Swope, Benedict, Jr.,	1				3
Swope, Benedict, Sr.,	1	1	1		2
Sprat, William	1				6
Tomkins, Edward	1				2
Talyor, Jonathan	1				3
Turney, Daniel	1				3
Turney, Michael	1				1
Thompson, James	1		2	1	3
Turner, George	1				1

Persons' Names Chargeable With the Tax	White Males Above 21	Above 16 and Under 21	Blacks Above 16	Blacks Under 16	Horses, Colts and Mules
Toney, Alexander	1				1
Trumbow, George	1				1
Utman, Peter	1				4
Utman, Joseph	1				7
White, George	1				2
Wornell, Richard	1		1		3
Williams, John	1				2
Whitley, Thomas	1				4
Williams, Thomas, Jr.	1		2	1	8
Williams, Thomas, Sr.	1		7	2	7
Williams, John	1		2	3	6
Warren, Burress	1				1
Ward, Thomas	1				1
Waddle, David	1				1
Williams, Elijah	1		1		2
Young, William	1				5
Zukledge, William	1	1			2
Calculated	5	1	1	7	11
	16	0	14	7	54
	17	2	1	0	40
	17	1	9	4	71
	18	4	9	1	81
	17	2	18	5	64
	18	3	4	4	62
	20	1	2	0	59
	16	3	5	3	48
	17	5	4	2	68
	17	0	13	2	48
	18	4	11	1	72
	19	3	4	0	69
	19	4	16	3	58
	20	2	7	1	57
Total Amount	254	35	118	33	862

I do hereby certify that the within Book is a true list of the Taxable Property within my District.

14th day Sept. 1789.   Charles Campbell
Lincoln to-wit

I have examined the foregoing list of Taxable property and find it (as corrected) a true copy.

Willis Green, C. L. C.

Persons' Names Chargeable With the Tax	White Males Above 21	Above 16 and Under 21	Blacks Above 16	Blacks Under 16	Horses, Colts and Mules
Ashby, Silas	1				2
Adams, Peter	1				1
Ackerman, Jane	Wm. Main				4
Allin, John	1		1		4
Adams, William, Sr.	Wm. Adams, Sr. Wm. Adams, Jr.				6
Adams, David	1				8
Alspach, David	1				
Avis, Mary		1			8
Allin, Robert	1		1		4
Arbuckle, John	1				2
Burch, Benjamin	1	1	2		2
Burch, Benjamin, Jr.					1
Barnett, John	1	1			4
Boyers, John	1				
Batest, John	1				
Blain, James	1				3
Bryan, James	1				3
Bentley, John	1	1			5
Boggs, John	1				4
Barnett, Robert	1				6
Balldock, Richard	1				
Brown, Morris	1				2
Burks, William	Wm.&Geo. Burks (2)	1			
Blain, Alexander	1		5		7
Black, Thomas	1				6
Ball, Thomas	1	1	3	1	10
Bunton, William	1				6
Burnside, Walter	1				4
Barbee, Elias	1	2			3
Brunk, Jacob	1				1
Black, Joseph	1				6
Brumpton, Bryan	1				2
Briscoe, Edward	1				2
Blain, Alexander, Jr.	Jno.Blain Alex. Blain, Jr.	1	3	2	9
Baily, Elisha	1				3
Briggs, Samuel	1				4
Cimbel, Stephen	1				
Collet, Isaac	1				2
Collet, Stephen	1				1
Cummins, Matthew	1				1
Cap, Martin	1				
Cotes, George	1			1	4
Christmon, Henry	1				

Persons' Names Chargeable With the Tax	White Males Above 21	Above 16 and Under 21	Blacks Above 16	Blacks Under 16	Horses, Colts and Mules
Craig, Sam'l	1			2	10
Crow, William	1		2	1	6
Cloyd, William	1				1
Crawford, John	1				5
Craddock, Robert	1		3	1	6
Cord, Christopher	1				
Caswell, John	1				3
Cox, James	1				5
Curry, John	1				8
Caufman, John	1				2
Carpenter, Elizabeth				3	5
Carpenter, Conrad	1				5
Carpenter, Adam	1				6
Childers, Goldsby	1				2
Curry, Sarah					2
Davis, Thomas	1				3
Davis, Jane		1			4
Day, John	1				4
Depaw, Charles	1				4
Davis, James	1		2	1	8
Daugherty, John	1	1	2		20
Darlington, Abraham	1				2
Donnally, Charles	1		2		4
Davis, Azariah	1				2
Dobson, Robert	1	1			5
Donan, David	1				3
Dobson, Joseph	1				2
Dodds, Andrew	1				5
Dodds, James	1				1
Dever, John	1				
Drummon, James	1				
Dooly, James	1				5
Ewing, Baker	1		3		11
East, Joseph	1				2
Elliott, George	1	2	2		5
Elliott, William	1				1
Eastin, William	1				
East, Neal	1				1
Fencounty, Joseph	1				
French, James	1				1
Ford, William	1		6	2	6
Freeland, Thomas	1				
Freeland, James	1		2	2	7
Freeland, John	1		2		6
Fourney, Nicholas	1				
Fresh, Gasper	1				
Givens, James, Jr.	1	1	2		7

Persons' Names Chargeable With the Tax	White Males Above 21	Above 16 and Under 21	Above 16 Blacks	Blacks Under 16	Horses, Colts and Mules
Givens, Robert, Jr.	1				6
Guthry, Elizabeth	Wm.Burns		2	1	10
Guthry, Robert	1				6
Graham, James	1				3
Gilmore, James	1				9
Gilmore, Samuel	2		1		4
Gray, Robert	1				2
Goodnight, Jacob	1				1
Givens, James	1				1
Givens, John	1				2
Givens, George	1	2	3		12
Garvan, Isaac	1				2
Gay, Thomas	1	2			4
Gan, William	1				1
Givens, Samuel	1				2
Gilmore, James	1				7
Helms, Marquis	1				3
Hunter, John	1		6		5
Hughes, John	1				1
Harvey, John	1				2
Hoopman, Jacob	1				3
Henderson, James	1				1
Hashfield, John	1	1			
Horine, George	1				2
Horine Michael	1				6
Hillicost, George	1	1			3
Hogg, Aron	1	1			3
Hansbrough, Moriah	1	2	2		4
Hite, Thomas	1				4
Harlin, George	1				7
Hambelton, James	1				1
Harrison, Thomas	1	1	1		1
Hardwick, William	1				3
Huston, Stephen	1				4
Huston, Mary		1	1		6
Helms, George	1				13
Helms, Leonard	1				3
Isaacs, John	1				6
Johnson, Noel	1		4	1	7
Johnston, Andrew	1				4
Jones, Arthur	1				1
Josselling, John	1		4	1	5
Johnston, Sam'l	1				4
Jackson, Christopher, and Christopher, Jr.	2		1		6
Jackson, Thomas	1				3
Josselling, William, and John Evans	1				3
Kirkpatrick, James	1			1	8
Kean, Sam'l	1		1		

Persons' Names Chargeable With the Tax	White Males Above 21	Above 16 and Under 21	Blacks Above 16	Blacks Under 16	Horses, Colts and Mules
Kean, William	1		2	1	3
Kilbreath, Evan	1				3
Knary, Christopher	1				2
Littler, John	1				7
Low, Sam'l	1				1
Lamb, Frederick	1		1		1
Lorger, John	1				
Logan, Nathaniel	1				6
Logan, Mathew, David and Jonathen....	3			1	11
Logan, James	1		1		5
Low, Edward	1				1
Marchall, Marchum	1				8
Mackey, James	1				1
McKenlas, John	1				
Martin, John	1		1		5
McCormick, Joseph	1				8
McCormick, Daniel and son Daniel	2		2		5
McCormick, William	1				5
Martin, John	1				4
McNight, Robert	1				4
Myers, Lewis	1				3
McMurray, Thomas	1				4
Magraw, John	1				1
Mansfield, John	1				1
Myers, Jacob and Thos. Buckner	2				4
Miller, Sarah					6
May, Humphrey	Robt. Mickleborough	1	2		3
Miller, John	1				4
Miller, George	1				2
Murral, George	1		2	1	7
Mason, William	1	1			5
Mason, James	1				1
Moore, Sam'l	1		3		2
Marchall, John T.	1				5
Morrison, David	1	1			3
Moore, Obidiah	1				2
Miller, William	1		1		7
Montgomery, John	1		6	2	6
McKenny, Enoch	1				1
McKenny, James	1		1		9
Mason, William	1				5
Naylor, George	1	1			1
Nealy, Isaac	1				1
Obannon, James	1				3
Patten, William	1		1		7

Persons Names Chargeable With the Tax	White Males Above 21	Above 16 and Under 21	Blacks Above 16	Blacks Under 16	Horses, Colts and Mules
Pitman, Thomas	1	1	1		6
Pope, Gasper	1				2
Peyton, Phillip	1				
Peyton, Valentine	1		1		5
Pope, George	1				6
Pope, Henrey	1		1		7
Peyton, Charles	1	1			1
Paton, Jacob	1				7
Lovey, Peyton		1			
Phillips, Charles	1	1			2
Pyton, Daniel	1				1
Perry, Richard	1	1			5
Retherford, John	1				4
Rickason, Timothy	1				2
Rock, James	1				
Reily, John	1				3
Rennex, Heney	1				2
Rennex, William	1				2
Ryan, John	1		2		2
Riddle, Moses	1				
Robinson, Hannah and Luke Robinson	1				4
Right, William	1				2
Robins, John	1				1
Richardson, Joseph	1				4
Ragland, John	1				1
Reynold, John	1				3
Rip, Christopher	1				10
Reed, John	1		4	1	8
Rees, William	1		2		5
Reynolds, Charles	1				9
Rayburn, Robert	1				2
Ross, Daniel	1				1
Ragen, Amos	1				5
Roberts, Alexander	1				1
Robinson, William	1				6
Stephens, Jacob	1				6
Sutherland, Uriah	1				2
Tyrus, Slanton	1				3
Smith, William	1	1			3
Smith, George	1				2
Sloon, John	1	1			7
Smith, James	1				1
Springate, William	1				4
Stone, Jacob	1				2
Shelby, Isaac	1		16	3	17
Smith, John	1		3	1	2
Steel, Paul	1				
Stephenson, James	1				1
Simpson, Sarah					1
Stone, Spencer	1				2

Persons' Names Chargeable With the Tax	White Males Above 21	Above 16 and Under 21	Blacks Above 16	Blacks Under 16	Horses, Colts and Mules
Smith, Thomas	1				1
Smith, Winstead	1				
Simpson, John	1				5
Smith, Scarlet	1				3
Smith, Jesse	1				2
Snider, Harmon	1				3
Smith, Thomas	1				3
Spears, Jacob	1			1	11
Stump, Jacob	1				2
Spencer, George	1				3
Shannon, Thomas	1				4
Smith, William	1				3
Smith, John (Shoemaker)	1				1
Sloan, William	1				2
Swinna, Moses	1	2	2		3
Swinna, Joseph and Chas.	2				2
Sharp, George	1				2
Shackleford, Sam'l	1	2	4	1	13
Sloan, John	1				1
Taylor, William	1	1			
Taylor, Frank	1				
Todd, Thomas	1		2		2
Thompson, William	1		1		5
Thompson, Alexander	1				2
Tibbs, Foushee	1		2	1	6
Underwood, John	1				1
Ulery, Peter	1				1
Veach, John	1				1
Vanwinkle, Michael	1	3			7
Vance, George	1				6
Wash, Benjamin	1				1
Wiley, William	1				
Warrin, James	1		1		13
Watherington, Wm.	1				
Warrin, William	1	1	4	1	22
Wray, William	1				1
Wilson, Sam'l	1				4
Williams, Chas.	1				
Woner, Peter	1				
Wiley, Aquilla	1				3
White, George	1				3
Young, Peter	1		1		1
Young, John	1	1	2		7
Yunt, George	1				4
Young, Jacob	1				6
Wilkines, John	1	1			3
Wiley, Benjamin	1	1			3
Watherington, Edward	1	1			7

Persons' Names Chargeable With the Tax	White Males Above 21	Above 16 and Under 21	Blacks Above 16	Blacks Under 16	Horse, Colts and Mules
Willis, Major	1		1	1	2
Willis, John					
Write, Jesse	1				2
William, David	1	1			1
Artgess, Henry	1				6
Berry, William, and John	1	1			4
Barnett, James	1				3
Barnett, John	1				3
Bennedick, John	1				3
Cary, John	1			1	3
Campbell, Joseph	1				6
Daugherty, Wm.	1	1			4
Freeman, Elisha	1				1
French, John	1				2
Givens, Samuel	1				2
Goldsby, James	1			1	1
Hilly, Francis	1				2
Havord, George	1				1
Jones, Thomas	1				2
Kenneday, Michael	1				1
Logan, Nahtaniel					
Logan, Hugh	1		1	2	8
Moore, Wm.	1				2
Moore, Geo.	1				1
Moore, Edward	1				2
McGill, Jno., and Hugh	2				5
McGill, Wm.	1				5
Mathew, Wm.	1	2			2
McKaffordy, Simon	1				1
Neal, Barnard	1	1			2
Neal, Geo.	1				3
Powell, Edward	1		4		7
Powell, Wm.	1			1	2
Willis, John	1		1		3
Ragon, Amos	1				5
Kerny, Dan'l.	1				2
Allcorn, Geo.	1				2
Black, Alexander	1				4
Phillips, John	1				4
Adams, Wm., Jr.	1				
Briggs, Benj.	1				1
Foreman, David	1				
Givens, Robt., Jr.	1				5
Gee, John	1				2
Holland, John	1				1
Joplin, John, Jr.	1				2
McKenney, Dan'l.	1				2
McKensey, John	1	1			8
Renix, James	1				6
Sloan, Alex	1				1

Persons' Names Chargeable With the Tax	White Males Above 21	Above 16 and Under 21	Blacks Above 16	Blacks Under 16	Horse, Colts and Mules
Renix, Wm., Jr.	1				6
Servant, Wm.	1				1
Southerland, Uriah	1				2
Stephenson, James	1				1
Tucker, John	1			1	1
Wiley, Benjamin	1				5
Young, Peter	1				2
Welch, James	1				3
McCain, Robert	1				3
Green, Willis	1	1	4	1	6
Horine, Jacob	1				2
Neff, Henry	1				4
	23	2	4	2	64
	43	8	9	5	137
	46	9	15	4	143
	39	5	22	5	135
	28	6	21	3	153
	41	7	23	5	159
	41	9	29	5	138
	37	3	11	9	154
	37	7	17	3	128
Total Amount	345	56	151	41	1211

William Reed Comr.,
Lincoln County, 1789.

I certify that I have examined the foregoing list of taxable property and find it as corrected to be a true copy. Given under my hand this 31st day of August, 1789.

Willis Green, C. L. C.

DEPARTMENT OF STATE ARCHIVES
LOGAN COUNTY TAX LISTS—1795

Logan county was formed from the western portion of Lincoln county in 1792, and comprised all the territory lying between Green river on the north, the North Carolina (Tennessee) line on the south, Elk Lick and Little Barren river on the east and the Mississippi river on the west. This territory included a district which has since been divided into twenty-five counties or parts of counties lying between the present counties of Green and Metcalfe and the Tennessee river, and also the whole of the territory known as Jackson's Purchase. This district was no further divided until Christian and Warren were formed in 1796.

In selecting a tax list for publication in this number of the Register, only two thin records of Logan county for the year 1795 could be found, and disappointment was felt at first at what seemed to be incomplete returns from such a large territory as was at that time included in Logan county, but comparison of the names on the lists herewith presented with data furnished by Collins' History of Kentucky, Perrins' History of Christian, Starling's History of Henderson and Rothert's History of

Muhlenberg counties has shown that practically the whole of the original county was covered, at least in the lists of personal property. The small number of landowners charged with tax would indicate that other lists of those charged with tax on lands have been lost. In fact, Finley mentions James Herndon as one of the commissioners, and we have no returns from him, although his name does appear on Reuben Ewing's list.

According to Finley's History of Russellville and Logan county, the first visitor to the site of Russellville was Morton Maulding "who came to the spring usually called Barclay's Spring in the spring of 1780." Morton Maulding (here called Maulden) appears on the list for 1795, as do Richard West and Ambrose Maulden, the Manskers, Ewings, Dromgooles, Burwell Jackson, "the richest man in the country," Rowland and George Madison (the latter afterwards dying in office as Governor of Kentucky), and many others who are handed down in history as men of importance in the county.

The part of Logan county which later became Warren is here represented by the McFaddins and Abraham Raymer, who is mentioned as the fast runner in Finley's history.

In what is now Christian county we find one of the commissioners of the tax, Charles Logan (later sheriff), Jonathan Logan, Justinian Cartwright, Young Ewing, who became the first circuit judge of the district, and Joshua Cates, mentioned by Perrin as one of the "later settlers," but who is mentioned by Finley as an early millowner on Big Whippoorwill.

Muhlenberg county is represented by Henry Rodes or Rhoades, the "Godfather of Muhlenberg," Henry Keith, Richard Morton and John Dennis. (See History of Muhlenberg County, by Otto A. Rothert.)

In Henderson county we find the name of Jacob Sprinkle and his brother Michael, who, as young boys, had been captured by Indians while hunting north of the Ohio, and had escaped after untold hardships to become settlers near the mouth of the Green river.

If time were taken for careful comparison with records of other counties since formed from Logan, there is hardly any doubt that settlers in each of them would be found in these lists except in the counties west of the Tennessee. That territory was still almost entirely occupied by the Chickasaw Indians after the abandonment of Fort Jefferson about 1782-3, and until it was bought from them by the commissioners, General Andrew Jackson and Governor Isaac Shelby in 1818.

The tax lists for Logan County for 1795, which were among the records of the Auditor's office. found in the basement of the old Administration building, appear on the following pages under appropriate headings.

A LIST OF TAXABLE PROPERTY IN THE DISTRICT OF REUBIN EWING, COMMISSIONER IN THE COUNTY OF LOGAN FOR THE YEAR 1795.

Persons' Names Chargeable with Tax	Males Over 16	Blacks	Horses	Cattle	Males Over 21
Armstrong, James	1		1		1
Abbot, James	1		2		1
Armstrong, Mosh	1		3		1
Asher, William	1		5		1
Armstrong, John, Sr.	1		2	22	1
Alexander, Matthew	1		1	8	1
Adkin, Haneh (?)					1
Anderson, Thomas					1
Allin, Elijah	1		9	38	1
Abbot, Samuel	1				1
Alexander, William	1		2	5	1
Anderson, Henry	1		2	14	1
Armstrong, John, Jr.	1		3		1
*Askey, Zachariah	1	2	13	15	1
Allerd, Hardy	2		2	8	2
Alexander, Ebenezer	2	4		13	1
Allen, William	2	4	1	13	1
Arrington, Charles					1
Armstrong, Abraham					1
Ander, John					1
Anderson, John					1
Anderson, Wiot					1
Ammons, John					1
Bratchy, John	1				1
Brown, John	1		6	19	1
Bryant, James			7		1
Baker, John	1		17	19	1
Bowie, Reason	1	8	11	23	1
Blakey, George					1
Burriss, John			2	17	1
Boyd, Daniel	1		3	3	1
Bellew, Thomas	1	4	2	25	1
Blayer, Andrew	1		1		1
Blayer, Thomas	2		4	12	1
Baulch, Amose					1
Barrow, John	2	2	6	10	2
Bozmon, Jacob	1		2		1
Boyd, John	1		3	10	1
Billingsly, John	1		1	5	1
Billings, Abraham	1		4	4	1
Boyd, Charles	1		1		1
Boyd, Andrew	1		6	22	1
Butcher, Gasper	1		3	20	1
Bryant, Edward	1		4	4	1
Brandond, John	1		2	5	1
Bell, Robert	1		1	6	1
Bishop, William	2		13	15	1
Barker, William	2		14	14	1
Bush, William					1
Buttler, William					1
Boyd, James	1		1	2	1
Byerstaff, John	1		1		1
Bay, Andrew	1		3	9	1
Billingsly, James	2	1	4	8	1

*Tavern license.

131

Persons' Names Chargeable with Tax	Males Over 16	Blacks	Horses	Cattle	Males Over 21
Barnes, Samuel	1		1		1
Buttler, John	1		9	4	1
Biggerstaff, Samuel	1		2		1
Buchannan, Jno.	3	2	2	24	1
Boyd, David	1			6	1
Bone, James	1		7	11	1
Bay, Caniday	1		2	2	1
Baly, John	2		2	14	1
Barnes, Jonas	1		1	5	1
Barnes, Frederick	1		1	4	1
Billings, William	1		5	9	1
Barnes, Andrew					1
Black, James					1
Ch.sum, Absolom	1		9	14	1
Cook, William	1		2	8	1
Chapman Thos.	2		3	28	1
Cox, John, Sr.	2		2	7	1
Cox, Samuel, Sr.	1	2	5	15	1
Chisum, John	1		8	5	1
Crabtree, William	1		1		1
Collins, Lewis	1	2	3	3	1
Cates, Joshua	1		7	14	1
Curd John	1	2	2	4	1
Cook, James, Sr.	1		1	19	1
Cox, John, Jr.	2	1	6	37	1
Cox, Phinis	1	2	7	56	1
Cook, James, Jr.	1				1
Cross Zachariah	1		6	13	1
Carnahan, Andrew	1		8	24	1
Craven, John	1		5	30	1
Cartwright, Thomas	1		3	10	1
Cook, Joseph, Jr.	1		4	7	1
Cox, William	1		2	2	1
Coats, William	1		7	15	1
Cumton, Varnell	1			11	1
Collins, William	1		1	15	1
Connely Timothy	1		1	4	1
Cravens, Elijah	1		2		1
Coats, Wilson	1		2	9	1
Comnton, Richard	1				1
Cumton, Levy	1	1	5	20	1
Cox, Samuel, Jr.	1		8	40	1
Carnahan, John	1		3	10	1
Cox, Fulken	1		5	18	1
Clerk Thomas	1		1	3	1
Corhern, George	1		1		1
Conner, William	1		3	11	1
Caldwell, Samuel	1	4	3	7	1
Cartwright, Just'n	1		3	7	1
Conner, Isaa					1
Choat, Squire	1		3	20	1
Cartwright, Peter	1		3	17	1
Coventon William	1		1		1
Cooper, Jobe	1		2		1
Corhern, John	1		4	14	1
Drumgoole, James	1	6	18	22	1
Dillender, Joseph	1		3	10	1

Persons' Names Chargeable with Tax	Males Over 16	Blacks	Horses	Cattle	Males Over 21
Davis, Thomas					1
Dial, Thomas	3		8	15	1
Dooley, Daniel	1		2	2	1
Drumgoole, Alexander	1		5	1	1
Downe, Ambrose	1	5	4	5	1
Dolihide, Aquilia	1		5		1
Dobb.ns, David	1				1
Dunn & Gorham	2	2	9	6	2
Dickason, Griffith					1
Daviss, Clem, Sr.					1
Daviss, Clem., Jr.					1
Dugin, Collonel	1		6	7	1
Eads, John	1		2	8	1
Eastis, William	1		1		1
Eads, Isaa	1		6	4	1
Ewing, Young	1	8	9	17	1
Ewing, John	1	4	2	9	1
Eastis, John	1		2	4	1
Ewing, Samuel					1
Edgar, William	1	2	3	4	1
Ewing, James	1		2	7	1
Ewing, Robert	1	6	6	25	1
Elem, John	1		2	19	1
Ewing, Chatham	1	3	5	6	1
Forde, Thomas	1		12	10	1
Fisher, John	1			4	1
Flemming, Ralph	1		3	7	1
Forgason, William, Sr.	1		3	8	1
Fiske, John	1		1		1
Forgason, William, Jr.	1		1		1
Finley Uzza	1		3		1
Finley, Norriss	1	3	2	4	1
Ferleigh, George					1
Fleener, Sarah			2	12	1
Frazer, George	1	1	4	28	1
Fisher, James	1		4	7	1
Felphs, Nicholas	1		1	2	1
Funkehouser, Christr.			2	5	1
Fisher, William	1		2	24	1
Fry, Bazel	1			10	1
Funkhouser, Christr.	1	3	7	30	1
Greaves, Frederick	1		2	3	1
Glover, Richard	1		1		1
Greaves, Anthony	1		3	12	1
Grimes, David	1		1		1
Gillmon, Joseph	1		2	9	1
Green, James	1		1	7	1
Grammer, John	2		6	13	1
Grammer, William	1		5	7	1
Gibbson, Gadi	2	5	5	17	1
Green, Jessee	1		9	10	1
Guffee, Alexander	1		6	15	1
Griffith, Christipher	1		2	11	1
Grason, Reuben	1		2	3	1
Grason, William	1				1
Gambrel, James	1		1	10	1

Persons' Names Chargeable with Tax	Males Over 16	Blacks	Horses	Cattle	Over 21 Males
Grigs, Julies					1
Goff, William					1
Goff, Thomas	1				1
Goff, Jessee	1				1
Goff, William, Sr.	1				1
Harrison, Jessee	1		3	6	1
Hood, William	1		1	7	1
Harlen, Joshua	1		1	3	1
Harden, Benjamine	1		4	9	1
Howard, William	1		1	3	1
Hudson, Ezekiel					1
Hamton, Caty			3	7	1
Herndon, Elisha	1		2		1
Henry, Thomas	2	2	7	14	1
Hargraves, Robert, Sr.	1		8		1
Hughs, David					1
Howard, John	1		10	36	1
Hendrix, Thomas	1		2	6	1
Howell, James	1				1
Hughs, James					1
Hany, David	1		2	6	1
Haw, Jacob	1		2	7	1
Herndon, James	1	12	5	20	1
Hudson, Thomas					1
Hughs, William					1
Henry, William	1		2		1
Handly, John	1		3	10	1
Harrison, William	1	10	23	25	1
Hays, Andrew	2		2		2
Hughs, David, Jr.	1		2	5	1
Hall, James	3		14	29	2
Hamton, Thomas	1	3	5	13	1
Herndon, Cornelius	1	4	1	8	1
Harris, William	1		4	10	1
Hutchcraft, John	1				1
Hughs, Jessee	1		3	14	1
Hensley, Charles	1		1	8	1
Hall, Edward	1		4		1
Hughs, William	1		1		1
Herndon, George	1	1	2	12	1
Hargreaves, Robt., Jr.	2		3	34	2
Harris, Jinkins					1
Hargraves, Willis	1		2	15	1
Harris, John					1
Hargraves, Hezekiah	1		2	8	1
Houghstedler, Jno.	1	1	7	20	1
Huker, Michael	1				1
Herrill, Robert					1
Holte, Danieal					1
Howard, Elihue					1
Jones, Stephen	1	2	2	5	1
Jones, James	1	1	1	4	1
Jackson, John	1	1	2		1
Jones, James, Sr.	1			1	1
Joy, Cumfort	1		2	8	1
Johnston, Nathen					1
Jackson, Burwell	2	2	4	8	1

Persons' Names Chargeable with Tax	Males Over 16	Blacks	Horses	Cattle	Males Over 21
Jones, David	1		1	4	1
Key, Thomas					1
Logan, Charles	1	3	2		1
Lemar, William	1		1	6	1
Lankford, Thomas	1				1
Lane, Robert	1		4	3	1
Lowry, Thomas, Sr.	2		5	4	1
Lawrence, John	1		5	5	1
Loggston, Thomas, Sr.	1		1	7	1
Loggston, Thomas, Jr.	1		2	8	1
Lacey, Alkanah	1		6	16	1
Loggston, James	1		1		1
Leemar, Samuel	1		2	8	1
Lewis. N. William					1
Lamm, John	1		2	12	1
Lowry, Thomas. Jr.	1		2	1	1
Lemar, Luke			3	7	1
Lacey, Lilel					1
Lacey, Nathariel					1
Loggston, William	1			30	1
Levaw, Abraham	1		1		1
Mcneese, John					1
Maxwell, John	1		2		1
Martain, Charles	2		3	2	1
Miller. John			3	7	1
Mcmillin, Hugh	1		2	11	1
Marshel, William	1		6	6	1
Mcbee, Silas	1	2	18	7	1
Morgan, Jeremiah	1		3	2	1
Memorn, Dominack	1				1
Montgomery, James	1				1
Mcfaddin, Andrew	1		2	22	1
Moor, William	1			6	1
McCutchen, James	1		6	22	1
Mckey, William	1		3	5	1
Mcmillin, William	2	1	3	14	1
Mcmillin, Thomas	1	2	11	19	1
Mars, William	1		10	22	1
Mcfaddin. Samuel	2		4	11	1
Maxey, Jessce	1		1	18	1
McCutchen. Robert	1		5	21	1
Megowan, Samuel	1		6	17	1
Madison, Rowland	1	18	7	40	1
Mcfaddin, William	1		1	10	1
Mosely, Thomas					1
Morgan, Joseph	1		4	16	1
McCutchen, Hugh	1			7	1
Maxwell, William	2		6	30	1
McClane, Matthew	1	3	9	110	1
Madison, George	1	8	2	5	1
Memorne, Domnack	1		2	7	1
McCurdy, Thomas (?)	1		5	17	1
Minday (or Murday), Samuel	1				1
Memorn, John	1		5		1
McCutchen, Samuel	1		7	17	1
Miller, Andrew	1	3	11	18	1

Persons' Names Chargeable with Tax	Males Over 16	Blacks	Horses	Cattle	Males Over 21
Marshal, John	1		2	20	1
McGoodwin, Daniel	1		3	9	1
Miller, George	1		3	16	1
Maulden, West	1	1	4	13	1
Mcfaddin, John					1
Mansker, George, Sr.	2		10	75	1
Maulden, Richard	1	1	2	14	1
Myers, Philip	1	1	5	21	1
May, Balaam	1		1		1
Moor, John	1		2		1
Mansker, George, Jr.	1		2	9	1
McCutchen, Jon'a, Jr.	1			11	1
Maulden, Morten	1	2	20	28	1
Morrow, Richard					1
Montgomery, Alx.	1		7	22	1
Morlen, Hugh	1		1		1
McDaniel, James	1		5	11	1
Musely, Thomas					1
McDaniel, Thomas					1
McClain, Ephrim					1
McLeane, James					1
McClain, Charles					1
McClane, Samuel					1
McPherson, John	2		1		2
McGinnis, Robt.					1
Morriss, William					5
Morris, John					4
Norriss, Ezekeial	1		4	17	1
Neel, John	1				1
Neal, Andrew	1		5	16	1
Neal, John, Sr.	1		2		1
Null, Nicholas	1		4	1	1
Newman, Simon	1		1		1
Neslor, Christo.	1		1		1
Neal, Thomas	1		3	20	1
Nancarow, John	1		3	6	1
Nelson, Abraham	1		4		1
Nesler, Joseph	1		1		1
Oneal, Hirham	1		6	13	1
Oneal, Jonithen	2	4	10	47	1
Oneal, Mitchel	1	1	6	10	1
Oxford, Samuel	1		2	1	1
Philips, Joseph					1
Puntany, Nelson	1		3	5	1
Puntany, Samuel	1		1		1
Palmore, Permenius (?)	1		8	10	1
Philips, John			1		1
Puntany, Aquilia	1		1		1
Painter, Joseph	2		4	8	1
Portwood, Ludy	1		4	6	1
Portwood, Paige	1		3	12	1
Pitmon, John	1				1
Parker, Thomas					1
Patterson, Thomas	1		1		1
Price, Mises (?)	1		3	2	1
Paul, Jacob	1			12	1

Persons' Names Chargeable with Tax	Males Over 16	Blacks	Horses	Cattle	Males Over 21
Pryer, John					1
Rutherford, Thomas					1
Ralston, Isaac	1		2	9	1
Reese, Charles	1		6	10	1
Ruhy (?), Edward	1		3	6	1
Reed, Leonard	2			4	1
R.ce, John	3		1	13	1
Rutherford Benjamine	1	1	4	12	1
Rutherford, James	1	2	10	17	1
Raymer, Abraham	1		1	8	1
Robert, Thomas					1
Reed, William	1		1	8	1
Reed, Edward			1	1	1
Rounsvill, Isaac	1	2	5	25	1
Raymer, Abraham, Sr.	2		2	14	1
Russle, Abraham	1		2	7	1
Rowland, Micajah					1
Russle, Handly					1
Sulliven, John					1
Steal, John	1		2	14	1
Shelby, Amose	1		5	4	1
Sutton, John	1		4	19	1
Scott, Jacob	1		4	22	1
Stamp, Frederick	1		3	39	1
Smith, Thomas	1		2	18	1
Showd (?), John	1		4		1
Standly, Abraham	1		2	7	1
Smith, Benjamine	1		2		1
Shurm, Nicholas	1			5	1
Staton, Charles	1		1		1
Sharp, Thomas					1
Simpson, William	1				1
Suggs, William	1	1	1	3	1
Staton, John	1		1	25	1
Stewart, John	1		1		1
Scott, Elias	1		1		1
Standly, David	2		12	44	1
Stewart, Charles	1	2	2	4	1
Sharp. Maxwell					1
Standly, John	1	1	5	12	1
Shannen, John					1
Slocum, John	1				1
Skillet, John					1
Shannen, Joseph	1	1	5	10	1
Suggs, Simon	1	1	3	2	1
Suggs, A. George	1	1	4	14	1
Shepard, James	1		1	2	1
Turney, Peter					1
Trawven, William					1
Tylor, James	1		1		1
Tope, Frederick	1		2	2	1
Thomson, John	1		2		1
Tigart, John					1
Tylor, Joseph	1		3	5	1
Tillee, John	1		1	6	1
Taylor, Elkin	2		4	9	1
Tillee, James, Sr.			4	14	1

137

Persons' Names Chargeable with Tax	Males Over 16	Blacks	Horses	Cattle	Males Over 21
Taylor, Moses	1	1	3		1
Thomson, Andrew	1		5	11	1
Tillee, James, Jr.			3	5	1
Taylor, Thomas	1		1		1
Tinnen, Lawrence					1
Taylor, Robert					1
Upton, John	1		1		1
Vanken, Peter	1				1
Williams, John	1		1	40	1
Williams, Thomas	1		3	13	1
Wall, Micajah					1
Williams, Rowland	1		3	3	1
Williams, Aron	1	3	4	16	1
Wise, Amose	1	3	4	12	1
Whitesitt, William	1	8	2	4	1
Ward, James	2			5	1
White, Hugh	1		3	8	1
West, Richard	3		8	20	1
Ward, Britten	1		2	17	1
West, Leonard	1		6	3	1
Wright, Stephen	1		2	6	1
Whiteaker, James	1		1	7	1
Waters, Barney	1		2	4	1
White, John, Jr.	1		1	4	1
Woocey, John	1		1	4	1
Ward, George					1
Williams, James	1		6	6	1
Ward, Brinkly	1		1		1
Wriley, John	3		6	17	1
Wallice, David	1				1
Whiteaker, Alex.	1		3	5	1
Ward, John	1	2	3		1
White, John, Jr.	1		3	7	1
Wilson, Samuel	1				1
Winkfield, William	1		3	15	1
Williams, Samuel					1
Woods, John	1		1		1
Willson, James	1	2	15	6	1
Wilcox, Thomas	1		4	8	1
Watley, Wiley					1
Young, Christopher	1				1
Young, William	1		2	15	1
Young, John	1		5	25	1
Young, Blood Aron					1
Youngblood, Henry					1
					474
					60
					534

I do hereby certify that their has remov'd to this County sence the 20 of March 60 free Males above the age of 21 that are Intitles to the Right of Electors which added to the above make 534.

RUBIN EWING, C. T. L.

138

A LIST OF LANDS IN THE DISTRICT OF REUBEN EWING, COMMISSIONER, IN THE COUNTY OF LOGAN FOR THE YEAR 1795.

Persons' Names Chargeable with Tax	County in Which Lying	Water Course	Quantity of Acres
Thomson, Andrew	Logan	Spring Creek	200
Billingsly, James	Logan	Gasper River	1,666
Butcher, Gasper	Logan	Whipperwill	200
Butcher, Gasper	Logan	Gasper River	150
Baker, John	Logan	Read River	180
Boyd, Daniel	Logan	Read River	100
Baly, John	Logan	Big barron	344
Barrow, John	Logan	Big Barron	50
Chapman, Thomas	Logan	Dracks Creek	200
Chapman, Thomas	Logan	Dracks Creek	200
Chisum, John	Logan	Gasper River	200
Cox, John	Logan	Gasper River	200
Chisum, Absolam	Logan	Gasper River	200
Cox, Phinis	Logan	Gasper River	200
Cates, Joshua	Logan	Whipperwill	57
Cartwright, Thomas	Logan	Read River	100
Dunn & Gorham	Logan	Whipperwill	100
Drumgoole, James	Logan	Read River	350
Drumgoole, James	Logan	Read River	100
Drumgoole, Alex.	Logan	Read River	50
Ewing, John	Logan	Read River	250
Ewing, John	Logan	Whipperwill	371
Frazer, George	Logan	Gasper River	50
Gilbert, John	Logan	Mudy River	480
Gilbert, John	Logan	Elk Lick	100
Graves, Anthony	Logan	Whipperwill	100
Harrison, William	Logan	Read River	250
Hargraves, Robert	Logan	Mudy Creek	200
Hendrix, Thomas	Logan	B. Barron	50
Howard, John	Logan	L. Mudy	284
Henry, Thomas	Logan	Read River	100
Herndon, George	Logan	B. Whipperwill	300
Hargraves, Willis	Logan	B. Mudy Creek	100
Handly, John	Logan	B. Mudy Creek	9,100
Herndon, James	Logan	Whipperwill	9,100
Houghstedler, John	Logan	Whipperwill	200
Herndon, Cornelius	Logan	Whipperwill	100
Jackson, Burwell	Logan	Gasper River	150
Jackson, Burwell	Logan	Mudy Creek	646½
Jackson, Burwell	Logan	Mudy Creek	540
Jackson, Burwell	Logan	Mudy Creek	350
Jackson, Burwell	Logan	Mudy Creek	500
Jackson, Burwell	Logan	Mudy Creek	123
Jackson, Burwell	Logan	Mudy Creek	143
Jackson, Burwell	Logan	B. Barron	750
Jackson, Burwell	Logan	B. Barron	232
Jackson, Burwell	Logan	B. Barron	300
Jackson, Burwell	Logan	B. Barron	66
Jackson, Burwell	Logan	Dracks Creek	466⅔
Jackson, Burwell	Logan	Dracks Creek	100

Persons' Names Chargeable with Tax	County in Which Lying	Water Course	Quantity of Acres
Jackson, Burwell	Logan	Gasper River	750
Jackson, Burwell	Green	L:ttle Barron	200
Jackson, Burwell	Logan	Green River	200
*Jackson, Burwell	Logan	Bigg Barron	300
McFaddin, William	Logan	Bigg Barron	55
McGowen, Samuel	Logan	Gasper River	150
Mosely, Thomas	Logan	Whipperwill	100
McFaddin, Andrew	Logan	B. Barron	700
McFaddin, Andrew	Logan	B. Barron	570
McFaddin, Andrew	Logan	Drakes Creek	500
McFaddin, Andrew	Logan	B. Barron	633
McFaddin, Andrew	Logan	Drakes Creek	170
McFaddin, Andrew	Logan	Read River	500
McFadd.n, Andrew	Logan	Cumberland	500
McFaddin, Andrew	Logan	Mudy River	263
Montgomery, Alex.	Logan	Whipperwill	100
Morgan, Jerimiah	Logan	Read River	100
Maulden, Morten	Logan	Whipperwill	400
Madison, George	Logan	B. Barron	400
Madison, George	Logan	Bays Fork	500
Madison, George	Logan	Mudy River	666⅔
Madison, George	Shelby	B'shers Creek	200
Miller, Andrew	Logan	Read River	1,774
Madison, Rowland	Logan	Big Barron	1,000
Mcmillin, Hugh	Logan	Read River	47
McPherson, John	Logan	Read River	1,000
McPherson, John	Logan	Read River	2,050
Nancarow, John	Logan	Gasper River	100
Nesler, Joseph	Logan	B. Barron	50
Newman, Simon	Logan	Mudy River	300
Raymer, Abraham	Logan	Big Barron	350
Standly, Abraham	Logan	Read River	200
Standly, David	Logan	Read River	200
Taylor, Joseph	Logan	Gasper River	60
West, Amose	Logan	Whipperwill	100
Woocey, John	Logan	Read River	100
Added up by me Max'l Sharp			5.557

"*The Tax on the hole of this Land as it Stands Stated I find to be 8..18 for the years 93 & 94."

A LIST OF TAXABLE PROPERTY IN THE DISTRICT OF CHARLES LOGAN, COMMISSIONER IN THE COUNTY OF LOGAN FOR 1795.

Persons Names Chargeable with Tax	White Males	Blacks	Horses	Cattle	Males Over 21
Adams, Matthew	1	2		3	1
Ashley, William	1			5	1
Barnett, Joseph					1
Bradley, Sam'l	1			5	1

Persons' Names Chargeable with Tax	White Males	Blacks	Horses	Cattle	Males Over 21
Barnett, Joseph	1	3	1	12	1
Barnett, William	1			2	1
Boyd, James	2		1	5	1
Barnett, Jacob	1			24	1
Barnett, Humphrey	1		1		1
Bradley, John	2		2	20	2
Burden, Joseph	1		2	50	1
Bukerstaff (or Bickerstaff), Benja.	1		1		1
Bowan, Ebenezar	1				1
Carpenter, Christo.	2		2	6	1
Cumpton, Varnald	1				1
Campbell, Robert	1				1
Cornerstock, Thos.	1				1
Cordery, John	1		3	10	1
Dinnis, John	2		4		1
Doutt, John	1			4	1
Davis, Benjamin	1				1
Davis, James	2	1	7	28	2
Ewing, Reuben	1		3	3	1
Eastis, John	2		2	8	1
Fransway, Norad	1			6	1
Friggs, Conrad	1				1
Fletcher, Peter	1		2	20	1
Faith, Alexander	1		1		1
Fouts, Lawrence	1				1
Gibbs, Sam'l	1		3	5	1
Gibbs, Robert	1		2		
Gibbs, Elizabeth			2	4	
Gibbs, William	1		2		1
Gibbs, Hugh	1		1		1
Hughs, John	1		1		9
Hughit, Russell	1	1	1	2	2
Harris, John	1			4	1
Hughs, Roland	1	1	3	8	1
Hardon (or Haidon), Jacob	2		2	5	1
Hopton, Stephen	1		12	26	1
Harden, Sam'l	1		2	10	1
Holly, Nathaniel	2			10	1
Hicks, Absolom	1		1	4	1
Hay, Micheal	1		4		1
Johnson, Nathan	1	1	5	10	1
Johnson, John	1				1
Inman, William	1		1	16	1
Knox, Hugh	1				1
Kirkindol, Adam	1		1	6	1
Kirkindol, Abner	1				1
Keith, Alexander	1				1
Kimble, Jesse	1			5	1
Knight, John	1		1	10	1
Keith, Henry	2		1	12	1

Persons' Names Chargeable with Tax	White Males	Blacks	Horses	Cattle	Males Over 21
Logan, David	1	5	4		1
Logan, Jonathan	1	4	2	5	1
Lawrence, Adam	1	4	10	40	1
Lawrence, George	1		2	4	1
Landers, Jacob	1		3	19	1
Mauldin, Ambrose	1	1	14	34	1
Mauldin, James	1		2	6	1
McEwing, Wm.	1		1	10	1
McCallister, Enos	3		2	1	2
Montgomery, Robert	1			11	1
Mason, Joseph	1				1
Mason, James	1		1	27	1
McRoberts, James	1		1	2	1
McElmurray, Jean				4	
McFadden, Jacob	1		4	19	1
McFadden, Sam'l	1		5	5	1
McMillin, Robert	1		1	5	1
McElmurry, David	1		1	1	1
McCoombe, John	1		1	15	1
Mortan, Richard	1		2	19	1
McFaddin, Shepherd	1		1	4	1
Noland, Abraham	1		1	2	1
Owens, Ezra	1			1	1
Ross, James	2		11	11	1
Rowen, Andrew	1				1
*Rhodes, Henry	2		5	16	1
Rhodes, Solomon	1		1	1	1
Rhodes, Daniel, Sr.	2		1	3	1
Rhodes, Dan'l, Jr.	1		3	5	1
Roberts, Obediah	4		7	14	1
Rolisson, Lawrence	2		1	8	2
Ramsey, Josiah	1	2	4	19	1
Ramsey, Jonathan	1		2	9	
Shelby, Moses	1	13	4	18	1
Slover, John	1		1	8	1
Simpson, Robert	1		1	2	1
Smith, John	1		1	1	1
Sprinkle, Micheal	1		2	3	1
Sprinkle, John	1		1	1	1
Smith, Thomas	1		1	2	1
Sprinkle, Jacob	1				1
Tyler, William	1		2	6	1
Tyler, Peter	3		3	11	1
*Thorn, Peter	1		1	3	1
Upp, Jacob	1			8	1
Vance, Patrick	1	2	1		1
Vaughn, Joseph	2	1	7	25	2
Wilcox, Charles	3		4	27	1
Wallace, William	1		2	14	1
Wortman, Henry	1		1		1

Persons' Names Chargeable with Tax	White Males	Blacks	Horses	Cattle	Males Over 21
Willingham, Thos.	1			32	1
Willingham, Isham	1		1	2	1
Worthington, Benja.	1		2	9	1
Worthington, James	1		1	10	1
White, Solomon	2		5	12	1
Wallace, George	1		1	4	1
Worthington, Joseph	1		2	5	1
Walker, John	1		1	5	1
Young, Nathan	1		1	2	1
	135	39	217	877	113
					37
					150

Logan County viz.: I do hereby certify that there has Come into my District sence the 1st of March 37 Males above the age of 21 that has the right of Electors which added to the above is 150.   CHAS. LOGAN, C. T. L.

*Tavern.

A LIST OF LAND GIVEN IN THE DISTRICT OF CHARLES LOGAN, COMMISSIONER, IN THE COUNTY OF LOGAN FOR THE YEAR 1795.

Owners' Names	County Where Lying	Water Course	Quantity of Acres
Cumptin, Varneld	Logan	Barren	520
Ewing, Reuben	Hardin	B. Creek	200
Johnson, John	Logan	Muddy	400
Keith, Henry	Logan	Muddy	200
Mortan, Richard	Logan	Green R.	300
Mason, Joseph	Logan	W. L. Creek	1,000
Mason, James	Logan	W L. Creek	200
Rhodes, Henry	Logan	Green R.	250
Rhodes, Henry	Logan	W. L. Creek	400
Shelby, Moses	Clark	Licking	500
Shelby, Moses	Logan	S. Creek	100
Shelby, Moses		Elkhorn	150
Logan, David	Logan	West Fork	228
Logan, Jonethan	Logan	W. Fork	207
			4,655

Logan County (towit) Sept. 10th, 1795.

    I do hereby certify that I have Examined the within agreeable to the Vouchers taken by the Commissioner and find it to be correct.

Test

    SAM'L CALDWELL, C. L. C.

MADISON COUNTY TAX LIST, 1788

List Found in Basement of "Administration Building," Old Capitol, May, 1922

Arranged for publication by Mrs. Jouett T. Cannon, Associate Editor.

"Taxable property within the district of Robert Rodes, Commissioner in the County of Madison for the year 1788."

Persons Names Charged With Tax	White Males Tithes	Blacks Over 16	Horses and Cattle
Anderson, Robert	1	....	1
Allason, Thomas	1	....	3
Anderson, John	1	....	a
Burgain, Jacob	1	....	6
Burgain, Isaac	1	....	10
Burgain, Denis	3	....	6
Blackwell, James	1	3	2
Boon, George	2	4	16
Barkkshire, Dickey	1	....	3
Blackwell, Armstead	1	....	1
Boon, Squire	1	....	6
Brown, George	1	....	3
Brockman, Thomas	1	....	1
Brinson, Zebulin	1	....	2
Burtin, Isaac	1	....	3
Ballew, Charles	1	....	1
Burtin, Samuel	1	....	4
Burtin, Allin	1	....	1
Butler, Thomas	1	....	2
Benit, Thomas	1	....	1
Calk, William	1	6	14
Clark, John	2	....	5
Crews, Thomas	1	....	4
Cook, Absalem	2	....	3
Clay, Green	1	1	7
Collier, John	2	....	2
Collier, James	1	....	1
Crews, David	2	2	13
Crews, Elijah	1	....	2
Cofer, Jacob	1	....	2
Carpenter, John	1	....	6
Cidwell, John	1	....	....
Davis, Elexander	1	....	2
Dosier, J. James	1	1	6
Dosier, Lenard	1	....	1
Debrell, Charles	1	3	6
Dosier, Zachariah	2	....	2
Dosier, James	1	....	1
Daniels, Nathan	1	....	3
Durbin, Christopher	2	....	2
Davis, Samuel and Davis, John	2	....	0
Durrum, James	1	....	1
Durbin, Edward	1	....	3
Dunham, William	3	....	7
Evens, Peter	1	2	1
Embry, Jessy	1	1	3
Embry, John	1	....	2
Embry, Joseph	2	2	8
Esten, John	1	—	1
Fletcher, William	1	—	3
Fowler, Joseph	1	—	1
Gentry, Richard	1	—	3
Gentry, David	1	—	4
Gogens, John	1	2	5
Grubbs, Higgason	1	—	15
Gaddy, Elijah	1	—	2
Hogges, Jessy	1	—	6
Herod, Edward	1	—	—
Harper, John	1	—	7
Hoon (or Horn), Christopher	1	—	6
Holley, Francis	1	—	3
Harris, Christopher	1	—	2
Harris, James	1	—	1
Hoon (or Horn), Aaron	1	—	4
Hoon (or Horn), Matthew	1	—	3
Hoy, William	2	10	6
Harris, William	2	4	9
Ham, William	1	1	8
Hervey, William Henry	.—	—	—
Hervey, John & William	3	1	5
Hopper, Moses	1	—	1
Hopper, William	1	—	4
Harket, Peter	1	—	1
Holland, William	1	—	2
Hall, David	1	—	7
Hill, Joel	1	1	2

Persons Names Charged With Tax	White Males Tithes	Blacks Over 16	Horses and Cattle	Persons Names Charged With Tax	White Males Tithes	Blacks Over 16	Horses and Cattle
Holley, John & Wilkason, John C.	3	3	13	Phelps, John, Jr.	1	....	9
Hall, James	1	....	1	Portwood, Page	3	....	9
Hendricks, James	...	....	9	Portwood, Loyd	1	....	1
Howard, Benjamin	1	....	4	Portwood, Thomas	1	....	3
Herndon, Owen	2	....	4	Portwood, Page, Jr.	1	....	6
Heartherly, Lenard	1	...	3	Phelps, John, Sr.	1	....	5
Jones, William	2	1	8	Redman, George	1	....	3
Jones, Irwin	1	2	5	Robards, Frances	1	....	2
Jones, Cad	1	....	3	Robards, Edward	1	....	7
Kerley (?), William	1	....	2	Robards, Nathan	1	....	4
Lorin, John	1	....	3	Robards, Elisha	1	...	3
Lanham, Thomas	1	....	4	Reyburn, Ralph	1	....	2
Lewis, Aaron	1	3	4	Reves, Grief	1	....	2
Logsted, Edward	1	....	5	Reid, Lenard	1	....	5
Logsted, Joseph	1	....	4	Rodes, Robert	1	4	10
Logsted, Thomas	2	....	3	Stone, Benjamin	1	....	4
Longstreth, Jonathan	1	....	1	Stone, Burgess	1	....	5
Loyd, Thomas	1	....	1	Stone, Valentine	1	2	4
Massie, Harris	1	....	2	South, John	3	1	3
Moor, Robert	1	....	12	Stephens, Thomas	1	....	3
Mise, Isaac	1	....	4	Sapinton, John, and Sapinton, Hanalas	2	....	6
McDaniel, James	2	....	2	Sapinton, John, Jr.	1	1	4
Merit, Joseph	1	....	4	Stalker, Thomas	1	....	1
McDaniel, Aaron	1	....	1	Sapp, John	3	....	2
Miller, Jacob	1	1	1	Stamper, Joshua Cp	1	....	1
Morgain, Mary	1	....	2	Smith, Thomas	1	....	1
McQueen, John	1	....	1	Searcy, Charles	1	1	9
McQueen, James	2	....	1	South, Mary	1	....	8
Moor, John	1	....	7	Salley, Stephen	1	....	2
Montgomery, James	1	....	2	Sapinton, James	1	....	3
McQueen, Joshua	1	....	1	Smith, Rev. (?)	1	....	2
Martin, Benjamin	1	....	2	Symes, Matthew	3	2	6
Million, John	1	....	1	Snell, Charles	1	....	1
Manion, James	1	....	3	Strauher (?), Thomas	1	....	4
Manion, Thomas	1	....	6	Sterns, Jacob	1	4	4
Noland, Henry	1	....	3	Skinner, Joseph	1	....	1
Nanby (?), John	1	....	2	Taylor, Joseph	1	....	4
Orear, William	1	....	3	Tudor, Valentine	1	....	4
Ocaley, William	1	....	2	Turner, Andrew	1	....	2
Ocaley, Benjamin	3	....	4	Towns, Oza (or Ola)	1	....	3
Oleor, George	1	....	1	Tudor, John	1	....	2
Procter, Nicklias, Sr.	....	1	...	Turpin, William	1	....	9
Procter, Benjamin	1	....	1	Tharp, Dodson	1	....	2
Procter, Page	1	....	...	Taylor, Francis	1	....	2
Parker, Edward	1	....	4	Terry, Othea	1	....	....
Pollard, William	1	....	3	Taylor, John	1	....	....

Persons Names Charged With Tax	White Males Tithes	Blacks Over 16	Horses and Cattle	Persons Names Charged With Tax	White Males Tithes	Blacks Over 16	Horses and Cattle
Tudor, Henry	1	....	3	White, James	1	....	1
Turpin, Elizabeth	—	....	1	Williams, William	2	....	6
Taylor, Frank S. (or L.)	1	....	4	Williams, Isaac	1	....	3
Williams, Edward	1	....	....	Williams, John	1	....	—
Williams, Philip, Henry and James	3	2	10	Walker, Asaph	2	4	8
Wilson, John	1	....	3	Walker, Stephen	1	....	1
Wells, Henry	2	....	2	Walker, James	1	....	1
Wiliams, Daniel	1	....	1	Weltch, Thomas	1	—	5
West, Richard	1	—	3	West, Johnnathan	1	—	5
West, Thomas	1	....	4	Woodrough, John	2	—	2
White, George	1	....	2	Woodrough, David	1	—	1
White, John, Jr.	1	....	8	William, Shadrach	1	—	5
White, John	1	....	1		231	81	694

Robert Rodes' return, Comm. for 1788.

146

DEPARTMENT OF STATE ARCHIVES
Madison County Tax Lists, 1792.

In selecting the tax lists of Madison county for 1792 for publication in this issue of the magazine some thought has been given to the fact that it may be interesting to compare the names of the residents in the first year of statehood with those in the lists of the pioneers at Fort Boonesboro in 1775, and in the "petitions" of the following years, as set forth in the very interesting article of Mrs. James W. Caperton, which also appears in this number, page 142.

Madison county was formed in 1785 from the eastern part of Lincoln, and included all or part of the counties of Garrard, Clay, Estill, Rockcastle, Perry, Laurel, Breathitt, Letcher, Owsley, Jackson and Lee. See Collins' History, vol. II, page 24. Mr. Collins did not include Bell and Harlan among those taken from what was originally Madison, and it is treason to question him, but the description of the boundaries of Madison, as set forth in petition No.......... to the *Virginia legislature* makes the line of *Washington county* one of the limits, and this must have been Washington county, Virginia, which was just over the mountains from Harlan. See Petition No. 27. Filson Club Publication, No. 27, page 84.

The three lists herewith presented were taken by William Caperton, Andrew Kennedy and John Adams, commissioners of the tax. A summary of all three lists is made in Caperton's return, which would make it appear that the whole county was covered by the three, but the absence of the names of a few men who are known to have been large landholders, such, for instance, as Gen. Green Clay, indicates that there was another list which has not been preserved. In the tax book for 1795 General Clay's land holdings cover three pages.

It would be interesting to make mention of some of the notables among the pioneers of this county of distinguished men, but the lack of space will prevent this, and Mrs. Caperton in her article tells in a most delightful way of the "first comers."

It may surprise some persons who are looking for the names of ancestors in this list not to find them under the proper initial, but a good many liberties were taken with spelling of proper names, and we find Phelps sometimes spelled *Felps*, Shackelford, *Sheckelford*, Wright, *Right*, and Chenault, *Shenault*.

A LIST OF TAXABLE PROPERTY WITHIN THE DESTRICT OF JOHN ADAMS, COMMISSIONER IN THE COUNTY OF MADISON FOR THE YEAR 1792.

Persons Names Chargeable With the Tax	White Males Above 21	White Males Above 16 and Under 21	Blacks Above 16	Blacks Under 16	Horses, Mairs, Colts & Mules	Cattle	Acres of Land
Adams, George	1		2	1	8	2	950
Arnold, John	1				6	6	
Allexander, Sarah					4	7	
Adams, Matthew	1				4	15	78
Arbuckle, Samuel	1				1	4	
Alcorn, John	1	1			5	9	
Adams, Feathergail	1			2	3	15	75
Adams, James	1	1	1	1	6	19	100
Adams, Robert	1				6	5	
Andrew, James	1				2	2	
Ardrew, David	1				3	5	
Arbuckle, James	1				1		
Arbuckle, David	1				1		
Alcorn, Robert	1				5	14	500
Alcorn, James	1				1		
Adams, Matthew	1				4	7	
Adams, George	1		2	3	4	5	
Anderson, James	1		1		3	8	242
Anderson, William	1				4	7	
Allon, William	1				2	10	
Adams, Luke	1	1			8	13	
Archer, John	1				4	13	
Boon, Josiah	1				3	18	
Best, Humphry	1	1	1	2	14	25	780
Barnett, James	1				5	7	
Best, Stephen	1				7		
Bull, Abraham	1				1	2	
Bryant, Jesse	1				1	6	
Bennett, Hardy	1				2	3	37
Boyles, John	1	1	3	3	5	20	
Brembel, Joseph	1				2	7	
Barnard, Charles	1				6	8	100
Bailes, Allexander	1				1	9	
Brown, Joseph	1				8	55	170
Brown, Robert	1						
Bonty, Alburt	1	1			9	31	
Burton, Allon	1			2	4	7	
Burton, William	1				3	12	
Burton, Abraham	1			1	7	10	
Burton, Robert	1	1	1	2	2	6	
Brockman, Thomas	1			1	1	8	
Burton, Isaac	1				5	10	
Barrow, Richard	1				1		
Bailey, John	1				1	2	
Bailey, Robert	1				2		
Bailey, Warrant	1	1					
Batts, Thomas	1		3	6	3	20	
Blann, Charles	1				6	7	126
Boyd, William	Ent.				1	3	
Brown, Beverley	1					4	
Brown, William	1				1		

Persons Names Chargeable With the Tax	White Males Above 21	White Males Above 16 and Under 21	Blacks Above 16	Blacks Under 16	Horses, Mairs, Colts & Mules	Cattle	Acres of Land
Bartlet, William	1		1	1	6	8	
Banks, Thomas	1	1	1	2	2	6	
Drown, Matthew	1				1		
Eryent, John	1				1	6	
Doyle, Alexander	1				2	8	
Bryant, John B. C.	1				7	4	
Black, James	1				3	12	
Brown, John	1		2	1	5	20	150
Brown, Charles	1				1		
Clythe, David	1				3	10	
Brinson, Stout	1			1	4	9	
Brank, Robert	1	1		2	9	21	
Barnett, Robert	1				5	9	
Barnett, Andrew	1				2	2	
Bruce, John	1		4	4	9	28	
Blair, Henry	1				1	2	
Barrett, William	1				2	3	
Beasley, James	1				2	14	
Boyd, Richard	1				1		
Beloo, Charles	1		1	1	1	5	106
Brown, Arabe	1		2		3	15	200
Brown, Barlett	1				2	2	
Brown, Absolom	1		1		7	9	100
Brown, Benage	1				1		
Brown, Fradrick	1				3	14	
Brasfield, Edward	1		3	6	4	15	
Clarke, John	1			1	3	9	
Clarke, Thomas	1				4	14	
Clark, William	1				2	17	
Cotney, John	1				5	8	50
Champ, William	1				7	22	200
Clarke, John S-6	1				4	5	568
Clarke, James	1						
Carpenter, Zapher	1	1			5	15	300
Crawford, William	1	2			13	16	180
Croucher, William	1				5	13	
Craig, James	1				2	2	
Chism, Elisha	1				2	3	
Cogswell, Jeramiah	1				2	4	
Cooley, Thadus	1				2	7	
Cooley, Wm.	1				3	11	
Crawford, Mary		1			4	10	100
Crawford, James	1				2	1	
Carr, James	1				4	9	
Cardwell, James	1			1	1	13	
Cockran, Samuel	1				4	6	
Clarke, John. Sr.	1	2			7	13	
Crawford, James P-S	1				9	25	150
Carpenter, John	1				3	5	
Clark, Thomas, Sr.	1	1			4	10	
Castain, John	1				3		
Childers, Goolsby	1				3	5	
Childers, Henry	1				3	1	

Persons Names Chargeable With the Tax	White Males Above 21	White Males Above 16 and Under 21	Blacks Above 16	Blacks Under 16	Horses, Mairs, Colts & Mules	Cattle	Acres of Land
Crawford, Alexander	1				1	9	64
Carson, John	1		1	1	3	14	100
Cumley, David	1				6	40	
Cockron, Denis	1				1	4	
Carr, Richard	1				3	20	
Doty, Francis	1				3	3	
Drinkerd, William	1				1	2	
Dougherty, William	1				2	3	
Dever, John	1	2	1	2	7	18	110
Dyer, Mary					6	11	
Dodson, Josep	1	2			11	68	
Denney, Alexander	1	1			9	35	200
Davis, John	1				7	13	400
Dickey, Robert	1	2			5	10	
Davis, John, Sr.	1		1		11	35	60
Davis, Samuel	1				2		
Dooley, Moses	1	1			7	22	340
Dooley, Abner	1				2		
Dunkin, George	1				2	11	79
Dunkin, Robert D.	1				4	1	
Dickey, George	1	1			7	8	
Dickey, John	1				1	8	
Daniel, Thomas	1				2	8	
Dehart, Ecklin	1				3		
Doty, John	1				12	50	
Dyer, Abraham	1				1		
Evins, Francis		1			2		
Evins, John	1				2	2	
East, North	1				3	14	65
East, James	1				1		
Finley, George	1		1	1	6	10	100
Finnell, Charles	1				3	5	
Finnell, William	2				6	16	150
Fitchjerral, John	1				5	14	
Faulkner, Thomas	1			1	3	27	200
Fish, Thomas	1				7	11	
Ford, John	1				4	13	
Ford, Peter	1	1			7	22	150
Franklin, John	1				1	4	
Francis, Henry	1		1	1	16	20	
Ferrel, William	1				2	1	
Finnell, James	1			1	3	7	50
Fields, John	1				5	9	
Francis, John	1		2	1	5	15	
Francis, Samuel	1				1		
Fenton, Bertholomew	1				21	36	
Fletcher, Thomas	1				2	2	
Glasgow, John	1				3	11	
Galaspey, William	1		1		2		140
Gordon, Robert	1			1	6	28	100

Persons Names Chargeable With the Tax	White Males Above 21	White Males Above 16 and Under 21	Blacks Above 16	Blacks Under 16	Horses, Mairs, Colts & Mules	Cattle	Acres of Land
Gulley, Thomas	1	1			5	15	
Gulley, Thomas, Jr.	1						
Gray, John	1				2		
Gray, Richard	1				1	5	
Guffey, Samuel	1				4	5	
Guffey, Jones	1				1	5	
Guffey, John	1					3	
Graham, Francis	1				1	11	
Green, Benjamin	1				2	9	
Gillett, Jonathan	1			2		8	
Gatliff, Charles	1	2			4	50	
Galahas, Patrick	1				3	2	
Graham, Mary		1			3	4	100
Gordon, Samuel	1				5	3	100
Gilcomb, Joseph	1					7	
Gill, Richard	1	1			2	6	
Gill, John	1				1	2	
Gill, Richard, Jr.	1				1		
Gibbs, Ezekel	1				1	1	
Gibbs, Jarimah	1				1	11	
Hamelton, Charles	1				3	11	120
Hinton, George	1				4	13	100
Harris, John	1				3	6	
Harris, Samuel	1				1	6	
Harris, James	1				3	2	
Harriss, Mary	1				5	6	200
Henin, Andrew		1			2		
Huston, Achibold	1				3		
Henderson, James	1	1	2		10	25	150
Hammon, Philip	1				3	21	50
Henderson, John	1				8	22	100
Henderson, Micheal	1				6	26	100
Harris, James	1				8	20	
Horn, Joseph	1	1			4	16	70
Hill, Robert	1				4	4	
Huntsman, John	1					5	
Huston, Robert	1				2	6	100
Hencely, David	1				8		
Hammon, Isral	1				2	13	
Haze, William	1				4	5	100
Hamm, Drury	1				6	6	
Hardwick, John	1				1	2	
Harris, Thomas	1				1	5	
Heagle, John	1				4	6	
Howhemmer, Henry	1				1	6	
Hows, William	1				1		
Hopkins, Eldridge	1				1	3	
Hill, Clemuel	1				4	10	100
Hopkins, John	1				2	4	
Harris, John	1				9	14	125
Hughs, Absolom	1				3	6	
Henry, Robert	1				10	35	
Hutchison, John	1			2	7	15	100

Persons Names Chargeable With the Tax	White Males Above 21	White Males Above 16 and Under 21	Blacks Above 16	Blacks Under 16	Horses, Mairs, Colts & Mules	Cattle	Acres of Land
Harris, Andrew	1			2	7	15	100
Holterman, Jacob	1				1		
Hagen, Jacob	1				1	4	
Hagen, Prosser	1				5	6	
Hicks, Daniel	1						
Hiett, John	1	1	2	4	13	40	
Hiett, Fredrick	1				5		
Hiett, Abner	1				2	3	
Hutchison, Laurance	1				1	2	
Hutchison, Charles	1				6	10	
Hennes, Henry	1				2	8	
Henderson, Robert	1		3	2	5	15	300
Hines, John	1				1	13	
Ingrim, Isaac	1		1	1	2	5	
Inglish, Charles	1		1		2	7	
Jones, Ellot	1				4	7	50
Johnston, Thomas	1				1	5	
Jobes, Daniel	1				1		
Jinnins, Ozias	1				1	1	
Jones, George	Exep.				1	5	
Johnston, William	1		1		2		58
Kennady, John, Jr.	1				2	13	50
Kincaid, William	1				4		
Kennaday, David	1			1	9	11	
Kennaday, James	1				5	11	100
Kennady, John, Sr.	1		2		5	3	300
Kennady, Thomas	1		7	9	54	180	4,813
Kergin, Joseph	1				2	6	
Keney, Peter	1	1			2	8	300
King, John P. S.	1			2	2	2	125
Kilpatrick, Hugh	1				8	7	100
King, Aaron	1				4	9	
Kennady, Andrew	1		1	3	17	40	27
King, John	1				2	5	
Kincaid, Robert	1				5	9	
Linch, William	1				6	6	
Littlepage, Epps	1				1	8	
Levingston, Thomas	1		1		4	16	
Lawson, Elihu	1				3	7	
Lawson, Aaron	1				1		50
Leach, Henry	1				4	13	
Lacewell, Henry	1				2		
Lyons, John	E				9	14	
Leveradge, John	1				4	30	171
Lace, Matthias	1				1		
Land, James	1						
Locker, John	1				1		
Lee, William	1					4	
Lowhorn, Thomas	1				1	3	
Lovelass, Veacheal	1				2	8	

Persons Names Chargeable With the Tax	White Males Above 21	White Males Above 16 and Under 21	Blacks Above 16	Blacks Under 16	Horses, Mairs, Colts & Mules	Cattle	Acres of Land
Lock, Richard	1				1	3	
Lock, Joseph	1				1	1	
Lavin, John	1				2	8	
Lewis, Thomas	1				1	7	169
Lewis, John	1				4	5	
Levy, Solomon	1			1	3	10	
Lear, George	1				4	11	100
Logan, Timothy	1				5	19	
McNeely, George	1				3	21	100
McNeely, Michael	1	1			4	17	100
McMurry, John	1				6	11	
McHuse, Moses	1				6	20	105
Miller, Nancy						19	100
Mobley, Benjamin	1				1	3	79
Montgomery, Joseph	1				2	18	
McCallister, Sarah					4	11	
Meholm, William	1				1		
Maxwell, Eazeleel	1	1	1	1	13	32	
McEneley, John	1					2	
Moore, Benton	1				2		
Maxwell, John	1				1	7	200
Miller, William B. C.	1				2	20	260
Merret, Stephen	1			2	1	19	63
Moore, Lodwick	1				5	12	290
Mitchel, John	1				4	23	
McCord, William	1				3	10	
Montgomery, John	1		1	1	4	11	150
Menise, Stephen	1				2		
Menise, Deniel	1				1	3	
Menise, John	1	1	1		4	19	100
Moore, Arthur	1	1			5	16	70
McElhenney, James	1		5		2	17	100
McNeely, David	2	1			3	8	100
McNece, James	1				1	4	
McNece, Jacob	1					2	
McFarlan, Walter	1					5	
McElway, Henry	1				2	1	
McLemass, James	1				1		
McNitte, Robert	1				1		
McClary, Samuel	1						
Mitchel, William	1				9	13	250
Miller, William, Jr.	1		1		5	6	50
Miller, William, Sr.	1		3	1	18	46	500
Morrow, William	1				2	8	
Murphy, Thomas	1				2	10	
Matthews, John	1				3	30	
Morris, James	1				2	11	
McMullen, John S. C.	1				2	9	
Miller, Andrew	1			1	8	8	43
Moore, Alexander	1				1	6	
McManis, Henry	1				2		
McDaniel, Neal	1				6	24	
McNeely, David, Jr.	1				2	5	

Persons Names Chargeable With the Tax	White Males Above 21	White Males Above 16 and Under 21	Blacks Above 16	Blacks Under 16	Horses, Mairs, Colts & Mules	Cattle	Acres of Land
McMillin, William	Exep.	1			4	6	
McMillan, Alexander	1				3	5	
Morris, Jesse	1				2	13	60
McMillen, John	1				1	3	
McNeely, John	1				2	5	
McCune, David	1				5	17	
McWhirter, James	1				6	11	74
Murphy, Zepheniah	1				2	12	
McMannes, Charles	1				1		
McDennel, William	1				3	10	
McFaddon, Hugh	Exep.				3	13	
Mounce, John	1				7	11	
Mobley, Clement	1				6	7	
Montgomery, Thomas	1		1		4	32	800
McNelly, James	1				2	14	
Maxwell, David	1	1			7	21	100
Nilson, William	1				2	1	
Nickles, Deniel	1				2	4	50
Nickles, Joshua	1				5	14	
Nichelson, William	1				4	5	50
Nucom, William	1				2	2	
Oliver, Andrew	1				2	7	
Owley, David	1				4	7	
Owley, William, Jr.	1				3	4	
Owley, Michael	1				6	23	
Owley, Christopher	1	1			6	18	
Owley, John	1				3	6	
Owley, Peter	1				19	40	400
Owley, Henry	1	1			10	26	200
Owsley, Thomas	1			1	1	8	
Owley, William	1				2	8	
Owsley, Thomas, Jr.	1		5	6	8	27	711
Patton, Phillip	1			1	5	19	
Provence, Mary				2	7	23	300
Provence, Andrew	1		1		2	14	
Pond, Griffen	1			2	3	24	
Pence, Henry	1				3		
Phillips, John	1				2	8	100
Patterson, John	1				11	16	200
Patterson, James	1				6	12	125
Patterson, Thomas	1				2	12	125
Patterson, William	1				6	4	100
Prier, Abraham	1				1	7	
Prochtor, Richard	1				1	6	
Partelow, George	1					1	
Peters, Jonathan	1				5	19	
Pointer, Thomas	1				2	7	
Partelow, Abraham	1						
Parris, Robert	1		2	2	4	26	
Phipps, George	1				1		
Poe, William	1				2	3	
Pearce, William	1				6	11	

Persons Names Chargeable With the Tax	White Males Above 21	White Males Above 16 and Under 21	Blacks Above 16	Blacks Under 16	Horses, Mairs, Colts & Mules	Cattle	Acres of Land
Russel, Edward	1				1		
Rice, Joseph	1				1	5	
Rennels, Richard	1		1	4	4	20	356
Ross, Ambrus	1			1	3	17	100
Ross, Thomas	1				2	2	
Reed, Alexander	1		2	8	5	32	175
Richey, William	1				4	12	
Rannolds, Henry	1		4	4	15	25	
Rennolds, Thomas	1		1		8	10	
Ryel, John	1				2	6	
Ratliff, John	1				3	9	
Rice, Samuel	1		2	4	4	25	250
Robinson, Mathew	1				3	19	
Rayburn, William	1				2	6	
Rice, John	1				1		
Robinson, James	1	1	1		7	11	
Spencer, Jesse	1				3	10	
Scott, Matthew	1				8	38	375
Small, John	1				2		
Smiley, Hugh	1				1	2	
Scott, Joseph	1				12	20	462
Smith, Rubin	1			1	4	9	
Salian, William	1				3	5	
Smith, James P. S.					4	3	100
Smith, James	1					5	
Stephenson, Pheabey		1			7	40	200
Slone, William	1				2	5	
Short, William	1				2	7	
Sruesberry, Allen	1				2	15	
Salley, John	1				1	15	
Sleaton, James	1			1	3	17	
Short, Joel	1	1			1	4	
Snett, John	1						
Stephens, Abraham	1				8	16	
Summers, John	1				2	8	95
Smith, John	1				3	13	156
Shesteen, Jesse	1				2	7	
Simpson, Charles	1	1			3	19	
Stringer, William	1				2	10	
Smiley, George	1	2			10	17	
Saunders, John	1				5	8	
Slevin, John	1				4	13	
Safley, John	1				1	3	
Stephens, John	1				6	15	
Smith, William	1				1		
Smith, Weadon	1			1	6	7	
Slaton, Tyre	1				2	12	
Shekelford, James, Sr.	1		1	1	2	5	
Shekelford, James, Jr.	1			1	1	6	
Terrell, William	1			1	2	35	
Terrell, Robert	1		6	9	5	20	50
Tolbert, Benjamin	1		1		2	4	

Persons Names Chargeable With the Tax	White Males Above 21	White Males Above 16 and Under 21	Blacks Above 16	Blacks Under 16	Horses, Mairs, Colts & Mules	Cattle	Acres of Land
Terrell, Edmund	1		3	3	9	22	616
Terrell, Joseph	1				9	6	
Tadford, David	1						
Terrell, Edmund, Jr.	1				3	1	
Tetor, George. Jr.	1			1	2	7	
Taylor, Edward	1				6	21	100
Turpin, Solomon	1				3	3	
Turpin, Moses	1					4	
Tetor, George, Sr.	1	1	2	4	6	20	500
Tetor, Samuel	1				6	12	
Turner, George	1				2	2	
Turney, Michael	1				2	7	107
Tipton, Thomas	1				1	8	
Vancleve, Abigail					5	17	
Vancleve, Jonathan	1				2	1	
Vanmeter, Isaac	1				5	10	
Waddel, Henry	1				3	11	
Walker, Alexander	1				1	20	200
Wheldon, John	1				3	20	
Wiley, James	1				2	5	
Wiley, Luke	1				3	1	
Wiley, William, Jr.	1				1		
Wiley, William, Sr.	1				2	5	
Watkins, Willis	1				3	2	
Wilcox, Edward	1				1		
Wilcox, John	1					8	
Woods, Samuel	1	2			9	31	450
Whealdon, Joseph	1				12	18	200
Wooden, Ruben	1				1		
Ware, Dudley	1	1			7	17	
Winscott, Isaac	1				4	17	
Walker, Richard	1				4	5	22
Wheeler, Eschelus	1				2	3	
Whitesides, Robert	1		1		1	4	
Wash, William	1				1	1	
Willis, Sherrod	1				5	20	
Willis, Drury	1				2	2	
Williams, Vincin	1		1	3	2	4	
Wallen, William	1	1			1	8	
Wallen, James ....Exempt		1			4	1	
Wolsey, George	1				5	14	
Walles, Oliver	1						
Walles, William	1				3	24	
Wallece, Michael	3	1	3	2	11	63	447
Wray, Joseph	1				3	12	175
Wilburn, Thomas	1				2	7	100
Yarberry, James	1				1		
Yarberry, Randol	1				2	1	
Yoter, Henry	1				5	9	
Younger, Joshua	1				5	7	
Adams, Walter	1			2	7	30	
Totel	449	60	108	148	1,748	4,873	17,683

John Adams, Comr.

MADISON COUNTY TAX LIST 1792.

A Book Containing a List of the Taxable Property in the Middle District in Madison County for the Year One Thousand Seven Hundred and Ninety-Two.

Andw. Kennedy, Com.

Dec. ye 8 dy 1792

Persons Named Chargeable With the Tax.	White Males Above 21	Above 16 and Under 21	Total of Blacks	Blacks Under 16	Horses, Mares, Colts & Mules	Cattle	Ordinary Licenses	Retail Stores	Covering Per Season	Acres of Land
Anderson, John, Jr.	1				3	7				
Anderson, Isaac	1				8	24				
Allcorn, John	1	1			6	12				
Allcorn, George	1					6				
Allcorn, James	1				1					
Allcorn, Robert	1									
Anderson, James	1		1	1	11	48				
Adams, John	1		1		8	20				250
Armstrong, John	1		2	1	4	5				
Anderson, John, Sr.	2		3	1	10	35				600
Atteson, William	1				1	3				
Anderson William	1				6	27				
Anderson, Samuel	1				5	8				
	14	1	7	3	63	195				850
Burton, George	1				3	6				
Butcher, William	1				8	26				
Bogie, Andrew	2	1	1		10	35				700
Butler, Nancy		1			6	19				
Butner, Isaac	1				1	4				
Barns, Mary					5	11				
Barnett, Joseph	1				6	12				248
Burnside, Robert	2				8	17				150
Barker, William	1				3	24				170
Bone, John	1		2	1	7	20				
Baugh, Joseph	1		1	1	3	13				
Baugh, Wm.	1		1	1	4	6				
Brown, William	1				2	10				100
Barnett, William	1				8	21				
Brown, Charles	1		1	1	3	4				
Black, John	3				3	52				490
Blackburn, William	1		2	1	4					
Baker, Thomas	1	2			9	12				150
Brinson, David	1				1					
Boggs, James	1		1	1	11	40				900
Baker, Robert	1				7	17				
Butcher, Richard	1				7	11				
Butcher, Joseph, Sr.	1				4	20				
Butcher, William	1				3	5				
Butcher, Joseph, Jr.	1					4				
Boyde, Samuel	1	1	1		4	19				100
Burriss, Charles	1		1	1	4	7				
Brinson, Zebulon	1	1			7	13				
Brown, Elias	1				4	10				
Baker, Rezen	1				3	9				220
Brown, Samuel	1				8	17				

Persons Named Chargeable With the Tax.	White Males Above 21	Above 16 and Under 21	Total of Blacks	Blacks Under 16	Horses, Mares, Colts & Mules	Cattle	Ordinary Licenses	Retail Stores	Covering Per Season	Acres of Land
Brisscow, William	1	1	1		6	21				114
Barns, Samuel	1				10	13				
Barret, Jonathan	1				2	10				50
Barnett, Mary					2	5				
Barnnett, James, Jr.	1				5	11				206
Boggs, Jóseph	1					4				
Berry, James	1	2	1	1	10	22				150
Berry, Garret	1				2	9				
Barns, Elias	1				4	18				
Barns, Abram	1				2	5				
Barns, Amos	1					3				
Barnett, James	1		6	2	7	35				
Barns, Shadrick	1				5	11				
	45	9	19	10	217	590				3,638
Carpenter, Edward		1			3	4				
Clark, Houton	1				2	9				
Creath, William, Sr.	1	2			9	20				77
Creath, William, Jr.	1				2	17				
Cochran, Samuel	1	1			5	24				266
Cochran, William	1				8	12				200
Cochran, Andrew	1		4	3	4	16				100
Cochran, James	1				5	13				258
Cambell, James	1				4	6				
Cambell, Charles	1				3	9				
Carlile, William	1				1	6				
Cloin, John	1				4	7				
Carley, William	1		2	1	4	23				1,500
Cambell, John	1				10	13				
Carson, Lindsey	1		2	1	7	2				
Carson, Robert	1		1		9	13				
Caperton, James	1				2	14				100
Clark, Jesse	1		3	1	7	19				
Cooper, Sershal	1				7	12				
Cochran, John	1	1			5	35				570
Cambell, Thomas	1	1			10	28				
Cavender, William	1		6	5	8	24				
Cavender, Charles, Jr.	1		1	1	8	21				
Cambell, Benjemen	1				1	17				
Collins, Thomas	1	2	5	3	3	4				
Caperton, William	1				8	21				
Carr, William	1				4	2				
Carvons, James	1				4	9				225
Carrier, Jonathan	1				2	2				
Cooper, Frencess	1		2	1	6	11				
Cooper, Branton	1				5	8				
Culdwell, Robert	1				2			1		
Crage, Thomas	1				1	4				
Cooper, Benjemon	1				3	15				
Chiles, James	1	1			3					
Conner, Daniel	1				3			1		

Persons Named Chargeable With the Tax.	White Males Above 21	Above 16 and Under 21	Total of Blacks	Blacks Under 16	Horses, Mares, Colts & Mules	Cattle	Ordinary Licenses	Retail Stores	Covering Per Season	Acres of Land
Cambell, Samuel	1		9	7	5	50				
Cavender, Charles, Sr.	1				5	5				
Calleway, Elizabeth			7	4	8	13				
Calleway, Richard	1		4	2	2	12				100
	39	8	46	29	189	518			2	2,396
Dunn, Richard	1				2	5				
Dunken, Benjemen	2				7	23				278
Dunstall, Richard	1	1	8	5	4	16				
Dickey, Ebenezer	1				3	22				
Donoho, Robert	1				1	6				
Deen, Robert	1				1	12				
Dougherty, Cornelus	1	1			11	31				177
Dougherty, Elenander	1				5	6				
Debrill, Charles	1		3	1	5	18				
Denham, John	1				3	2				
Donnelson, Andrew	1	1			4	9				100
	12	3	11	6	45	150				555
Eaton, Isaac	1					2				
Ellot, John	1				1	16				
Enyeart, John	1	1			12	16				
Enyeart, Abraham	1				7	32				
Estell, William	1		4	3	5	21				198
Evens, Thomas	1				4	12				
Englhish, Stephen	1		1	1	4	20				
Estell, Boudy	1		1		11	42				450
Estell, Samuel	1	2	6	3	9	52				1,800
	9	3	12	7	53	218				2,538
Forbush, Robert	1				4	8				50
Fouller, James	1				1					
Fariss, Moses	1				5	10				
Freeman, Samuel	1		1		9	16				100
Fariss, Michal	1				4	18				50
Fariss, Thomas, Jr.	2				9	34				160
Fariss, Cayor	1				1	10				70
Fariss, Thomas, Sr.					6	13				
	8		1		39	109				430
Gaddy, Elisha	1				3	6				100
Goolow, William	1		3	1	3	12				575
Goody, George	1				4	1				
Gilbert, Micah	1				1	10				50
Gleen, William	1		1	1	7	30				
Gorden, Richard	1				6	5				
Green, Stephen, Jr.	1				2	3				
Green, Stephen, Sr.	1		3	2	18					

Persons Named Chargeable With the Tax.	White Males Above 21	Above 16 and Under 21	Total of Blacks	Blacks Under 16	Horses, Mares, Colts & Mules	Cattle	Ordinary Licenses	Retail Stores	Covering Per Season	Acres of Land
Green, Martin	1				6	13				
Gentry, David	1				3	16				100
Gass, David	3		1		18	100				850
Gutridge, John					1					
Gentry, Richard	1		4	3	7	60				100
Gleen, Joseph	1				3	8				
Gleen, Martin	1					4				
Gleen, Hugh	1	1			5	2				
Guinn, Mathew	1		3	2	2	31				
	19	1	15	9	77	319				1,875
Hains, Even	1				8	21				
Hancock, William	2	2			19	20				900
Hennery, William	1				1	3				
Harris, David	1				1					
Howard, Hannah					2	14				
Howard, William	1				4	14				
Hutton, Hennery	1				5	15				
Hawkins, Joseph	2	1			9	40				
Hubbort, Durret	1					1				
Hubbert, Eusebus	1		6	4	2	9				
Houston, Andrew	1	1			4	12				100
Harvey, William, Sr.	1		5	4	2	6				
Henderson, Richard	1				6	5				
Hancock, Stephen	2		3	1	10	34				
Hendrickson, John	1				2	5				125
Hammor, Abraham	1				4	6				50
Hawkins, Nickless	1		5	2	11	25				388
Harbour, Elisha	1				12	20				
Hawkins, Nathen	1		9	5	2	14				
Hays, Charles, Sr.	1				3	4				
Hays, Charles, Jr.	1				1					
Harvey, William, Jr.	1				3	10				
Ham, William	2		3	2	7	30				100
Hubbert, Joseph	1					3				
Holland, Wm.	1				1	9				75
Hammelton, John	1	2			3	17				67
Hieatt, Joseph	1				5	31				
Horn, William	1				2	7				
	31	6	31	18	129	375				1,305
Isbell, Danniel	1				1	2				
Johnson, Hennery	1				2	10				
Jones, Charles, Jr.	1				2	9				
Jones, Ames	1				1	5				
Jones, Charles, Sr.	1	1			6	20				
Jemmeson, Joseph	1				7	14				
Jacson, William	1				1					
Jones, James	1				1	4				

Persons Named Chargeable With the Tax.	White Males Above 21	Above 16 and Under 21	Total of Blacks	Blacks Under 16	Horses, Mares, Colts & Mules	Cattle	Ordinary Licenses	Retail Stores	Covering Per Season	Acres of Land
Jones, John	1				9	11				
Jones, Joseph	1				7	12				
Jones, Thomas	1				6	12				
Jones, Francess	1				3	4				
	11	1			45	103				
Kenney, Elenander	1									
Kennedy, Joseph	1		3	1	9	40				1,300
Kirkpatrick, Robert	1				8	24				46
Knox, Robert	1				2	6				
Knox, John	1				2	7				
Kidwell, John	1					4				
Kinkaid, John	1				4	28				300
Kinkaid, David	2		1		14	50				300
Kinkaid, James	1				10	38				100
Kinkaid, Andw.	1				3	4				
	11		4	1	52	201				2,046
Lee, Richard	1				5	5				
Land, Thomas		1			5	8				
Lee, George	1				2	10				
Lee, William	1				2	1				
Linch, David	1				3	1				
Lewis, Nathenneel	1				7	8				
	5	1			24	33				
May, Jesse	1				2	9				
McMullen, James	1				1	5				
Mobbly, Benjemen, Sr.	1				3	10				100
Mobbly, Edward	1				2	12				
Mobbly, Benjemen, Jr.	1				3	6				100
Moppon, Curnelus	1				2	16				
Moore, David, Sr.	1				6	16				
Milton, Charles	1				1	4				
Mise, Jeremiah	1				1	2				
Moss, Edward	1				3	6				
Morrison, William	1	1	7	4	9	37				400
Moores, Hennery	1	1			6	22				
McNutt, James	1				9	50				150
McLean, John	1				8	12				100
Mason, William	1				4	45				
Marten, William	1		4	3	3	17				
McGuire, Thomas	1				7	14				
Miller, Hennery	1				2	4				
Mitchel, John	1				4	13				
McGuire, William	1				15	16				220
McCollerster, James	1		1	1	2	2				
Morrow, Samuel	1				6	16				
McNutt, Francess	1				9	37				200

Persons Named Chargeable With the Tax.	White Males Above 21	Above 16 and Under 21	Total of Blacks	Blacks Under 16	Horses, Mares, Colts & Mules	Cattle	Ordinary Licenses	Retail Stores	Covering Per Season	Acres of Land
Maxwell, Thomas	1	1			11	24				
Maxwell, Bazel	1				3	15				
Mathews, Joseph	1				1	9				
Moor, William, Sr.	4				8	31				950
McCullah, William					3	8				100
McCormack, James	1				2	3				50
Moor, David, Jr.	1				2	12				250
Marter, Oney			1	1	2	6				
Mackey, Elenander	1	1			14	38				300
Masae, Harris	1				6	8				
Millar, John	1		8	5	19	50				400
Massae, David	1				4	5				100
Mackey, John	1				1					
	37	4	21	14	181	580				3,420
Noon, Jean					5	16				
Nickeson, John	1				2	12				
Noble, David	2				2	20				60
Nolen, Jesse	1				3	18				
	4				12	66				60
Oeve, Isaac	1				4	16				100
Oeve, Eleanander	1									
Oeve, Elizabeth					9	14				
	2				13	30				100
Proctor, Nickless	1				2	25				
Proctor, John	1		1		5	6				
Pasley, James	1				1					
Phelps, John, Sr.	1				10	9				
Phelps, Cary	1				4	17				
Potter, Thomas	1	1			1	9				100
Proctor, Joseph	1				1	12				
Price, James	1				3	15				
Potter, Elisha	1				1	3				
Pullens, Lofty	1				4	10				50
Paton, Jacob	1				7	13				200
Preator, Edward	1				6	13				
Perry, Jeremiah	1		1	1	3	7				
Parten, James	1				3	2				
Pinkson, Bazel	1	1			2	7				
Paris, Moses					2	11				
Phelps, John, Jr.	1			1	1	10	1			
Paton, Yelberton	1				4	45				400
Prator, John	1	1	1		8	20				
Petijohn, Mollerster	1				6	8				
	18	3	4	2	80	242	1			750

Persons Named Chargeable With the Tax.	White Males Above 21	Above 16 and Under 21	Total of Blacks	Blacks Under 16	Horses, Mares, Colts & Mules	Cattle	Ordinary Licenses	Retail Stores	Covering Per Season	Acres of Land
Quick, Benjemen	1				6	20				
Quick, Jacob	1	2			5	11				
	2	2			11	31				
Roads, Robert	1		9	6	10	50				
Right, John	1		1		3	7				
Robertson, Samuel	1		2	2	5	19				
Reed, John	2	1	5	4	9	30				
Robertson, James, Sr.	1				8	16				
Robertson, David	1				6	11				
Roberts, Francess	1				7	9				
Rogers, Antony	1				4	9				
Robertson, William	1	2	15	11	8	14				451
Robertson, James, Jr.	1				1	8				
Robertson, John	1				3	2				
Roberts, Nathen	1				4	11				
Riggs, Beththuel	1				5	9				50
Randolph, Charles	1				2	11				
Roberts, John	1		1	1	15	23				
Reed, John, Sr.	1	1			4	49				300
Reed, James	1				2	20				
Reed, John, Jr.	1				1	6				
Right, Gideon	1				1					
Retherford, John, Jr.	1		2		4	10				
Retherfor, John Sr.	1	1	2	1	2	8				
Reed, Elenander	1				7	34				
Robertson, Thos.	1	1			4	10				
	24	6	37	25	115	366				801
Shakleford, Carter	1				2					
Smith, Bennet	1				3					
Salley, Stephen	1				5	7				
Stepp, John	1	2	1		10	22				92
Snow, Elizabeth					2	4				
Smith, Joshua	1				1	7				
Stephensen, James	1		2	1	38	45				
Snoddy, John	1		3	1	18	100				250
Shurley, Charles	1				2					569
Shurley, Catrenah					11	14				
Sersy, Esa	1		1		5	13				150
Sawers, John	1				1	8				
Selfe, John	1				2	16				
Stepp, James	1		2		4	14				
Smith, Thomas	1		1		3	10				
Stevens, Peter	1				3	4				
Skidmore, Thos.	1				6	4				
Smith, William	1				1	4				
Stagner, Barney	1		3	1	7	26				200
Stevens, Jacob	1				4	12				
Sheels, Edward	1					4				
	19	2	13	3	128	304				1,261

Persons Named Chargeable With the Tax.	White Males Above 21	Above 16 and Under 21	Total of Blacks	Blacks Under 16	Horses, Mares, Colts & Mules	Cattle	Ordinary Licenses	Retail Stores	Ferries	Acres of Land
Turnner, Phillip	1		1	1	9	12				
Turpin, Nathen	1									
Travis, Danniel	1	1			11	5				
Titus, Joseph	1				8	21				
Turnner, John, Sr.	1			1	4	16				
Turnner, John, Jr.	1				4	7				
Turnner, Thomas	1				5	23				
Turpin, William	1		1		8	16			1	25
Taylor, Peter	1		3	1	16	34				1,696
Turnner, James	1				5	12				
Turnner, John	1				2	12				
Taylor, John	1				2	5				
Thomas, Jesse	1				3	3				
Turnner, Edward, Jr.	1				4	4				
Turnner, Thomas	1		2	2	3	6				
Tuder, Elizabeth					2	5				
Tuder, Hennery	1	1			4	10				
Turnner. Edward, Sr.	1				4	7				
Trousdail, John	1		1	1	2	5				
Trotter, David	1		3	2	4	22				1,400
Talbert, Haile	1		11	6	13	37				300
	20	2	26	14	110	262			1	3,421
Warren, Thomas	1		1	1	7	43				500
Wald, Richard	1				5	10				86
Wells, John	1	1			11	23				
Woods, John	1		5	2	10	70				1,100
Woods, Archible	1	2	7	4	17	73				1,800
Woods, Peter	1		7	6	6	22				200
Woods, Andw.	1		1	1	3	9				100
Wallace, Michal	1		2		7	20				
Wisdom, John	2	1			6	27				
Wisdom, Thomas	1				3	10				400
Woods, Adam	1	1	2	1	16	28				
Wilson, James					4	7				
Woods, William	1		2		3	10				
Watson, Joseph	1				7	10				
Westremen, Charles	2				6	6				
Williams, Benjemen	1				4	3				
Williams, Shadrick	1				5	7				
Wheeller, Benjemen	3		2		2	22				250
White, Blecher	1				1	2				
Williams, John	1				4	16				
Williams, Wm.	1		2	1	4	36				
Wolfscail, George	1				17	36				100
West, Joseph	1									
Walker, Asaph	1		10	6	5	31				300
Walker, Stephen	1				2	1				
Walker, James	1				1					
Walker, William	1				1					
Williams, Phillip	1	1	7	5	5	9				
Williams, Hennery	1				5	3				
Williams, James	1				6	6				

Persons Named Chargeable With the Tax.	White Males Above 21	Above 16 and Under 21	Total of Blacks	Blacks Under 16	Horses, Mares, Colts & Mules	Cattle	Ordinary Licenses	Retail Stores	Ferries	Acres of Land
White, John	1				1	2				
White, Equilli	1				2	4				
Williams, Edward	1				9	13				50
Wood, Abraham	1				1	14				
Wolfscail, William	1				11	16				
Wolfscail, Joseph	1	1			12	31				100
Williams, Caleb	1				6	10				
Wilburn, Zacariah	1				6	9				100
	41	7	28	27	221	639				5,086
Young, John	1	2			13	42				150
Young, William, Sr.	1				11	14				
Young, William	1					2				
Young, William, Jr.	1				2	11				
Yeats, John, Jr.	1				2	12				
Yeats, John, Sr.	1				5	12				200
	6	2			33	93				350
A	14	1	7	3	63	195				850
B	45	9	19	10	217	590				3,638
C	39	8	46	29	189	518		2		3,396
D	12	3	11	6	45	150				555
E	9	3	12	7	53	213				2,538
F	8		1		39	109				430
G	19	1	15	9	77	319				1,875
H	31	6	31	18	129	375				1,805
I	1				1	2				
J	11	1			45	103				
K	11		4	1	52	201				2,046
L	5	1			24	33				
M	37	4	21	14	181	580				3,420
N	4				12	66				60
O	2				13	30				100
P	18	3	4	2	80	242	1			750
Q	2	2			11	31				
R	24	6	31	25	115	366				801
S	19	2	13	3	128	304				1,261
T	20	2	26	14	110	262			1	3,421
W	41	7	48	27	221	639				5,086
Y	6	2			33	93				350
Total	378	61	285	168	1,838	5,421	1	2	1	32,382

Andrew Kennedy Com.
Decr., ye 8 dy 1792.
Madison Courtt
I hereby Certify that I Have Examined the within Lists & find them to be true Copies.
Testi Will Irvine Clk M. C.
Rec'd Decr 11th 1792.

32382
17066
25948

76018

Persons Names Chargeable with the Tax.	White Males Above 21	White Males Above 16 and Under 21	Total Blacks	Blacks Under 16	Horses, Mares, Colts & Mules	Cattle	Acres of Land
Adley, James	1				1	2	
Anderson, John	1	1			3	16	
Adams, John	1				1	8	
Anderson, Robert	1				2	6	
Antrobus, Wm.	1				2	10	
Brucks, Lynch	1				2	3	
Burgin, Isaac	1				11	12	200
Burgin, Jacob	1				9	6	150
Brucks, Robt.	1				1	2	
Baxter, Benjamn.	1				1	5	
Baxter, Elizabeth					1	8	
Baxter, George			1				
Burton, Saml.	1			1	3	12	140
Bennet, Thos.	1				1	4	40
Brucks, Henry	1				7	5	
Blyth, Wm.	1				2		
Brown, George	1				4	6	
Brown, Henry	1	1			6	5	137
Burnum, John	1			1	1	4	50
Berry, Wm.	1				2		
Burgin, Charles	1				6	7	
Bruner, George	1				1	8	
Benton, Richd.	1				1	6	
Burnum, Henry	1				2		
Boone, John	1				5		
Boone, George	1		4	10	14	81	637
Boone, Squire	1				1	3	
Burgin, Danes	1				6	8	
Boone, Jonithan	2				6	3	
Bridges, Wm.	1			1	2	10	107
Briges, Isham	1			1	1	6	
Boone, Squire, Sr.	1				5	10	
Burnum, Henry	1				3	4	
Blackwell, Amsted	1				4	5	100
Blackwell, Sarah			3	5	4	15	100
Bratton, John	1				5	14	50
Barton, Joshua	1				4	18	100
Bellew, Charles	1				7	14	50
Butler, Thos.	1				2	6	125
Bruner, Christon	1					2	180
Batterton, Benjn.	1				1	5	
Batterton, Henry	1	2			3	13	68
Brown, James	1				4	6	
Barker, Elias, Sr.	1	1			6	12	200
Barker, Elias, Jr.	1				4		
Barker, Joseph	1				3	4	100
Baxton, Barthel	1				3		
Barnet, George	1				3	4	
Blackwell, James	1				2	7	
Curle, Archd.	1		1	2	4	13	100
Calk, William	1		5		20	53	200

Persons Names Chargeable with the Tax.	White Males Above 21	White Males Above 16 and Under 21	Total Blacks	Blacks Under 16	Horses, Mares, Colts & Mules	Cattle	Acres of Land
Con, Josiah	1				4	4	60
Cruse, Thos.	1				2	10	
Carpenter, John	1				10	53	500
Colly, Charles	1				2	4	
Crews, Jaryh.	1				2	5	200
Cook, Wiles	1				2	2	
Clark, Godfree	1				1	6	
Coffee, Jesse	1		2	3	5	11	
Clark, John, Sr.	1				2	13	115
Clark, John, Jr.	1				2	9	200
Colier, James	1				3	9	
Colier, John	1				5	13	100
Croock, Osias	1				1		
Crews, David	1	1	2	1	13	35	2,200
Crook, Absalom					3	10	100
Clay, Thos.	1		3	7	7	10	
Davis, John	1				5	3	40
Davis, Solomon	1						100
Dunbare, Wm.	1				2	9	
Dunbare, James	1						
Durbin, Edward	1				4	10	
Durbin, Joseph	1				4	8	
Durbin, Christopher	1	1			4	13	
Dosure, Lanard	1				2	6	100
Dosure, Zachariah	1				3	6	325
Durbin, John	1				1	3	
Doloson, Robt	1				3		
Durbin, Thos.	1				2	4	
Datharge, Killes	1				4	8	
Davis, Zachariah	1				1		
Dosure, Thos.		1	1		5	6	300
Davis, Alexander	1				4	11	150
Davis, Thos.	1				2	5	
Dooley, Jacob	1				5	6	100
Dumpart, Danial	1				2	4	24
Dunking, Gabril	1				1	10	
Dunham, Wm.	1	1			5	10	150
Ellison, Thos.	1				3	10	
Embre, Talton	1		2	3	2	24	185
Estin, John	1				4	12	
Embre, Joseph	2			4	10	38	165
Ellison, Joseph	1				4	31	123
England, David	1				2	3	50
Evens, Peter	1		1	1	2	16	100
Evens, Edward	1				1	2	
Fowler, Richd.	1				3	12	100
Fowler, Benjn.	1				2	2	
Foot, Thos.	1				1		
Farel, John	1				2	11	
Fox, John	1				3		
Flacher, John	1						

Persons Names Chargeable with the Tax.	White Males Above 21	White Males Above 16 and Under 21	Total Blacks	Blacks Under 16	Horses, Mares, Colts & Mules	Cattle	Acres of Land
Fowler, Matthew	1	1			2	7	80
Forbis, Alexander	1					3	
Fox, Saml.	2	2	4	3	5	13	
Fowler, Jerimiah	1				4	10	100
Fort, Frederick	1				1	4	
Fowler, Joseph	1				3	7	100
Flat, John	1				2	5	
French, James	1		2	2	16	27	200
Felphs, Joseph	1	1			12	24	350
Felphs, George	1				9	18	100
Gray, Thos.	1				1	5	
Gray, Leaven	1				2	3	
Guthry, Levi	1				2		
Gaff, John	1	1			4	6	85
Gass, John	1				3	9	85
Gutry, Wm.	1		2	2	3	10	100
Gum, William	1				6	10	200
Hopper, Wm.	1				3	10	
Hacket, Peter	1				4	15	
Howard, Henry	1				3	8	
Holly, Richd.	1		2	6	5	24	60
Haney, Henry	1				2		
Hockaday, Isaac		1			3		
Harris, Christopher	1		5	4	15	43	700
Hatherly, Lanerd	1				3	8	106
Hill, John	1		3	3	6	13	
Harrias, (?) Wm.	1				3	10	
Howard, Benjn.	1				3	12	162
Herendon, Oan	1	1			6	14	200
Herendon, John	1				2	3	
Hill, James	1				2	5	
Hall, William	1				2	2	
Haney, Wm.	1		5	4	6		
Harok, Samson	1						
Hill, Joel	1		1		6	25	200
Hill, James	1		1		2	2	
Hall, Squire	1				2		
Hopper, Wm.	1				2	5	
Harris, Richmd.	1				4	11	
Hopper, Moses	1				2	6	
Hall, David	1				8	20	820
Hoy, Sarah		1	2	2	3	5	
Hendricks, James	1		3		7	11	300
Herrod, Edward	1				1	9	100
Hodges, Jasey	1				4	7	100
Horn, Christopher	1				8	19	50
Horn, Asron	1				4	16	67
Horn, Matthew	1				3	7	50
Henderson, Robert	1				5	5	
Henderson, David	1				2	6	
Hambleton, Patk.					1	2	
Hambleton, Wm.					2	2	

Persons Names Chargeable with the Tax.	White Males Above 21	White Males Above 16 and Under 21	Total Blacks	Blacks Under 16	Horses, Mares, Colts & Mules	Cattle	Acres of Land
Harris, Sherwood	1				4	7	80
Howard, Clament	1				1	3	25
Harris, Benjn.	1				1	7	
Holly & Wilkerson	2		3	3	18	45	400
Irvine, Wm.	1		3	3	9	23	480
Jones, Georgewall |?)	1				1	4	
Jones, Mosias	1		1		2	4	100
Jonson, John	1	1			1	4	
Jones, Thos.	1				1		
Jonson, James	1				5	17	100
Jones, Cad.	1				1	8	
Jomes, Irvine	1		2	2	3	30	200
Jones, William	1	2	1		7	12	206
Jaffries, Henry	1		1		3	10	
Jate, Stephen	1	1			2	15	
Kelly, Samuel	1	1			7	10	
Linch, Edward	1				1	2	
Lewis, Wm.	1						
Logsdon, Thos.	1				2	2	
Logsdon, Edwd., Jr.	1	1			3	16	192
Logsdon, Edwd., Sr.					1		
Lorocon, (?) John	1	1			3	9	
Lowry, James	1			1	6	11	
Logsdon, John	1				1	2	
Logsdon, Thos., Sr.	1				5	6	
Longe, John	1				1	3	
Loyde, Saml.	1					4	
Lowis, Aaron	1	1	4	2	6	23	536
Lunicks, Charles	1				1	3	
Login, David	1					4	55
Linn, Patrick	1					3	
Lackey, James	1				4	9	
Lackey, Andrew	1				7	10	250
Lackey, James, Sr.					3	1	
Lackey, Thos.	1				3	9	
Moore, James	1			1	3	3	300
Moore, John	1						
Mullens, Gabl.	1		2	2	3	8	
Mcguire, Daniel	1				5	5	
Mcqueen, Joshua	1				3	12	100
Montgomery, James	1				3	9	
Manion, Thos.	1				6	10	
Magee, Rafe	1				1	3	
Moore, John, Sr.	1				6	13	162
Moore, John, Jr.	1				2		
Million, Travise	1				2	6	
Morton, Benjn.	1				2	7	200
Mcglockling, Curn. (?)	1				1	4	
Mise, Isaac	1				6	11	

Persons Names Chargeable with the Tax.	White Males Above 21	White Males Above 16 and Under 21	Total Blacks	Blacks Under 16	Horses, Mares, Colts & Mules	Cattle	Acres of Land
Million, John	1				1	6	
Million, Robt.	1				1	5	
Marton, James	1	1	8	5	5	31	300
Moore, Robt., Sr.	1		1		5	17	700
Moore, George	1				3	9	
Mcdaniel, Aaron	1				3	6	50
Mcdaniel, James	2				3	20	100
Mcdaniel, David	1				1		
Malot, John	1				2		
Mcqueen, James	1				3	14	
Moore, John	1	1			9	8	405
Marchal, George	1				1	5	
Manion, James	1				3	9	120
Magee, Robt.	1				5		
Maddick, Nathl.					2	2	
Mcdaniel, Franc.	1				3	10	
Maclary, Michael	1						
Miller, Jacob	1		1	1	9	14	118
Nave, Lanard	1				5	6	12
Nuby, John	1				4	15	
Noland, William	1	2			7	20	
Newland, Abram	1			1	11	24	200
Noland, Henry	1	1			3	3	100
Oldom, Jasey	1	1	2	4	10	21	100
Oldom, Richd.	1		2	2	5	19	100
Orchard, John	1				5	9	100
Orchard, Wm.	1						
Oller, George	1	1			2	6	112
Okaly, Benjamin	1				4	10	147
Orchard, Alexander	1				1	2	
Odon, Thos.	1					3	50
Orear, William	1			2	8	12	270
Portewood, Page, Jr.	1				10	10	100
Portewood, Page, Sr.	1				6	11	100
Portewood, Elizabeth					4	11	100
Partetow, Solomon	1						
Pursley, Benjamin	1				1	6	
Proctor, Page	1				1	10	50
Pits, Levy	1						
Powel, William	1				2	5	
Pollen, Wm.	1				2	2	
Pursley, Benjn, Sr.	1			1	7	19	500
Portewood, Lude	1				3	1	
Portewood, Thos.	1				6	13	120
Portewood, Saml.	1				3	2	100
Parham, Thos.	1				4	7	
Proctor, Nicols	1						
Rice, Hieriam	1				4	4	
Roland, Henry	1				1	5	
Roland, Richd.	1				2	5	

Persons Names Chargeable with the Tax	White Males Above 21	White Males Above 16 and Under 21	Total Blacks	Blacks Under 16	Horses, Mares, Colts & Mules	Cattle	Acres of Land
Rush, John	1				3	5	67
Reid, Leonard	2	1			4	4	
Ridman, George	1				2	18	100
Roberds, Wm.	1				3	4	
Raburn, Robin	1				2	5	35
Roberds, Nathan	1				4	7	50
Rush, Peter	1				3	10	
Smith, Carr	1				6	16	150
Scott, David	1				7	9	100
Steel, John	1				5	7	100
Sapp, John, Jr.	1				1	4	100
Srawborn, Thos.	1				7	20	320
Sappington, John, Sr.	2				3	14	40
Sappington, John, Jr.	1		1		7	29	100
Smith, James	1				3	12	100
Sappington, James	1				6	12	100
Shenault, Wm.	1	1		1	7	14	128
Shenault, David	1				1	2	
Sercy, Richd.	1				3	9	
Subastian, Wm.	1				3	7	
Sapp, John, Sr.	1	1			4	18	
Simonds, John	1					5	
Strainge, Stephen	1				2	7	
Stivers, William	1				1	5	
Southerland, Lanty	1				2	4	
Skinner, Joseph	1				4	9	
Smith, James	1				1		
Smith, Moses	1				3	10	
Stephens, John	1				1	9	
Stockstil, Shadrick	1				1		
Shelton, Thos.	1		1		12	18	200
Seburn, Jacob	1				3	10	50
Spilmon, George	1						
South, William			1		2	4	
South, Zadiciah	1				6	11	125
Lucy, Sercy	1	1	4	1	7	20	100
Sercy, Charles	1			1	3	7	50
Sercy, Richd., Sr.	1				3	5	100
Stivers, Edward	1					6	
South, John	1	2	1		7	9	150
Stivers, Reubin	1				1	3	
Starnes, Jacob	1		1	3	16	24	260
Stone, Benjn.	1	1			4	14	100
Stone, Valentine	1	1	4	6	5	16	170
Stockstil, Wm.	1				1		
Stockstil, Saml.	1					3	
Steen (or Stan), Edward	1				2	6	
Stuart, Allexander	1				5	7	
South, Saml.	1		2	5	5	11	100
South, Weldon	1			1	3	7	100
Sapington, Hartly	1				3	11	100

Persons Names Chargeable with the Tax.	White Males Above 21	White Males Above 16 and Under 21	Total Blacks	Blacks Under 16	Horses, Mares, Colts & Mules	Cattle	Acres of Land
Trible, Andrew	1	2	2	2	3	21	
Tod, Thos.	1				5	4	
Tharpe, Dotson	1				2	8	125
Tod, Joseph	1	2			9	12	
Taylor, Thos.	1				4	15	
Teddor, Volentine	1				3	7	
Terpin, Nathan	1					4	
Teddor, John	1				3	10	
Turner, Edward	1	2			11	31	190
Taylor, Joseph	1				4	12	
Taylor, Frans., Jr.	1				4	19	
Taylor, Frans., Sr.	1				3	6	
Townsen, Joshua	1		1		7	12	100
Timberlake, Richd.	1				8	16	100
Timberlake, John	1				5	2	
Townsen, Oswald	1				3	13	200
Turpin, Wm.	1				1	1	
Turpin, Elisah.		1			1	11	
Tinsher, William				1	1	5	300
Thompson, Saml.	1		1	1	9	14	118
Tharpe, Dodson, Jr.	1						
Tivis, Thos.	1						
Tivis, Robert	1		1	1			
Vinson, Wm.	1				1		
West, Nathl.	1				2	3	100
West, Wm.	1				3	15	135
Walker, James	1		1	3	6	15	259
Wheeler, John	1			1			
Wells, Joseph	1				4	9	
White, James	1				2	11	
Wilkerson, Presley	1				3	10	
Woodrough, James	1				2		
White, John	1				8	30	200
West, Richd.	1				2	3	86
Weagel, Jacob	1				3	5	
Weagel, John	1				6	6	
West, Jonathan	1				4	3	100
Whitloe, Pleasant	1				2	6	
Williams, Wm.	1	2			6	12	200
Williams, Jacob	1				3	6	
Wilson, John	1				3	13	100
Winscot, Joseph	1				1	10	
Wilcocks, David	1	1	1		2	9	
Wilcocks, George	1				5	7	
Welch, Thos.	1				8	10	84
White, David	1				3		
Woodrough, David	1				1	4	100
Williams, Shadrick	1				5	12	50
West, Thos.	1	1			4	10	50
Williams, Arthur	1				2		
Wood, Francis	1				4	19	75
Woodrough, John	1			1	4	14	220

Persons Names Chargeable with the Tax.	White Males Above 21	White Males Above 16 and Under 21	Total Blacks	Blacks Under 16	Horses, Mares, Colts & Mules	Cattle	Acres of Land
Wells, Robert	1				4	9	
Wells, David	1				7	14	395
Total	350	53	106	123	1,294	3,152	25,948
Adams	449	60	108	148	1,748	4,873	17,683
(Kennedy)	378	61	285	168	1,838	5,421	32,382
(Total for Madison Co.)	1,175	174	499	439	4,880	13,446	76,018

Wm. Capterton, Comr., 10th Decmr. 1792.

Madison, towitt:

I hereby Certify that I have Examined the within List and find them to be a true copies. Test—Will Irvine, C. M. Cur.

MERCER COUNTY TAX LIST—1789

NOTE—It will be noticed that the names on this list are arranged alphabetically by the Christian name, not the surname, as is common. For instance, the name of Absolem Yager is found in the A's, and not in the Y's, as might have been expected.

It is to be regretted that this list taken by William Green evidently did not include the tithables in the whole of Mercer County, which at that time still had its original bounds. The absence of the names of Judge Harry Innes, Judge Thomas Todd, George Muter, James Harrod and some others who are well known to have been living in that part of Mercer now included in Boyle County as early as 1786, indicates that another Commissioner took the list for that part of the County.

List of Taxable property within the District of Wm. Green commissioner for the county of Mercer for the year, '89.

Absolom Attkisson	*Cornelias Yager	Joseph Bunch
*Abram Bluford	Christopher Smith	*John Brown
Abner Eastwood	*Daniel Barbee	James Bryan
*Adam Fisher	Daniel Burchel	Jonathan Boone
Andrew Gimlins	*David Cesar	James Brown
Ambris Garrott	*David Finley	*John Burks
Andrew Hare	David Gates	*John Barbee
Andrew Hugh	Elkanah Allen	John Barbee, Junr.
Abrm Kimberlin	Elizabeth Allin	James Carddwell
Alexander Lewis	*Elizabeth Bowman	John Chiles
Adam Smith	Edward Fry	Jeremiah Clemons
*Aaron Vancleave	*Elias Fisher	John Davis
Absolem Yager	Ely Garrott	*James Davis
Andrew Barbee	Elijah Harlow	*James Dismukes
Addam Bell	Edward Polly	James Edwards
Benjamin Davis	Elijah Holsclaw	Jacob Engleman
Benjaman Egerton	Edward Turpin	James England
Benjamin Price	Friend Carter	James Forsyth
*Barnet Fisher	Frank Roach	Jacob Fulkerson
*†Benjamin Grayson	George Hughs	James Jones
Charles Anderson	Gabriel Rice	*John Harrison
*Charles Alford	Gideon Watts	*John Harrison, Jr.
*Charles Burks	George Wm. Downs	*John Henderson
Charles Bland	*Henry Balinger	John Holloway
Charles Chatwell	Henry Blankenbiker	Jacob Holsclaw
Caleb Dannellee	Henry Daugherty	*John Letcher
Charles Degroas	*Henry Greiders	James Leatch
**†Christopher Greenup	Henry Jeffris	James Lawrance
Claben Harlow	Henry Yocum	Jacob Myers
Claten Holloway	Isaac Finley	Josiah Miner
Charles Isom	John Archer	John Meguire
*Christopher Singleton	John Singleton	Joshua Powel
Charles Spelman	James Alcorn	*James Ownbey

*James O. Ricey
Jane Richay
James Robinson
*John Roberts
Joseph Scott
James Smith
John Shewmaker
James Scott
*James Stone
*James Smith
James Taylor
Joshua Thurman
Joseph Tyre
John Vagers
*Joseph West
John Willis
John Yocum
John Yocum
James Buncher
*Little Bery Roach
Lipscomb Norrell
Lewis Washburn
*Martin Frazer
Mary Garrett
Michael Harlow
Michael Hampton
*Mark Howard
Margaret Morrow
Mikle Myers
Moses More
M. Nagle
Michael Quigley
Michael Woods
Mathew M. Key
Nicholas Blankenbiker
Nathan Rice
*Nicholas Willhite
Obadiah Wright
Peter Bucher
Peter Biles Felt
Philips Caldwell
*Peter Keney
P. Tardiveu

*Peter Watts
*Philip Yeiser
Robert Alcorn
Rings Atkins
*Robert Baker
Richard Burk
*Robert Bowman
*Richd. Barber
*Richd. Balinger
Robt. Cox
Roger Devine
Richd. Gray
Ruben Kemp
Richd. Peter, Junr.
Richd. Peter
Richd. Overton
*Samuel Brookins
Samuel Bush (physician)
Sam Blankenbeker
Samuel Brewer
Simon Engleman
*Stephen Fisher
Samuel Harlow
*Samuel Irvin
*Samuel McDowell
Samuel Peter
Stephen Roberson
*Samuel Scott
*Samuel Shelton
Samuel Finley
Thompton Burks
*Townson Fugett
Thomas Harlow
Thomas Henry
Teter Huffman
Thomas Jeffress
Thomas Thornbury
Thomas Lewis
Thomas Miner
Thos. Threlkeld
*Thos. Turpin
Thos. Turpin, Junr.
Wm. Anderson

*William Arnold
Wm. Allcorn
Wm. Allen
Wm. Basset
Wm. Bunton
*Wm. Curry
Wm. Crump
Wm. Daviss
Wm. Downing
*Wm. McDowel
*William Gaines
William Graves
*William Green
*William Hughs
*William Hogan
William Hugh
*William Jeffris
William Lamm
William Lee
William Lusk
Wm. Mays
Wm. Nation
*Wm. Peter
*Wm. Robinson
Wm. Shumaker
Wm. Smith
†Walter E. Strong
*Wm. Thrailkeld
*Wm. C. Wakeland
Wm. Watts
Zachariah Allen
Z. Bunch
*Z. Cumpton
*Z. Taylor
Total
153 white tithables
    above 21.
43 white males above 16
    and under 21.
176 slaves.
2 ordinary licenses.
4 carriage wheels.
6 stud horses.

Mercer County:

I do hereby Certify that the foregoing five pages contain a true Copy of William Greens Book of Taxable property for the Year 1789.

Teste

Tho. Allin, ck. mc.

*Slave holder.
**Four wheeled carriage.
†Ordinary license.

175

DEPARTMENT OF STATE ARCHIVES—
Mercer County Tax Lists—1795

NOTE

Mercer County was formed by an Act of the Virginia Legislature passed October 1785 which provided: "That from and after the first day of August next the County of Lincoln shall be divided into three distinct counties, that is to say: So much of the said county bounded by a line beginning at the confluence of Sugar Creek and Kentucky river; thence a direct line to the mouth of Clark's run; thence a straight line to Wilson's Station in the fork of Clark's run; thence the same course continued to the line of Nelson county; thence with the said line to the line of Jefferson county; thence with that line to the Kentucky river; thence up the said river to the beginning, shall be one distinct county and called and known by the name of Mercer." (The rest of the Act provides for the creation of Madison county). See Hening's Statutes at Large, Vol. 12, age 118.

The boundaries of Mercer county as set forth above included all that part of the present county of Franklin which is south of the Kentucky River, and the greater portions of Boyle and Anderson counties.

The Tax Lists herewith presented are for 1795, ten years after the creation of the county of Mercer, and twenty-one years after James Harrod and his company built the first town in Kentucky at Harrodsburg. They include the names of heads of families for the whole of the original county, for although the Act providing for the creation of Franklin was passed in November 1794, it did not become effective until May 1795, and after the Tax returns were made for that year. This is clearly indicated by the fact that Thomas Lillard, who was listed in Mercer in 1795, became the Commissioner for the Tax for the lands lying South of the Kentucky in Franklin County in 1796, and in that year returned practically the same names that were on Gabriel Slaughter's list for Mercer in 1795.

It is regretted that the space required did not permit the publication of the lists which gave the number of acres of land and the watercourse on which it lay, but the returns for lands and personal property were made separately, and as the latter contained practically all the names on the former and many more besides, it was thought best to use it. Attention is called to the large number of horses and cattle in proportion to the population.

List of Taxable Property Within the District of James Clark, Commissioner of the County of Mercer for the Year 1795.

Persons Charged With the Tax	Blacks	Horses	Cattle
Ayres, Azariah			
Anderson, Benja.			
Akin, Daniel		1	
Adom, David		8	38
Allen, Grant	10	6	30
Anold, Grace	1	3	15
Ashby, George		2	5
Alon, Henry		1	2
Ayres, Joseph		9	17
Allison, John		1	12
Atwood, James		2	4
Abernathy, Robert		3	1
Arnett, William		4	6
Burton, Allen	1	1	1
Burns, Arthur		3	5
Boucher, Amos		1	
Brewer, Abraham		7	24
Bridges, Absolom		1	
Bennett, Ann	6	4	4
Bilbo, Archd.		5	8
Blagrave, Ban't	1	1	2
Bowman, Benj'n			
Bull, Bennett		3	11
Beall, Benjamin	10	8	45
Barnett, Charles			4
Boyls, Charles			7
Brewer, Daniel		1	
Banta, Daniel		4	28
Bryan, David	6	3	11
Bice, Dennis		3	16
Butlar, Edward			
Blagrave, Henry	1	3	11
Banta, Henry	1	3	11
Blagrave, Harrison	1	2	3
Banta, Henry, Admrs.	6	8	46
Brewner, Jacob		1	8
Brown, John		4	14
Brumfield, Job		5	8
Brewer, John		4	18
Brickey, Jarrot		2	1
Berry, John		6	16
Butlar, Joseph		3	9
Burch, John		2	
Bottom, John	3	9	24
Bridges, John	8	23	13
Butlar, John		1	4
Butlar, John		1	2
Butlar, Jessee			1
Butlar, James		4	8
Brown, James		6	26
Brinton, Robt.		5	11
Boucher, Peter, Sr.		5	12
Boucher, Peter, Jr.		1	
Banta, Peter		9	25

Persons Charged With the Tax	Blacks	Horses	Cattle
Bottom, Robt.		2	7
Barnett, Susanna	1	3	3
Banta, Samuel	1	9	29
Bennett, Sam'l		1	7
Bottom, Turner		3	
Bilbo, Wm.	1	5	8
Barbee, Thos.	9	9	54
Bottom, Wm.			
Brumfield, Wm.	2	5	18
Clark, Alexander		4	9
Connine (or Cozine), Andrew		2	5
Cox, Cheston		1	
Cup, Christopher		1	12
Campbell, David		2	7
Coovert, Daniel			7
Carvan, Edward		1	
Clark, Francis	7	5	25
Caldwell, George, Jr.	5	13	20
Cole, George		2	2
Conder, George		2	5
Caldwell, George, Sr.	33	29	96
Coats, George	2	6	12
Couzine, Jarrot		3	11
Commingore, Henry		3	9
Collette, Isaac		8	18
Cox, Isham		1	
Coffman, Isaac		11	14
Coovert, Isaac		2	8
Crawford, James		2	4
Copeland, James		3	7
Conder, John		5	
Cochran, John	4	6	18
Crow, Jacob	2	5	19
Commingore, John		6	24
Clark, Jessee		1	2
Crump, Joshua		3	6
Chiles, John, Jr	3	8	22
Chiles, John, Sr.	4	3	7
Clarkson, Joseph		3	4
Champion, John		1	
Cole, Jessee		1	
Coalter, John		7	20
Chilton, John		5	9
Cochonhom (?), Jacob		2	7
Clark, James	1	6	13
Cowan, John	14	18	60
*Chambers, John		1	
Colwell, John		9	24
Cook, John	7	4	19
Campbell, Josiah		8	18
Cole, Joseph	5	4	21
Copland, John		2	7
Campbell, John		1	3
Commins, Matthew		3	6

*Ferry.

177

Persons Charged With the Tax	Blacks	Horses	Cattle
Caldwell, Robert	18	19	67
Cannon, Robert			2
Cox, Richard		3	12
Conner, Thos.			
Champion, Thos.		3	8
Cogg, Thomas			
Cruchfield, Wm.		2	11
Cole, William		1	
Cann, Wm.		6	17
Crowdus, Wm.		9	25
Clarkson, Wm.		1	
Dye, Avery Constable	2	2	6
Debond, Abraham		3	5
Demott, Abraham		4	18
Davis, Azariah		3	1
Damewood, Boston		3	12
Damaree, Cornelius		4	13
Dickin, Charles	1	5	2
Davis, Edward		1	7
Davis, Edward, Sr		7	35
Darland, Garrot	3	5	22
Dickey, Joseph		3	8
Davis, John		1	
Day, John		2	13
Davidson, James		2	2
Drye, Jacob		9	11
Davis, James	1	2	
Durham, John, Jr.		1	
Durham, John, Sr.	1	6	20
Davis, Joseph	1	14	22
Davis, Jessee			
Davis, Jacob		4	15
Daugherty, Jas.	14	11	42
Dickin, Joseph	2	7	7
Demott, Laurence		2	8
Doran, Patrick	2	16	19
Davis, Peter		1	
Durham, Sam'l	7	8	31
Dunn, Sam'l	5	21	61
Daugherty, Wm.		4	
Depuis, Wm.		3	
Embree, John	1	1	7
Ewing, Samuel	2	6	18
Eastland, Wm.	5	8	16
Field, Barnett			
Field, Benjamin	10	11	11
Franklin, Claibon			
French, Henry	1	9	19
Field, Henry			
Follis, Isaac	1	2	11
Floyd, Morris		1	
Fulkenson, Philp.	1	7	18
Field, Rubin			
French, Sam'l		3	6
Fisher, Stephan	1		

Persons Charged With the Tax	Blacks	Horses	Cattle
Freeman, Thos.	3	6	17
Field, William	3	9	30
Galagher, Charles		2	11
Gage, Daniel		2	2
Gates, Elijah	3	7	14
Gillilan, Hugh			
Gilbot, John W.	3	4	6
Grover, Issiah		5	5
Gashwiller, Joseph		9	21
Grant, John		1	
Gritton, John		5	15
Gates, James	8		10
Gash, Michal, Sr.	7	5	17
Gash, Michal, Jr.			5
Guant, Mary		6	12
Givins, Martha	6	5	25
Gibbin, Megan	1	5	7
Galagher, Patrick		1	
Gray, Robert		4	14
Gash, Thomas		1	5
———, George Travis		2	7
Gibson, Thomas	1	4	13
Gibson, William		1	2
Goderd, William			
Gates, William	10	4	17
Guthree, William	4	10	16
Hanna, Adom		4	9
Hutching, Aaron	8	4	13
Harrod, Ann	1	3	5
Huff, Abram		2	8
Hill, Burril		2	1
†Hughes, Barnabas		1	
Howard, Charles		5	15
Houts, Christopher	4	11	22
Harlin, George		6	18
Hail, Hannah		1	5
Hall, Henry, Sr.	1	3	11
Hall, Henry, Jr.		1	1
Hess, Henry		4	7
Hanna, James		4	21
Hollin, John B.		1	1
Harbison, John		3	17
Hughes, John	1	1	2
Henderson, John	5	3	22
Harlin, James	8	21	60
Hines, John		1	6
†Hart, John	2	1	1
Hopewell, John		2	8
Holin, John		3	6
Harmon, Michal		1	4
Hunter, Nancy			7
Hill, Robert	1	6	15
Harbison, Rachel	4	6	14
Hope, Richard		5	28

†Retail store.

Persons Charged With the Tax	Blacks	Horses	Cattle	Persons Charged With the Tax	Blacks	Horses	Cattle
Hanna, Stephen	2	5	40	Miller, Daniel		1	5
Harrison, Thos. G.		5		Murphy, Daniel		4	2
Harbison, Thos	5	7	11	Miles, Elisha			
Hanna, Thomas	1	1	2	‡McKendry, Edwd.			2
Hall, William	1	2	5	May, Henry	2	1	
Hines, William		1		Montgomery, Hugh		1	2
Hunter, Zachariah		1		Miles, Isaac		2	
				Miles, Isaac, Sr.			3
Irvin, Abraham	12	11	57	Miles, John		3	5
Irvin, John	1	8	16	McGinnis, Jno., Sr.		7	13
Irvin, Robert		3	2	McGinnis, Jno., Jr.		4	6
				Mitchell, James		4	17
Jones, Allen	1	1	5	Myles, John		2	17
Jones, John		3	7	Montfort, Jas.		4	15
Jimmerson, James		1	8	Mansfield, John	3		3
Jinkins, Jonathan	2	6	34	McCaddoms, Jas.		1	1
Jones, Martin		1	4	McGraw, John		3	11
Jinkins, William		1		Moss, John	2	2	8
Jinkins, Wm., Sr.		4	12	Miner, Jacob		1	11
Jinnins, William		1	5	Mahan, John	2	5	19
				Miner, Larkin		3	4
Knox, David	7	7	14	McNeel, Laughlin			
Kerr, James		12	60	Montfort, Peter		7	9
Kenton, Mary			6	Morgan, Philip		3	13
King, Philip		2		Mitchell, Robt.		3	12
King, Thomas		1		McIntire, Robt.	1	5	10
Kelly, Timothy		3	6	Maloney, Robert	7		2
Kirkland, Thos.		6	16	McGinnis, Sam'l	4	4	1
Kennady, Wm.	1	1		McGinnis, Thos.			10
				Meglaughlin, Thos.			4
Ludewick, Christian		2	14	Martin, William		2	6
Lawrence, David	6	3	11	Moss, William	2	2	2
Lillard, Ephraim			2	Moore, William	5	1	5
Lillard, Edward		1		McGinnis, Wm.	1	3	5
Lillard, John	18	12	33	Montgomery, Wm.			
Lillard, James		3		Martin, Wm.	7	10	6
Lawrance, John	8	14	18	Miles, Zephaniah		1	
Lawrance, Joseph		4	5				
Lawrance, James			5	Nation, Edward		5	6
Latimar, John		1		**Nicholas, George	48	10	200
Latimar, Jacob		4	7	Nourse, William	2	4	18
Looney, Jonathan		11	17	Noel, William		2	4
Laws, Jeremiah		4	3				
Little, John		4	18	Owans, John		4	16
Lyster, John		1	8	Owans, Jeremiah		6	
Low, Lawrance		1	2	Owans, Thomas			3
Lunkirt, Peter		1					
Lawrance, Robert		2	6	Prewitt, Anthony	6	5	13
Lamb, Susanna			3	Powell, Charles		1	
Latimer, Sam'l				Philips, Charles		2	2
Latimer, Sam'l, Sr.		5	10	Potts, David		5	21
Little, Thomas		6	10	Prewitt, David	1	5	19
Laws, Thomas		6	21	‡Prewitt, Isham, Jr.	3	7	24
Liggon, Thos.	4	4	5	Pawlin, Isaacker	13	4	12
Lockmon, Vinson		3	6				
Long, William		1	3				
Moss, David	1						

‡Ordinary license.
**Carriage with 4 wheels and 94,240 acres of land.
‡Ordinary license.

Persons Charged With the Tax	Blacks	Horses	Cattle
Prewitt, Isham	2	1	
Pipes, John		1	
Potts, Jonathan		1	
Phillips, James		4	15
Puryear, Jessee		1	7
Potts, Jeremiah		1	
Price, John	1	3	2
Patterson, John		6	12
Philips, Mary		6	10
Perrigoe, Robert		3	12
Price, Robert	2	2	7
‡Pipes, Slyvanus		2	15
Pancake, Simon			
Patton, Samuel		2	6
Price, William H.	1	1	2
Price, Wm., Jr.			1
Price, Wm., Sr.	10	8	
Parks, William		3	2
Rankin, Adam	6	5	6
Radford, Elijah		2	1
Ripidan, Frederick		9	36
Reed, George			
Royalty, Isham		2	7
Richardson, John		2	1
Rodgers, John	2	12	29
Rock, John		2	5
Reynerson, Joakim		2	5
Ramsey, James		2	6
Rains, James		4	7
Razor, John			2
Rowland, John		3	2
Rollins, James		4	7
Rochester, John	7	5	5
Reeves, James		2	4
Roberds, Lewis	3	1	
Richardson, Margt.	5	5	18
Rowland, Robert		6	12
Reynerson. Reynes		3	15
Royalty, Thomas		1	2
Robards, Wm. S		2	4
Sutton, Ann	1	4	10
Smith, Armistred	1	2	2
Spencer, Amasa		4	12
Smock, Barna		4	18
Stewart, David A.		1	5
Stone, Elisha			
Shipley, Edward	2	9	
Shipley, George		10	22
Smith, George, Sr.		2	21
Smith, George, Jr.		2	4
Smith, Godfrey		4	
††Sparrow, Henry		4	12
Sage, Henry		1	1

††Stepfather of Nancy Hanks.

Persons Charged With the Tax	Blacks	Horses	Cattle
Sortor, Henry		1	5
Smock, Henry		2	
Sage, John		2	15
Sparrow, Jas. B.		1	
Sortor, John		1	3
Sparrow, John		3	2
Staton, Jehu		5	6
Splmon, James			4
Sandefur, Jas.		5	3
Sparrow, Jas. B., Sr.		1	9
Sparrow, Mary		3	9
Shaw, Matthias		2	4
Simmons, Moses		2	
Stone, Nimrod		2	10
Sheafer, Peter		3	2
Sebring, Rulef		2	4
Stemmons, Stephen		2	8
Shaw, Thomas			
Splmon, Thos.		2	11
Stewart, Thos.		1	
Smith, Thos.		1	
Stone, Thos.		3	6
Skelton, William		2	
Smith, William		2	4
Thornsburg, Amos		1	4
Thompson, Archibald		9	31
Tolley, Cornelius		2	7
Thompson, David		2	
Thomas, Edward		1	
Thomas, Henry		2	9
Thornsburg, Joel		2	2
Taylor, Jackson			
Thompson, John		3	
Thomas, John			5
Taylor, Leonard	1	3	16
Thompson Lawrence		5	12
Thomas, Masse		2	10
Thompson, Thos,		2	13
Thompson, William	2	8	41
Thompson, Wm.		4	7
Thomas, William		2	8
Thompson, William		1	7
Tolly, William		4	8
Taylor, William	4	7	16
Vannonsdol, Abraham		1	1
††Vorhis, Albert		7	24
Vannoy, Anderson		1	1
Vorhis, Cornelius		5	13
Vannorsdol, Cornelius		2	4
Vanorsdol, Christopher		2	
Vorhis, Cornelius		4	11

††(100 acres on Six Mile Creek, in Shelby Co. One of the "Low Dutch" Colony, as no doubt almost all the men whose names appear in the V's were.) It will be noted that none of them were slaveholders.

Persons Charged With the Tax	Blacks	Horses	Cattle
Vanorsdol, Cornelius		1	5
Van Nuys, Cornelius		4	11
Vorhis, Francis		8	21
Vanderipe, Harmon		3	8
Vannorsdol, Isaac		1	
Vannorsdol, Isaac		4	13
Van Nuys, Isaac		5	21
Vannorsdol, John		2	3
Vannorsdol, James		3	12
Vandevier, Peter		3	6
Vannest, Peter		1	2
Watkins, Asolum	13	10	6
Whiteneck, Abraham			2
Walker, Alexander		6	3
†Warran & Barbee			
Willer, Bottle			8
Weeks, Benjamin		2	7
Wright, Denis	1	7	6
Whiteneck, John		1	2
Willis, Joseph	3	9	32
Whitehouse, James		1	4
Wilson, James	8	20	29
West, Jeremiah		1	2
Walkup, John		3	14
Wilson, John		7	15
Westerfield, Jas.		3	12
Wren, John	1	2	5
Williams, John	1	5	10
Wren, Nicholas		5	7
Walker, Philip	8	6	23
Walker, Robert		4	
Webster, Richard		2	8
Whitwell, Robert		1	
White, Randolph		2	6
Williams, Thos.		3	4

†Retail store.

Persons Charged With the Tax	Blacks	Horses	Cattle
West, Thomas			
Whiteside, Thos.		4	
Willis, William		2	4
Whitehead, Wm.		2	7
Wilham, William			
Young, Jacob		6	9
Total	577	1,670	4,609

White males over 21.................... 487
Carriages with 4 wheels 1
Ordinary licenses 3
Retail stores 3
Ferries 1

Mercer County, Sct.
I do hereby certify that the foregoing fourteen pages contains a true list of the taxable property taken in by James Clark for the year 1795 agreeable to the certificates filed in my office.

Teste

THOS. ALLIN, C. C.

The Amt. of Taxable property taken in by Jas. Clark, Comr. for Mercer County for 1795.

	No.	
Slaves	577	L 43. 5. 6
Horses	1,670	41.10. 0
Cattle	4,609	28.16.17
Stud horses	13	9. 5.
Ordinary licenses	3	9. 0.
Carriages	1	1. 4.
Retail stores	3	30. 0.
Town lots	49½	533.14.
First rate land	19,711	29.11. 4
Second rate land	148,632	111. 9. 5
Third rate land	182,341	68.11. 4

A List of Taxable Property Within the District of Gabriel Slaughter, Commissioner of the County of Mercer for the Year 1795.

Persons Charged With the Tax	Blacks	Horses	Cattle
Ashby, Jesse		5	12
Arnold, Stephen		2	15
Armstrong, Robert	1	5	23
Adams, William	1	6	14
Arbuckle, John		1	3
Arnold, Jane			5
Ashby, Henry	1	2	3
Adams, Martin		4	6

Persons Charged With the Tax	Blacks	Horses	Cattle
Adams, Frances		1	5
Armstrong, Richard	4	2	5
Adams, George		1	15
Adams, William		1	
Adams, James			
Armstrong, John		16	29
Adams, Sam'l		12	48
Armstrong, Allexr.		4	20
Armstrong, Edwd.		1	
Ashby, Stephen	7	14	18
Arnold, John	2	9	34
Armstrong, Willm.		7	21

181

Persons Charged With the Tax	Blacks	Horses	Cattle
Ashby, George		1	6
Armstrong, Allexr.		6	2
Anderson, Josiah		6	7
Ashby, Henry	4	1	4
Adams, Samuel		10	13
Ashby, Stephen		1	
Allright, Adam		1	6
Abbet, William		1	
Armstrong, Robert		5	18
Allexander, Willm.		1	3
*Ashby, Danniel	2	4	10
Ashby, Peter		3	8
Addams, Thomas		1	4
Anderson, James	1	1	2
Arnold, John		3	8
Arnold, James	3	5	22
Armstrong, John		2	4
Ashby, John		2	5
Adams, John			1
Arnold, Stephen		2	
Bowman, Thos.		1	30
Boyd, William		4	8
Brown, Robt.		10	22
Bymson, Joseph		2	5
Buntain, Andw.	4	6	22
Baker, Robert	5	3	28
Bennet, Benjn.	3	11	15
Byrns, John	2	2	16
Batey, George			
Brown, James	1	2	4
Bowman, Benjn.		1	
Baker, Reubin		1	
Baker, Thomas		1	
Brown, Presley		3	3
Butler, John		4	14
Beall, Thomas		1	7
Buntain, John		2	9
Bohon, Walter		8	15
Bohon, Benjn.		5	15
Baker, James		1	
Burris, Nath'l	2	6	11
Brown, George		1	5
Barrow, John		2	11
Bailey, John		1	7
Bailey, Rebaka			2
Bohon, John		3	12
Bain, Leroy		2	6
Blizard, James		2	17
Beck, John		1	
Buntain, John		5	16
Boyd, James		1	
Brown, Chars.	6	7	7
Burford, Daniel		2	2
Butler, George	8	5	15
Buchannan, James		2	18
Bratton, George		1	

Persons Charged With the Tax	Blacks	Horses	Cattle
*Bush, Mathias	3	8	7
Bigham, John		5	10
Branson, Hannah		1	4
Bushong, Jacob		2	
Buchanan, George		1	
Berry, Reubin	3	5	25
Buchannan, John		2	7
Brown, John		7	5
Bryant, Christo.			
Burris, Samuel		3	7
Berry, Christian		2	1
Buchanan, George		6	18
Black, Sam'l		1	8
Burton, Eliz.	8	4	8
Berry, Searcy		3	10
Board, Philip		10	14
Bohanan, Austin		4	5
Bratton, Robert			
Brite, Jacob		3	11
Banion, John		3	7
Bruer (or Bruce), Vincent			1
Bogart, Corns.		4	16
Buchanan, Allexr.		5	
Boon, Jonathan			
Bennet, Timothy		1	4
Brown, Scott	2		
Beriman, John			
Briant, Zachariah		3	
Barrow, Wm.		2	
Buntain, John	6	5	29
Clark, John			
Crocket, Hamilton		1	8
Curry, James		3	15
Coffman, Ellenor		3	8
Carmikel, Patrick		2	8
Caldwell, Robert	2	4	13
Cantrill, Joshua		1	9
Christian, Thomas			
Campbell, William		1	15
Curry, John		6	13
Cockanon, John		1	2
Chaimberlain, Robt.			4
Cantrill, Zebulon			2
Curry, James		3	18
Campbell, Henry		1	4
Crawford, Lory			2
Casy, Peter	9	16	80
Casart, Mary		2	8
Curry, William		3	19
Clark, Charles		1	9
Curry, James		2	
Cathey, Hugh		7	10
Cahoon, John		2	11
Curry, Andrew		1	
Colier, Jonathan		9	15

*Retail store.

Persons Charged With the Tax	Blacks	Horses	Cattle	Persons Charged With the Tax	Blacks	Horses	Cattle
Canning, William		4	3	Delaney, Eliab			1
Chissum, George	2			Douthit, Silce?	1	4	21
Curry, John		5		Davis, John	3	2	8
Crocket, Anthony	5	5	53	Davis, John		1	
Choice, Cirus		1		Dickey, David		1	1
Callahan, Dennis				Despourt, Christo.		2	14
Crawford, William		2	7	Dodson, William			1
Crocket, William		2	10				
Cary, Ebenezer		2		Evins, Robert		2	3
†Crawford, Thomas	5	4	37	Emmerson, Jesse	1	6	8
Currens, James	1	4	19	Everley, John		2	13
Curry, William		20	37	Erven, William		3	24
				Ellis, Dannel		1	
Debenport, William		3					
Driskill, David		3	11	Forsithe, Mathew		3	12
Dorson, William		1	11	Flanagan, Mary		1	
Dean, Richard		1		Follis, Isaac		5	24
Delany, Josh.	4	5	20	Forrester, Samuel			
Denny, Robt.		2	24	Foreman, David		1	15
Dean, Summers		2	6	Faris, Elijah	1	3	12
Davis, William		2	9	Freeman, Benjn.		2	5
Dickey, Samuel		4	9	Furguson, Willm.			4
Demoree, John		3	10	Freeman, Rosanna		1	3
Devine, Samuel		1	4	Forrister, Thom.			
Dowden, Nath'l		3	17	Faris, Major		1	3
Dean, Henry	1	6	20	Foby, Richard		3	
Dean, John				Forrister, Willm.		1	
Dean, Thoms.	4	3	30	Forrester, Nath'l			1
Debon, Joseph, Jr.		5	4	Foby, James			2
Dunn, Benjn.		2	11				
Dean, Leaven		3	9	Graves, Leonard		4	17
Digs, Thomas		3	6	Gates, David			
Davis, Theodorus		10	16	Gibson, Henry		4	16
Downey, John		1	8	Graham, Sam'l			
Dean, William		1		Goudy, John		3	11
Devine, Margaret		1	2	Glasgow, Obediah		1	
Devine, John				Gordan, Betty		4	12
Denton, Thomas	1	6	13	Gordan, William		2	6
Debon, Joseph		7	12	Goodnight, John		7	20
Dunn, Alexr.			3	Graham, Samuel	6	7	1
Dean, Willm.		3	7	Griffin, Barney,		1	
Durmit, Edwd.		1	4	Goodnite, Henry		5	14
Denny, John		1	8	Gilmore, John		4	4
Davis, George		2	11	Graham, Sam'l	6	5	26
Duree, Albert		2	4	Grimes, Amous		2	6
Davis, Thomas		5	13	Gullion, Robert		3	18
David, Charles		2	8	Goodnite, Abram.		2	12
Daniel, William	5	3	2	Grimes, Stephen	1	1	
Darneby, Edward	3	7	20				
Davidson, Josiah		2	2	Hungate, John	2	2	10
Drawyer, Henry				Hughey, Ephream		1	2
Davis, Lemuel		2	6	Hammilton, Archd.		5	15
Davis, Theodorus, Jr.				Howley, Dennis		5	17
Divine, Andrew		1	8	Hungate, Charles		2	
Davis, John				Higgins, William		5	15
Dickey, John		3	7	Holman, Richard		2	12
				Hutton, Samuel		1	13

†Ordinary license.

183

Persons Charged With the Tax	Blacks	Horses	Cattle	Persons Charged With the Tax	Blacks	Horses	Cattle
Haner, James		5	9	Jett, James	1	5	7
Huff, Thomas	2	3	21	Jack, Samuel		1	8
Hungate, Charles		9	14	James, Thomas		3	1
Hutton, James		4	14	Jones, David	1	2	22
Hale, John		4	25	Jordon, Patrick			
Hill, Thomas		2		Jones, Thompson M.			
Hendrix, Isaac			2	Jones, John		9	19
Hog, Aaron		4	10	Johnston, Robert		3	19
Huff, William		2	12	Jones, Mason	7	7	5
Hornback, James		2	8	Johnston, John		4	5
Hoblet, Boston		1	1	Jones, Fieldon			
Hutton, Samuel		2	2	Jordon, Peter		9	19
Hammond, Willm.				Kinkade, James		3	11
Holms, Rosanna		1	10	Kirkland, John		5	10
Hopewell, Thos.		1	5	Kinney, Richard		4	10
Hart, Samuel		2	3	Keyn, Patrick		2	6
Hunter, Robert		3	12	Kelly, Daniel		3	21
Hendrix, John			2	Kelly, Jacob		2	8
Hammond, Edwd.		1	6	Kelly, John		3	11
Hoboy (?), Philip		2	8	Kelly, Samuel		2	14
Hungate, John		4	4	Kirkindoll, Jacob		4	5
Horine, George		2	3	Kennedy, Ezekiel	1	6	16
House, John		2	5	Kesler, Henry		1	4
Hart, Charles		7	14	Kulp, Jacob		2	11
Hale, Jesse		6	13	Kermikle, Peter		3	7
House, Levy		3	5	Kennedy, William			
Hammilton, Mary		5	7	Kinney, Daniel		2	8
Harbison, James		9	3				
Hensley, William		1	11	Logan, Thomas		3	25
Hardin, Nicholas				Long, John		1	14
Hammond, Jas.		1		Lipsey, John		3	7
Huff, Charles		1	2	Lee, Sammuel		2	3
Husk, Edward		3	7	Lock, Joseph		5	17
Higgins, Henry	6	5	10	Ledgerwood, James	3	6	18
Hoboy, Andrew		1	3	Lock, James		2	14
Harris, John				Lyon, Samuel		3	14
Hogshead, Will.				Lucas, Leah		1	3
Haydon, Noah		5	12	Long, William		3	7
Hutton, Joseph	1	1	8	Long, Jacob		2	11
Hart, David		4	18	Lee, William Jr.		4	3
Hammond, Hudson		1	6	Long, Abraham		2	
Hendrix, Will.		1	5	Long, George		3	5
Huver, George		1	2	Lankford, Larkin		1	
Hart, David		3	12	Logan, Thomas		4	15
Hart, John		1	9	Lillard, John, Jr.	3	4	13
Hammond's Heirs				Lee, William		2	9
Hale (or Hall), Palmer		5	20	Lightfoot, John	14	12	41
Higgins, Ellinor		3	8	Lawler, James		5	6
Huff, Richard		1	3	Lapsley, Margaret	7	3	7
				Lillard, Thomas	6	7	22
Irvin, John				Light, Jacob	6	5	9
Isham, William	3	3		Lyster, Peter		2	9
				Lucas, Jesse		1	
Jones, Moses		2		Lucas, Richard		4	6
Jones, Jabok		3	11	Leonard, Willi		3	7
Jones, Thomas		3	17	Lampbert, John		3	5
Jones, Joseph		5	16	Lyan, David		4	13
Jackson, Thomas		1	12	Lyan, James		3	16

Persons Charged With the Tax	Blacks	Horses	Cattle	Persons Charged With the Tax	Blacks	Horses	Cattle
Lyan, Ezekiel		2	24	McCoun, James		2	11
Lacewell, John		1	2	McClure, Allexr.		9	25
Long, Samuel		1	11	Miles, John	7	5	3
Lock, Jacob		2	9	Moore, Zebulon, Jr.		2	7
Lyan, Joseph		6	16	Moore, John	1	6	10
Lock, Benjn.		1	7	Molton, John		1	2
Lyan, John		3	8	MaCormack, John		2	2
Lykins, William		2	2	Moore, John		2	6
Lock, Jeradus		1		Mayhall, Timothy		2	3
Lawless, Benjn.	6	3	14	McKinney, Joseph		2	4
				Moore, Thomas		5	24
McClain, James		4	9	McAfee, George	3	10	26
McCample, John		1	10	Moore, Thomas			
McGuire, James		1	23	Moore, William			
McClure, Stale		1	2	McFatridge, William		1	2
McAfee, Robert	1	5	15	McNew, John		3	3
McBrayers, Hugh		2	2	May, William		5	10
McBrayers, John		1		McClary, Sam'l		3	9
Moore, Joseph		1	10	McGuire, David		1	
McMicle, James		2	13	Mitchell, James		1	
Moore, Zebulon		2	13	McNight, William		2	10
Moore, Charles		5	24	McBrayer, James		3	3
Minter, William				McClaw, Thomas		1	1
Maun, Beverly		4	20	McCastlin, Margaret		3	8
Miller, Henry		7	13	Mitchell, Robert		2	12
McCastlin, Richard		3	6	McCoun, John	1	3	6
McAfee, James	1	9	37	McGuire, Joseph		1	2
McGee, John		8	25				
Mayhall, William		3	10	Newton, Peter		1	5
McFaddin, Hugh		2	17	Neele, Nathan	2	7	10
Meaux, John	40	25	51	Newman, Henry			4
McAfee, John		1		Nation, William		1	5
Moore, Mary		2	6	Nation, George			5
McGuire, Lawrance		1		Nation, Joseph		1	7
McDannel, William		3	5	Neele, Abraham		2	13
McDannel, James		2		Ney, Samuel		3	13
McGuire, Jesse				Neele, Robert		1	
McCamey, Robt.		2	18	Neele, Elias		1	8
Murphy, Cath'n		3	8	New, John		1	2
McCormack, George		2	7	New, James		2	3
Martin, James G.		3	9	Nokes, George		4	9
Mitchell, Joseph F.		3	8				
McGary, Hugh			5	Ormsby, John			1
Moland, Jesse		1	3				
McClain, John		2	15	Payton, Henry		2	
McCullough, James		4	9	Paxton, Thomas	1	2	7
Munday, Emond.	6	12	24	Prather, Henry	3	12	24
Modecit John	1	1		Petty, Rody	1	2	5
Morris, Richard		3	5	Pidcock, Horatio		1	2
McCoun, John	4	5	25	Paddock, Willm.		2	6
Molton, John		2	4	Powel, Charles	6	5	16
McAfee, Sam'l		7	29	Poague, Robert	8	3	8
Moore, Simean		3	12	Poague, Joseph			6
McCoun, James	10	5	24	Parr, Aaron		3	5
Miller, George		3	4	Peter, Richard, Sr.		3	4
Moore, Daniel		2	4	Pollock, Thomas		2	7
Moore, Austin		3	6	Parker, Isaiah			3
				Phemister, John		3	4

Persons Charged With the Tax	Blacks	Horses	Cattle
Potter, John		1	2
Prior, John		3	5
Passmore, Augustine		4	14
Pennybaker, Wyan		3	2
Prather, Thomas	1	6	12
Peter, Samuel		2	10
Quigley, Elizabt.			5
Robertson, John		4	9
Robertson, Henry		2	9
Richmond, Willm.			
Robertson, William	4	6	20
Russel, John		1	12
Ray, John		3	11
Ransdall, Willi		1	
Rollins, Joseph		1	
Robertson, James	3	7	26
Ransdal, Wharton		1	
Righthouse, Thomas		3	2
Rizley, Daniel			
Ransdal, John		1	
Robertson, Alexr.		2	12
Ryneason, Barnet		1	11
Robertson, Joseph		4	6
Robertson, Robert		1	
Reuby, Peter		2	8
Ray, James	6	7	15
Robertson, William		6	37
Robertson, William		6	3
Ruth, John		1	2
Ragin, Amos		3	9
Ransdal, Zachariah		1	
Richey, Stephen			
Rice, William M.		1	4
Rice, William B.		3	7
Richey, James	1	1	5
Robertson, James		5	5
Rucker, Ephriam		2	10
Slaughter, Gab'l	6	6	14
Stephens, Samuel			
Sutterfield, Benjn.			
Stokes, Thomas			2
Shields, James		5	13
Simmons, Thomas			
Stalkup, Emmon		2	6
Shouce, Christian		2	7
Shouce, Jacob		2	1
Smelcer, Paulcer	1	2	6
Shearly, William		1	12
Salmon, John		3	5
Sutterly, John		1	
Spalding, Thomas		6	8
Salmon, Nath'l		1	
Smith, William		1	
Sage, John		2	7
Suttle, Henry		6	19

Persons Charged With the Tax	Blacks	Horses	Cattle
Sutterfield, John		1	
Scoonover, David		1	
Shepherd, William		6	8
Senate, Richard		2	10
Sharp, Solomon		2	10
Shaddock, John	2	4	
Steel, Menian (or Ninian?)		3	11
Sutterfield, Edwd.		6	12
Shofner, Henry		4	10
Stewart, William		3	9
Stilts, John		1	3
Smith, William		1	1
Smith, Thomas		2	1
Spurr, Jesse		3	13
Shepherd, William		1	
Steen, John		2	2
Springate, William		3	16
Stilwell, John		2	15
Slaughter, Jesse	12	6	14
Slaughter, Robert, Sr.	14	8	16
Sharp, Robert			
Simpson, Robert		1	
Stokes, Catherine		2	4
Shoemaker, Even			3
Sanford, John	1	1	
Stilwell, John		4	37
Shoemaker, Jesse		1	2
Smith, Thomas		2	2
Sharp, Abraham	2	6	25
Satterly, Samuel	3	1	6
Smith, Thompson		2	1
Stepleton, John		3	17
Stewart, Robert		4	
Silvertooth, Mary		2	7
Sillers, Jerimiah		2	9
Smithy, Thomas		2	11
Smith, Thomas		1	5
Smith, Stephen		5	4
Stunitt, John		2	4
Smith, Jerimiah			
Sage, Alexander			3
Smith, Edward		4	12
Thompson, George	30	15	43
Thomas, Joseph	2	1	8
Timmins, Tulliver		3	4
Thompson, Leon'd	12	3	6
Threldkeld, John	7	12	30
Tracy, William		2	
Turpin, Thomas		2	2
Talbot, Isham	2		
Threldkeld, Daniel	1		
Thompson, Even		5	5
Thomas, John	1	4	16
Tharp, Perry		3	10
Thompson, Lawrance		2	5
Timmons, Stephen		3	9
Talbot, Isham, Sr.	3	4	7

Persons Charged With the Tax	Blacks	Horses	Cattle	Persons Charged With the Tax	Blacks	Horses	Cattle
Thompson, James		7	18	West, John		1	8
Terhune, Garrett		5	11	Webb, Sam'l		3	7
Thukston, Thomas		3	6	Woodcock, Joseph		3	10
Thomas, Elisha		3	12	Woods, Sam'l			10
Thomas, Anna		2	4	William, David		10	60
Talbot, Edmund		4		West, William		1	1
Thompson, Rodger	42	4	40	Watts, William			3
Thompson, John		1		Willis, John		2	10
Timmons, George		4	10	White, James		4	18
Timmons, Sam'l		4	13	White, William			3
Thomas, Ozwell		2	3	Wilson, Samuel			
Tracy, John		1		White, James		2	6
Thompson, Joseph		3	15	Ward, John		5	15
Thickston, William		2	9	Wilson, Thoms.	2	7	33
Tolly, Isham		1	3				
Tuthero, Michael		2	7	Yocum, Mathias		6	25
Thompson, James				Yocum, Matthias, Jr.		3	5
Thompson, Henry		2	11	Yocum, Jesse	6	8	15
Tracy, Sam'l		1	6				
				Zeanes, Martha			
Vibert, George			1	Zicklidge, William		2	4
Vories, Court		3	10				
Vanneys, Isaac, Jr.		2	3	Total 623	479	1,820	5,485
Vories, Jacob		2	7				
Vanberkle, Peter		1	4				
Vanderslice, Benjn.		2	1				

Slaves 479   L 30:18:6
Horses 1,820   45:10
Cattle 5,485   34: 5:5¼
Ordinary license 1   3: 0:0
Stores 2   20: 0:0
Studs 11   7: 4:0
1st rate land 8,182   12: 5:3
2nd rate land 104,629   78: 9:4½
3rd rate land 134,201   50: 1:6

Mercer County, Sct.

I do certify that the foregoing twenty-six pages contains a true list of taxable property taken by Gabriel Slaughter for the year 1795 agreeable to the certificates filed in my office.

Teste:

THO. ALLIN, C. C

Persons Charged With the Tax	Blacks	Horses	Cattle
White, James		2	2
Wilson, Thomas		5	24
Warren, Peter		3	5
Wilcoxin, Aaron	1	3	18
Woolfork, Joseph	9	6	21
Warner, George			
Weond, Mathias		2	4
Whitler, John	2	2	
Willis, Edward		3	16
Willis, Joseph, Sr.		1	10
Williams, Beverly		3	10
Wickersham, Sampson		1	2
Wells, William		3	1
West, Joshua		1	3
Walker, Peter		5	16

A List of the Taxable Property Within the District of Wm. Gaines, Comr. for Mercer County for 1795.

Persons Charged With the Tax	Blacks	Horses	Cattle
Atkenson, Abraham	3	4	16
Allford, Charles	1	7	25
Allford, Jacob (Penchr.)		5	9
Allin, Zachy.		3	4
Allin, Eliz.		1	4

Persons Charged With the Tax	Blacks	Horses	Cattle
Allin, Wm.		6	1(
Adair, John	8	7	2:
Anderson, Wm. (Cohe)		3	:
Anderson, Cornelius			
Anderson, Wm.	3	2	:
Atten (or Alten), Addrien	1	3	1(
Allcorn, Wm.		1	:
Allin, Thos.	6	8	2'

Persons Charged With the Tax	Blacks	Horses	Cattle
Barbee, John	10	10	44
Barbee, John, Jr.		4	23
Barbee, Dan'l	1	4	12
Bryant, Wm.		3	7
Bowlin, Henry		1	3
Banta, Cornelius		4	9
Bowman, John	7	9	20
Barlow, Ambrouse		2	9
Barlow, Aaron			
Brown, Jerimh		3	7
*Brown, Wm.	1	3	10
Brown, Scott	2	2	
Brown, John		1	2
Banta, John	1	5	16
Banta, Peter, Sr.		8	30
Banta, Albert		8	18
Banta, Petrus		6	18
Banta, David		3	7
Banta, Jacob		2	8
Bellowfelt, Peter		3	16
Bellow, Philip		1	3
Ballenger, Richd.	7	9	16
Ballenger, Richd., Jr.	5	1	6
Bennet, Stephen		3	16
Back, Joseph		2	7
Blanton, Joshua	2	2	14
Black, David		4	14
Bunch, Richd.		2	7
Bunch, Joseph		4	13
Bunch, Charles		2	14
Bunch, Calloway	3	4	10
Blankenbeker, Nichs.		6	14
†Baker, Fredk.	4	3	3
Bulger, Dan'l	1	1	4
Burks, John	1	2	3
Bruner, Petèr	2	5	15
Burtchum, Benajah		2	10
Burks, Charles	3	1	5
Burks, Tompson	3	2	4
Bice, Cornelius		2	4
Broaddrick, Wm.		2	1
‡Burney, James			
Bushong, Henry		3	7
Barns, George		3	11
Bell, Adam		3	10
Bogart, James			
Britt, James	1	4	1
Bruner, John		2	5
Buford, Abram.	2	2	1
Buford, John	2	3	12
Buford, James	10	12	19
Blankenbeker, Henry	1	4	14
Bell, Tho.			
Burriss, Wm.			1

*Tavern license.
†Tavern.
‡Store.

Persons Charged With the Tax	Blacks	Horses	Cattle
Craddock, Robt.	7	4	14
Chapline, Abram.	10	12	25
Conrin, Jerrerd	3	1	5
Conrin, Hannah	2	6	21
Corn, Joseph		1	5
Corn, Sollomon		5	29
Corn, Timothy		2	9
Corn, Edward		1	3
Corn, Aaron		3	2
Cobourn, Susannah		3	2
Colter, Thos.		4	7
Canary, Christian		7	18
Coomes, Richd.		2	4
Cumpton, Zach.	8	5	20
Causby, Charles		2	3
Clemmons, Sam'l		2	3
†Clemmons, Jeremiah	5	2	11
Craig, Robert		2	7
Caldwell, John		1	4
Colvin, John		1	13
Calvin, John		5	8
Clemmons, Joseph			4
Cape, John	1	4	1
Curd, Newton	6	3	8
Ceasar, David	1	1	2
Danily, Caleb		3	12
Demmeree, Peter		7	22
Demmeree, Sam'l		6	18
Demmeree, Davd.		4	10
Demmeree, Da (S. J.)		2	3
Downs, W. George		2	4
Davis, Joseph	10	10	22
Davis, Charles		5	11
Davis, Benj.			
Davis, James	4	8	16
Davis, Sam'l		6	15
Davis, James (Overs)		1	3
Davis, Joshua	17	2	1
Davis, Wm.		5	23
Demott, Peter		2	12
Demott, John		2	5
Dismukes, James	1	3	8
Dismukes, Joseph	1	1	
Dismukes, Wm.		1	
Downing, Rachel		2	12
Downing, John		2	
Denney, Sam'l		1	11
Daniel, Wm.		4	8
Dooley, Sam'l		3	9
Davidson, John		2	6
Dungan, Nathan		2	11
Dunklin, John	2	2	
Denniston, Robt.		1	1
Davy, Free		3	5
Dolley, Owen		1	5
Davis, Thos. T.	7	6	22

†Tavern.

Persons Charged With the Tax	Blacks	Horses	Cattle	Persons Charged With the Tax	Blacks	Horses	Cattle
England, James		3	3	Harriman, John		3	11
Edrington, Benj.		3	4	Higgins, Gideon	11	3	10
Edrington, Wm.		2	2	Harlin, John		4	6
Embree, Joseph	1	2	5	Humble, Mic'l	4	11	35
Edmondson, Philip		2	5	Humble, Paul		3	16
Edwards, James				Hauks, Lewis		4	6
				Hughs, Edward		5	6
Froman, Jacob, Jr.		2	10	Hodgson, Phinehas		1	
Froman, Jacob	14	12	33	Harris, James		2	3
Fugate, Townsin	2	5	15	Harris, Overton	5	3	11
Firney, Nich.		2	8	Hughs, Wm.		4	17
Finley, David	1	17	36	Hodges, Andrus		4	15
Finley, John		4	5	Huffman, John		2	7
Fisher, Stephen	12	19	85	Hufman, Peter		3	11
Fisher, Adam	6	8	38	Hennon, Abell		1	4
Fisher, Barnet	3	11	31	Harris, Sam'l		1	10
Fisher, Elias	3	8	29	Hanlin, Partrick		1	2
Fisher, Benja.	3	4	6	Handy, Wm.		4	8
Fisher, Joseph		1		Handy, Jessy		1	
Fairley, Peter			2				
Flanigan, Partrick		6	13	Jones, Gab'l		2	7
Flanigan, Tarrance		3	15	Ison, Charles		5	12
				Ison, James		3	3
‡Gillaspee, David	10	11	28	Johnson, James		2	11
Grider, Jacob		3	4	Irvine, Sam'l	5		1
Grider, Henry	3	5	19	Jeffrees, Dan'l		4	4
Grider, Christo.		3	7	Jeffrees, Wm.		4	8
Grider, Tobias		1		Jinnings, Jonath.	5	4	16
Gimlin, Andrew		7	14	Jinnigs, Dianna	3	3	12
Gordon, Ambro.	6	5	10				
Gray, John		2	10	†Kanaday, Benj.	3	1	1
Garrott, Ambr.		8	16	Kalfrus, Fredk.	1	1	6
Gaines, Wm.	3	6	27				
Grayham, Tho.		3	4	Lamme, Wm.		8	20
Gibson, Jonathan		3	3	Lewis, Joseph	21	4	20
Gillbert, John		1	3	Lewis, Alexr.		3	12
Grayham, James		4	4	Lewis, Richd.	1	1	1
Garr, John		1	3	Larrance, Sam'l	2	6	3
Goshon, Mark		5	7	Larrance, Isaac			9
Grayham, Tho.		7		Larrance, James		2	3
Green, Henry		1	4	Legrange, Aaron			
Grayham, James	2	3	2	Letcher, Benj.	9	6	28
Gill, Tho.	1	3	9	Letcher, Eliz.	5	5	11
Greenup, Christo.	3	3	7	Leach, James		3	
Henderson, John	1	2	8	Lanwell, Sam'l			2
Headdrick, Joseph		1	4	Lashbrook, Wm.		7	4
Holsclaw, Jacob, Jr.		4	2	Lashbrook, John		2	
Hancock, Ann		2	6	Lasswell, Peter		3	15
Holloway, Mary		4	5	Long, John		1	13
Hogan, Wm.	2	4	8	Langsdon, Charles		1	
Hogan, John		2	7	Lists, George		1	5
Hogan, James (Fayette)	2	2	14	Lobb, Eliz.	3	1	11
Harrison, John	14	6	18				
Hutton, James		1	7	McDowell, Sam'l	11	12	57
Haggin, John	7	9	34	McDowell, Sam'l, Jr.	9	8	20
Harrison, John, Jr.	11	7	20	McDowell, Wm.	16	12	59

‡Store.   †Tavern.

Persons Charged With the Tax	Blacks	Horses	Cattle	Persons Charged With the Tax	Blacks	Horses	Cattle
McDowell, Joseph	2	3		Pairtree, John		2	7
Mon, Sam'l John		3	10	Protsman, John	1		4
McMurtry, James		1	10	Poor, Robert	7	7	23
Megill, John		6	13	Poor, John	1	3	9
Mehee, Wm.		1	3	Peters, Wm.	2	1	5
Mehee, Lydda		3	6	Parrish, Benjn.		2	2
McQuie, Wm.	4	7	17	Philips, John		8	20
Meginnis, Hezekiah		5	3	Pebargan, George		2	6
Meginnis, John	1	3	11	Polley, Edward		4	12
Moosby, Robt.	20	8	37				
Moosby, Joseph	8	3	14	Rice, Nathan		3	9
Moosby, David	8	6	14	Robertson, Alexr.	10	7	29
Meginty, James	8	4	22	Robertson, Margt.	1		7
Montgumree, James	2	8	29	Robertson, Mich			
Montgumree, Sam		3	9	Robertson, Sarah		1	3
Myars, Mich'l		8	25	Robertson, Steph.		3	8
Myars, Peter			5	Railsback, John		3	11
Meginnis, Tho.	1	7	15	Robards, Eliz.	20	9	6
Marrs, Sam'l		3	6	Robards, George	7	6	23
Marrs, M. Henry	1	2	20	Robards, Joseph		4	
Marrs, Barnabas		2		Robards, Jessy	4	4	13
McDannold, Angi (?)		4	9	Rice, Polley	1	3	6
‡McDannold, Sam		1		Rice, John		2	17
Meguire, Larrance		2	9	Rice, (Rev.) David	2	13	27
Mckinney, Charles	17	12	43	Rice, Andrew		4	12
Mckinney, Wm.		5	1	Rice, Benjn.	2	4	6
McKinney, Reaney				Rice, Gab'l		4	6
McBride, Wm.	1	2	16	Rice, Jessy		1	2
Mercer, Tho.		1	3	Rose, Lewis	7	14	45
Martin, Anna		2	7	Reed, John		1	2
Moore, Wm.			8	Renshaw, Sam'l	2	4	4
Martin, Lewellin		1	3	Roney, Roger		5	16
McDoo, John		3	6	Roney, Mary		1	9
Miller, Henry			2	‡Rochester, John			
Meloney, August		1	2	Roach, Littlebory		2	4
Miles, John		2	5	Ramey, Matthew		4	
McMurtry, Alexr.				Ramey, Wm.		3	
Mckinney, Tho.		2		Reed, John		1	3
Mecombs, Patty		2	9	Reed, Benjn.		2	4
Menear, Abrm.	1	2	5	Raines, Wm.		1	
Measlin, David		7	12	Reatherford, Eliz.	1	1	
Moore, Wm.		5	4				
Myars, Jacob		5	19	Smith, Jno. (Colo.)	7	11	25
				Smith, Jno. (Capt.)	11	13	30
Nickum, Micha.		3	8	Smith, Jno. (Taylor)	1	4	26
Noel, Barret	1	7	17	Smith, Jno. (Black S.)	9	2	2
Noel, Scott			2	Smith, Jno. (Son of Jam.)	4	3	4
Nutgrass, Gray		1	7	Smith, Wm.		1	
Neal, Charles	2	4	2	Smith, Zach.	3	7	38
				Smith, Wm. (Dect.)	7	9	20
Ownby, James	5	7	11	Smith, Eliz.	2	4	9
Oglesby, Wm.	6	5	8	Smith, Thomas		5	14
				Smith, James	6	11	78
Pirkins, Benj.	11	5	18	Smith, Hugh		3	12
Pirkins, Joseph	4	4	3	Smith, Jessy	2	2	
Pirkins, Reuben		2	5	Smith, Aaron		1	4

‡Store.

‡Store.

190

Persons Charged With the Tax	Blacks	Horses	Cattle	Persons Charged With the Tax	Blacks	Horses	Cattle
Smith, Edwd.		5	11	Tipton, Wm.		2	
Singleton, Christo.	5	5	16	Toney, Jessy		1	2
Singleton, Christo., Jr.		1	3	Turner, Charles	1	1	
Scott, Joseph		1	4	Tirpin, Hugh		1	2
Scott, James	1	5	13	Tompson, Arthur		1	3
Scott, Sam'l	1	6	9	Troxel, Fredk.		4	17
Scott, Sam'l, Jr.		3	4				
Spilman, Charles	6	4	13	Vorouse, Jno. (Blue)		4	16
Spilman, Benjn.		3	6	Vorouse, Abrm,		2	
Shelton, Sam'l	5	2	9	Vorouse, Luke		4	10
Slaughter, James	7	7		Vorouse, Cornelius		2	9
Slaughter, Robt.	3	3	8	Vorouse, James		6	
Shelladay, Edwd.		1	3	Vanosdol, Sim. (Maj.)		6	15
Shelladay, George		3	19	Vanosdol, Luke	1	6	31
Shelladay, Andrew		2	7	Vanosdol, Simson		3	8
Shelladay, Hester		6	13	Vannuys, Peter		2	11
Sneed, Tho.	6	4	2	Vanbrike, Larrance		2	8
‡Strong, E. Walter	4	2	8	Vance, Wm.		4	15
Stone, James		7	19	Vandiver, Henry		3	8
Sorter, Jacob		2	7	Vandiver, Cornelius			7
Surthern, Wm.	3	5	6	Vantreece, Hartman		2	4
Swinney, John		1	9	Vantreece, Imman (?)		2	1
Swinney, Rosanh.		1					
Swinney, Micajah		2	2	†Waggener, John	4	7	15
Summers, John	1	6	21	Wilhoit, Nicho.	8	6	35
Stroher, Abm.		2		Wren, Vincent	3	2	11
Shy, Jessy	1	2	3	Woods, Mich'l		4	13
Shy, Sam'l		1	4	Woods, Sam'l, Jr.	4	5	30
Sled, Wm.		3	14	Wood, Isaac	6	4	9
Smock, John		3	10	Wall, Jacob		2	2
Shields, Wm.		11	16	Wall, Jacob, Jr.		1	1
Sowder, Michl.		2	4	Wall, Gab'l	1	2	6
Schooling, Josep.	1	7	13	Wall, Francis		1	3
Shearro, Ann		1	2	Wall, Robt.		1	2
Shuman, George		1	5	Watts, Peter	3	8	20
Speed, James	12	14	50	Watts, Gideon	1	3	10
Scott, George		10	25	Wright, Fran.		1	
Shy, Robt.				Williams, Joseph		1	4
				Wilson, Francis		3	4
Taylor, Sam'l	2	9	19				
Taylor, Jno. (by Allford)		1	5	Yeizer, Philip	3	1	8
Taylor, John	2	4	15	Yagar, Cornls.	2	7	30
Taylor, Uriah	2	5	9	Yagar, Joshua	1	4	12
Taylor, Clayton			4	Yagar, Abs.		5	11
‡Tillfair, Isaac	1			Yocum, Henry		3	10
Templain, John		8	27	Yocum, Jno. (Young)		2	9
Tirpin, Tho.	4	5	9	Young, Peter		1	4
Tirpin, Henry	3	3	8	Young, Tho.		1	
Tirpin, Edmond	1	1	4				
Tilford, Jerimiah	10	7	41	Total 432	761	1,508	4,419
Tommas, John		4	7				
Threlkeld, Wm.	2	9	23				
Todd, John		2	2				
Tompson, John	17	5	11				
Terhune, Wm.		3	9				
Thornbery, Tho.		4	6				

‡Store.

Mercer County, Sct.

I do hereby certify that the foregoing thirteen pages contain a true list of the taxable property taken in by William Gaines

†Tavern.

for the year 1795 agreeable to the certificates filed in my office.

Teste:

THO. ALLIN, C. C.

The total amount of taxable property in Mercer County pr. Commrs. returns:

Slaves	1,817	L 136: 5: 0
Horses	5,058	126: 0: 0
Cattle	14,513	90: 0: 0
R. stores	8	80: 0: 0
O. licenses	7	21: 0: 0
Studs	38	26: 8: 0

Billiard tables	3	30: 0: 0
Town lots L 1,069	16.0	1:12: 2¾
Carriages	1	0:16: 0
1st rate land	53,895	80:16:10
2nd rate land	658,887	494: 3: 1¾
3rd rate land	864,936	324: 7: 0
		L 1,412:11: 4

To an additional return of Gab'l Slaughter:

2nd rate land	121,907	91: 8: 7
3rd rate land	23,632	8:17: 2¾
		1,512:17: 1¾

192

STATE ARCHIVES—MONTGOMERY COUNTY

(Editor's Note)—The following data, taken from original records on file in the Archives of Kentucky, in the custody of the State Historical Society, is of particular value for the reason that the Court House of Montgomery County with practically all its contents was burned in 1864.

The Tax Lists for 1797 give names of the male residents over twenty-one, with the amount of land owned. The star indicates slave holder; † indicates tavern license; ‡ indicates retail store.

The marriage and death records copied by Miss Hattie Scott are taken from the Vital Statistics records which were made under an Act of the Kentucky Legislature between the years 1852 and 1862, and filed with the Auditor of Public Accounts during those years.

The lists of early civil and military appointments are taken from the original Executive Journals of Governor Garrard's administration, and the Act forming the County, from the original enrolled Bills of 1796.

The county of Montgomery was formed from part of Clark County under an Act of the Kentucky Legislature, approved December 14, 1796, as follows:

"Be it enacted etc.—
"Section 1. That from and after the first day of March next, all that part of the County of Clark lying northwardly and eastwardly of the following bounds, towit: beginning at the Bourbon line at a red oak tree marked C. L. on the side of the road leading from Mountsterling to Paris, thence a straight line to strike the dividing ridge between Hingston's and Stoner's waters, where the road leading from Winchester to Mountsterling crosses said ridge; thence the same course continued, crossing Red river, until it strikes the Kentucky river, shall be one distinct county by the name of Montgomery.

A Court for the said County of Montgomery shall be held by the Justices thereof to be named on the first tuesday in every month after the said division shall take place in such manner as is provided by law in respect to other counties. * * * The Justices * * * shall meet at the House of William Conner in the said County upon the first Court day after the said division shall take place, * * * and proceed to appoint a Clerk and fix upon a place to hold Courts as near the center thereof as the situation and Convenience will admit * * * and proceed to erect Public buildings etc."

On December 17th, 1796 the Governor, James Garrard, issued the following commissions:

To be Justices of the Court of Quarter Sessions for the County of Montgomery, Jilston Payne, James McIlhaney and James Poage; to be Justices of the Peace and County Court, Enoch Smith, Robert Dougherty, Bennett Clarke, James Ward, William Rosenborough, Jesse Woodruff, William Ellis, Joseph Colvin, William Robinson, John Hardwick, James Turley and David Hughes. Sheriff—Nelson Hackett; Coroner—John Hambleton.

On February 8th, 1798 the Governor "laid off a new regiment (of Militia) being the XXXI, to be included in the county of Montgomery, and appointed James Poage Lieutenant-Colonel Commandant, Andrew Swearingham Major of the 1st Battalion, & Samuel Downing Major of the 2nd Battalion."

The following Company officers were commissioned for this Regiment:

Captains—William Farrow, Daniel Paton Matthew McClung, Samuel Burchem, David Black, John Mockbee & William Rodgers, David Wilcox & Micajah Harrison.

Lientenants—David Hathaway, Abihu Anderson, Enoch Smith, William Stafford, Thomas Moore, Caleb Litton, Jacob Langston, Joseph Simpson, John Judy, James Lasy Uriah Wilson.

Ensigns—Michael Paul, Beverly Kirtley, Lewis Cheatham, William Fleming, John Pritchett, John Heringford, Isaac Montgomery, John Terrel, John Nickels & John Wilson. Cornet—(Of Cavalry Co.) Jeremiah Davis.

A BOOK FOR THE AUDITOR GEORGE MADISON ESQUIRE A. P. A. COMMISSIONERS BOOK
1797

MONTGOMERY COUNTY

Persons names	Acres land
*Anderson, Nicolas	687
Arthur, James	
*Arthur, Stephen	
Anderson, Wm.	
Armstrong, Robt.	
Allen, John	
Anderson, Abihue	
Anderson, James	
Adkins, Tho.	
Arbuckle, Jas.	
Arbuckle, Saml.	
Arbuckle, John	

B

Berry, John	
Badger, Oliver	
Brown, Wm.	
Brunt, Wm.	
Brown, John	
*Bell, Wm.	149
*Biggers, Wm.	
Butler, Bazel	
Baker, Moses	
Burress, John	
Burress, John Jr.	
Burton, John	

Persons names	Acres land
Bunch, Henry	
Bunch, Clark	
Bunch, Sabia	
Brannam, Tho.	
Bradburn, Frankey	
Bradshaw, James	
Bartlett, Joshua	
Boayers, Henry	
Bogard, James	
Barnet, Jonathen	50
Barnet, Abner	
Burton, John Senr.	150
Bradly, Edw.	90

C

Craig, Robt.	
*Campbell, Duncan	
Crafford, Alxdr.	
*Clark, Bennet	200
*Campbell, John	100
*Coons, Jacob	
Crawford, James	
Colliar, John	
Cooper, Geo.	
Cooper, Henry	100
Coffy, Ambrouse	20
Carter, Wm.	104
Curral, Dudly	
*Crump, Mary	200
Also	1000
Crump, Richd.	
*†Conner, Wm.	
*Colvell, Joseph	400

D

*Davis, Lemark	113
*Downey, Saml.	
*Davis, John	500
Davis, Enock	
Darnal, Cornelous	
Darnal, Henry	
Day, Wm.	50
Darnal, Danl.	
Dowden, Nathnl	
Dobbins, Saml.	
Dobbins, Jas.	
Dunlap, Jas.	
Dewitt, Paul	
Dewitt, Peter	150

194

Persons names	Acres land	Persons names	Acres land
Dewitt, Barnet		Hill, Gabriel	
Dewitt, Henry		Higgins, Wm.	
Dewitt, Martin		Hatten, Jno.	
Dunlavy, Danl.		*Hardwick, Jno. Jnr.	
Dickey, Robt.		Haneline, John	
*Dyer, John		*Hardwick, John Senr.	
		*Hammon, Philip	
E		Hensley, Joseph	
*Ellison, James		Hedge, Mathias	
Ellison, John		*Hodges, John	
East, North		*Hodge, Andw.	
*Elledge, Isaac		Hodge, Hamilton	
		Harper, John	400
F		Harper, Charles	
Fowler, John		*Hadden, Saml.	
*Farrow, Wm.	1000	Hall, Aaron	
Also	300	Hurly, James	150
Also	200	Hanks, John	100
Frakex, Joseph	100	Hanks, Peter Senr.	
Fraim, Wm.	200	*Hanks, Wm.	100
*Fowke, Geo.	782	Homes, John	150
*Fuqua, Jos.	50	Hatheway, Davd.	
*Fuqua, John	100	Hedge, Levy	
Forguson John		Halloway, John	
Fowler, James		*Hodges, William	
Fletcher, John	400		
Finly, John		**I**	
Fursythe, Jacob		Ingland, Stephen	
Faning, John			
Finly, David		**J**	
		*Jones, Wm. Junr.	
G		Jones, Ambrous	
Griffen, Anthony		James, Tobias	
Griffen, Terry		Julin, Stephen	
Griffen, Richd. Senr.	127¼	Johnston, Wm.	
Golden, Wm.		*Jones, Wm. Senr.	
*Gooden, Patrick	217½		
Also	57	**K**	
Gilmore, Jaramiah		Kenady, John	
Griffen, Richd. Jnr.		*Kenady, Merady	
		Keeton, Wm.	
H		Kilbreath, John	
*Hall, Wm.	200	*Kirtley, Beverly	
Hardwick, Geo.	50	Keeton, Isaac	
Hawley, Benjm.		Knox, Moses	
Harlow, Tho.			
Harlow, Susana		**L**	
Hodges, Geo.		Lacy, Moses	50
*Hart, James	46	Lockert, Levy	
*Hart, Wm.		Logan, Davd.	
Harrison, Micajah		Lysle, Henry	

195

Persons names	Acres land	Persons names	Acres land
Lane, Tho.		Also	500
Lee, James		Also	500
		*Poage, James	666
M		Also	250
Morriss, Christo.		Also	190
Morriss, Jacob		Purks, James	
McClunge, Mathew		Paul, Michael	
McDannal, Wm.		*Payne, Jilson	600
McDannal, Jno.	300	Parkhurst, Jno.	
Megary, Danl.		Parish, Benjm.	
Munroe, Arthur		Proctor, Richd.	
Masse, Tho.	128	*Payne, James	
Morriss, Saml.		Preast, Geo.	
Meek, Bazel		*Phelps, Avingdon	
Musset, John	200	*Peaton, Danl.	
McGuire, John			
Megill, James	200	**R**	
Martin, Henry	560	Riggs, Isaac	
*Martin, Ezariah		Rogers, Wm.	
Miller, Elizabeth		*†Roberts, John	220
Means, John		Also	400
Motly, John		Riggs, Greensberry	296
*Metear, William	400	Raibourn, David	
Montgomery, Patrick		Roberts, Edw.	
Miller, John		Rolen, Robt.	
*Morlen (Mortin?), Lucy		Rector, Danl.	100
*McMillen, Jas.	1500	Robeson, Absolam	
Myers, Joseph		*Reamy, Saml.	
		Raiborn, Henry	
N		†Raibourn, Geo.	
Nickles, Geo.		Riden, Wm.	
Nickles, John		Robeson, James	
Nickles, Tho.		Riggs, Silace	
Nickles, Robt.		Riggs, Jas.	
*Nickles Joseph		Riggs, Isaac	
Nickles, Wm.		*Reid, Wm.	400
Neely, James			
Newton, Tho.		**S**	
Nortin, Wm.		†Stewert, John	
		Stevens, Jahue	
O		*Stevens, Tho.	136
OHair, Michael		*Sanford, Henry	
*Owsley, William	118	Sewell, James	
Oxer, Michael		Stoker, Jonathan	
Oxer, Simon		Stoker, Abram	981
Owefield, Elias		Strange, Berry	
		Strange, Stephen	
P		Steeples, Tho.	
*Payne, William	500	Sweet, Jacob	
Also	90		

Persons names	Acres land
Stewert, Joseph	
See, Coonrod	
See, John	
Smith, Wm.	
Smith, John	
Stillwell, John	
Spurgeon, Saml.	
Summers, John	50
Smith, Anthony	
Stevens, John	
*Sanders, Wm.	
Scroggins, Humphrey	
*Smith, Wm.	370

T

Trimble, John	
*Thompkins, Archebal	
Turpen. Wm.	71
Turpen, Isaac	
*Thuston, Ezekeil	
*Treadeway, John	28¾
Tolin, Chas.	150
Tatman, John	100
Thomas, John	
*Turley, Leonerd	
Thompson, James	
*Troutman, Peter	
Thompkins, Jas.	

W

Wilkeson, Drury	
*Wooldridge, William Senr.	
Watts, John	
Wright, Jessy	
Wills, John	1000
Woodruff, Jessey	100
Walker, James	
Webster, William	
*Watson, Saml.	
*Walker, Robt.	
*Wills, Jas.	316
Wells, Wm.	
Wilson, Alexdr.	
Wilson, Moses	
Wilson, Wm.	
Wilson, Andw.	
Wilson, Geo.	
Williams, Danl.	80
*Wilkeson, Moses	150

Persons names	Acres land
Williams, Edw.	787
Woodland, Wm.	
Woodland, Absolam	
Woolf, Andw.	
*Woodward, Chesly Junr.	
*Wren, James	300
Ward, James	
*Wells, John Senr.	100
Wells, Haston	
Wills, Wm.	
Williams, John	
Williams, Mason	

Y

Young, Joseph	200
Yoecum, John	
Yoecum, Geo.	

(total(Amt. of land forwarded

1st	2d	3d	Amt. this
6410	14457	1800	book
			£84 16 4

Town Lotts

Persons names	Acres land
Myers, Jos.	½
Troutman, Peter	11¼
Conner, Wm.	12½
Hoges, Wm.	¼
	Val. T. lotts
	£522
No. Whites above 21	282
Whites above 16 under 21	45
Blacks above 16	97
Total blacks	222
Horses &c.	1027
Ordinary License	5 £15
Retail Stores	1 5
Stud Horses & rates covering	
9 £7	3 0
Town Lotts & their Value	24½ acres
	£524

Montgomery County—Sct.

I do hereby Certify that the a foregoing are a true copy taken from the Vouchers returned to my Office by Joseph Colvill Esquire Commissioner of the Tax for the year 1797. Given under my hand as Clerk

of the County aforesaid this 25th Day of
December 1797

Teste

M. HARRISON, CMC

Note—* slave-holders
   ‡ Ordinary License
   † Retail Stores.

MONTGOMERY COUNTY TAX LISTS—1797—

William Thompson, Commissioner of the
Tax for the Year 1797, Book for the Auditor,
George Madison, Esq.

Persons chargeable with the tax	Acres of land
Alkeah, Jno.	133-
Allen, Jno.	
Almon, Thos.	60-
Allen, Joseph	
Alexander, Jno.	
Alexander, Randolph	
Alexander, Thos.	
Alexander, Jas.	50
Allington, Dud	
Allington, Jonathan	
Ard, John	
Atkinson, Thos.	200
Anderson, Henry	
Adams, Elijah	
Anderson, Robt.	
Armstrong, Robt.	134
" "	2000
*Armstrong, Jas.	134
" "	2000
Alphrey, Jas.	
Archer, Jno.	
Armstrong, Thos.	
Allison, John	
Adin, Thomas	
Allington, Jacob	
Allen, Wm.	
Alexander, Randal	50
Arthur, Wm.	
Allen, Jno.	
*Alexander, David	

B

Bracking, Robt.	
Burcham, Jno.	50

Persons names	Acres land
Barr, Wm.	
Barr, Jas.	
Barrior, Abraham	
Barrior, Richard	
Barrior, Frederic	
Brackenridge, Jas.	
Bracken, Jas.	
Berry, Margaret	
Brinson, David	
Bates, Wm.	
Blan, Alexander	
Brinsley, William	
*Berry, Jas.	
Burcham, Saml'.	196
Battleton, Amor	
Balla, George	250
Brook, Toss (?)	
Butler, Ignatious	
Blackburn, Ben.	
Brown, Andrew	
Byor, Philip	
Butler, Thos.	
Bonard, Hezekiah	
Brown, Moses	
Burnes, Charles	
*Brown, Thos.	1000
" "	300
" "	2000
Balla, Warren	
Bomer, Benjamin	
Brumajim, James (?)	
Barker, Joseph	
Bracken, Matthew	
Briggs, Jno.	
*Berry, George	25
Boid, Wm.	3525
Brown, Quilor	
Brown, Wm.	
Brown, Daniel	
Bridges, Wm.	400
Brown, Jno.	
Butner, Edward	
*Butler, Edw.	
Brothers, Rbt.	
Brothers, Absalom	
*Brown, Jno.	
Bulkhannon, Henry	
Black, Wm. Snr.	
*Black, Ezl.	

198

Persons names	Acres land
Black, Wm. Jnr.	
Butler, Jno.	100
Brooks, Abijiah	1131
Boid, Jno.	
Bengol, David	
Burbridge, Rollen	
Blakeman, Moses	
*Boid, Thos.	
Baldridge, Daniel	
Baldridge, Robt.	
Balla, Robt.	
Balla, Wm.	
Balla, Jno.	
Boid, Richard	
Barnes, Elijah	50
Burton, Allen	59
Burcher, Jas.	
Brown, Robt.	
Brown, Jno.	
Blan, Wm.	110
Barnard, Jas.	
Briant, Anderson	80
Beaty, Daniel	100
Beaty, George	100
Beaty, Jno.	180
Black, Thos.	
Buck, Coonrod	
Black, David	100
Beaver, Coonrod	
Berry, Alexander	
Barry, Jno.	
Batry, Thos.	200
Bennefield, Robt.	
Brinson, Tabulor	
Brown, Jas.	
Butt, Edmond	
Brown, Daniel	
Barnes, Charles	
Becraft, Abraham	
*Brackenridge, Robt.	100
Do	150
Bradshaw, Thos.	150
Blair, Jas.	
Blackburn, Saml.	
Bigs, Andrew	
Barnard, Jno.	

Persons names	Acres land
C	
*Caldwell, Kingcaid	
*Caldwell, Wm.	100
Do	100
Carr, Jas.	
Chism, Elijah	
Cooks, Wilis	75
Craig, Jas.	
Cowgill, Daniel	
Cassaty, Peter	
Caldwell, Jas.	
Cogswell, Jedediah	
Clark, Jno.	
Crockett, Robt.	
Cawhorn, Thos.	
Cooley, Ebenezer	
Cook, Richard	
Cowan, Thos.	
Crooks, Jno.	
*Caldwell, Jno.	
Culberson, Wm.	
Cracraft, Wm.	
Cracraft, Thos.	
Cannon, Newbill	
Cracraft, Wm. Senr.	
*Cartmill, Andrew	
Carrol, Bartley	
Cartmill, Thos.	
Carroll, Andrew	
Canaday, Wm.	
Carrol, Andrew	
Carrol, Jno.	
Cline, Jno.	
Conyghym, Thos.	
Cilgore, Jno.	
Cent, Jno.	
Coshaw, Jno.	
Cox, Jno.	
*Collins, Josiah	100
Do	2000
Do	745
Do	40
Cowhorn, Cornelus	
Cox, John	
Cross, Philip	
Conyear, Isaac	100
Conyear, Matthew	
Cantrol, Joshua	400
Cantrol, Zabulon	

Persons names	Acres land
Connely, Arthur	
Crosse, Michael	
Colliver, Joseph	70
Collins, Dudley	
Caldwell, Jno.	
Cofer, Reuben	
Cheat, Augustean	
Caven, Moses	
Commons, Jno.	
Cassaty, Wm.	
Cassaty, Thos.	
Cassaty, Peter	
Cassaty, Peter Jnr.	
Cassaty, Jno.	
Carpenter, Daniel	
Carpenter, Michael	100
Cassaty, David	100
Coiles, Peter	
Closer, Michael	
Cowhorn, Wm.	
Carrol, Leroy	100
Cassatty, Wm.	100
Clemons, Roger	
Coswell, Jno.	
Combs, Daniel	
Chambers, Alexander	
Clark, Jas.	
Clark, Francis	
Crawford, Jno.	
Cuningham, Jas.	
Carter, Solomon	
Cave, Benjamin	
Cheatam, Leonard	
Clemon, Jno.	
Coons, Jno.	
Coffee, Jas.	
Carr, Wm.	
Cofer, Reuben	
Cutrite, Peter	
*Cowing, Jno.	
Clark, George	
Casteldine, Jno. Snr.	
Castledine, Jno. Jnr.	
Casson, Adam	250
Cockeowing, Jno.	
*& Company	1922
Do	1200
Do	2314

*Owing, John Cockey.

Persons names	Acres land
Do	4000
Do	224
Do	600
D	
Dale, Thos.	
Dick, Abraham	
Downing, Andrew	
Dougherty, Rbt.	
Davis, Harrison	
Davis, Jas. Jur.	
Deskin, Daniel	
Davis, Nathaniel	
Duncan, Isaac	
Davis, Luke	150
Davis, Joseph	
Davis, Isaac	150
Duncan, Isaac	
Davis, Wm.	
*Doggett, Thos.	
*Downing, Jno.	
Dougherty, Wm.	
Davis, Jas.	
Duncan, Andrew	
Donahue, Joseph	
Dedman, Wm.	
*Denne, Saml.	
*Donnelson, Wm.	
Darnald, Jno.	844
Darrnald, Wm.	
Dedman, Saml.	65
Dusdal, Jas.	25
Danald, Reuben	
Darnald, Thos.	
Ditch, Jno.	
Davie, Benjamin	
Daniel, Jno.	
Downing, Jas.	
Downs, Robt.	
Dene, Saml.	
Denne, Jno.	
Dotson, Joseph	
*Davis, Thos.	
Drinkard, Wm.	
Davis, Jno.	
Davis, Benjamin	
Davis, Aron	
Danel, Daniel	
Dun, Daniel	150

Persons names	Acres land
Davis, Jas. Jnr.	
*Davis, Jas. Snr.	300
Dula, Ephriam	
Davie, Henry	

E

Persons names	Acres land
*Elliott, Jno.	
Evens, Wm.	
Evens, Francis	
Evens, Thos.	
Evens, John	
Elliot, Ralph	
England, David	
Eberman, Wm.	
Eberman, Michael	
Eberman, Jacob, Jnr.	
Eberman, Jacob Snr.	
Evens, Richard	
Evens, Jas.	
Elliot, Jas.	
*Ellin, Wm.	200
Elliott, Rich.	
Evens, Jas.	
Ewing, Wm.	
*Ewing, Robt.	

F

Persons names	Acres land
Flemon, Jas.	140
*Fugate, Josiah	300
Do	1000
Forguson, Thos.	
Fuland, Robt.	
Fugate, Randolph	
Forgia, Jno.	
Fletcher, Thos.	
Forgia, Alexander	
Forgia, Hugh	
Frad, Jno.	
Forgusson, Wm.	
Fletcher, Gillison	
Fustad, Anthony	100
Forbis, Hugh	1000
Do	1000
Do	1000
Do	1000
Do	160
Francis, Saml.	
*Fort, Peter	100
Foley, Daniel	
Fitchgarrel, Joseph	

Persons names	Acres land
Fort, Frederic	
Finne, George	
Fletcher, Jilson	

G

Persons names	Acres land
Gattson, Wm.	
Guill, Thos.	
*Gooch, Thos.	500
Guell, George	
Graham, Wm.	
Gragg, Saml.	196
Garrel, Jno.	
Grayson, Jno.	
Goodpasture, Jno.	
Goodpasture, Solomon, Jnr.	
Goodpasture, Solomon, Snr.	
Goodpasture, Abraham	
Goodpasture, Conelus	
Gudgull, Andrew	
Geary, Jas.	
Gammon, Richard	
Gray, Wm.	
Green, Edmond	
Gibson, Saml. Snr.	
Gibson, Saml. Jnr.	
Gibson, Jas.	
Gray, Joseph	
Goodpasture, Isaac	
Gore, John	
*Gore, Benjamin	
Gragg, Saml.	
Gilkinson, Wm.	
Godfrey, Jno.	
Gillaspie, Simon	
Gugil, Jacob	
Graham, Jas.	
Grimes, James	

H

Persons names	Acres land
Headen, Balemus	
Harbenson, Robt.	
Harbenson, Archibald	
How, Saml.	
Herring, Shadwick	
*How, Joseph	
Harrow, Saml.	
Hill, Elizabeth	
Hopkins, Henry	
Hopkins, Francis	
Hopkins, Robt.	

Persons names	Acres land	Persons names	Acres land
Hopkins, Wm,		Hinds, Jas.	
Hopkins, Eldridge		Hendricks, Wm.	50
Hamilton, Elliot		*Higgin, Moses	
*Hamilton, Jno.		*Higgin, Jesson	100
Hostetter, Isaac	100	Hon. Jones	
Do	118	Hunt, Thos.	
Hendricks, Jacob		Herring, Sarah	
Hendricks, Absalom		Hedes, Enoch	
Hendricks, Noah		Hood, Luk	
Haskings, Gregory, farmer,	72	*Higgin, Wm.	318
Haskings, Jno.		Do	250
Haskings, Jas.		Do	100
Hayslet, Wm.		Higgin, Jas.	
Haysler, Jas.		Hamilton, Saml.	
Hendricks, Enoch		*Higgin, Jno.	100
Hendricks, George		Herring, Wm.	
Hunt, Thanz (?)		Hansley, Davis	
Hackings, Thos.		Hansford, Henry	
Hoga, Jno.		Hays, Jeremiah	
Huke, Wm.		Harper, Jas.	
Hendricks, Nimrod		Harper, Betty	400
*Hamilton, Abner		Hening, Sarah	
Hendron, Taylor		Harper, Thos.	
Hutton, Alexander		Helms, Peter	
Horton, George	59	Harmon, Jno.	
Harrow, Jas.	200	Herreford, Andrew	
Hickman, Mary		Herreford, Jas.	
Hunter, Margaret		Herreford, Jno.	
Hening, Daniel		Hedrick, Jacob	
Hill, Joseph		*Harthorn, Jas.	
Henton, Thos. Snr.		Henry, Moses	
Hinton, Joseph		Henderson, Jno.	
Henton, Thos. Jnr.		Heaton, Jno.	
Harlow, Michael		Hendron, Nimrod	
Harris, Wm.			
Hill, James		**I**	
Hews, David	250	Iles, Thos.	
Do	400	Ingrim, Uriah	
Do	700	**J**	
Hamilton, Jno.		Jones, Cad	60
Hank, Peter		*Jones, Thos. Jnr.	
Hamilton, Archibald		Jones, Frank	
Hansford, Wm.		*Jones, Thos. Snr.	
Hews, Jas.		Jones, Benjamin	
Hatherway, Philip		Jones, Jas.	
*Hatherway, Johnathan		Jarobus, Thos.	
Hendron, Jnó.		Jeffrey, Joseph	
Holmes. David		*Jameson, Jno.	500
Hackett, Nellson		Jerrel, Jno.	

Persons names	Acres land	Persons names	Acres land
Judah, Winepush		Lindsey, George	705
Johnston, David		Luvet, Wm.	
Jones, Charles		Luvet, Thos.	
Jones, Thos.		Luvet, David	
Judah, Jno.	200	Luvet, Nancy	
Jameson, Thos.	2030	Luvet, Ignatious	
*Jameson, Jas.		Lemons, David	
Jeffreys, Henry	190	Logan, Wm.	
Jenkins, Jno.		Lamasters, Benjamin	
Julin, Stephen		Lasey, Jas.	
Johnston, Andrew		*Lasey, Wm.	
Johnston, Jno.		Likings, Isaac	
Jenkins, Elijah		Lamasters, Richard	
James, Benjamin		Luwherge, Jas.	
Jones, Benjamin		Lamasters, Richard	
Jones, Abigail		Liviston, Henry	
Jarrel, Walter	60	Litton, Calib	100
Julin, Stephen		Linch, Danniel	
Jenkins, Wm.	34	Lamasters, Coonrod	
Jackes, John			

K

Kingcaid, David			
Kehley, Daniel			
*Knox, Jas.			
King, Joseph			
*Kingcaid, Jno.	150		
King, Joseph			
King, Jeremiah	244		
Kelly, Thos.			
*Kirk, Alexander			
Kehely, Jno.			
Kays, Jno.			

M

Mola, Joseph	75
Mcdowel, Rbt.	
Mitchell, Jno. Jnr.	
Mitchell, Thos.	
Mitchell, Rbt.	
Mulany, Wm.	
Marberry, Lewis	
Marberry, Joel	
Massey, Catherine	
McHenry, Jas.	
Mafarsen, Jesse	
Mccullum, Jno.	
Mcclanahan, Jas.	
Moffet, Wm.	100
McBride, Peter	
*Magary, Robt.	100
Mulberry, Jno.	
McClure, Jean	
Morrow, Rbt.	120
Mounts, Jno.	
*Moore, Rbt.	
McEntire, Alexander	500
Magary, Daniel	
*McMullen, Jno.	
Mcclure, Thos.	200
Murphy, Ralph	
Morrel, Thos.	
Montgomery, Thos.	

L

Linagar, Jesson	
Linagar, Wm.	
Lessoherage, Jno. (Lockridge?)	300
Lane, Jno.	
Langston, Jacob, Snr.	
Langston, Isaac	
Langston, Jacob, Jnr.	
Lion, Thos.	
Lonsdale, Wm.	
*Lane, Jas.	105
Lancaster, Joseph	50
Lancaster, Jno.	
*Love, Elizabeth	100
Lisle, Jno.	100
Little, Nathaniel	

Persons names	Acres land	Persons names	Acres land
Mulane, Wm.		*Marshall, Jno.	
Musselman, Henry		Moore, Thos.	
McChaney, Jas.	150	Martin, Janaway	
Mappin, Jno.		Moses, Edward	
Morgan, William		Montgomery, Jos.	
Mcglockling, Neal		Montgomery, Jas.	
Mcglocking, Jno. Snr.		Montgomery, Saml.	
Mcglocking, Jno. Jnr.		McEntosh, Anguish	
Mcglockling, Hugh		Moore, Joseph	
Mcquem, Thos.		Miller, George	
Murray Phenie		Miller, Jacob	100
Martin, Russel		McClelland, Alexander	
Mccorman, Jas.		Moore, Thos.	
Mitchell, Jno. Snr.		May, Nicholas	
Mccorman, Wm.		Mounts, Jno.	
Mennefee, Richard		Mcclure, Thos.	
Mounts, Jno.		Munroy, Jno.	
Mockabee, Jno.		Morgan, Ralph	
Mulane, Jno.		Monday, Saml.	
Mcgyre, Jno.	90¾	Miyear, Wm.	
Mccarty, Jno.		Miyear, Joseph	
Montgomery, Thos. Snr.	652	McCullah, Jno.	
Montgomery, Jos.		Mcdows, Jas.	
Montgomery, Thos. Jnr.		McHugh, Wm.	
Montgomery, Isaac		Murtin, Charles	
Mumly, Jas.		Mosess, Moses	
†McClintic, Wm.		McEntosh, Jno.	
McNabb, Jno.		Moore, Quinton	200
Miller, Rbt.		Do	50
McDugle, Rbt.		McVeters, Daniel	300
McEntire, Jno.	600	Morriss, John	
Do	566½	Mappin, Jas. Jnr.	
Do	100	Mappin, Jas. Snr.	100
Do	200		
Do	23	**N**	
Do	750	Nelson, Saml.	
Do	107	Nailer, George	300
Do	250	Norris, Jno.	
Do	500	*Nicholas, George	17000
Do	100	Do	3300
McDaniel, Ruben	200	Do	1000
McDaniel, John		Do	1500
Martin, Sarah		Do	1500
Milton, Thos.		Do	1000
Maguha, Wm.		Do	5000
Mason, Pleasant	53	Do	8000
*Meyear, Henry, Jnr.	300	Do	1500
Meyear, Henry Snr.		Do	2500
Marshall, Hubbet		Do	5000

Persons names	Acres land	Persons names	Acres land
Do	200	Do	2000
Do	75	Do	2000
Do	4500	Do	1000
Do	4,000	Do	1000
Do	3000	Do	1000
Do	250	Do	365
Do	100	Do	2113½
Do	1000	Do	304
Do	30	Do	450
Do	500	Do	2000
Do	500	Do	2000
Do	320	Do	550
Do	4639	Do	1000
Do	4000	Do	4093
Do	1225	Do	500
Do	800	Do	6000
Do	8000	Do	600
Do	3030	Norris, Jacob	
Nicholas, George & Breckinridge	5000	Noble, Jno.	
Do	2000	Nelson, Wm.	
Do	800	Norton, David	
Do	3000	Nelson, Thos.	
Do	666⅔	Newkirk, Elias	

O

Persons names	Acres land
Do	300
Do	1500
Do	666⅔
Do	4800
Do	250
Do	500
Do	1000
Do	500
Do	500
Do	565
Do	237
Do	1000
Do	40
Do	800
Do	1000
Do	3550
Do	1125
Do	3647
Do	7500
Do	8000
Do	5000
Do	2500
Do	2750
Do	9531
Do	1715
Do	5662

Persons names	Acres land
Owing, Joshua	100
Oxford, Jno.	
Owing, Joshua	
Osburn, Wm.	
Okely, Edmond	
Okely, Wm.	119
Okely, Christopher	116¼
Okely, Pleasent	
Okely, Thos.	
Offill, Elzaphen	
Offill, Samuel	
Oberturf, Martin	
Owings, Ely	
Offill, Jno.	
Oden, Thos.	
Owings, Nathan	200

P

Persons names	Acres land
Patton, Jas.	100
Parson, Jno.	
Prater, Jas.	100
Peter, Jonathan	
Poore, Jeremiah	
Paine, Warfare (?)	
Parker, Edward	

Persons names	Acres land	Persons names	Acres land
Purvis, Wm. Jnr.		Robinson, Wm.	300
Purvis, Wm. Snr.		Rhea, Alexander	100
Philson, Jas.		Rhea, Elizabeth	
Pick, George		*Robinson, Jno.	200
Peyton, Henry	250	Richardson, Jonathan	
Poore, Jeremiah	315	Reeds, Wm.	
*Parrish, Joseph		*Rolls, Nathaniel	
Paul, Michael		Routt, George	
Pritchett, Philip		Rosebrough, Wm.	
Poor, Holloway		Rosebrough, Jas.	
Pratt, Zapheniah		Roger, Wm.	175
*Patton, Robt.		*Roger, Jas.	350
Patton, Jno.		Roger, Saml.	
Patton, Joseph		Ryon, George	
Pebler, Frederic		Rifle, David	
Plick, Jno.		Ringgo, Cornelius	
Price, Thos.		Rouds, David	
Pritchett, Jno.		Robinson, Ben.	160
Pibler, Michal		Rader, David	
Pibler, Peter		Reeves, Joseph	
Pyle, Nicholas		Roberts, Phillip	
Pyle, Wm. Jnr.		Radcliff, Stephen	1000
Pyle, Wm. Snr.		*Riddle, Wm.	96
Pyret, Allentine		Ramsey, Rbt.	
Pervis, Wm. Jnr.		Rogers, Jno.	
Pervis, Wm. Snr.		Ramsey, Wm.	
Parish, Benjamin		Rhoads, Jacob	
Paterson, Thos.		Ramsey, Saml.	
Pyle, Jno.		Rease, Jno.	
Parker, Ezl.		Reake, Wiett	
Pierce, Jno.		Richards, Robt.	
Phemous, Saml.		Richards, Josiah	
Parsons, Ezl.		Richards, Wm.	
Price, Lewis		Richards, Juley	
Phebous, Saml.		Remer, David	
		Rogers, Patrick	
R		Rafferty, Jas.	
Roberts, Jno.	128	Railes, Wm.	
Do	200	Relley, Thos.	
Do	100	*Ramey, Jno.	213
Do	97	Roger, Stephen	
Roberts, Edw.		*Roger, Wm.	100
Ringgo, Saml.		Rue, Henry	
Ringgo, W. Jr.		Reyburn, Ralph	
Ringgo, Joseph		Rice, Joseph	
*Ringgo, Peter	1000	Rice, Jas.	
Ringgo, Henry		Reyburn, Wm.	40
Robinson, Hugh		Reyburn, Wm.	
Ross, Jno.		Riblen, Wm.	350

Persons names	Acres land	Persons names	Acres land
Rogers, Thos.		*Somers, Elijah	60
Rogers, Joseph		Steel, Laurence	50
Rook, Patrick		Steel, Rbt.	
Rock, Jno.		Simpson, Jno.	
*Radcliff, Zapheniah		Smith, Enoch	
		Do	500
S		Do	1000
Shulse, Joseph		Do	500
Sharp, Moses	162	Do	500
Do	150	Do	800
Soseby, Dnl.	100	Do	500
Soseby, Thos		Singhorse, George	
Stogsdell, Veachel	100	Stodgdill, Ben.	
Smith, Walter		Sinclair, Job.	
Somers, Jno.		Simpson, Joseph	200
*Sutherland, And.		Somers, Jno.	600
Stewart, Jas.		Smith, Enoch	
Sharp. Robt.		Smith, Henry	
*Stafford, Wm.	75	Stephen, Elijah	
Stafford, Henry		Smith, Jno.	
Sire, Jno.	330	Swim, Moses	23½
Snediger, Isaac		Saftly, Jno.	
Snediger, Moses		Smith, Jno.	
Sprout, Jno.		Skidmore, Joseph	
*Stone, Richard	400	Stephens, Ben	
Sarrency, Caml.	100	Shastean, Jesson	
Sarrency, Jacob		Shastean, Jas.	
Sarrency, David		Stewart, David	100
Shavers, George		Sample, George	
Smith, Michael		Sidner, Laurence	
Steel, Jacob		Scott, John	
Swin, Alexander	501	Shawver, Peter	
Sanklin, Andw		Stewart, Ben.	
Smith, Jas.		Sample, George	
Skidmore, Saml.	400	Smith, Jno.	
Shrout, Peter		Stephenson, Elijah	
Shook, David		Smith, Americah	
Shout, Edw.		Skinner, Jonathan	200
Smith, Patrick		Smallwood, Been	
Steel, Jno.		Swift, Wm.	
Shulie, Christean			
Shulse, Henry		**T**	
Story, Jno.		Tarrel, Jno.	
Stott, Adam		Thornton, Wm.	
Switzer, Abm.		Thompson, George	700
Smith, Peter		Turner, George	
Sanson, Elizabeth		Thomas, Saml.	
Steel, Jno.		*Thompson, George	125
Stean, Edw.			

Persons names	Acres land
Do	100
Trimble, Jas.	
Thompson, Dvd.	
Thomas, Joel	
Titsworth, Ben	
Titsworth, Jas.	
Tompson, Isaac	
Thompson, Francis	
Titsworth, Margaret	
Trocksell, Adam	
Trocksell, Jno.	
Trocksell, Frederic	
Trocksell, David	
Trumbow, Jacob	
Trumbow, Jno.	
Trumbow, Jacob	
Taylor, Joseph	
Taylor, Edmond	
*Tolbert, Isham	300
Do	3000
Do	1272
Tanner, George	
Thompson, Lewis	
Trotter, Christopher	
Thompson, Jno.	
Thompson, Thos.	
Tap, Jno.	107
Trimble, David	
Tipton, Thos.	
Turner, Jos. Snr.	
Turner, Jos. Jnr.	100
Turner, Wm.	50
Turner, Thos.	
Trotter, Dick	17
Tackett, Jno.	
*Turley, Jas.	100
Thompson, Joseph	
Turguire, Moses	
Taylor, Frank	
Thomson, William	184

U

Underwood, Reuben	
Underwood, Jehue	

V

Vinson, Wm.	
Veneton, Abm.	
Veneton, Isaac	

Persons names	Acres land
Varson, Daniel	
Vinson, Daniel	

W

Willson, Jas.	
Woolsey, George	
Wilkinson David	
Walden, Ben	
Walls, Christophel	200
Whitecraft, Jno.	150
Wood, Jno.	
Williams, Joseph	
Wick, Moses	
Williams, Philip	
Williams, Thos.	
Williams, Nathaniel	
Wright, Jas.	
Williams, Philip	
Willson, Joseph	
Willson, Uriah	
Willson, Thos.	
Willson, Jeremiah	1000
Do	100
Williams, Frederic	
Westner, George	
West, John	
Warfield, Calep	
Walter, Peter	
Warner, Jacob	
Williams, David	
*Warrick, Jacob	
Warren, Jno.	
Williams, Henry	
Willson, Uriah, Snr.	
*Wilcox, David	100
Wood, Rbt.	
Ward, Jas.	
Ward, Wm.	
Wood, Malcam	
Williams, Jno.	
Ward, Washington	
*Wiett, Frank	300
Warmsley, Thos.	
Warmsley, Wm.	
Wools, Philip	
West, Jonathan	
Woodard, Saml.	
Watson, Wm.	

Persons names	Acres land	Persons names	Acres land
Watson, Jacob		Young, Wm.	
*Watson, Saml.		York, Ezekiel	
Watson, Jas.		York, Charles	
*Williams, Rolley	100	Yates, Wm.	
Wiett, Thos.		*Yates, Joshua, Snr.	300
Waid, Dawson	89	Do	200
Waid, Joseph		Yates, Joshua	26
Watson, Eseriah		Yokeam, George	
Wills, Jno.		Yokeam, Jno.	
Wimer, John		Yokeam, Wm.	
Wayne, Ephriam		Yokeam, Frank	
Waid, Dawson, Jnr.	60	Yarbrough, Jno.	390
Wallace, Olliver			
White, Charles			
White, Jno. Snr.			
White, Jno. Jnr.			
Willson, Wm.			
Weagle, Jacob			
Welch, Thos.			
Waid, Jas.			
White, Jno.			

Y

Yardley, Wm.	200		
Young, Ephriam			

Montgomery County, Sct.

I do hereby Certify that the Aforegoing are a true copy taken from the Vouchers returned to my office by William Thompson, Gent. Commissioner of the tax for the year 1797. Given under my hand as Clerk of the County Aforesaid this 3d day of November 1797.   M. HARRISON.

NELSON COUNTY TAX LISTS—1792

An Act for dividing the county of Jefferson into two distinct counties—

"Be it enacted by the General Assembly, That from and after the first day of January next, the county of Jefferson shall be divided into two distinct counties by Salt river; and that part of the said county lying south of the said river shall be called and known by the name of Nelson, and all the residue of the said county shall be and retain the name of Jefferson. That a court for the said county shall be held by the justices * * * to be named * * to meet at Beardstown, in the said county, * * * and fix upon a place for holding courts * * and thenceforth the said court shall proceed to erect the necessary public buildings at such place, and until such buildings be completed, to appoint any place for holding courts they shall think proper. * * *

"Section III—*That it be further enacted,* That the value of the courthouse and other public buildings in the said county of Jefferson shall on or before the first day of January next, be ascertained and fixed by William Pope, George Slaughter, Philip Barbour, William Oldham, Isaac Cox, Andrew Hinds and Benjamin Pope or any four of them, who shall make return * * of such valuation to each of the courts of the said counties of Jefferson and Nelson; and the court of the said county of Jefferson shall within twelve months after the return is made, levy on the tithables in their county, and pay to the court of the said county of Nelson, the proportion of such valuation, according to the number of tithables in that part of said county of Jefferson at the time the expence of the said buildings was levied by the court of the said county of Jefferson. * *

"October, 1784."

See Henning's Statutes at Large, Vol. II, pages 468-69.

It is to be regretted that the earliest Tax Lists of Nelson County which have been found by the Historical Society are for the year 1792, eight years after the county was formed, but it is believed that those here presented cover all of the original territory included in Nelson except that part which was cut off for the county of Washington in June, 1792. Hardin county was formed under an Act passed November, 1792, *after* the list below was taken, and this latter Act did not become effective until February, 1793.

The territory covered by these lists and that covered by the lists of Washington County tithables (published in the January number) cover the whole of the original Nelson County.

A LIST OF THE TAXABLE PROPERTY TAKEN IN NELSON COUNTY BY BENJ. FRYE

I do hereby certify that the following list of Taxable property is a true copy of an original list filed in my office by Benj. Frye, Gent, of the Commissioners of the Tax for the County of Nelson.

Given under my hand this 5th day of
January, 1793.

(Signed) BEN. GRAYSON, Co. Cl.

Persons names	Acres land
Able, Edmund	150
Adams, John	50
Aden, Henry	
Able, William	500
Andrews, Willm.	100
Allen, Benjm.	125
Allen, David	
Adams, M. Sam	400
Ambrose, Jacob	768
Allon, William	100
Able, George	91
Atherington, Peter	134
Atherington, Moses	
Atherington, Benjn.	66
Atherington, Arong	100
Atherington, Aren	
Ashby, Thomson	150

B.

Black, Charles	
Bull, Thomas	880
Bunch, Lenard	347½
Brown, James	300
Brashear, Nary (?)	126¾
Boyce, Joseph	
Bozoth, Jonathan	
Brown, James	125
Black, Anderson	
Bohs, Ignatius	140
Brown, Robert	
Baird, James	300
Brady, Morris	1200
Braden, Robert	
Briggs, Thomson	
Briggs, William	169½
Blackburn, Isaac	
Blackburn, David	
Baird, James, Jr.	200
Ballard, Proctor	300
Bland, Osten (?)	100
Brown, Jereboam	150
Brewer, Peter	
Belew, John	
Borman, Jewit	
Borman, Willm.	208
Burney, Willm.	

Persons names	Acres land
Bray, Henry	450
Bray, John	
Bray, Peter	
Bray, Willm.	
Black, Sarah	
Bird, Edward	65
Bringle, Christian	
Brihmer (?) Jacob	325
Briant, Frank	
Barnet, Thomas	49
Burns, Micheal	125
Brown, James	300
Beall, Walter, Jr.	
Brown, John	
Bethell, Willm.	200
Bealer, Cristopher	200
Brooks, James	600
*Beall, Walter	
Briant, Alexander	
Burnet, John	456
Baird, Mary	

C

Cowen, M. Elexr.	
Chinwoth, Willm.	1021½
Caldwell, James	200
Clark, David	
Coxen, W. Leven	650
Clark, Mary	
Crepps, Elisah.	200
**Clure, Mc. Willm.	
Cuntryman, Henry	282
Chambers, James	
Cuntryman, Jacob	
Crew, Henry	
Carley, Mc. Isaac	232
Clements, John	108¾
Caster, Elisabeth	
Cremer, John	72
Caster, James	
Caster, Shedrick	300
Craven, John	200
Cissel, Ignatius	80
Cissel, Joseph	
CayMc, John	50
CayMc, Daniel	150

*Retail store.
**Evidently intended for Wm. McClure.
The same form was use for McCarley, Mc-
Clay, McDaniel, McGomery, etc.

Persons names	Acres land	Persons names	Acres land
Crutcher, Thos.	300	Cochren, James	
Cotten, Ralph		Collard, Joseph	350
Cleaver, Willm.	259	Crew, John	
Connay, John	112		

D

Cissel, Peter		Dewit, Zachariah	
Camren, M. James	100	Davis, Joshua	300
Carns, Barshaba	114	Dorsey, Charles	
Craven, Jerimiah	100	Davis, John	80
Coventree, Willm.	100	Dorherty, Richd.	108
Clane Mc, Willm.		Donohoo, John	100
Clark, Thos.		Daley, John	
Carter, Mesheck	400	Dorsey, Beall	112½
Carter, Joseph		Denny, Willm.	
ClaneMc, John	50	Devers, Henry	340
Cox, Gabriel	450	Downs, Jonathan	50
Cravens, James	200	Devers, Thos.	
Crutcher, James	100	Devers, Richd.	
Carter, Ben	300	Dorson, John	50
Clark, John	200	Ditch, Jonathan	
Clark, Joseph	87	Dacon, James	100
Claton, Joseph		Doherty, James	300
Calhoon, George	1070	Davis, John	1050
Clark, Margaret		Dewit, Elisha	
Collard, Elijah		Dewit, James	
Cleaver, Benjn.	100	Dunn, Veneer	
Camren, John	220	Daniels Mc. Elexr.	
Clark, Wilford		Duncan, John	200
Clark, Richd.			

E

Campbell, Michel	483	Esrey, (?) John	400
Cleaver, David		Erwin, John	230
Coy, Daniel		Evans, Josiah	
Chambers, Hymeas		Eaglin, Willm.	
Cotton, Nathaniel	320	Eaglin, Richd.	
Calvin, James			

F.

Calvin, John		Foster, Anthony	482½
Colvin, Luke		Floyd, John	300
Carnahan, Adam		Floyd, Nathaniel	
Clifton, Samuel		Foster, Robert	200
Coy, William		Funk, Martin	
Chamberlen, Anthony	180	Finley, Rubin	
Carter, Nicholas	200	French, Joseph	
Culver, Jonathan	70	French, Raphel	50
Crooks, James	300	French, Ignatius	150
Cotton, Willm.		Finch, John	65
Carnahan, John		Floyd, Henry, Jr.	
Crutcher, John		Floyd, Henry	200
Cleaver, Willm., Jr.	212	Foushe, Daniel	103
Cavner, Gerrit	40	Fowler, Benjn.	
Cleaver, Stephen			

212

Persons names	Acres land	Persons names	Acres land
G		Hill, Atkinson	250
Grabel, David	200	Hayes, Bennet	220
Gour, (?) Laurence	150	Hagen, Clement	
Gray, David	50	Huchens, John	
Gardain, Henry		Honeyman, Stephen	
Graham, John		Harris, Thos.	
Glase, Adam	375	Hoback, Anderson	
Green, Benjamin	50	Hoback, Volentine	
Gobel, Benjn.	180	Hoback, Anderson, Jr.,	
Gristy, Clements	50	Hoback, Isaac	
Grinnel, Jeremiah	70	Hoback, Micheal	
Garner, Richd	40	Hanks, Willm.	
GomeryMc, Basel	68½	Hanks, Joseph	150
Grinnel, Joshua	130	Hill, John B.	300
Grinnel, Arnel	60	Head, Cuthbert	300
Gobb, Samuel		Hill, Willm.	103
Grayson, Benjn.		Hagen, Edward	300
Gatch, Fredrick	100	Hagen, Walter	
Gilky, Willm.	175	Hagen, Ignacius	170
Gilky, John	779	Haden, Henry	
Gray, James	300	Haden, Willm.	150
		Haustings, Charles	
H		Harris, James	
Hall, Mary		Houstown, John	160
Harris, Isaac		Hays, Joseph	
Hatfield, John	150	Hatfield, Jonas	100
Hatfield, Thos.		Hicks, James	42
Hatfield, Edward		Hunter, John	50
Hahn, Peeter		Hubbard, Ephraim	
Howard, Thos.		Harrison, Cuthbert	4153
Hines, Thos.	2000	**J**	
Harned, Jonathan	100	Jefferies, Moses	325
Harned, Edward		Jackson, John	150
Harned, Innes	200	Johnson, Ephraim	100
Hammelton, James	100	Jefferies, Joseph	100
Harned, Willm.	120	Johnson, Jeddiah	100
Harned, Jonathan, Jr.	100	Johnson, Ezekiel	
Hufman, Aaron		Jones, John	
Hinton, Samuel	200	Jackson, John	
Hobbs, Joshua	375	Jones, Saml. P.	
Holmes, William	30	Johnson, Elexander	346½
Hook, Benedick		Johnson, Robert	
Harrison, George	735	Johnson, Thos.	
Harrel, Caleb		Johnson, Peeter	50
Hackley, James	244	Jarboe, Joseph	
Heroild, Chester		Jarboe, T. Jesse	
Herald, James		Jee, Jesse	100
Hart, Himy	300	Johnson, Leonard	206½
Harden, James		Jarboe, John	

Persons names	Acres land	Persons names	Acres land
K		Morten, Saml.	
King, Wuthers	900	Montgomery, Sam.	
Kennedy, John	875	Morten, Richd.	3815
Kester, Willm.	180	Martin, Edward	125
Kester, Willm., Jr.		Miles, Seth	
Kester, John		Mattingly, Joseph	100
Keith, Elexander	100	Milligen, Will	50
Kindle, Benjn.		Morehead, Charles	425
Keith, Willm.	200	Merrifeild, Thos.	
Kennedy, Charles	325	Miller, Charles	100
Kelly, William	50	Mattingly, Baxter	
Kelly, John	200	Mattingly, Richd.	
Kester, Paul		Mills, John	50
Kindle, William		Mills, Elizabeth	
Kyser, Henry		Medcalf, James	
King, John		Millender, David	
King, Cornelius	222	Mosterson, Thos.	
Kindle, Worden		Mosterson, Willm.	
King, George		Mosterson, Willm. Jr.	
King, Peeter	100	Masterson, John Jr.	152
KinsayMc, Enoch	225	Masterson, Hugh	
KimMc, William	100	Mills, Ethelbert	
		Macatee, Leonard	
L		Miles, Edward	
Lamb, Fredrick		Morgan, Charles	
Lowe, Richard	100	Masterson, Hugh, Jr.	
Luie, Abner	588	Masterson, Jerry	250
Lincoln, Hannaniah		Miles, Henry	132
Luie, William		Melton, John	225
Luie, David	171	Macatee, Thos.	150
Lasby, Solomon		Medcalf, Ignatius	50
Latham, Richd.	627	Miller, Ebineser	200
Langley, Thos.		Masterson, John	
Latham, James		Masterson, Zack	
Lasby, Benjn.	150	Miller, Jacob	
Lewis, Bijah		Millender, Caty	
Lowney, Thos.		Masterson, Charles	400
Lonsdale, Isaac	455	Merriman, Zachah.	380
Lemon, John	435	Mayo, Joseph	
Lee, David		Mattingly, Phillip	25
Lee, William	225	Morrison, Isaac	
Lee, Willm., Jr.		Merry, Calvin	
Leonard, James		**N**	
Lewis, John	120	Neel, Samuel	200
Lee, Josiah	540	Neuman, Thos.	750
Lineh, Charles	400	Neal, Briant	200
Laird, John		Norris, Henry	
Laird, Ezekiah		Norris, Phillip	
Lee, John		Norris, Rodolph	140
Lewis, Joseph	28622½		

214

Persons names	Acres land	Persons names	Acres land
Napper, Willm.		Rogers, James	1000
Neel Mc, John		Ruby, Asa	130
Nobb, Widow		Rogers, Mathew, Jr.	83
O		Rogers, Mathew	300
Ormsby, W. John		Reed, George	300
Owen, William	475	Robertson, John	
Ormsby, Stephen		Robertson, George	100
P		Rogers, William	
Pound, Thos.	100	Rapier, J. Richd.	743
Phillips, Sam.	180	Read, William	33
Panley, John		Roberts, Thos.	
Pursley, Thos.	400	Richey, John	460
Prior, Simon		Reed, John	400
Parker, Richd.		Ross, John	100
Pursley, James		Reede, Asher	
Potinger, Sam., Jr.	100	Reid, Phillip	
Patent, Daniel	100	Roberts, Willm.	
Pee, Jacob		Ross, Joseph	150
Pairgmint, (?) Sarah		Reed, Joseph	200
Potinger, Saml.	1000	**S**	
Phillips, John	250	Sweets, Thos.	
Peek, Canellem	100	Sandress, Joseph	
Peek, Francis	50	Slater, John	
Pike, Archible	50	Samuels, Willm.	
Pater (or Paten), Elisha	100	Stigler, Samuel	150
Pennebaker, Peeter		Stroodes, Willm.	
Pursley, Dennis		Spriggs, Levin	100
Pursell, Edmund		Smith, James	
Parker, James		Shafer, Jacob	300
Pain, Frank	100	Summers, B. Will	
Prutsman, John	100	Stephens, James	100
Price, Edward		Strange, Phillip	
Pickrell, Willm.		Stewart, Willm.	
Paten, Elias		Samuel, James	189
Q		Shields, John	100
Quirk, John	200	Shehan, Bostain	
Quirk, Henry		Slaughter, Frank	525
Quirk, Tunas	200	Slaughter, Thos.	
Quirk, Andoen		Snider, John	100
R		Snider, Samuel	
Ricketson, Timothy		Settle, Joseph	
*Rhea, John		Stephens, Solom.	
Rowan, Willm.		Stewart, Charles	
Rychey, John		Seals (or Scales), John	50
Rickets, Peeter		Shannasa, Willm.	
Runner, Micheal	132	Stallens, Samuel	
		Shaw, John	165
*Retail Store.		Sutherlin, John	1105
		Snauter, Thos.	25

Persons names	Acres land
Storm, John	
Smith, John	
Smith, Charles	
Scott, Daniel	
Scott, Willm.	300
Scaggs, Mary	200
Scaggs, Jeremiah	
Smith, Laurence	228¾
Stidger, Peeter	
Shepherd, Adam	1400
Shain, Frank	200
Smyth, Samuel	400
Shain, William	
Slaughter, James	

T

Persons names	Acres land
Teets, Michael	
Turner, Joseph	
Turner, Matthew	
Turner, Denham (?)	
Townsend, Samuel	
Thomas, Isaac	48
Taylor, Thos.	50
Tibbs, Joseph	
Thomson, Athanatius	100
Tucker, Peeter	
Trasy, Rasamus	
Taylor, Benj.	
Tanneyhill, Sarah	
Thomas, James	
Thomson, Robert	
Tucker, Joseph	250

U

Persons names	Acres land
Urie, Zachariah	

V

Persons names	Acres land
VayMc, John	200
Vittiton, Saml.	170
VayMc, John, Jr.	200
Vittiton, Stephen	170
Vessels, James	100
Vowels, John	200

W

Persons names	Acres land
Wheatley, Thos.	
Willson, Daniel	50
Worth, Richd.	
Wiseman, John	400
Williams, Evan	300

Persons names	Acres land
Willson, John	30
Watson, Richd.	50
White, Andrew	100
Winfield, Jonah	
Wood, John	
Woods, J. John	
Willson, Willm.	100
Williams, Thomas	
Walker, Henry	
Withrow, James	
Withrow, John	
Willet, George	
Willet, James	
Willet, William	300
Willet, Samuel	400
Wathen, Jeremiah	
Williams, Edward	300
West, Nicholas	
Wimset, Ignatius	60
Willcox, William	310
Willcox, Ezra	
Williams, Noah	
Williams, Thos.	

Y

Persons names	Acres land
Yocum, Jacob	
Younger, Kinnard	
Yasel, David	
Yocum, Matthias	
Younger, Henry	72

Whole amount of list brought forward.

Whites above 21	Whites	Total Blacks.	Blacks.	Horses	Cattle	Land
564	88	398	207	1,378	3,922	95,386
	4	7	8			
561						
565	95	413	221	1,453	4,193	101,824

(Signed) BENJN. FRYE, C. T.

216

A LIST OF TAXABLE PROPERTY
WITHIN THE DISTRICT OF
GABRIEL COX
COMMISSIONER IN THE COUNTY OF
NELSON FOR THE YEAR 1792

Name	A	Acres
Anderson, Jeremiah		200
Asby, Stephen		20
Ash, John		82
Ash, Ruben		45
Applegate, Stacy		
Applegate, Samuel		
Anderson, Sus'nah		
Anderson, John		
Ash, Joseph		
Andrews, Isaac		75
Arnold, Richard		75
Arnold, Charles		86
Anderson, William		100
Anderson, James		
Allen, William		100
Allen, James		40
Adams, James		897
Anderson, William		100
Anderson, James		
Anderson, Robert		
Adams, William		
Adams, Elisha		
Adams, William		
Allen, James		600

Name	B	Acres
Bland, David		166
Brown, Samuel		200
Brown, Nathaniel		300
Bland, John		
Bowls, James		
Barker, Aaron		116
Bennet, John		
Bennet, William		
Brown, John		50
Brown, Johnson		100
Brown, Samuel		100
Bell, John		200
Burch, Christopher		
Brown, John		200
Brown, Joseph		50
Barker, Thomas		40
Bidwell, Daniel		30
Batman, John		45
Brewer, George		100

Name	Acres
Brewer, Charles	
Brewer, Thomas	
Bennet, Joshua	100
Bennet, John	100
Basey, William	
Basey, Richard	72
Bennet, Thomas	
Bailey, Silas	
Bennet, John	150
Bennet, Daniel	
Bridgwaters, Samuel	
Baird, William	65
Baird, Alexander	50
Bridgewaters, Leve	50
Best, Cornelius	
Boulderback, Jacob	50
Briggs, John	
Berry, Enoch	100
Berry, George	105
Berry, William	150
Bruce, William	200
Bruce, Turner, Jnr.	200
Briscoe, Walter	200
Brown, John	
Brown, Walter	
Briscoe, Parminus	400
Blue, Uriah	
Bland, John, Jnr.	375
Bland, William	100
Bland, Samuel	120
Bane, Thomas	250
Barker, Robert	
Bye, John	
Bruce, George	75
Burket, William	102
Bell, John	600
Buky, Rudolphus	
Bogard, Cornelius	
Butcher, Henry	
Bowen, Sutliff	
Bruce, James	88
Burk, Thomas	
Bushart, Jacob	
Brockham, Will	
Burkot, Abraham	
Burket, Eliazer	100
Batsel, John	107
Bane, Joseph	

Name	C	Acres
Conner, Richard		200

Name	Acres	Name	Acres
Clark, George	111	Clark, Thomas	40
Cary, Joseph		Canbur, William	90
Cooper, Beryamen	100	Combs, William, Snr.	2050
Cain, Patrick		Combs, William, Jnr.	
Crawford, John		Combs, Enoch	
Clark, Jude		Crawford, Hugh	112
Combs, Edward	100	Chalfant, David	
Combs, John	80	Case, Samuel	94
Combs, Thomas		Crane, Robert	
Combs, Nelson	100	Coper, William	
Clark, Samuel	50	Crawford, Hugh, Snr.	
Cotton, Edmund		Crawford, Samuel	
Combs, David	88	Crume, Ralph	673
Combs, Edward	100	Crume, Moses	
Clark, William	30	Collinsworth, Edmond	
Cotton, John	100	Crumes, Jesse	100
Cotton, Temple		Cotton, Henry	
Case, David		Cox, James	44
Conner, Daniel		Caulk, Thomas Ward	112
Cain, Matthew	78	**D**	
Curry, William	10	Dukes, Nicholas	
Connel, James		Drury, Mary	
Case, William	50	Davis, Hugh	
Case, James	100	Duncan, Henry	210
Case, William, Jnr.,	80	Drake, Cornelius	100
Case, John		Duker, Jacob	400
Case, Nathaniel	50	Duncan, James	
Coin, Andrew		Drake, Moses	
Cox, David	443	Drake, John	
Cox, Benjamin	300	Drake, James	80
Carfman, Joshua	220	Daugherty, Michael	194
Cunningham, Frank	100	Denton, Israel	
Clark, David		Dale, Abraham	200
Clark, Benjamin	100	Davis, Henry	212
Clark, Benjamin, Jnr.		Dodson, William	300
Clark, John		Dozer, James	50
Crest, Nicholas, Snr.	150	Dugan, James	
Conner, James		Duncan, Samuel	100
Collins, William	45	Duncan, George	100
Collins, Zebulon	230	Davis, Jesse	350
Crest, George	233	Davis, Warren	160
Cummins, John	150	Davis, James	
Chalfant, Thomas	200	Davis Isaac	100
Case, Jacob	137	Davis, Travin	200
Chalfant, Abner	150	Davis, Henry	68
Crest, Henry	900	Dozer, John	400
Crest, Nicholas, Jnr.	350	Dorsey, Greenberry	100
Connoway, Joseph	320	Duncan, Charles	150
Crutchner, George	140	Duncan, Rawleigh	

Name	Acres
Duncan, Benjamin	333
Davis, George	67
Davis, Giles	201
Dunbar, James	
Donley, Michael	50
Davis, Moses	160
Dawit, Peter	
Devore, Price	
Davidson, William	75

E

Name	Acres
Evins, Gilbert	120
Edwards, William	200
Evins, Caleb	100
Eldridge, Job	112
Enlows, Abraham	
Enlows, Joseph	
Enlows, Mordecai	
Enlows, John	
Enlows, Joseph, Snr.	250
Enlows, Henry	
Evans, David	300
Eldridge, Samuel	
Estup, Alexander	200

F

Name	Acres
Ferguson, Joshua	600
Frakes, John	
Froman, Jacob	200
Folkes, John	360
Finch, William	
Funk, Henry	
Fetherkele, Euly	50
Fetherkele, George	
Forman, Joseph	388
Flek, Peter	
Forman, Thomas	100
Frakes, Philip	
Frakes, John	
Frakes, John, Snr.	100
Frad, John	
Fowler, Zacheriah	
Falkner, Thomas	
Froman, Paul	1500
Ferguson, Joseph	150
Ferry, Daniel	100

G

Name	Acres
Gier, Samuel	200
Green, Leven	400
Guthrie, Adam	218
Gauff, William	62

Name	Acres
Goodwine, Abraham	
Gilkey, Edward	
Gray, Presley	100
Gray, William	100
Gray, Drakeford	177
Glover, Uriah	100
Goodwine, John	205
Grable, Joseph	200
Goodwell, Daniel	
Goodwell, James	
Grigsby, Nathaniel	
Grigsby, Natle, Jnr.	100
Graham, James	100
Graham, Christopher	200
Gray, William	
Greathouse, Herman	300
Goldsmith, Saml.	30
Gaither, John	521
Glen, David	1400
Galtoway, John	100
Graves, Philip	

H

Name	Acres
Howard, James	200
Howard, John	180
Howard, Joseph	75
Hammond, Job	148
Hammond, Gervin	250
Hammond, Gervin, Snr.	
Hughs, John	175
Howard, Samuel	75
Herron, John	50
Herron, William	180
Hobbs, Joseph	1017
Hawkins, John	100
Hawkins, Thomas	
Hughs, John	250
Herod, William	
Hogland, James	200
Hogland, Abraham	150
Hogland, Amos	150
Hogland, Moses	
Houston, William	
Heady, Stilwell	12
Heady, Thomas, Snr.	135
Heady, James	240
Hardesty, Caleb	50
Huff, Lawrence	83
Heady, Thomas, Jnr.	620
Holtzclaw, James	106

219

Name	Acres	Name	Acres
Holtzclaw, Kelly H.		Jordon, John	100
Haywood, John		Jordon, George	
Harris, Joseph		James, Joseph	200
Harris, James		Jrevine(?), Joseph	400
Harris, Stephen	300	Jones, William	345
Harris, Susanna		Johnson, John	
Hobbs, Joshua	170	Jennings, Isreal	130
Hobbs, John	178	Joseph, Negro	
Haycraft, Joshua		**K**	
Hughbanks, James		Kennedy, William	150
Habbert, Thomas	140	King, Thomas	150
Herrald, Moses	333	King, Robert	
Herrald, James	200	Kincaid, Samuel	150
Hay, Adam		Korah, Nathan	
Hughs, William, Snr.		King, Smith	100
Hughs, William, Jnr.	125	King, William	
Houston, John	133	Kauffman, Christian	
Hughs, James	50	Kirts, Cunrod	300
Harrison, Joshua	80	Kirts, George	150
Harrison, Greenberry	60	Kimbly, Andrew	500
Hobbs, Eli	100	Knot, Basil	
Harris, Sarah		Kirts, Martin	50
Heavenhill, Oliver		Kirts, Jacob	
Higgins, Henry		King, William	
Harris, Bambo, Negro	25	King, John	50
Hogland, Margaret	100	King, William	1784
Herman, Asahal		King, Elijah	
Harris, Nathaniel	430	King, Abner	
Hinton, Stephen	50	Kirkham, Robert	200
Holt, Thomas		Kinchloe, Thomas	140
Hopkins, William	250	Kauffman, Jacob	700
Hay, Felty		Kennady, Robert	
Hall, Arthur		Kinchloe, Lewis	
Hinton, John	92	Kinchloe, William	200
Hynes, Andrew	11900	Kinchloe, Stephen	
Hart, George	170	Kerns, Peter	200
Hahn, Peter		Kiervick, John	
Hill, William	100	Kirtus, John	
Humphrey, William	300	Kirkendolpher, Christo	
Herald, Moses, Snr.	666	**L**	
Herrald, William	2500	Lambert, Abraham	50
Herrald, Isaac		Lewis, Thomas	497
Herrald, John		Lindsey, George	
Herod, Richard		Lesley, Alexander	100
J		Langsford, Nicholas	
Jinkinson, Joseph	100	Lancaster, Raphel	100
Jones, David	142	Lee, John	100
Johnson, James		Lucust, Abraham	
Jackson, William		Lucust, John	

Name	Acres	Name	Acres
Lucust, Abrah, Snr.	120	Massey, Joshua	
Leaton, Joseph		McMachen, John	350
Lent, William	188	McGrue, Joseph	170
Lee, John	360	McGee, John	3350
Lout, Daniel	250	McGee, Patrick	1850
Leewright, Catherine	100	McFawl, David	50
Loan, Benjamin	100	McKinley, John	
Lee, Peter		Martin, Thomas	
Lenty, Nicholas		Mullikin, James	100
Lewis, John	850	Mullikin, Borton	
Leaton, John	100	Marks, George	1000
Leaton, Zach		McDonald, John	
		Murphy, Gabriel	200
M		Marguis, Christopher	150
Maeher, James M.	200	Marguis, James	
May, David	1140	Marquis, William	50
McDonald, Redm	176	May, John	
Moore, Nicholas	50	Mason, George	
McDonald, John	300	McClennen, William	100
McCarty, Jonathan	150	McCullum, James	100
McKay, Richard	200	Melton, Moses, Snr.	500
McGinnis, John		McKinley, James	
Morehead, Armd	268	Melton, Moses, Jnr.	
McKinley, Michl.	82	Moore, Jesse	
McLam, Mary		Melton, Richard	100
Miller, Henry		McCullough, James	
Maffet, Will	200	Morton, Thomas	100
McCasland, John	200	Morgan, Samuel	100
May, Gabriel	1557	Miles, Jesse	
McCullum, Jo	100	Mitchell, George	150
McCullum, John		Mitchell, Frederick	100
Moore, John	100	Mulen, Isaac, Snr.	100
Murry, John	75	May, William	39459
McGrew, Dolly	100	McKinney, Mary	
McDowell, Robt.		Modrel, John	
Martin, John		McHatton, William	150
McMachen, Richd.	200	McClung, William	400
McCasland, John	70	Malin, Isaac, Jnr.	
McKinley, John	65	Matthews, Paul	50
McDonald, Archyd	150	**N**	
McLaughlin, Jesse	225		
McKinley, Jno.	65	Neel, John	75
McKinley, William	50	Neel, Spencer	
McMullen, Will		Nugent, Robert	75
Marshall, John	60	Nugent, Willoughby	
Marshall, Mark		Neel, William	
Martin, Will		Nickles, Valentine	100
Marshall, William	250	Newboldt, Sarah	
Marshall, Robert	84	Nall, John, Jnr.	
Montgomery, Thomas	385	Nall, John, Snr.	200

Name	Acres	Name	Acres
Nail, James	470	Roberts, Abner	
Newman, John Posey		Reeves, Samuel	
O		Reed, David	100
Osburn, Samuel	500	Restine, John	60
Osburn, Nicholas	150	Ross, Lazarus	
Owens, William	440	Ritchie, John	
Ogdon, Benjamin	40	Randol, Henry	130
Overall, John	170	Ruble, Isaac	200
Overall, Thomson	100	Ruble, Jacob	
Overall, Nathaniel		Russel, James	
Overall, William	100	Russle, Daniel	
Overlin, William		Randolph, Thomas	60
		Redmund, Thomas	50
P		Redmund, John, Jnr.	
Polke, Charles, Snr.	440	Redmund, John, Snr.	105
Phipps, John		Roberts, Benjamin	
Pringle, John	150	Roberts, William	
Polke, Charles, Jnr.	140	Robertson, John	460
Pursel, Benjamin	100	Robertson, William	400
Patton, Ebenezar		Riland, Richard	
Pope, Benjamin		Ruby, Lawrence	165
Pittman, Joseph		Ridgway, Samuel	93
Pursel, Lawrence		Ridgway, Joseph	100
Payne, Samuel	200	Roman, Andrew	
Payne, Jonathan		Rose, Edward	
Pawe, Jeremiah		Raleigh, Henry	
Payne, Jonathan			
Paddock, Ebenezar	150	**S**	
Piety, Sarah		Spilman, Henry	100
Persons, Moses	150	Shields, John	
Parker, John		Staple, James	100
Patrick, Lydia		Small, William	
Prather, Richard		Samuels, John	
Prather, Thomas		Stone, John	502
Paul, Ann		Stilwell, John	25
Paul, Jonathan	550	Stillwell, Joseph	60
Pannerbaker, Wiand	400	Stillwell, Joseph, Jnr.	
Pannerbaker, Will	450	Shaddock, James	26
Pearman, Samuel	1159	Simpson, John	55
Pearman, Randol		Stephens, Saml.	100
Polke, Edmund	500	Smiley, William	775
Polke, Thomas	200	Stewart, James	100
Pryer, John		Silkwood, Barzalla	
		Sturgeon, Robert	50
R		Sturgeon, James	25
Robertson, John		Spencer, Spier	
Rodgers, Daniel	50	Simpson, Thomas	400
Redmund, Richard		Sturgeon, John	25
Ross, James	100	Scott, Arthur	
Ryan, Michael		Sturgeon, Jerome	
Rodgers, Andrew	150		

Name	Acres
Sturgeon, John	40
Stallard, Walter	100
Stevens, Ruth	150
Severns, Daniel B.	
Stilwell, Obadiah	59
Southward, James	
Steel, James	100
Shanks, Zacheriah	200
Slone, Bryant	
Strother, Benjamin	
Slaton, John	
Sands, James	400
Stark, James	142
Stark, Jonathan	100
Shoptaw, John, Snr.	150
Shoptaw, Andrew	
Shoptaw, William	
Shoptaw, John	
Stark, William	
Stilwell, Richd.	
Samuels, Robert	
Scott, Thomas	
Severns, John	93
Suttler, Abraham	12
Shumate, Nimd.	
Shumate, Margaret	135
Smithers, Thos.	
Singleton, Benr.	
Smith, David	40
Smiley, James	
Stark, Shristor	
Stovall, Ralph	
Stoner, John	524
Sands, William	48
Stovall, Hezekiah	100
Stovall, John	
Stovall, Bartholomus	
Simmons, Richard	290
Simonton, Robert	100
Simnson, Levi	102
Simmons, Verlinaer	52
Simmons, William	
Standiford, Ephraim	
Sevan, Jusrinan	
Shane, Edward	100
Smith, Mary	
Smith, William	22
Strickley, John	
Sevan, Edward	

Name	T	Acres
Shots, John		
Solomon, Negro		
Summers, William		30
Spencer, Thomas		200
Smith, Dennis		
Tucker, George		
Tucker, John		
Taylor, Daniel		
Thomas, Edward		200
Traux, William		85
Troutman, Jacob		200
Tichenor, Joseph		
Tichenor, Daniel, Jnr.		
Tichenor, Daniel, Snr.		2500
Taylor, William		200
Temple, David		
Truman, Edward		100
Thomson, James		100
Thomson, Anthony		
	U	
Underhill, James		25
Underwood, Joseph		50
Umppreys, William		
Unsil, Abraham		
Unsil, John		126
Unsil, Frederic		
Unsil, Henry		
	V	
Vowls, Matthew		200
Vaughan, Andrew		300
Vebbert, George		
	W	
Williams, Simpson		75
Wiley, Stephen		
Wiley, Jacob		
Woodsmall, James		
Woodsmall, George L.		
Wakefield, John		200
Wakefield, Daniel		
Worman, John		
Worman, Joseph		100
Woodsmall, James		100
Wright, Jonathan		
Wright, Gabriel		
Wise, Henry		260
Wathers, Benjamin		125
Walker, Ann		
Wise, Daniel		
Woodward, Michael		

Name	Acres
White, James	
Wise, Jacob	
Wells, Edward	
Welsh, William	130
Wilson, James	
Watson, James	
Williams, James	
Wooley, William	
Wible, Adam	147
Wilson, Robert	760
Wilson, John	220
Wilson, Vance	200
Wakefield, Matthew	166
Williams, John	
Williams, Samuel	50
Watson, Henry	300
Watson, William	
Wells, Abraham	100
Wilson, William	
Williams, Parrot	50
Wolf, Peter	
Wise, Caleb	100
Willes, Matthew	100
Wise, Richard	
Wise, Adam	
Wisehart, George	
Wright, Eli	100
Woods, James	124
Wallace, John	
Wilson, Robert, Jnr.	250
Work, Samuel	

Y

Young, Peter	200
Young, John	120
Young, Bryant	160
Young, William	112
Yoder, Jacob	

I do hereby certify that the within List of Taxable propery is a true Copy of an original List filed in my office by Gabriel Cox, Gent. one of the Commissioners of the Tax. for the County of Nelson. Given under my hand this 5th day of January, 1793.

BEN GRAYSON, Cl. P. T. N. Co.

A LIST OF TAXABLE PROPERTY TAKEN IN NELSON COUNTY
BY James McMAHON

I do hereby Certify that the following list of Taxable property is a true copy of an original List filed in my office by James McMahon, Gent. one of the Commissioners of the Tax for the County of Nelson. Given under my hand this 5th day of January, 1793.

BEN GRAYSON, Cl. Crt. N. C.

Name	A	Acres
Avit, Richard		
Atherton, John		
Ashcraft, Danl.		
Ashcraft, Jedidiah		2539
Alamilton, George		
Anderson, Jonathan		120
Anderson, Hannah		
Arndo, Joseph		
Atherton, Aaron		
Atherton, Jno., Jnr.		
Anderson, John		
Allentharp, John		227
Abbot, William		
Abbot, James		150
Atkisson, Jesse		
Anderson, Joseph		100
Ashby, Bladen		1700
Alex, Vesy		

B		
Buckner, William		15000
Barby, Elias		1000
Briver, Samuel		
Barthnap, Peter		100
Bozorth, John		354
Baird, Robert		
Barnett, Joseph		
Burnett, Jno.		
Burks, Samuel		
Black, Joseph		200
Belpher, Berry		
Burks, Isham		
Bethar, John		
Burks, Nicholas		
Brunts, John		100
Bryant, John		15

Name	Acres	Name	Acres
Bush, Christopher	700	Dodge, Josiah	400
Bush, William		Dickens, Ephriam	200
Brownfield, William		Dewitt, Henry	100
Brainer, Adam		Demoss, Peter	
Barnett, Alexander	7	Duncan, Samuel	
Brown, Patrick	700	Deen, Richard	150
Burrace, Booze		Dispain, Peter	
Bell, Zephimah	100	Dudley, Thomas	
Barton, Theophilis	557½	Dye, Isaac	400
Brown, Thomas	400	Defevers, John	500
Bozorth, David		Dobson, Joseph	100
Bozorth, Abner		Dobson, James	100
Bell, Robert		Dawes, Joseph	50
Bell, Henry		**E**	
Byers, Daniel	250	Eastwood, John	
Brownfield, Rich.	174	Elliot, William	
Brownfield, Edw.	200	Easter, Adam	
Barton, Phebe	1465	**F**	
Barnett, William		Fitch, Walter	
Blevans, Nathan		Flint, John	
C		Fought, George	
Casinger, Andrew		Frazier, Alexander	100
Close, George		Fausch, Solomon	
Case, Elizabeth		Foster, Fredrick	
Crist, Jacob		Friend, Isaac	
Culbertson, John		Foster, Henry	
Clem, John	100	Fairby, Andrew	127
Cooper, Job		**G**	
Casinger, Solomon (Snr.)	159	Gray, Jonas	
Casinger, Joseph		Greenwall, Joseph, Snr.	75
Coleman, Martin	7	Greenwall, Joseph, Jnr.	100
Callaway, Chesley		Gardiner, George	
Coombs, Andrew		Gum, Shepherd	500
Cumstock, William		Glenn, John	
Connolly, Timothy		Grass, Henry	
Chisam John	116	Goodwin, Thomas	
Coy, John, Jnr.	300	Goodwin, Isaac	200
Coy, John, Senr.		Glenn, Joseph	
Chisam, James	80	Gill, William	250
Chisam, Richard	250	Goodwin, Samuel, Snr.	400
Cumpton, Richard		Goodwin, Saml., Jnr.	
Cameron, Anguish	100	Gilliland, Thomas	
Crail, Richard	112	Greenwall, John	
Childers, Sarah		Gardiner, John	
Campbell, Michael		Greenwalt, Lewis	75
Claycomb, Bolson		**H**	
D		Handon, William	
Dye, Job		Hartt, Josiah	
Derimiah, John	300	Hargis, Thomas	

Name	Acres
Hall, John	135
Haynes, William	
Howell, John	100
Hoback, John	
Hazel, Caleb	100
Hodgen, Robert	1093
Hynch, George	50
Harmon, Thoms.	
Hornbeck, Abram.	
Hoop, Sarah	
Hoop, Benjamin	
Hall, John, Snr.	
Holeman, John	
Hendricks, James	
Harden, Daniel	400
Hargas, John	
Hynns, Isaac	
Helen, Thomas	4760
Highbough, George	
Harris, Samuel	800
Haycraft, Saml.	200

I

Name	Acres
Inlow, Abram.	
Inlow, Isam	850
Isabel, James	100

J

Name	Acres
Jolly, Nelson	
Jackson, Chriso.	
Jackson, Jesse	
Jayne, Mathias	
Jackson, Chris.	3½
Jackson, Leroy	
Johnson, Benjn.	100
Johnson, Jno.	

K

Name	Acres
Kalin, Asa	300
Kilpatrick, Joseph	1100
Kelleham, Patrick	
Kitter, Coonrod	462¼
Kieth, Henry	7
Kilpatrick, Moses	200

L

Name	Acres
Logdon, Wm.	
Lyon, James	320
Lee, William	300
Lee, Charles	
Lyons, James, Snr.	
Lerew, Isaac	950

Name	Acres
Lyndon, Danl.	500
Lyndon, Jacob	3685
Lee, Frederick	

M

Name	Acres
Martin, Aquitta	
Malone, John	
Miller, Earnest	400
Makentire, Thos.	
Miller, Peter	
Morgan, Elenor	
McComas, Magt.	200
Miller, Christr.	300
Miller, Henry	
McClure, David	100
McGrew, James	
Miller, Wm.	
Matthews, Wm.	920
Matthews, Wm., Jnr.	100
Miller, Adam	
Miller, Saml.	550
Montgomery, Simpson	
McPack, James	75
McColgin, Jno.	200
Matin, Saml.	165
Miller, John	
Mosley, Robert	
Miller, Nicholas	
McFarlin, Abr.	

N

Name	Acres
Nees, Henry	

O

Name	Acres
O'Donald, John	
Osbourn, Benjm.	
Osbourn, Ebenezer	

P

Name	Acres
Parepoynt, Frans.	619
Patrick, Benjn.	
Powers, Hannah	
Powers, Isaac	7
Peace, Simon	
Priest, David	
Phelps, Nicholas	
Phelps, William	70
Peper, John	
Phillips, Philip	1046
Peterson, Thos.	
Powell, Ann	
Pittman, Sarah	250

Name	Acres	Name	Acres
R.		**T**	
Radley, Ichabud		Trent, Bryan	50
Rhodes, Henry		Therman, John	
Richards, Nathan		Turner, James	
Rollins, Aaron	150	Tinsley, James	
Rollins, Edward	240	Taylor, Will Thos.	100
Rice, Nicholas		Thomas, Evan Jam's	
Rorick, Reuben	100	Thos., Jno.	1000
Robertson, John		Thompson, Uriah	
Rhodes, Danl.	7	Taylor, Philp	7
Rhodes, Jacob	200		
Read, Andrew	100	**V**	
Redmond, Thomas	450	Vetittoe, Daniel	420
Rager, Burkett	187	VanWinkle, Alexander	
Rollinger, Stephen	209	Vantz, William	307
		Vanmeter, Jacob	2862
S		Vanmatre, Jno.	
Swank, John	100	Vantreese, Jonas	
Smith, Edward		Vanbruso, Jacob	
Sharp, Wm.		Vantriese, Jno.	1400
Spingston, Peter		Vantz, Alexr.	300
Shivcly, Jno.		Vanadake, Martin	8½
Shiveley, Jacob		Vanmatre, Jacob, Snr.	4833
Shiveley, Michael		Vanmatre, Jacob, Jnr.	
Skaggs, Moses		Vanschoyck, Jno.	100
Skaggs, Henry	200		
Skaggs, David		**W**	
Skaggs, Solomon	100	Walker, Jno. Jones	
Shakles, Richard	200	Welsh, Nicholas	
Scisney, Mary	200	Winters, Samuel	
Scott, James		Wooldridge, Richd.	
Skaggs, Wm.	200	Walters, Barnabas	
Sideburn, Charles	200	Watkins, James	100
Skaggs, Sarah		Walters, Jno.	
Studdart, Saml.		Wilhelm, Alexr.	
Skaggs, James	200	Watkins, Saml.	400
Skaggs, Jno.		Wise, Valentine	
Skaggs, Henry, Jnr.	117	Wyse, Jacob	
Saunders, Saml.	400	White, William	
Saunders, Joseph		Winchester, Richd.	189½
Saunders, Saml., Jnr.		Wilson, Samuel	
Skaggs, Thos.		Williams, Thomas	
Skaggs, Archibald		Walters, Conrod	360
Shutt, Jacob		Walters, Nancy	
Swan, Hugh		Wooldridge, Jno.	
Saunders, Mary		Woolart, Isaac	
Shutts, Mathias	7	Wetherholt, Jacob	
Shaw, Bannans	200		
Schoonover, David		**Y**	
Springtow, Joseph		Yootsler, Jacob	
		Young, James	

DEPARTMENT OF STATE ARCHIVES—SHELBY COUNTY TAX LISTS, 1795.

A List of Taxable Property Taken and Returned by Thomas Shannon Esquire, Commissioner of the Tax for Shelby County for the Year 1795.

WM. McDOWELL, ESQ., Auditor of Public Accounts.

Persons Named Charged With Taxes	Horses	Cattle	County	Water Course	Acres of Land
Adams, David	2	15			
Adams, John, Jr.	1	2			
Adams, Hugh	1	2	Shelby	Roberts Creek	100
Adams, John	3	27			
Archer, Joseph	5	16		Gisses Creek	100
Adams, Samuel	2	1			
Adams, Frances					
Adams, William	2	10			
Adams, William, Jr.	1	3			
Adams, David, Jr.	1				
Allin, James	2	9	Shelby	Buck Creek	350
Anderson, John	1	5			
Ashby, Stinson[1]	2	6	Shelby	Buck Creek	100
Ashby, Beady	3	8	Shelby	Buck Creek	100
Ashby, Beady			Shelby	Buck Creek	100
Akers, Joseph	1	8	Shelby	Snake Run	107
Allin, Andrew	2	7	Shelby	Snake Run	250
Allin, John	1	14	Shelby	Snake Run	250
Ashcraft, Elizabeth	2	2			
Applegate, Benj.	4	3			
Ballard, Bland W.	3	20	Shelby	Bullskin	100
Ballard, Bland W.			Jefferson	Pond Creek	600
Ballard, Bland W.			Jefferson	Pond Creek	325
Ballard, Bland W.			Jefferson	Harrods Creek	325
Burns, Thomas					
Ballard, James	5	17	Shelby	Bearshears Creek	100
Ballard, James			Shelby	Bearshears Creek	156½
Ballard, James			Shelby	Buck Creek	200
Bradshaw, John					
Bradshaw, Thomas[2]	9	21	Shelby	Gisses Creek	800
Brenton, Henry	1	11	Shelby	Gisses Creek	167
Brenton, Robert					
Bennett, Daniel	3	6	Shelby		

Persons Named Charged With Taxes	Horses	Cattle	County	Water Course	Acres of Land
Brenton, John	1	6			
Buttler, William[3]		7	Clark	Main Licking	200
Breading, Richd.	4	23	Shelby	Plum Creek	200
Billea, Peter	7	26	Shelby	Bullskin	470
Burkes, George	1				
Best, John	2	7			
Barker, William					
Buskirk, John	4	9	Shelby	Bearshears Creek	318
Buskirk, John			Shelby	Bearshears Creek	200
Buskirk, Michael	1	5			
Builderback, Jacob	4	7			
Bailey, Robert	3	6	Shelby	Buck Creek	100
Bailey, Robert			Shelby	Buck Creek	571
Brawdy, William	5	12	Shelby	Plum Creek	120
Boyls, David	7	23	Shelby	Plum Creek	200
Baskett, John[11]	3	7	Shelby	Buck Creek	100
Bowman, John		8			
Blades, Eli	4	6			
Bennett, Daniel	1	10	Shelby	Elk Creek	100
Beadle, Johnathan	3	7			
Boyls, John					
Creed, Elijah	2	11			
Crawford, John	1	9	Shelby		
Collins, William	2	7	Shelby	Beech Creek	150
Churchill, Richd.	1	4	Shelby	Gisses Creek	100
Connelly, John[4]	1	6	Shelby		
Connelly, Thompson		6		Snake Run	70
Cox, Johnathan[11]	3	19			
Chitwood, John	1				
Chitwood, Amos	1				
Chitwood, Seth	2	1	Shelby		
Cook, Moses	3	8		Roberts Run	215
Clark, Lewis					
Chambers, Alexr.[1]	2	2			
Conneley, William	3	8			
Cash, Warren	2	8	Shelby	Beech Creek	100
Clutter, Simeon[6]	2	6		Jeptrey Creek	50
Crawford, Robert[4]	3	10	Shelby	Gisses Creek	150
Carlin, Thomas[5]	4	30		Bearshears	1,400
Carlin, Thomas			Shelby	Salt River	400
Carlin, Thomas			Shelby	Bearshears	400
Craveston, George	6	23	Shelby	Salt River	200
Crawford, John	1	10			
Carlin, John	1				
Collins, William E.	2	8	Shelby	Elk Creek	500
Cuntryman, Jacob	2	9			
Crawford, Isaac	3	5			
Combs, Thomas	2	4			
Cunningham, Francis	6	14	Shelby	Salt River	250
Cunningham, Francis			Nelson	Long Creek	108
Crawford, Thomas	3	1			
Crawford, Moses	7				
Crawford, James	2	2			
Crist, George[6]	3	12	Shelby	Salt River	50
Case, Jacob	2	6	Nelson	Cox Creek	137

Persons Named Charged With Taxes	Horses	Cattle	County	Water Course	Acres of Land
Crawford, Nathan			Shelby	Gisses Creek	1,500
Crawford, Nathan			Nelson	Cox Creek	350
Crawford, Nathan			Nelson	Cox Creek	300
Crawford, Nathan			Shelby	Clear Creek	500
Crawford, David			Jefferson	Harrods Creek	1,000
Crawford, David			Hardin	Nolin	1,000
Crawford, David			Shelby	Kentucky	1,250
Dugan, Hugh	2	20	Shelby	Beech	139½
Down, John					
Duncan, James[4]	5	17			
Davis, John	1	9	Shelby	Gisses Creek	100
Downing, Wm.					
Dilling, John					
Denboe, Solomon		10	Shelby	Gisses Creek	64
Dodson, John		2	Shelby	Elk Creek	50
Elder, John	1	2			
Ellis, Isaac[5]	4	21	Shelby	Bullskin	500
Evans, Thomas	2	10			
Easters, William		13			
Edwards, David	3	16	Shelby	Jeptrey	100
Edwards, David			Hardin	Hardin	450
Edwards, Isaac	1	16	Hardin	Hardin	550
Evans, James	1	2			
Evans, Robert	1				
Evans, William	2				
Evans, David[4]	1				
Eakins, John	2	10			
Eakins, Alesr.[4]	1	2			
Ellitt, Thomas	1	7	Shelby	Beech Creek	200
Eastin, Redwood					
Ferguson, William	8	18			
Fields, Abraham[6]	2	11	Jefferson	Pond River	200
Flickoner, Peter		4			
Ferguson, William			Shelby	Gisses Creek	406
Ferguson, James			Shelby	Beech Creek	140
Frowman, Thomas[4]	7	18	Shelby	Plum Creek	200
Fields, Cane	1	8	Shelby	Gisses Creek	60
Gasuway, John	1	5	Shelby	Jeptry	100
Goodwin, Thomas	2	5			
Gage, John	1	2			
Gregory, John	4				
Gardner, Thomas	2	19			
Gasuway, Richard	1	11	Shelby	Jeptry	200
Gwinn, Thomas I.[7]	4	21	Mason	Fleming Creek	1,500
Gregory, Richard	3	12	Shelby	Clear Creek	180
Garner, James	1				
Garrott, Isaac	1				
Goban, William	7	23	Shelby	Plum Creek	200
Graves, Edmund	2	10	Shelby	Beech Creek	200
Griggsby, Charles	4	12	Shelby	Beech Creek	100
Garrott, Nathan	1	10	Shelby	Jeptry Creek	160
Gray, Robert	1	15	Shelby	Jeptry Creek	150

Persons Named Charged With Taxes	Horses	Cattle	County	Water Course	Acres of Land
Garrott, John	2	9	Shelby	Gisses	68½
Garrott, William					
Garrott, Morris					
Cragg, David	4	8	Shelby	Gisses	117½
Glaize, Nathanl.[4]	4	8	Shelby	Bearshears	164
Gage, Aaron	1	4			
Glenn, William[4]	2	10			
Gamble, Wm.	3	4	Shelby	Gisses	100
Hughes, Benjamin[6]	3	27	Shelby	Long Run	400
Hughes, Benjamin			Shelby	Long Run	200
Hughes, Benjamin			Shelby	Jeptry	1,000
Hill, Firgus	1				
Humphrey, John	1				
Hester, Mathias	2	9			
Humphrey, Merry		8			
Hansberry, John	3	8			
Hunter, Henry[3]	3	18	Shelby	Tick Creek	352
Huss, Benjamin	1				
Horms, John	2	4			
Humphrey, George	3	14	Shelby	Beech Creek	208
Haff, Luke[1]	4	6	Shelby	Clear Creek	2,000
Hucklebury, Jacob	1	7			
Holms, Andrew	6	14	Shelby	Gisses Creek	300
Harrison, John[4]	3	11	Shelby	Beech Creek	400
How, John	3	10	Shelby	Gisses Creek	718
Hill, Hardy	4	21	Shelby	Salt River	400
Hill, Able	1	7			
Hickling, Hugh[1]	2	6			
Helmes, William[6]	3	19	Shelby	Gisses Creek	450
Helmes, William			Shelby	Busha Pond	1,400
Hansley, Richardson[4]	2	10			
Hammons, Joseph		1			
Hansley, Johnathan	1	2			
Hardmon, Joseph	1	4	Shelby	Beech Creek	71
Hardmon, Solomon	1	12	Shelby	Snake River	108
Hardmon, Johnathan	3	2			
Hardmon, David	4	14	Shelby	Snake River	71
Haile, Levy					
Jacobs, Samuel	2				
Johnston, David	1	9			
James, George	1	5			
Imgrim, Archer	3	10	Shelby	Beech Creek	100
Ingle, John, Jr.		5			
Ingle, John	1	10	Shelby	Plum Creek	115
Johnston, John[4]	2	8			
Johns, John	2	16			
Jrehes (?), Robert	2	18	Shelby	Wolf Run	200
Johnston, James		8	Shelby	Beech Creek	69½
Johnston, William	4	21	Shelby	Bearshears	200
Kindle, Thomas	1	8			
Knight, John[3]	4	17	Shelby	Bullskin	120
Knight, John				Floyd Fork	675

Persons Named Charged With Taxes	Horses	Cattle	County	Water Course	Acres of Land
Kindle, Ewell	1				
Kennady, Samuel	1				
Kencade, Robt.	2	29	Shelby	Bearshears	160
Kencade, Robt.			Shelby	Bearshears	50
Kaster, William, Sr.[6]	4	18			
Kaster, Paul	1	4			
Kaster, William	2	7			
Karr, Absolom	2	10	Shelby	Elk Creek	400
Kykindall, Peter	3	12	Shelby	Gisses Creek	125
Lucas, Abraham	2	8			
Leatherman, Peter	2	7			
Lucas, John	1	7			
Lockey, Jeremiah[4]					
Lee, William	2	4			
Lively, William					
Lowrey, Robert	2	2	Shelby	Gisses Creek	100
Logan, Benjamin[9]	10	70		Bullskin	1,400
Leatherman, Christian[4]	4	8	Shelby	Beech Creek	550
Leatherman, Christian			Bourbon	Boones Run	2,000
Leatherman, Christian			Bourbon	Boones Run	1,000
Leatherman, John	2	9	Shelby	Beech Creek	750
Logan, James[5]	5	7			
Leamon, Robert	1	6	Shelby	Bearshears	214
Leamon, Robert			Shelby	Bearshears	89
Leamon, Robert			Shelby	Beech Creek	200
Leamon, Robert			Shelby	Bearshears	300
Leamone, John[3]	3	13	Shelby	———? R.	210
Lucas, Abraham	2	5			
Liston, Edmund	1	8			
Leanard, Charles	2	5			
Lasley, Robert	3	8	Shelby	Elk Creek	300
Lasley, Robert			Shelby	Bearshears	70
McIntire, John	1	1			
Maddox, Absolom	1				
Miner, Thomas	3	9			
Maddox, Wilson	2	16	Shelby	Gisses Creek	150
Monroe, William[4]	1				
McWait, Henry	4	29	Shelby	Clear Creek	500
McWait, Henry				Long Run	300
Martin, John, Jr.	2	17	Shelby	Bearshears	150
Monroe, George	1				
McDowell, Charles	7	17			
Maddox, Dan	2	4			
Monroe, Phillip	1	1			
Miller, David	1	3	Shelby	Beech Creek	100
Miller, Conrod	1	1	Shelby	Beech Creek	100
McWait, James	3	16			
McMannass, John	1	9	Shelby	Jeptrey	100
Morton, James[4]	4	17	Shelby		
Meeks, John[4]		1			
Murphey, James	3	10	Shelby	Beech Creek	130
McCormack, Wm.	3	3			
Millon, Alexr.	1	2	Shelby	Beech Creek	300
McGinniss, John		4	Shelby	Gisses Creek	82

Persons Named Charged With Taxes	Horses	Cattle	County	Water Course	Acres of Land
McCourtney, John	1	9			
May, William[4]	4	13	Shelby	Plum Creek	182
McCorle, Samuel	1				
McCormack, Peter	4	9	Shelby	Salt River	70
Miser, John	1	4			
Miller, Isaac	2	3			
McMahan, James[4]	5	17			
Montgomery, George		8			
Mellon, Isaac	1	2	Shelby	Gisses Creek	150
Mattenly, James	2	4	Shelby	Gisses Creek	250
Mattenly, James			Shelby	Gisses Creek	50
McIntire, Archibald	2	22	Shelby	Bullskin	116
Martin, Sarah[5]	1	6			
McDaniel, James, Sr.	2	12	Shelby	Bearshears	274
McDaniel, James	1	7	Shelby	Beech Creek	200
McDaniel, Daniel	3	15			
McBride, Robert					
McDaniel, Alexr.	1	2			
Morgan, Lenard	1	11	Shelby	Beech Creek	125
McCortney, James	1	4	Shelby		
McClain, David[6]	2	10	Shelby	Gisses Creek	100
McCinly, James	1	4			
McCleland, Joseph	1	3			
Martin, John	2	8			
Mairtin, Nimrod					
Mairtin, Thomas	1	5			
McCarter, Robert	2	9			
Morgan, Ahle	1				
Neald, William[4]	2	12	Shelby	Roberts Run	100
Nowlin, Lewis		9			
Neald, William	1	5	Shelby	Beech Creek	138
Newman, Henry		3	Shelby	Beech Creek	125
Newman, Jacob[4]	10	40	Shelby	Clear Creek	300
Owen, David	2	8	Shelby	Gisses	400
Owen, Brackett[10]	6	37	Shelby	Clear	1,334
Owen, Brackett			Shelby	Clear	46
Osburn, Johnathan	1	2			
Organ, John	1				
Osburn, Michl.[4]		1			
Price, William[4]	7	30	Shelby	Besherres	250
Price, William			Logan	Green River	600
Price, Frederick	5				
Pirkins, John	2	8	Shelby	Gisses	50
Parks, Culberson	4	4	Shelby	Bersheares	200
Price, David	1		Shelby	Beshears	198
Paule, Andrew[8]	4	13	Shelby	Beech Creek	200
Pounds, Joseph	2	14			
Pounds, Thomas	2	18			
Polly, James	1	5			
Pirkins, John, Sr.[4]	3	14	Shelby	Gisses	250
Pirkins, William	1	4			
Peek, John	4	10			
Paddon, Johnathan	2	4	Shelby	Gisses	100

Persons Named Charged With Taxes	Horses	Cattle	County	Water Course	Acres of Land
Pyatey, Thomas	2	6	Shelby	Gisses	150
Phigley, Simeon	3	27			
Patton, Ebenezer	5	13	Shelby	Beshears	400
Polke, Charles[4]	6	9	Shelby	Gisses	100
Quirk, James					
Reid, Alexr.	2	10			
Roberts, Agness	3	17	Shelby	Roberts Run	200
Rodman, Hugh	2	13			
Riland, Nicholas[12]	1	3			
Ross, John					
Romine, Christy	1	8	Mercer	Salt River	200
Romine, Christy			Shelby	Gesses Creek	100
Romine, Christy			Shelby	Kentucky	257½
Richardson, James[13]	2	22	Shelby	——? Run	100
Robins, James[12]	1				
Richey, Thomas	3	10	Shelby	Jeptry Creek	148
Reid, David	2	10	Shelby	Elk Creek	100
Reid, Jousha	3	10	Shelby	Elk Creek	89
Reid, Caleb	4	13			
Reid, Barnett	1	10	Shelby	Elk Creek	50
Reid, George[12]	7	1			
Reiley, John	1	7			
Ruelile, Jacob	2	8	Shelby	Gesses Creek	71
Richey, William[12]	2	14	Shelby	Bershears	100
Roberts, Benjamin[13]	3	19	Shelby	Meadow Run	226
Roberts, Benjamin			Hardin	Ruff Creek	3,421
Roberts, Benjamin			Shelby	6 Mile Creek	400
Roberts, Benjamin			Shelby	6 Mile Creek	400
Roberts, Benjamin			Shelby	Beech Creek	439
Roberts, Benjamin			Shelby	—— Creek	100
Roberts, Benjamin			Shelby	Pattons Creek	2,500
Roberts, Benjamin			Jefferson	Pond Creek	1,086
Roberts, Benjamin			Shelby	Fox Run	500
Roberts, Benjamin			Shelby	Drinnings	500
Roberts, Benjamin			Jefferson	Cain Run	1,508
Roberts, Benjamin			Washington	Rolling Fork	400
Roberts, Benjamin			Nelson	8 miles from Ohio	600
Roberts, Benjamin			Jefferson	Cain Run	500
Roberts, Benjamin			Shelby	Long Run	500
Robert, William	2		Green	Russell & Wolf Creek	3,555⅓
Robert, William			Green	Russell Creek	378
Robert, William			Green	Cumberland	176
Robert, William			Green	Russell Creek	546
Robert, William			Green	Russell Creek	240
Robert, William			Green	Russell Creek	100
Robert, William			Green	Glenn Creek	1,500
Robert, William			Green	Cumberland	490
Robert, William			Logan	Red River	420
Robert, William			Logan	Red River	257
Robert, William			Logan	Scags Creek	200
Robert, William			Logan	Muddy River	475
Robert, William			Logan	Red River	325
Robert, William			Logan	Red River	200
Robert, William			Logan	Red River	90

Persons Named Charged With Taxes	Horses	Cattle	County	Water Course	Acres of Land
Robert, William			Logan	Red River	300
Robert, William			Logan	W. Fork	135
Robert, William			Logan	Clifty Creek	130
Robert, William			Logan	Pond River	325
Robert, William			Logan	Little River	400
Robert, William			Logan	Pond River	100
Robert, William			Logan	Muddy River & Creek	366⅔
Robert, William			Logan	Sinks of Beaver	600
Robert, William			Logan	Green River	300
Robert, William			Logan	Green River	352
Robert, William			Logan	Big Barren	500
Robert, William			Logan	Muddy River & Creek	2,000
Robert, William			Logan	Big Muddy & Pond R...	333⅓
Robert, William			Logan	Little River	100
Robert, William			Logan	Russell Creek and Green River	1,500
Robert, William			Logan	Russell Cr. and waters of Big Barren	666
Robert, William			Green & Logan	Big Barren & Green R.	666
Robert, William			Green	Russells Creek	800
Robert, William			Shelby	Ohio	3,000
Robert, William			Washington	Rolling Fork	1,000
Robert, William			Logan	Muddy River	200
Robert, William			Logan	Muddy Creek	150⅔
Robert, William			Green	Russells Creek	300
Robert, William			Shelby	E. Fork Mill Creek	682
Robert, William			Shelby	Clear Creek	1,100
Robert, William			Logan	Red River Fork	275
Shannon, Samuel[1]	4	19	Shelby	Bullskin	560
Shannon, Samuel			Shelby	Mulberry	400
Shannon, Samuel			Shelby	Meadow Run	400
Shannon, Samuel			Shelby	Bullskin	417
Shannon, Samuel			Hardin	Ohio	560
Shannon, Samuel			Hardin	Ohio	560
Shannon, Samuel			Shelby	Gisses Creek	273½
Shannon, Samuel			Shelby	Clear	533
Shannon, Samuel			Shelby	Gisses	400
Shannon, Samuel			Shelby	Fox Run	200
Shannon, Samuel			Shelby	Drinnings	102½
Shannon, Samuel			Shelby	Drinnings	900
Shannon, Samuel			Shelby	Bullskin	217
Shannon, Samuel			Shelby	Bullskin	2,034
Shannon, Samuel			Shelby	Bullskin	1,071
Shannon, Samuel			Shelby	Bearshears	131
Shannon, Samuel			Shelby	Benson	400
Shannon, Samuel			Shelby	Bearshears	577
Shannon, Samuel			Shelby	Drinnings	129
Shannon, Samuel			Shelby	Mill Creek	300
Shannon, Samuel			Green	Red River	550
Shannon, Samuel			Hardin	Ohio	560
Shannon, Samuel			Shelby	Clear Creek	990
Shannon, Samuel			Shelby	Bullskin	275
Shannon, Samuel			Shelby	Drinnings	875
Shannon, Samuel			Shelby	Ohio	200
Shannon, Samuel			Mason	Ohio	800

Persons Named Charged With Taxes	Horses	Cattle	County	Water Course	Acres of Land
Shannon, Samuel			Shelby	Drinnings	500
Shannon, Samuel			Jefferson	Cain Run	1,500
Shannon, Samuel			Bourbon	Stoners Fork	2,000
Shannon, Samuel			Bourbon	Hancock Fork	1,680
Shannon, Samuel			Bourbon and Fayette	Green Cr. & David Fork	1,868
Shannon, Samuel			Nelson	Cox Creek	560
Shannon, Samuel			Nelson	Salt River	580
Shannon, Samuel			Bourbon	Flat Creek	560
Shannon, Samuel			Bourbon	Green Creek	2,140
Shannon, Samuel			Jefferson	Cedar Creek	560
Shannon, Samuel			Shelby	Clear	200
Simpson, James[14]	4	19			
Shaver, David	2	5			
Spelding, C. Moses					
Smith, William	1				
Sharp, Anthony[15]	2	4			
Stephenson, Robert[15]	4	9			
Standley, David	3				
Standley, Joseph	3	13			
Spencer, Spear	1	5			
Seeff (or Suff), John					
Scipes, M. John	1	8			
Stump, Frances	2	8	Shelby	Beech Creek	200
Spencer, Walter	2	6	Shelby	Beech Creek	125
Shannon, Alexr.	2	4			
Shephard, John	2	4	Shelby	Beech Creek	100
Scipes, Joseph[16]	2	11	Shelby	Beech Creek	312
Smith, Jinney	1	5			
Spencer, John[15]	3	8	Shelby	Bearshears Creek	214
Sebastian, Samuel					
Starks, Joseph	2	15	Shelby	Wolf Creek	398½
Starks, John	3	12			
Starks, William	2	7			
Starks, James[16]	5	13			
Shaw, Jacob	1	8			
Suiye (?), James	1	2			
Stillwell, John	2	11	Shelby	Elk Creek	149
Stillwell, Joseph	2	6	Shelby	Elk Creek	50
Starks, Christopher[17]	4	21	Shelby	Elk Creek	300
Sally, William	1	2			
Starks, Daniel[16]	4	16			
Steel, James[17]	3	5			
Stark, Johnathan		3			
Stark, David[16]					
Stark, Johnathan, Jr	2				
Stark, Johnathan		3			
Stark, Jacob	1	3	Shelby	Elk Creek	126
Steppleton, Andrew	1	3	Shelby	Beech Creek	244
Stone, Benjamin[15]	2	3			
Short, Charles	2	3			
Short, William	1	4			
Sharp, John	1	6	Shelby	Gisses Creek	100
Smith, John[16]					
Scott, John[15]	5				
Stephens, Samuel	2	5			
Silkwood, Berzilly	3	7			

Persons Named Charged With Taxes	Horses	Cattle	County	Water Course	Acres of Land
Stergan, Robert	4	9			
Stergan, John	3	9			
Stergan, John, Jr.	3	10			
Stergan, Jeremiah		5			
Scott, Arter[16]	2	15			
Shannon, Thomas[16]	5	15	Shelby	Clear Creek	300
*Tilford, James	1				
Tatgard, (Teagard?), Basell	1		Shelby	Beech Creek	150
Tucker, Peter		8			
Thomas, William	1	2			
Tucker, Jacob[16]	2	11			
Tichener, Jacob		17			
Taylor, James	1				
Tirey, John		1			
Tracey, Nathaniel	2	16			
Thompson, John	1	1			
Todd, John[16]	6	32	Shelby	Gisses Creek	162½
Tater, Robert (?)	7	25	Shelby		
Taylor, Robert, Jr.	2	12			
Taylor, Robert	7	25	Shelby	Tick Creek	286½
Taylor, Robert			Shelby	Gisses	637½
Taylor, Robert			Shelby	Drinnings	500
Taylor, Robert			Shelby	Drinnings	300
Tichener, Joseph	3	6	Shelby	Snake Run	100
Veach, George	3	28	Shelby	Buck (or Beech) Creek	150
Ulrey, Daniel	1	3	Shelby	Snake Run	108
Ulrey, Jacob	2	5	Shelby	Bearshears	100
Winlock, Joseph[18]	3	23	Shelby	Bullskin	294
White, Peter	1		Shelby	Bullskin	100
Williamson, John	1				
Whiteker, Isaac	2	15			
Whiteker, Elisha	1	4			
Wright, John[18]	3	11	Shelby	Jeptry Creek	103½
Wright, John			Shelby	Beech Creek	200
Whiteker, Martha[19]	3	19	Shelby	Clear Creek	200
Whiteker, Abram	2	18	Shelby	Clear Creek	522
William, John	2	13	Shelby	Wisers Run	200
William, John			Shelby	Kentucky	257½
Whiteker, Charles		3			
Wilson, John	1				
Whiteker, Elijah	4	26	Nelson	Cedar Creek	150
Wood, John	3	10	Shelby	Beech Creek	100
Washburn, George	4	11	Shelby	Beech Creek	100
Whiteker, Levy[19]	1	1			
West, Nathaniel	3	4			
Whiteker, Jessee	4	2			
White, Joseph[20]	5	5	Shelby	Elk Creek	150
Woodard, Michael		3			
Whiteker, John[20]	3	10			
Whiteker, Aqualla	11	33	Shelby	Clear Creek	1,000

*Retail store the property of I. Waggoner.

237

Persons Named Charged With Taxes	Horses	Cattle	County	Water Course	Acres of Land
Whiteker, Aqualla			Shelby	Fox Run	700
Waymond, Edmund	2	2			
Wells, Edward	2	3	Shelby	Beech Creek	100
Wise, Daniel	1	5	Shelby	Gisses Creek	100
Winnentvandander ⎫ Winnint ⎭	2				
Young, John[18]	12	28	Shelby	Clear Creek	325
Young, Edward		4			

Total Amount of Taxable Property Taken by Thomas Shannon, Comr. for Shelby County.

Whites over 21 years	383	
Whites over 16 and under 21	59	
Total blacks	141	L.10,11,6p
Blacks under 16	67	
Horses	842	21, 1,0
Cattle	3,087	19, 5,10
Ordinary license	1	3
Stud horses	6	3, 6,0
Retail stores	1	10, 0,0
		67, 3,4p

First rate land	16,169	23/ pr. hund.	L. 24. 4. 9
Second rate land	76,025	@ 1/6 pr. hund.	57. 0. 4½
Third rate land	32,450	@ /9 pr. hund.	12. 3. 4½
Town lots L.464.18			0.13.11¼
Studs	10		5.19. 0
R. stores	3		30. 0. 0
O. licenses	1		3. 0. 0
Slaves	282		21. 3. 0
Horses	1,446		36. 3. 0
Cattle	6,015		25. 1. 3
			L.215. 8. 8½
			67. 3. 4½

State of Kentucky,
  Shelby County,
    July the 8th, 1795.

282. 12. 4¾

This is to Certify that having compared the within List of Taxable property with the Original vouchers taken and returned by Thomas Shannon, Esquire, Commissioner of the Tax for said County and find the same to be a true List.

And having Examined the other Lists with this one find them to be true copys of each other.

                                                          Tese.
                                                          JAMES CRAIG, Clk.

[1] 1 black.
[2] 5 blacks.
[3] 1 black, 1 ordinary license.
[11] 4 blacks.
[4] 1 white male between 16 and 21.
[5] 2 blacks.
[6] 2 white males over 21.
[7] 9 blacks.
[8] 2 white males between 16 and 21.
[9] 14 blacks.
[10] 3 white males between 16 and 21, 10 blacks.

Persons Named Charged With Taxes	Horses	Cattle	County	Water Course	Acres of Land
Armstrong, James[1]	1	9			
Anderson, William	1	3			
Asher, William	1				
Ashby, Silas	2	4			
Adcock, Edmund	1	1			
Brackett, John[2]	5	16	Shelby	Guesses Creek	200
Bowling, George	2	4			
Brinton, Joseph		7			
Boone, John, Jr.	1		Shelby	Fox Run	141
Boone, Jonathan[3]	9	19	Shelby	Clear Creek	500
Boone, Jonathan			Shelby	Clear Creek	180
Bennet, Sanford	2	7	Shelby	Tick	50
Brenton, James	1	8			
Boles, James[4]	3	9	1 lot in Shelby-ville		
Baker, Richard	3				
Burton, Jarrard	1	13			
Burton, Martha Ann	1	8			
Beard, Thomas[5]	10	17	Shelby	Guesses Creek	800
Boone, Isaah	1		Shelby	Fox Run	250
Boone, Isaah			Shelby	Guesses Creek	120
Buran, Phillip	1	3			
Buran, William[6]	3	5			
Boone, John Sr,[3]	3	4			
Boone, William[3]	2	12	Shelby	Fox Run	300
Boone, William			Shelby	Bullskin	275
Brenton, John	1	10			
Boone, Squier, Jr.	3		Shelby	Fox Run	300
Bean, Lewis					
Bull, Abraham	2	6			
Bryan, Morgan					
Brakett, Burrell	1				
Buran, Ibey	3	11	Shelby	Drhenans Lick Creek	
Boyd, Benjamin	1	12			
Boone, Samuel	4	17			
Boone, Moses	3	10			
Brackett, Phil					
Booth, John	1				
Boyd, George	5	7	Shelby	Beech	
Brackett, Hawkings	1	9			
Baker, Elijah	3	15			
Bowling Syms	1	20			
Brenton, Henry	1	7			
Byrk, Richard	1		Shelby	Fox Run	500
Chisholn, Walter			Not known	N. Fork of the Root-ing (?) Salt River	680
Craig, James	1				
Clark, Jacob	1	1			
Calvert, Daniel	2	16			
Conway, Hugh	2	17	Shelby	Bullskin	100

239

Persons Named Charged With Taxes	Horses	Cattle	County	Water Course	Acres of Land
Coleman, Bathsheba		3	Shelby	Fox Run	500
Chapman, Nathan	1				
Carman, Isaac	2	2			
Carman, Mary	1	6	Shelby	Fox Run	200
Carman, Caleb	1	1			
Coon, George	1				
Cooper, Segen	3	19	Shelby	Clear Creek	130
Carr, James	1	14			
Carr, William	1	11			
Colgin, Daniel	9	25	Shelby	Clear Creek	500
Caplenner, Harry	4	25			
Carr, John	2	5			
Cooper, William	3	16	Shelby	Bullskin	600
Cooper, Samuel	2	7			
Cornwell, John	2	10	Shelby	Drhenanslick	172½
Clines, Peter	1	6			
Clines, Nicholas	1	4			
Colelasher, Jacob	2	9			
Colelasher, Abraham	1	7			
Creamour, James	1	1			
Cull, Hugh	1	9			
Carr, James	1				
Clark, Reuben	1				
Collet, John	1		Not known	Mudy River	400
Clynes, John	2	22	Shelby	Tick Creek	300
Chatman, Joshua		2			
Crim, Clary	2	4			
Crim, Peter	1	13	Shelby	Tick Creek	100
Carlin, Peter	2	9	Shelby	Drhenans Lick	100
Crockel, James	1	5			
Cooper, Jonathan	3	10			
Daniel, Martin	1	13	Shelby	Beech Creek	400
Daniel, Martin			Shelby	Clear Creek	422
Daniel, Robert			Bourbon	H. F. Licking	1,920
Daniel, Robert			Bourbon	H. F. Licking	400
Daniel, Robert			Harrison	Fork Lick	17,456
Daniel, Robert			Not known	A coperish mine	7
Daniel, Robert			Harrison	Raven Creek	43
Daniel, Robert			Fayette	Hickman	300
Daniel, Robert			Nelson	Ohio	1,000
Daniel, Robert			Nelson	Coxes Creek	195
Daniel, Robert			An island	In the Ohio	400
Daniel, Robert			Nelson	Simpson Creek	400
Daniel, Robert			Lincoln	Kentucky	150
Daniel, James		1			
Daniel, John		1			
Ditto, William	2	5			
Duncan, Benjamin	2	14			
Duncan, Nimrod	3	18	Shelby	Tick Creek	130
Daniel, Thomas			Shelby	Kentucky	1,000
Darnald, Olever (?)	3				
Dennan, Anthony					
Daniel, Colman	4	7	Shelby	Clear Creek	58
Demoree, Peter	2	3			
Dement, George	2	4			

Persons Named Charged With Taxes	Horses	Cattle	County	Water Course	Acres of Land
Dennan, William	2				
Dennan, John	1	2			
Demoree, Abraham	2	4			
Ditto, Henry			Shelby	Little Kentucky	1,000
Ditto, Henry			Shelby	Drhenans Lick	872
Demoree, Samuel	3	17			
Ervin, Joseph	3	10	Shelby	Drhenans Lick	200
Ervin, Robert	3	10	Shelby	Drhenans Lick	200
Ellerson, Robert	2	32	Shelby	Mulbury	725
Elwood, James					
Farley, Daniel	2	11	Shelby	Mulberry	50
Fountain, William			Not known	Pages Creek	1,000
Favour, Samuel					
Fisher, James	3	20			
Forgerson, Arther	4	11			
Fisher, Zachariah	1	11			
Ford, Ezekiah	2	6	Jefferson	Floyd Fork	146
Ford, Ezekiah			Shelby	Clear Creek	200
Favour, Caleb	1	5			
Fleming, Enoch	1	4			
Forgerson, Kinder	1	1			
Fields, Abner			Shelby	Beech Creek	100
Fields, Abner			Jefferson		66
Fields, Abner, as agent for Joseph Roberts			Shelby		700
Fields, Abner, as agent for Joseph Roberts			Shelby		1,000
Fields, Abner, as agent for Joseph Roberts			Shelby		1,000
Fields, Abner, as agent for Joseph Roberts			Jefferson		1,000
Fisher, Elias					
Grisham, James		7			
Griffe, John	3	16			
Gimmerson, Abraham	1	9			
Gorden, David	1	3	Shelby	Tick Creek	131
Griffin, Ralph	3	32			
Greenwood, Philip	2	8	Shelby	Drenings Lick	143
Glass, Robert	2	7	Shelby	Mulbury	300
Gratehouse, Isaac	4	15	Shelby	Mulbury	200
Harris, James			Jefferson		11,400
Hall, William	1	10	Shelby	Guesses Creek	600
Hall, William			Shelby	Tick Creek	150
Hall, William			Shelby	Benson	560½
Hall, William			Nelson	Beech Fork	400
Hawkings, Clabon					
Harris, John	5	12			
Hobbs, Jacob	2	7			
Hensley, George	2	8	Shelby	Mulbury	50
Hughes, Thomas	1	8			
Hensley, Samuel		6			
Harris, Daniel		4			

Persons Named Charged With Taxes	Horses	Cattle	County	Water Course	Acres of Land
Harris, George	1	2			
Hoke, Henry	2	20			
Hogland, Moses	1	8			
Hogland, Jamimah	1	3			
Hogland, James	3	33	Shelby	Clear Creek	254½
Holman, George	1	7	Shelby	Mulbury	400
Hogland, Nancy	4	9	Shelby	Drennings Lick	100
Horton, Thomas					
Hemphill, James	1				
Hensley, James		2			
Howard, Allen	1	9			
Hunter, Samuel	2	12			
Howard, James					
Harris, Jonathan					
Harris, William	2	5	Shelby	Clear Creek	159
Harris, William			Not known	Green River	100
Junkins, Anthony	4	16	Shelby	Tick Creek	100
Junkins, Anthony			Nelson	Mill Creek	600
Jacobs, William	1	3			
Johnson, John					
Johnson, Andrew					
Infield, Thomas	2	10			
Jones, John	2	7			
Jones, Isaac	3	5			
Junkins, Samsetot	4	26	Shelby	Guesses Creek	100
Kipheart, John	3	13			
Kilbreath, David		9			
Kilbreath, James	1	5			
Kipheart, Abraham	2	2			
Kipheart, Jacob	3	16	Shelby	Drennings Lick	300
Kipheart, Charles	2	8			
Kipheart, George		2			
Kerling, Joseph	1				
Kinder, Peter, Sr.	3	17	Shelby	Big Bullskin	150
Kinder, Peter, Jr.					
Kiser, Frederick, Jr.		3			
Kiser, Frederick, Sr.	6	14	Shelby	Fox Run	130
Katchum, Daniel	5	30			
Kiser, John					
Lowden, Robert	3	15	Shelby	Drennings Lick	266
Liget, John	1	5			
Laphety, John	2	4			
Laswell, William	3	7			
Lawson, John	1	10			
Laphety, Barney		6			
Lemaster, Caty	1	12	Shelby	Drennings Lick	200
Lambert, James		13			
Lowden, Thomas	1	7			
Lapety, Benijah	2	3			
Lemaster, James	1	10	Shelby	Drennings Lick	207½
Lively, Guilham	4	29			
Long, Anderson	5	18	Shelby	Clear Creek	250

Persons Named Charged With Taxes	Horses	Cattle	County	Water Course	Acres of Land
Mounee, Samuel		4			
Munson, Allen					
McClellen, Daniel	5	29	Shelby	Big Jepsey	300
Meryfiel, Mary		4			
McClure, Joan	2	8			
McClure, James	7	11			
McClure, William	1	9			
McKindley, Samuel	2	13	Shelby	Drhennans Lick	200
McGahha, Arther	3	5	Shelby	Clear Creek	150
Morris, Harry	3	4			
Morris, Joshua	7	20	Shelby	Ohio	1,190
Morris, Joshua			Shelby	Bullskin	196
Morris, Joshua			Franklin or Woodford	Elkhorn	1,220
Moore, Abraham	3	12			
Meryfield, Reece	2				
Meryfield, Allen	2	10			
Meek, John, Jr.	2	15			
Montgomery, John					
Meek, Jacob	2	7			
Mack, Jeremiah	1	2			
May, George	2	17			
Medcalf, Thomas	1	4			
Meek, John, Sr.	5	25			
McClure, John					
Medcalf, James	2	6			
Medcalf, William	3	21			
Meddeek, Emanuel	1	10			
McMund, Allenr	2		Shelby	Clear Creek	500
Moore, John		4			
Medcalf, John		15	Shelby	Clear Creek	120
Masten, John	1	2			
Montgomery, Allenr	3	12			
Morris, William			Shelby	Mulberry	2,000
Morris, William			Shelby	Big Benson	1,000
Marten, Aron	2	12			
Marten, Peter	2	7			
Marten, Lewis	1	2			
Morrow, William	3	15			
Marten, William					
Morris, John	3	8	Jefferson	Floyds Fork	8,000
Meek, Basel	1	5			
Minor, Thomas			Shelby	Guesses Creek	100
Meriwether, Nicholas		7	Shelby	Clear Creek	760
Meriwether, Nicholas			Shelby	Ohio	3,000
Meriwether, Nicholas			Shelby	S. Fork Clear Creek	500
Meriwether, Nicholas			Franklin	Hammons Creek	1,000
Meriwether, Nicholas			Hardin	Green River	1,351
Meriwether, Nicholas			Formerly Nelson	Nole Lynn	500
Meriwether, Nicholas			Nelson		600
Meriwether, Nicholas			Hardin	Clover Creek	2,972
Meriwether, Nicholas			Jefferson	Beargrass	1,434
Meriwether, Nicholas			Jefferson	Beargrass	666
Meriwether, Nicholas			Jefferson	Ohio	
Meriwether, Nicholas			Jefferson	Ohio	
Meriwether, Nicholas			Jefferson	Beargrass	30

Persons Named Charged With Taxes	Horses	Cattle	County	Water Course	Acres of Land
Meriwether, Nicholas			Harrison	Hinkston	2,000
Meriwether, Nicholas			Harrison	Hinkston	
Meriwether, Nicholas			Harrison	Hinkston	2,562
Meriwether, Nicholas			Campbell	Licking & Ohio	1,466⅔
Meriwether, Nicholas			Campbell	Big Bone	533
Noel, Basel	3	12			
Nield, Elias	2	5	Shelby	Mulberry	575
Neeley, Joseph	1	9	Shelby	Tick Creek	138¼
Norman, William					
O'Neal, Bryant	5	18			
Owen, John	5	6	Shelby	Clear Creek	209
Owen, Abraham			Shelby	Gesses Creek	453
Owen, Abraham			Shelby	Gesses Creek	12
Paris, Robert	12	32			
Price, John	5	3			
Pickens, John	2	4			
Porter, David	2	5			
Peter, John	3	6	Shelby	Clear Creek	860
Porter, Jane	2	25			
Patterson, John	1	12	Shelby	Bullskin	10½
Piper, Henry	1	2			
Patrick, Robert	1	4			
Pritchard, James	2	13			
Peter, Thos.	1	1			
Parker, Thos.	2	13			
Parker, John	4	15			
Pryor, Samuel	2	3	Shelby	Mulberry	275
Right, Obedick	1	2			
Robertson, James			Shelby	Plumb Creek	2,200
Rollins, Aaron	1	11			
Robins, Rachel		10			
Romine, James		5			
Ryker, John	4	5	Shelby	Bulskin	100
Ryker, Gerades	2	9	Shelby	Bullskin	100
Robins, Vincent	1	6	Shelby	Clear Creek	50
Right, David	5				
Ryker, Samuel		15	Shelby	Bullskin	50
Rue, Richard	2	16	Shelby	Drennans Lick	400
Standiford, David	1	10	Shelby	Clear Creek	400
Standiford, David			Shelby	Clear Creek	525
Standiford, David			Shelby	Clear Creek	100
Standiford, David			Shelby	Little Kentucky	500
Standiford, David			Shelby	Big Kentucky	1,000
Standiford, David			Shelby	Drenins Lick	525
Standiford, David			Jefferson	Floyd Fork	500
Smith, John		5			
Swearingen, Van	2	2	Shelby	Gesses Creek	282
Steel, Adam	2	6			
Sills, Adam	5	6	Shelby	Tick Creek	61
Smock, Jacob	3	4			
Samples, Sam'l					
Swinney, James	5				

Persons Named Charged With Taxes	Horses	Cattle	County	Water Course	Acres of Land
Samples, David	3	3			
Simpson, Soloman	3	9			
Scantling, Alex'd					
Smither, Nicholas	4	10	Shelby	Drenings Lick	350
Simpson, Joseph	2	2			
Smith, David	2	23			
Scott, James	6	40	Shelby	Clear Creek	391
Scott, James			Jefferson	Floyds Fork	250
Singleton, Philip	5				
Smith, Susanna		13	Shelby	Drennins Lick Creek	400
Sullivan, Jeremiah	1	3	Shelby	Bullskin	37
Shepherd, Martha	1				
Shepherd, James	1	7			
Singleton, Rich'd	4	2			
Shepherd, Davis	1	6			
Simpson, Agnes	3	9			
Storm, Jacob	1	7			
Smock, Charity		7			
Smilie, Robt.					
Shepherd, Christ'r		2			
Smith, Nathan	5	5			
Skidmore, John	2	9			
Shannon, John	6	12	Jefferson	Floyd Fork	800
Talbot, Ezekiel	1	10	Shelby	Gesses Creek	100
Talbot, Ezekiel			Clark	Red River	500
Townsen, Light	3	13	Shelby	Tick Creek	100
Teagen, John, Sr.	2	26	Shelby	Bullskin	100
Teagen, John Jr.					
Teagen, William	1	10	Shelby	Clear Creek	62½
Talbot, Isham	3	8	Shelby	Mulberry	300
Talbot, Isham			Clark	Red River	1,200
Talbot, Isham			Scott	Lick Creek	3,008½
Tucker, George	2	8			
Thorn, Elizabeth		8	Shelby	Drennins Lick	140
Taylor, Richard		5			
Underwood, John	1	14	Shelby	Mulberry	333⅓
Underwood, Nathan		4	Shelby	Mulberry	
Underwood, Jacob	3	11	Shelby	Mulberry	
Underwood, Joseph	3	8	Shelby	Tick Creek	
Vancleave, John	2	9	Shelby	Bullskin	300
Vancleave, John, Jr.	5	1			
Vancleave, Benj'm	5	13	Shelby	Bullskin	400
Vancleave, Benj'm			Shelby	Six Mile Creek	300
Vancleave, Benj'm			Shelby	Drennings Lick	300
Yount, George	4	14	Shelby	Tick Creek	150
Yount, Nicholas	2	3			
Yount, John	1	6			
Fullenwider, Jacob	3	17	Shelby	Bullskin	200
Fullenwider, Jacob			Shelby	Bullskin	

¹ 3 blacks.
² 10 blacks.
³ 1 black.
⁴ Retail store.
⁵ 2 blacks.
⁶ 5 blacks.

245

State of Kentucky,

Shelby County, July the 7th, 1795.

I do hereby certify that having compared the within list of taxable property taken and returned by Coleman Daniel, Esqr., Commissioner of the Tax for said County with the Original Lists; and find the same to be accurately done. And having examined the said List with the three Other Lists, find them to be true Copies of each other. Given under my hand the day and year aforesaid.

JAMES CRAIG, Clk., S. C.

Amount of Taxable Property Taken by Coleman Daniel, Shelby County.

	383		
White males	314		
	697		
White males over 16 and under 21	38		
Total blacks	142	at 1/6 per head	L. 10—13
Blacks under 16 years	75		
Horses	604		15— 2
Cattle	2,928		18— 6
Stud horses	4		2—13
Retail stores	2		20
LAND—			
First rate land	7,515	@ 3/ pr. hun.	L. 11- 5-5
Second rate land	43,505	@ 1/6 pr. hun.	32-12-6
Third rate land	77,414	pr. hun.	28-13-1
Amount of taxes paid for 92, 93 & 94 L.58-0-9½			139" 5"
			215" 8" 8¼
			354"13" 8¼

I do hereby Certify that having compared the Original Lists returned by Coleman Daniel, Commissioner, and find the same to be true list. Given under my hand this 27th day of Nov., 1795.

James Craig, Clk.

The Auditor of Public Accounts.

Additional List.

Persons Named Charged With Taxes	County	Water Course	Acres of Land
Boone, John, Jr.	Shelby	Six Mile	1,000
Crawford, Nathan	Green	Green River	1,100
Collet, John	Jefferson	Pond Creek	10,000
Collet, John, for John Ryley	Jefferson	Pond Creek	7,031¼
Crawford, Nathan for Binnett Henderson	Shelby	Plum Creek	2,351½
Davis, James	Green	Pittmans Creek	300
Dupuy, Joseph, for Charles Seaman	Not known	Waters of Licking	500
Dupuy, Joseph, for Lewis Craig	Shelby	L. Kentucky	2,000
Dupuy, Joseph, for Lewis Craig	Franklin	Twinns (Creeks)	2,000
	Shelby	L. Bullskin	3,511½
Dupuy, Joseph, for John Tylor	Shelby	C. Creek	2,000
Dupuy, Joseph, for John Tylor	Shelby	Kentuck	1,000
Dupuy, Joseph, for John Tylor	Not known	L. Benson	1,000
Dupuy, Bartholomew	Shelby	Drenning Lick	3,500
Dupuy, Bartholomew	Shelby	Plumb Run	3,500
Dupuy, Bartholomew	Shelby	Floyds Fork	3,500
Dupuy, Joseph, for Robt. Tylor	Shelby	Drinnings Lick	720
Dupuy, Joseph, for Charles Seaman	Shelby	Drinnings Lick	1,000
Dupuy, Joseph, for Jonah Seaman	Shelby	Fox Run	500
Daniel, Robert	Hardin	Not known	1,000
Daniel, Robert		Burning Spring	1,000
Daniel, Robert		Green River	500
Daniel, Robert	Hardin	Green River	600
Daniel, Robert	Nelson	Nollin	1,000
Daniel, Robert	Hardin	Wolf Creek	1,000
Daniel, Robert	Hardin	Wolf Creek	1,000
Daniel, Robert	Shelby	Floyds Fork	8,843
Daniel, Robert	Hardin	Green River	1,228
Daniel, Robert	Hardin	Nollin	1,000
Daniel, Robert	Hardin	Nollin	2,000
Daniel, Robert	Washington	Shawnee Lick	400
Daniel, Robert	Shelby	C. Creek	200
Daniel, Robert	Shelby	Ohio	300
Daniel, Robert	Nelson	Ashes Creek	1,000
Daniel, Robert	Jefferson	S. River	555
Daniel, Robert		Green River	500
Daniel, Robert	Hardin	Green River	2,000
Humphries, George, for Samuel Stump.	Shelby	B. Creek	288
Marshall, George, for John Withers	Shelby	C. Creek	1,000
Medcalf, Thomas	Shelby	C. Creek	95⅓
McCleland, Danl., for E. McCleland	Shelby	C. Creek	200
Medcalf, Thos., for Wm. Medcalf	Shelby	C. Creek	100
Myers, Jacob	Lincoln	Cumberland	1,000
Myers, Jacob	Lincoln	Cumberland	5,000
Myers, Jacob	Lincoln	Laurel	10,000
Myers, Jacob	Lincoln	Laurel	418

Persons Named Charged With Taxes	County	Water Course	Acres of Land
Owen, Abraham	Lincoln	Rolling Fork	1,000
Paris, Robt. for John Howe	Fayette	B. Kentucky	100
Paris, Robt. for John Howe	Scott	Eagle Creek	1,000
Robert, Wm., for Joseph Roberts	Shelby	C. Creek	700
Robert, Wm., for Joseph Roberts	Shelby	C. Creek	300
Robert, Wm., for Joseph Roberts	Shelby	C. Creek	800
Robert, Wm., for Joseph Roberts	Shelby	Gesses Creek	1,000
Robert, Wm., for Joseph Roberts	Shelby	C. Creek	1,000
Robert, Wm., for Joseph Roberts	Mason	Licking	1,000
Robert, Wm., for Joseph Roberts	Hardin	Pittmans Creek	2,904½
Robert, Wm., for Joseph Roberts	Hardin	Barrens	1,000
Robert, Wm., for Joseph Roberts	Logan	Muddy Run	1,500
Robert, Wm., for Joseph Roberts	Jefferson	Pond Creek	1,000
Shannon, Thos.	Green	Pittmans Creek	300
Sullivan, James, for Aron Sullivan	Shelby	Fox Run	200
Shannon, Alexr.	Shelby	C. Creek	315
Wilcox, John	Shelby	Fox Run	250
			49,106

DEPARTMENT OF STATE ARCHIVES—TAX LIST OF WASH-INTON COUNTY—1792.

(Editor's Note:—Washington County was formed from part of Nelson under an act signed by Governor Isaac Shelby, June 22nd, 1792. This first county of the new State of Kentucky was named for Gen. George Washington, and in the act authorizing its erection it is described as follows: "From and after the first day of September next that part of Nelson beginning on Salt River where the boundary line between Nelson and Mercer crosses the same, thence down the said river to the mouth of Crooked Creek or what is by some called Lewis Run, thence a straight line to the mouth of Beaver Creek, a branch of Chaplains Fork, and thence down Chaplains Fork to the Beech Fork, thence down the Beech Fork to the mouth of Hardins Creek, thence a straight line to the Big Knob Lick near the Pottingers Creek, thence a straight line to the mouth of Salt Lick Run, emptying into the Rolling Fork on the south side, thence up the main branch of the said run to the ridge dividing the waters of the Rolling Fork from Green River waters; thence eastwardly along the said dividing ridge to the line dividing Lincoln from Nelson, thence with the same to the Mercer line, thence along the line between Nelson and Mercer to the beginning, shall be one distinct county and called and known by the name of Washington and all the residue of the said county shall be called by the name of Nelson."

The act further provided that the justices who should be appointed for the new county should meet at the house of Francis Simbrill to "appoint and qualify a clerk and fix upon a place to hold courts in the said county at or as near the center thereof as the situation and convenience will admit of."

Washington County continued under the same boundary set forth above until 1827 when a small part of it was taken to form the southern portion of Anderson. In 1834 the whole of the southern portion of Washington was cut off to form Marion County.)

Tithables	Blacks	Horses	Cattle	Acres of Land
Allin, William		5	12	500
Allen, David		1	3	
Adams, Peter		3	13	50
Alvey, John	1	4	10	200
Allen, Archibald		3	13	
Askin, Phillimon		3	6	100
Askin, Edward	2	1	5	350
Askin, Phillimon, Jr.			6	
Alvey, Joseph		1	4	144
Abel, Samuel	10	4	27	
Abel, Joshua	6	3		482
Abell, Barton	1	2	4	
Alvey, Thomas G.	1	2	4	100
Alvey, Robert		1	5	96
Abell, Robert	9	5	9	441½
Burcham, David		2	9	100
Barlow, Jacob		5	13	50
Barlow, Cornelius		1		
Barlow, Lewis		1	10	25
Brownfield, James		9	19	
*Berry, Richard	2	10	34	600
Barlow, Michael		1	4	
Barlow, Christopher		3	13	100
Brothers, Cornelius	1	3	11	264
†Brewer, William		2	4	70
Brown, Anthony		3	5	45
Brown, Ann		2	5	107
Brothers, John		3	3	

*2 tithables.
†3 Tithables.

Tithables	Blacks	Horses	Cattle	Acres of Land
Boon, John	4	3	8	
Brown, Bazil		3	12	
Bozworth, Henry		3	14	50
Bennet, Benjamin		2	4	100
Burdyne, Betty	2	5	10	300
Bringle, George		1	1	500
Beal, Richard		6	21	250
Brown, Benjamin	4	3	16	250
Briggs, Ebenezer		4	5	350
Barlow, Henry		3	13	100
Briscoe, Edward		1	2	
Baxter, William		3	7	
Buckman, Ignatius		7		250
Bland, Rachel		5	10	
Brown, Raphael		1		
Bords (?), William	1	4	23	115
Brothers, Cornelius, Jr.		2	3	
Brunts, James		3	8	
Bennit, Sam'l			1	
Briscoe, Jeremiah	2	11	36	1,100
Bullock, John	5	5	13	400
*Brunt, Peter		4	9	86
Blackburn, William		3		
Brown, Coleman	4	5	36	315
Briggs, William				230
Caldwell, William	14	6	27	500
Clark, David		2	2	
**Caldwell, John	11	5	15	650
Cavenhaven (?), Joseph		3	9	100
Clark, Shadrack		1	9	
Cissel, Rhody		3	9	
Cissel, Barnabas		1	7	50
Clifton, Burdit	4	3	12	
Clifton, Baldin		4	6	1,181
Clifton, Howsan		12	19	
Cummins, Peter	1	6	20	
Cissel, John B.	1	4	22	130
Carlisle, James		3	12	
Carlisle, John	1	2	8	
Carlisle, William		2	8	
*Chesnut, William		1	1	150
Chandler, Robert	1	6	9	
Cartwright, Joseph		3	8	300
Cunningham, John		7	19	200
Camburn, Ignatius		1	4	
Catlin, James		1	3	
Case, Reuben		2	6	
Case, Elizabeth		2	2	
Crume, Daniel		5	17	233
Clements, Thomas		1	4	
Claland, Phillip	9	5	13	
Catlin, Theory		4	6	
Catlin, Seth	3	4	14	
Chamberlin, Thos.		4	10	50
Cox, Richard			5	

*2 tithables.
**Retail store.

Tithables	Blacks	Horses	Cattle	Acres of Land
‡Coppage, Moses		6	19	
Caffey, Benjamin		4	3	
Cissel, James		1	9	125
Camburn, Thomas			2	
*Camburn, James		1	2	
Camburn, John B.		2	19	250
Cummins, Thomas		3	9	
Crawford, Abell		2	5	50
Camburn, Henry		4	4	
Camburn, William		1	5	
Cash, Caleb		2	7	
Crawford, John		1	9	
*Caldwell, David	9	9	16	300
Cissel, Joshua				
Davis, Robert		3	10	500
Davis, John		2	10	500
Duncaster, Charles		1	7	
Dant, John B.	7	3	13	100
Dant, Joseph	2			
Davis, David		2	12	150
Daily, Bend't		1	10	100
Davis, Phillip		3	12	
Dickin, William	2	3	12	162
Davidson, John		8	15	202
Dicken, John	1	2		500
Dennis, Samuel		2		
Dean, Benjamin		3	15	75¼
Dyer, John		5	14	
Dyer, William		7	25	200
Dyer, John, Jr.				
Dufner, Jacob		1		
Dawson, George		1	1	
Doom, Jacob		11	26	850
Duel, William		1	5	
Dowdal, John	7	7	19	
Depu, William				
Dowling, James		2	10	
Ewing, Charles	2	4	8	800
Ewing, George	2	3		
Eves, Mastin Hearst	4	6	25	500
Elder, William	1	3	4	
Elder, James		3	4	200
Elder, Ignatius	1	2	3	
Edmonson, John		2	4	
Edmonson, Patty	1	2	1	2,000
Eliston, Thomas	1	4	16	
Elder, Joseph	1	4	4	
Elliott, Stephen	3	4	10	260
Elliott, Thomas		6	11	125
Evins, John			1	
Elliott, Edward		1		
Froman, Isaac		4	7	200
Fickle, Benjamin		2	5	50

‡5 tithables.
*2 tithables.

Tithables	Blacks	Horses	Cattle	Acres of Land
Ferry, James		1	1	400
Flemming, John			2	
Fagan, Michael				
Fowler, Charles		1	8	
French, James		1	9	
*Finwix, Thomas	2	2	13	100
Gray, Joseph	28	32	125	2,576
Grayham, David			9	
Gilkey, David		10	13	150
Gough, Charles		2	3	150
Gough, John B.		1	7	
Grimes, John		8	18	250
Grimes, Francis		5	10	250
Gilliham, Clement		1	6	400
Griffy, Samuel			2	
Galliway, John		4	12	
Galliway, Robert		5	7	
Gaither, Cornelius				
Grunwell, Charles		3	3	100
Grayham, Marcus		4	9	
Graves, Charles		1	4	50
Grant, Adam		3	5	220
Grigory, Richard	5	6	37	150
Grigory, Smith		2	9	
Gibbs, Benjamin	2	6	12	
Grundy, Gardum (?)		7	10	
Grundy, John	2	14	22	
Grundy, George	2	8	16	
Grundy, Samuel	2	16	2	
Grundy, Elizabeth	10	8	30	
Grundy, Robert		8	16	
Hardin, Benjamin	10	8	27	800
Harrison, Thomas	1	1	2	
Hardin, John P.		3	19	696
Hardin, Martin	5	5	20	1,000
Hardin, Henry		1	8	100
Hardin, Ann	1	2	15	200
Hardin, John, Jr.			7	100
Hardin, Big John		1	8	
Hupp, George		5	9	142
Hickman, Ezekiel		1	5	50
Hays, William		5	20	223
Hudgel, Joseph		2	7	44
Hudgel, John		1		
*Haydon, Baziel	16	9	34	243
Haydon, Stanislaus	1	2	6	
Haydon, Bennet	2	2	35	45
Haydon, Charles	1	2	4	
Hand, John		1	3	100
Heard, John B.		3	5	
Holland, Henry		3	4	400
Harding, John		2	14	75
Howard, Caty		1	5	25
Harding, Thomas		3	8	100

*2 tithables.

Tithables	Blacks	Horses	Cattle	Acres of Land
Harding, Robert		3	13	100
Howard, Charles		3	7	25
Head, Edward	2	6	4	
Head, Henry		2	2	
Hine, Thomas		2	4	
Hill, John		2	1	
Hughes, Robert	1	6	8	100
Hendrickson, Leonard			7	30
Hardin, Jane	7	9	26	2,700
Hopson, William		3	4	
Hald, John		1		
Hald, Caleb			4	
Hawrigan, Patrick		13	8	250
Hamilton, James		4	7	
Hamilton, Isham	1	3	8	
Hindman, James		1	3	
Haydon, John		2	3	350
Haydin, William		5	12	200
Hilton, William	1	1	5	
Hilton, Henry H.				
Hager, James		2	2	150
*Harding, Stephen		11	19	
Halliday, John		2	12	200
Handly, James		8	37	379
Handly, Alexander	1	3	4	
Hunter, Alexander		3	12	
Hitchens, James		1		
Hardin, Marck	3	11	40	2,750
Harbison, John		3	8	
Hill, Thomas	5	1	10	
Hardin, Absolom				
Hardin, Moses		2	6	
Hamilton, Leonard	8	7	2	600
Hamilton, Clements				
Hardin, Ede				
Hundley, Anthony				
Hundley, Josiah				
Holms, John	1	5	19	
Jones, William	1	1	11	100
Jeremiah, Thomas				
*Jackson, John		11	15	400
*Jackson, William		16	15	200
Jarbow, John B.		4	11	
Jarbow, Henry		4	4	
Jones, Balaam	3	4	5	1,400
Jackson, John				
Kennison, James		1	1	
Kennison, Joseph			3	
Kyles, Thomas		2	9	137
Keeling, Thomas		1	3	
Keeling, Benjamin		2	6	28
King, John E.	1	4	5	
Kendal, Thomas		1	8	
Kirk, James		1	7	28
Kennison, James		4	5	

*2 tithables.

Tithables	Blacks	Horses	Cattle	Acres of Land
Kirk, Henry		3	6	
Kennet, Charles		3	19	500
Kelly, William				
Kendrick, William		11	23	200
Keeling, William		3	6	50
Keeling, James			2	
*Kimberlin, Jacob		4	40	200
Kilerause (?), Robert		2	6	
Kendall, Davis		1	7	
Kendal, William		1		
Liston, Joseph		2	4	100
Logan, Robert	4	4	12	450
Lincoln, Mordicae		1	2	100
‡‡Lincoln, Bathsheba		1	10	
Litsen, Susanna		3	17	200
Lee, Phillip	4	4	12	168
Lucas, Ignatius		1	2	
Lucas, Henry		2	7	130
Little, Jane	2	4	10	
Luallin, John			5	100
Leonard, William		2	4	
Long, John		4	8	
Murry, Charles		5	15	150
Mudd, Luke		5	11	100
Mock, Daniel		2	8	100
Mattingly, Clements		3	6	
Milburn, Joseph		4	9	85
*Manning, John		2	4	
Mattingly, Robert		3	9	100
Mattingly, William		2	6	50
Mattingly, Ignatius		3	3	360
Mattingly, Leonard		2	11	
Mills, Ignatius	2	3	3	360
Mattingly, Luke		2	9	
Mattingly, John		3	10	100
Mattingly, Leonard		2	16	181½
McKay, George		2	6	64
Mock, Jacob		3	5	
Murphy, Hays		5	10	
Mercer, George		4	12	20
Morrison, Hugh		2	3	
McKee, William			2	
Morgan, Patrick		4	8	
McIntire, Thomas		3	10	250
Mastin, William		1	4	
Moore, John			3	
*McKay, Hugh	6	9	18	500
Myers, Michael		8	9	100
Myers, Jacob		5	22	200
Myers, William				100
Martin, Nathaniel		4	13	
Miles, Mary		1	8	
McMurry, James		2	19	
Medlock, Isham				

‡‡Grandmother of Abraham Lincoln.
*2 tithables.

Tithables	Blacks	Horses	Cattle	Acres of Land
McKay, Samuel	4	6	12	250
Mann, John		3	4	
McMurry, John	1	8	19	1,000
McKay, John	1	3	3	
McKay,, Hugh, Jr.		3	6	
Mann, Asa		6	2	
McColgan, Edward	1	6	17	100
Muldraugh, John	1	6	28	780
McClure, John			1	
Miles, Joseph		1	2	124
Montgomery, Edw'd		3	5	
Montgomery, John		1	3	
McAtee, Henry		2	2	150
Montgomery, Elisha		1	4	
Miles, Wilford		1	7	
Mattingly, John		2	1	
Merridith, William			2	
Miller, John				
Mann, Moses		6	4	
McColgan, James		2	1	
McKee, James		2	2	175
Neighbours, John		1	2	100
Neely, David		2	9	50
Nicholas, Abiel			6	50
Newton, Ignatius			1	
Newton, John N.		7	11	100
Neely, James		3	4	100
Neely, John		3	3	
Nowlin, Lewis			2	
Nell, John		1	4	
Notingham, Phillip	1	5	3	833
Nalle, John				
Oneal, James				
Orr, Samuel	2	3	8	500
Overlin, John		2	7	200
Odair, John		2	1	
Pottinger, Samuel		2	10	160
Penn, Matthew		9	11	
Peterson, Henry		4	7	100
Payn, Charles		1	1	
Pike, William	1	2	4	
Peak, Robert		2	8	125
Perry, John	2	3	13	550
Phillips, Andrew		5	7	
*Piles, William		7	25	
Piles, Richard		4	8	
Parsans, James		1	4	50
Powell, Thomas		2	16	
Pane, Jonathan		5	11	
Pane, Samuel		2	7	
†Purdy, John		7	13	800
Peackston, James		2	4	67
Pyburn, Lewis		8	17	100

*2 tithables.
†3 tithables.

Tithables	Blacks	Horses	Cattle	Acres of Land
Patrick, Samuel		3	4	
Phillip, Fredrick		1	5	45
Pryor, Peyton		4	7	
Pearce, Thomas	1	7	30	630
Phillips, Benjamin		6	21	
Pike, John	1	2	10	100
Phillips, Thomas		8	28	300
Phillips, John	2	12	25	400
Phillips, William		7	9	100
Pottinger, William				
Peters, Peter	4	4	13	225
Parker, Richard	7	6	40	2,913
Parker, Robert	1	2	13	
Queen, Elijah		1	1	
Row, Adam		1	2	
*Rounder, Joseph		1	10	100
Robertson, Samuel	4	4	22	347
Reaves, Nathaniel		1		
Reyny (?), Thomas		3	9	50
Russel, Charles		2	7	100
Ray, Absolom		5	2	400
Ray, Benjamin		5	15	840
Ray, Richard		3	16	400
Ray, John		10	17	512
Robins, Aaron		2	3	
Robins, Mary		1	4	100
Rickets, Zachy		1	4	180
Riggs, William		4	12	200
Rout, George			5	
Robins, John	3	4	14	50
Ryon, James		3	16	200
Ridge, William		3	4	133¾
Robins, John		2	8	
Richards, George		4	10	250
Ray, William		4	4	
Ray, Joseph			8	
Ray, Nathaniel		5	7	
Ray, William		4	4	
Rutter, James	2	11	27	
Robertson, George		6	25	200
Rayly, John B.		1	8	
Rayly, John		1	5	100
Rayly, Henry S.		1	4	
Rice, William	3	5	19	1,500
Rice, Larkin				
Rice, Jesse		1	2	
Riney, Jonathan		2	9	
Riney, Clements			2	
Riney, Bazil	1	1	2	100
Roach, Francis				
Rounder, Molly		1	4	
Shewbard, John			2	
Stout, Aaron		2	1	
Shread, John		1	3	25
Stapleton, John		3	14	100

Titables	Blacks	Horses	Cattle	Acres of Land
Sibert, Peter		4	20	150
Swearingin, Charles		2	6	
Slack, William		3	15	200
Slack, Randolph		2	15	200
Slack, Randolph, Jr.		4	7	
*Smock, Henry	4	8	18	704
Smith, William		1	1	
Snelling, William		2	4	200
Snelling, Hugh	6	5	11	150
Smith, Thomas		11	45	
Scott, George		8	22	100
Seaton, William		5	6	
Stillwell, Ann		4	4	57½
Stillwell, Daniel		2	3	40
Smith, Presley	6	12	30	300
Smith, Benjamin		3	4	75
Scandland, Benj.				
Stapton, Scarborough		2	7	400
Stayton, Thomas		4	14	292
Silvers, Samuel	1	10	14	250
Steyton, Obed		3	10	
Simbrill, Francis		6	13	250
Speaks, Barzella		1		
Sherald, Arrington		3	9	
Sherrald, Elisha		7	11	
Steal, Paul		2	6	
Springer, John		3	23	200
Shread, Peter		2	6	
Silvers, John		10	16	550
Sandusky, Antho'y		10	19	491
South, Henry		1	1	
Sandusky, John		10	13	
Simpson, Thomas	1			600
Simpson, John	1			800
Ship, Richard		6	6	
Springer, Isaac		5	13	1,000
Smith, Nicholas	1	2		
Spaldin, Benedict	7	4	13	441½
Sims, John		4	11	
Sutton, William			1	
Stalcup, Hannah		1	9	100
Spencer, Michal		1	6	50
Speaks, Rebecca		3	9	
Springer, Ann		4	6	300
Smith, Stapton		1	4	100
Shoemaker, William		4	12	
Tobin, Robert	2	2	30	
Talbot, Edward		1	7	
Trunum, Thomas		3	8	400
Thompson, Joseph		1	3	150
Thomas, Owen		3	8	100
Thomas, Harding		5	10	
Thomas, Isaac		3	16	
Thomas, Lewis		2	15	900
Thomas, Enos		2	6	100
Thomas, Henry		3	10	100
Templin, Terah		1		300

Tithables	Blacks	Horses	Cattle	Acres of Land
Taylor, John		4	6	100
Taylor, Cleyton		2	2	
ªVaughan, Samuel	2	5	34	150
Vancleave, Aaron	1	5	8	100
Walton, Matthew	15	10	39	3,400
Waters, Phillemon		6	9	314
Wynman, Christian		6	18	
Wynman, Lewis		2	7	
Winset, Raphael		1	10	80
Winset, Stephen		2	7	100
Wade, John, Jr.		1	3	
Wade, Greenbury		1	6	
Wade, Joseph		5	11	25
Wright, Thomas		10	22	349
Wheler, Zadock		2	6	
††Weldon, Vachael				
Wright, Thomas		1	7	
Wilñng, Thomas		1	3	
Wynman, Christian, Jr.		5	14	100
Washburn, Phillip		2	7	200
Wade, John		6	16	50
Wood, Henry		8	16	300
Waller, John	5	8	17	700
Walker, William	2	6	13	
Weathers, James		2	4	170
Whitesides, Samuel		3	6	
Wilson, Josiah		10	16	500
Whitecotton, James				
*Walker, Phillip		9	9	
William, Wright (?)		1	6	100
Wilson, Agnis		6	40	
Williams, Isaac		3	12	
Whitcliff, Charles	9	9	25	400
Wheatly, Leonard		1	2	
Wright, William		2	9	744
Walker, Thomas		1	5	
Weekly, John				
Young, Samuel		1	9	100
Yates, Zachary		4	5	
Yates, Thomas	3	4	3	
Yoder, Jacob	4	3	10	
Total	382	1,695	4,720	79,417¾

*2 tithables.
††Name crossed out.

Washington County, Sct.
I hereby certify that I have examined the within list of taxable property according to law, and find it (as corrected) to be a true copy.

Teste: John Reed, C. C.

A List of Deeds admitted to Record in the County Court of Washington between the first day of September, 1792, and the last day of January, 1793.

Parties	Quantity Land	When Admitted to Record
John Alvey to John Caldwell..............................	100	October Court
Same to William Allen....................................	202	Same
Same to William Keeling...............................	50	Same
Same to Benjamin Keeling............................	28	Same
William Dyer to John Raley................................	100	Same
John Phillips to William Dicken.........................	170	December
Same to Thomas Wright.................................	100	Same
Same to James Kirk..	28	Same
Same to Thomas Staton, Jr..........................	50	Same
Francis Simbrill & w. to Jno. Reed, Jr.............	250	Same
Dudley Brown to Jno. Bullock............................	800	January
	1,878	

Test: John Reed, C. W. C.

DEPARTMENT OF STATE ARCHIVES
WAYNE COUNTY, KENTUCKY.

In connection with the Reminiscences of Capt. Micah Taul, the first Clerk of Wayne County, whose name is signed to the original Tax Lists in the Archives of Kentucky, it is believed that the following data in regard to the county will be found interesting to the descendants of the early settlers of that section of the State.

The boundaries of the county as originally laid out are described in the Acts of the Kentucky Legislature as follows:

"An Act for the erection of a new County out of the Counties of Pulaski and Cumberland.

Approved December 18, 1800.

"Section 1—Be it enacted by the general assembly, That from and after the first day of March next, all that part of the counties of Pulaski and Cumberland, included within the following bounds, that is to say—beginning at the mouth of Indian Creek, on the Cumberland river and running up the same by Sanduskie's cabin, to the road that leads from Capt. Thomas Johnson's to Major Alexander McFarland's on Indian Creek; thence to the top of Poplar mountain; thence with the same until it intersects the State line; thence east with said line so far that a north line will strike the mouth of Rock Creek on the main south fork of Cumberland river; thence down the same to the begining, shall be one distinct county and called and known by the name of Wayne.

* * * *

Section 3—The justices to be named in the commission of the peace for the said county of Wayne. shall meet at the house of Henry Garner, in the said county * * * on the first court day after the said division shall take place * * * and shall proceed to fix upon a place for the seat of justice for said county, and proceed to erect the public buildings at such place &c. &c.

* * * *

Section 6—An be it further enacted, That the inhabitants of said county of Wayne, shall proceed to vote for and choose a representative at the courthouse of Pulaski county until they shall be entitled to a separate representation agreeably to the ratio heretofore fixed by law, any custom or usage to the contrary notwithstanding."

* * * *

The inconvenience experienced by the inhabitants of Wayne in complying with the last section of the foregoing Act, was expressed in the following:

"An Act erecting the County of Wayne into an Election Precinct.

Approved December 13, 1802

"Whereas, the citizens of the county of Wayne, are compelled to attend at the court-house in the county of Pulaski, to vote in all elections, and it appears that in consequence thereof they are subject to considerable expence and trouble, having to travel a great distance, and to cross the Cumberland river; therefore,

"Sec. 1—Be it enacted &c., That the citizens of the county of Wayne, entitled to vote, shall, in all elections in future wherein they have a right to give their suffrage, vote at the court-house of the county of Wayne, and the elections shall be held in like manner, and the sheriff and officers conducting the same shall be subject to like penalties, and entitled to the same allowance for their services, as are by law prescribed in similar cases."

The Executive Journal shows that on December 20, 1800, Governor James Garrard appointed the following gentlemen Justices of the Peace of Wayne County, all to serve "during good behavior":

Samuel Newell, Hugh McDermit, Isaac Crisman. Charles Debril, Martin Symes, Edward N. Cullom, James Montgomery. James Jones, Rawleigh Clark, Samuel Hinds and James Evans. John Francis, Sheriff. James Johnston, Coroner.

On June 13, 1801 the names of North East and Joshua Beck were added to the list of "Justices" and Joshua Jones was appointed County Surveyor.

The customary military organization of the county of Wayne was effected by the appointment on December 15, 1802, of the following: Colonel, Charles Debrel; Major 1st Bat. Isaac Christman; Major 2nd Bat., Thos. K. Edgeman as officers of the 53rd Regiment which was "laid off," by Executive order of December 10 of that year.

WAYNE COUNTY TAX LISTS—1801

Persons Chargeable with the Tax. (First 3 names beginning with A illegible.)	Acres Land
Ayres, Samuel	200
Andrews, Daniel	
Alexander, Nich	200
Ard, Reuben	
Alexander, Archd.	
Alexander, Jos.	200
Alexander, Andw.	
Bain, (or Baird) Jos.	600
Barrow, Daniel	200
Bond, Joseph	280
Beason, Isaac	200
Bows, Thos.	
Beck, Joseph	
Bartleson, Zach	325
Balch, Thos.	
Burton, Geo.	200
Barnet, James	
Bartleson, Wm.	
(3 names illegible)	
Blevins, Elisha	
Baird, Wm.	700
Beason, Henry	
Bogard, Jas.	
Cooper, Frederick	
Coffee, John W.	150
Cammerl, Elijah	
Clark, Js.	
Chaney, Francis	
Crabtree, Isaac	200
Cooper, Corn	
Cooper, Wm.	
Castellon, Thos.	
Carigin, Hugh	
Davis, John	
Dabney, Benjamin	
Dinsmore, John	
Dooley, Joseph	
Denny, Sam'l	200
Denny, John	
Dean, Francis	
Dean, Joshua	
Dean, Michl.	
Dodson, Martha (Adm. Jo Dodson decd.)	
Dodson, Wm.	
Dibrell, Chs.	400

Persons Chargeable with the Tax.	Acres Land	Persons Chargeable with the Tax.	Acres Land
Ewing, David		Jones, John	
Evans, Jas.	200	Jones, Joshua	195
Evans, (Illegible)		Jones, Wm.	
Francis, Sam'l	200	Johnson, John	55
Forbes, Sam'l	200	Overstreet, Js.	
Francis, Jno.	200	Pierce, Hugh	200
Franklin, Jas.		Right, Sam'l	
Franklin, Elijah		Ruby, James	
Franklin, Wm.		Ruby, Thos.	
Guffee, Ephraim		Rogers, Geo.	200
Guffee, Ephraim (Jr. in 1803)		Robinson, Wm.	
Guffey, Henry	200	Singleton, Geo.	200
Garner, Henry	200	Smiley, Thos.	150
Garner, Vincent	140	Smiley, Geo.	300
Green, Rob.		Stevens, Jos.	200
Grace, John		Simpson, Thos.	200
Hinds, Jos., Jr.		Simpson, Wm.	
Hinds, Jos., Sr.	100	Simpson, Christo.	
Harris, Jas.		Sullens, Peter	
Harris, Jas., Jr.		Simpson, Wm.	
Hicks, Mashack		Simpson, Jas.	
Hornback, Jas.		Simpson, Js.	
Harbert, Jas.		Small, Matt	200
Harbert, Mat.		Small, Wm.	
Hancock, Benj.		Small, Henry	
Hancock, Wm.		Small, John	
Hancock, Js.		Small, Thos.	150
Hancock, Jesse		Turner, Geo.	150
Hatfield, Val.		Thompson, Alex.	170
Hancock, Benj.	200	Thompson, Js.	
Harris, Richd.		Thomas, Joseph	200
Huffaker, Xopher	200	Wright, Jesse	100
Hammons, John, Jr.	200	West, Isaac	200
Hammons, Jno., Sr.	400	West, Solomon	150
Hammonds, Woodson			
Hammonds, Leroy			
Huffaker, Jacob	200		
Hinds, Joseph (Capt. 1803)	100		
Jones, Jas., Esq.	200		
Jones, John			
Jones, James			
Jackman, Wm.			
Jackman, Thos.			
Ingram, Wm.			
Isbell, Godfrey	200		
Jones, Elliotte	200		
Johnson, Thos.	200		

Total Amount of Taxable property—

162 Acres of 1st rate land
10,351 Acres of 2nd rate land
200 Acres of 3rd rate land
113 White Males above 21
14 White Males bet. 16 & 21
28 Blacks above 16
62 Toatal Blacks
276 Horses, Mares, &c.
1 Stud Horse at 12 for Season

(Signed) Edwd. N. Cullom, Com.

Wayne County, Sct.,

As Clerk of the County Court of Wayne I hereby certify that I have compared this book with the vouchers returned to my office by Edward N. Cullom, Esq. & find it to be a true transcript from the former.

Given under my hand this 28th day of July, 1801, and tenth year of the Commonwealth.

(Signed)—Micah Taul

TAX LIST OF WAYNE COUNTY—1801

Persons Chargeable with the Tax.	Acres Land
Allcorn, James	150
Allen, Js.	
Bailey, Wm.	350
Brock, Wm.	
Bartlet, Joshua	
Beatty, John	145
Beatty, Wm.	
Black, Nathl.	
Betheny, Richd.	
Bennett, Zach	
Burnett, Bond	
Beatty, Robt.	400
Cullom, Edmd. N.	200
Cullom, Wm.	200
Coger, Nicholas	150
Cole, Stephen	
Cole, Fennie (?)	
Combs, William	
Crabb, Stephen	
Carson, Sam'l.	
Cowan, Thos.	
Cowan, John	
Cooper, Jacob	200
Carson, Roger	
Clack, Rolly	200
Christall, Richd.	
Chrisman, Isaac	200
Daniel, Jas.	
Davis, Baxter	200
Davis, James	
Davis, Benj.	
Davis, Samuel	
Dunn, Timothy	200
Dodson, Thos.	200
Dodson, Jesse	
Dodson, Leond.	

Persons Chargeable with the Tax.	Acres Land
East, North	100
Egman, Kimble	200
Emberson, Walter	
Emberson, Wm.	
Emberson, Francis	
Farmer, Thos.	
Goodin, James	100
Garrard, Benj.	
Goodin, Richd.	200
Hunter, Edw.	350
Hancock, Wm.	150
Hancock, Jas.	
Hancock, Simon	
Hudgins, Moses	200
Harle, W.	
Hinds, Sam'l	250
Hinds, Levi	200
Hart, Charles	
Hooser, Isaac	
Hooser, Jacob	300
Hooser, Sampson	
Ingram, Js.	400
Ingram, Sam'l	200
Johnson, Jas.	
Kilwell, Jno.	320
Kenneday, Thos.	
Larcher, Jos.	
Long, Jno.	396
Martin, Benj.	200
Martin, John	150
Maxwell, Jno.	
Morris, Jno.	
McDermid, Hugh	200
Montgomery, J.	
Matthews, Jos.	265
Martin, Ann	
Mercer, Nichs.	
Mercer, Jones	
Mattix, Edwd.	
Miller, Andw.	400
McCarkle, Alex.	
McCastland, Andw.	
Nicholas, Jno.	150
Nicholas, Js.	100
Norton, Martha	200
Norton, Jacob	
Neville, Samuel	362
Nicholas, Js.	

Persons Chargeable with the Tax.	Acres Land	Persons Chargeable with the Tax.	Acres Land
Nicholas, Stephen		Sharp, Wm.	200
Kilgore, Chs.	200	Sharp, Mat	
Kerley, Benja.		Shores, Reuben	
Keeton, Isaac		Stacey, Jesse	
Linney, Charles		Stone, Thomas	200
Linney, Henry		Sanders, Zach.	
Linsey, Mark		Stogden, Masik.(?)	
Levington, John		Simpson, Joshua	
Lair, Wm.		Simpson, Moses	
McWhirter, James		Simpson, Reuben	
Merrit, Thos.		Smith, Matthew	
Mullins, Wm.	200	Sheeks, David	
Matney, Charles		Sheeks, Geo.	800
Montgomery, Jos.		South, John	
Mingo, Jos.		Stogdon, Peter H.	200
Mounts, Absolum		Shoats, Gabl.	
Meadows, Isaac		Shatteen, Jesse	
McCullom, Thos.	200	Sims, Martin	200
McKemie, Jno.	200	Stanley, Jesse	200
McHenry, Jas.		Stanley, Richd.	
McGown, (or Gover) And.	400	Scott, John	
Norman, Thos.	200	Smith, Wm.	
Nicholas, Francis		Saunders, John	200
Oats, Roger	200	Saunders, Frank	
Owens, John	100	Stevenson, John, Sr.	
Owens, Wm.		Stevenson, John, Jr.	
Price, Abraham	279	Sleyton, Jas.	
Payne, Phil.	200	Simpson, Thos.	
Polate (?), Tobias		Sharp, John	195
Potts, John	200	Smith, Davd.	
Paris, Ezekiel		Shores, Wm.	
Parks, Soloman		Stevens, Isaac	200
Price, Nath'l		Shrewsberry, Drury	
Paris, Ezekiel(?)		Tinford, Wm.	
Potts, Nathaniel	200	Taylor, Dan'l	
Preist, Samuel		Tackett, Wm.	
Preist, Wm.	200	Turner, John	
P—ceafull, John		Troxall, Jacob	
Rue, Matthew L.		Turpin, Aaron	200
Robards, John		Troxall, Xpher	
Read, James		Troxall, Peter	
Robins, Wm.		Ussery, Richd.	
Read, John	200	Ussery, Wm.	200
Robins, Richd.		Upton, Benj.	
Rogers, Elijah		Van Winkle, Abra.	
Ryan, James	200	Vandeveer, Thos.	
Russell, James		Valliant, Robt.	
Ray, Wm.	200	Wheeler, Jos.	

Persons Chargeable with the Tax.	Acres Land	Persons Chargeable with the Tax.	Acres Land
Woods, Sam'l		Wolfscale, Geo.	200
Wade, Richd.		Wade, John	
Watts, James		Wallace, Ro.	200
Wade, Joseph		Watkins, Benj.	
Wade, Dawson		Walker, Js.	200
Wade, Wm.		Yocum, Geo.	200

Total Amount—14,209 Acres of 2nd Rate land
1,259 Acres of 3rd Rate
231 White Males above 21
43 above 16 and under 21
31 Blacks above 16
59 total blacks
473 horses, mares, &c.
3 Stud horses

(Signed)—John Taul, Com. Tax W. C.

Wayne County, Sct.   Summary—

This book being examined appears to be a true transcript from the vouchers retd. to my office by John Taul, Com. of the tax for the part' of Sd. County that was taken from Cumberland.

(Signed)—Micah Taul, C. W. C.

Anderson (cont.)
Cornelius 187
Hannah 224
Henry 4, 31, 131, 198
Isaac 157
James 115, 148, 157, 182, 194, 217
Jeremiah 217
John 4, 115, 131, 144, 166, 217, 224, 228
John (Jr.) 157
John (Sr.) 157
Jonathan 224
Joseph 31, 50, 224
Josiah 182
Nicolas 194
Reuben 50
Richard C. 87
Robert 144, 166, 217
Robt. 198
Samuel 157
Sus'nah 217
Theop's 31
Thomas 131
William 148, 157, 217, 238
Wiot 131
Wm. 4, 175, 187, 194
Wm. (Cohe) 187
Andrew, James 76, 148
Andrews, Alexan. 50
Daniel 261
Isaac 217
Willm. 211
Angel, Martin B. 66
Anold, Grace 177
Anthony, Jonathan 76, 80
Antrobus, Wm. 166
Apperson, Richd. 50
Applegate, Benj. 228
Daniel 50
John 98
Richard 82, 87
Sam'l 87
Samuel 82, 217
Stacey 82, 217
Thomas 98
Arbuckle, David 148
James 148
Jas. 194
Jno. 47
John 121, 181, 194
Sam'l 194
Samuel 148
Archer, Benj. 4
Jno. 198
John 148, 174
Joseph 228
Joshua 82, 87
Archibald, Murphy 73
Ard, John 198, 261
Arms, William 44
Armstrong, Abraham 131
Armstrong, Alex'r 12, 181, 182
Edwd. 181
James 23, 131, 239
Jas. 198
Jno. 47
John 115, 157, 181, 182
John (Jr.) 131
John (Sr.) 131

Armstrong (cont.)
Mosh 131
Richard 181
Robert 181, 182
Robt. 31, 47, 194, 198
Thos. 198
Willm. 87, 181
Wm. 12
Arndo, Joseph 224
Arnet, Stephen 106
Arnett, David 108
James 31
William 177
Arnold, Charles 217
Elisha 4
Humphrey 115
James 31, 182
Jane 47, 181
Jas. 47
Jno. 47
Jno. (Jr.) 47
John 4, 31, 148, 181, 182
Josiah 98
Nicholas 31
Reuben 115
Richard 217
Stephen 47, 181, 182
William 4, 175
Arrington, Charles 23, 131
Arskins, Edwards 63
Artgess, Henry 127
Arthur, Ambrose 106
James 194
Stephen 194
Thomas 12
Thos. 106
Wm. 198
Arthurs, John 58
Aryes, Samuel 31
Ash, John 217
Joseph 217
Ruben 217
Ashbrook, John 4
Ashby, Absolom 76
Bailie 4
Beady 228
Bladen 224
Daniel 76
Danniel 182
David 98
Enoes 76
Fielding 98
George 177, 182
Henry 181, 182
Jesse 181
John 76, 182
Peter 182
Silas 121, 239
Stephen 76, 181, 182, 217
Stinson 228
Thomson 211
Ashcraft, Danl. 224
Elizabeth 228
Jediah 4
Jedidiah 224
Asher, Bartlett 98
Dill 106
John 106
William 131, 239
Ashhumst, Robert 31
Ashhurst, Robert 31
Ashley, Joel 31
William 23, 140

Ashworth, John 66
Samuel 66
Askey, Zachariah 131
Askin, Edward 249
Phillimon 249
Phillimon (Jr.) 249
Astor, Samuel 50
Asturgus, James 87
James (Sr.) 98
John 87
Atchison, John 23
Mary 23
Atherington, Aren 211
Arong 211
Benjn. 211
Moses 211
Peter 211
Atherton, Aaron 224
Jno. (Jr.) 224
John 224
Atkenson, Abraham 187
Atkins, Rings 175
William 115
Atkinson, Joel 108
Joseph 12
Thos. 198
Atkisson, Jesse 224
Atten, Addrien 187
Atterberry, Elijah 66
Elisha 66
J. 66
Michael 66
Michall 66
Simeon 66
Solomon 66
Thomas 66
Atteson, William 157
Attkisson, Absolom 174
Atwell, Richard 66
Atwood, James 177
Aulsup, John 106
Joseph 106
Aulverson, Wm. 106
Ausbon, Edmund 106
Auston, Nathaniel 76
Avis, Mary 121
Avit, Richard 224
Aygleton, Wm. 4
Ayres, Azariah 177
Joseph 177
Samuel 261
Thomas 4
Bacey, William 98
Back, Joseph 188
Badger, Oliver 194
Badgley, Robert 50
Badley, Andrew 44
Baggley, Thomas 106
Bags, Andrew 32
Bailes, Allexander 148
Bailey, James 108
John 108, 148, 182
Rebaka 182
Robert 92, 115, 148, 229
Silas 217
Warrant 148
William 115
Wm. 263
Baily, Elisha 121
Bain, Jos. 261
Leroy 182
Matthew R. 67
Baird, Alexander 217
Delley 23
James 211
James (Jr.) 211
Jos. 261

Baird (cont.)
Mary 211
Robert 224
William 217
Wm. 261
Baites, Ephraim 31
Baker, Bris 106
Elijah 115, 239
Francis 44
Fredk. 188
George 50
James 182
Jas. 47
John 32, 131, 139
Moses 194
Reuben 47
Reubin 182
Rezen 157
Richard 108, 239
Robert 157, 175, 182
Robt. 47
Thomas 157, 182
Thos. 47
Balch, Thos. 261
Balderidge, Robt. 108
Baldin, John 31
Baldridge, Daniel 199
Robt. 199
Baldwin, Elisha 23
James 87
Jehu 82
William 23
Baley, James 106
Balinger, Henry 174
Richd. 175
Ball, Benjamin 115
Elizabeth 108
James 108
Thomas 121
William 108
Zopher 4
Balla, George 198
Jno. 199
Robt. 199
Warren 198
Wm. 199
Ballard, Bland 92
Bland W. 228
James 92, 228
Proctor 211
Balldock, Richard 121
Ballenger, John 106
Richard 106
Richd. 188
Richd. (Jr.) 188
Ballew, Charles 144
Balley, John 67
Ballinger, Richard 107
Bally, Groomsbright 4
Baly, John 132, 139
Bane, Joseph 217
Leroy 47
Thomas 217
Banion, John 182
Banks, Linn 115
Reubin 115
Thomas 149
William 115
Banta, Albert 188
Cornelius 188
Daniel 177
David 188
Henry 177
Henry (Admrs.) 177
Jacob 188
John 188
Peter 177

Banta (cont.)
Peter (Sr.) 188
Petrus 188
Samuel 177
Barbee, (?) 181
Andrew 174
Daniel 174
Dan'l 188
Elias 121
John 174, 188
John (Jr.) 174, 188
Thos. 177
Barber, John 4
Richd. 175
Barbour, Philip 210
Barby, Elias 224
Barker, Aaron 217
Elias (Jr.) 166
Elias (Sr.) 166
Joseph 166, 198
Lewis 23
Robert 217
Thomas 217
William 131, 157, 229
Barkkshire, Dickey 144
Barkster, James 108
Barlow, Aaron 188
Ambrouse 188
Christopher 249
Cornelius 249
Henry 250
Jacob 249
Lewis 249
Michael 249
Barnard, Charles 148
Gilbert 106
Jas. 199
Jno. 199
Barnes, Andrew 132
Charles 199
Elijah 199
Frederick 132
Jonas 132
Joseph 23
Joshua 44
Samuel 132
Barnet, Abner 194
Edward 115
George 166
Humphry 77
James 261
Jonathen 194
Joseph 77
Robert 115
Thomas 211
Barnett, Alexander 225
Andrew 149
Charles 177
Humphrey 141
Jacob 77, 141
James 13, 127, 148, 158
John 121, 127
Joseph 140, 141, 157, 224
Mary 77, 158
Robert 121, 149
Susanna 177
Thomas 12
William 77, 141, 157, 225
William (Jr.) 13
William (Sr.) 13
Barnnett, James (Jr.) 158
Barns, Abram 158
Amos 158

Barns (cont.)
Elias 158
George 188
Mary 157
Samuel 158
Shadrick 158
Barr, Jas. 198
Wm. 198
Barrackman, Jacob 4
Barret, Jonathan 158
Barrett, M. Andrew 32
William 149
Barrior, Abraham 198
Frederic 198
Richard 198
Barrow, John 131, 139, 182
Daniel 261
Richard 148
Wm. 182
Barry, Jno. 199
Barthnap, Peter 224
Bartle, John 4
Bartleson, Wm. 261
Zach 261
Bartlet, Anthony 32
Henry 51
James 32
Joshua 263
Mary 87
William 149
Bartlett, Elijah 67
John 50, 98
Joshua 194
Bartley, Matthew 31
Barton, John 13
Joshua 166
Phebe 225
Theophilis 225
Basey, Edmund 82
Richard 217
William 217
Baskett, John 229
Basset, Wm. 175
Bates, James 67
Thomas 67
Wm. 198
Batest, John 121
Batey, Geo. 47
George 182
Batman, John 98, 217
Thomas 98
Batry, Thos. 199
Batsel, John 217
Batterton, Benjn. 166
Henry 166
Battleton, Amor 198
Thomas 148
Baugh, Joseph 157
Wm. 157
Baulch, Amose 131
Baunty, Albert 108
Bax, Joseph 13
Baxter, Benjamn. 166
Elizabeth 166
George 166
Samuel 32
William 250
Baxton, Barthel 166
Bay, Andrew 131
Caniday 132
Baylor, Walter 108
B.Bullet, Clxr. 4
Beadle, Johnathan 229
Beak, John 31
Beal, John 4
Richard 250
Bealer, Christopher 211

Beall, Benjamin 177
 Thomas 182
 Walter 211
 Walter (Jr.) 211
Bean, Lewis 239
Beard, Archibald 59,
 60
 Archd. 59, 60
 Daniel 60
 Richard 60
 Robert 77
 Samuel 50
 Thomas 239
Beasley, James 149
Beason, Henry 261
 Isaac 261
Beatty, Cornelius 87
 John 263
 Robt. 263
 Thomas 88
 Wm. 263
Beaty, Daniel 199
 George 199
 Jno. 199
Beaver, Coonrod 199
Beck, John 182
 Joseph 261
 Joshua 261
Becraft, Abraham 199
Beeson, Mejor 44
Belew, Charles 23
 John 211
 Thomas 23
Bell, Adam 188
 Addam 174
 George 67
 Henry 67, 225
 Jacob 67
 John 13, 32, 217
 Robert 131, 225
 Tho. 188
 Thomas 31, 50
 Thos. 47
 William 50, 82
 Wm. 194
 Zephimah 225
Bella, Peter 92
Bellew, Charles 166
 Thomas 131
 Philip 188
Bellowfelt, Peter 188
Beloo, Charles 149
Belpher, Berry 224
Belt, Josiah 98
Belue, Stephen 106
Belveal, Samuel 4
Bemet, Timothy 182
Bemson, Joseph 98
Bengot, David 199
Benham, Peter 4
 Robert 214
Benit, Thomas 144
Bennedick, John 127
Bennefield, Robt. 199
Bennet, Benjamin 250
 Benjn. 182
 Daniel 217
 Evans 77
 Evens 80
 John 217
 Joshua 217
 Sanford 239
 Stephen 188
 Thomas 217
 Thos. 166
 William 217
Bennett, Ann 177
 Benj. 47

Bennett (cont.)
 Daniel 228, 229
 Hardy 148
 Larkin 23
 Sam'l 177
 Stanford 92
 Timy. 47
 Zach. 263
Bennit, Matthew 31
 Sam'l 250
 Thomas 32
Bentley, John 121
Benton, Richd. 166
Benvel, Timothy 4
Berd, Robert 77, 80
Beriman, John 182
Bernett, William 67
Berrimon, Thomas 108
Berry, Alexander 199
 Benjamin 31
 Christian 182
 Enoch 77, 217
 Garret 158
 George 198, 217
 James 23, 158
 Jas. 198
 John 127, 177, 194
 Joseph 44
 Margaret 198
 Reuben 31
 Reubin 182
 Richard 249
 Ruben 77
 Samuel 31
 Searcy 47, 182
 Washington 2, 4
 William 77, 127,
 217
 Withern 44
 Wm. 31, 166
Berryman, Jno. 47
 Thos. 47
Bescom, Henry 44
Best, Cornelius 217
 Humphry 148
 John 229
 Stephen 148
Bethar, John 224
Bethell, Willm. 211
Betheny, Richd. 263
Betts, William 13
Bias, Jeremiah 115
Bice, Cornelius 188
 Dennis 177
Bickerstaff, Benja. 141
Bidwell, Daniel 217
Biggers, Wm. 194
Biggerstaff, Samuel 132
Biggs, Francis 67
 Stephen 67
Bigham, John 182
Bigs, Andrew 199
Bilbo, Archd. 177
 Wm. 177
Billea, Peter 229
Billings, Abraham 131
 William 132
Billingsley, John 131
Billingsly, James 131,
 139
Bimson, Jos. 47
Bird, Edward 211
 Matthew 67
 Robin H. 67
 Wm. 67
Birdsong, Shedruck 13
 Wm. 13

Bishop, George 98
 William 131
Black, Alexander 31,
 127
 Anderson 211
 Andrew 77
 Charles 211
 David 12, 13, 188,
 193, 199
 Ezl. 198
 Hugh 108
 James 31, 67, 108,
 132, 149
 James (Jr.) 31
 John 31, 106, 157
 John (Jr.) 31
 Joseph 31, 121, 224
 Moses 67
 Nathl. 263
 Paterick 108
 Robert 32
 Sam'l 182
 Samuel 32
 Sarah 211
 Thomas 13, 121
 Thomas Bell 44
 Thos. 199
 William 77
 Wm. (Jr.) 199
 Wm. (Sr.) 198
Blackburn, Ben. 198
 David 211
 George 31
 Isaac 211
 Saml. 199
 William 157, 250
 Wm. 12
Blackwell, Armstead
 144
 Amsted 166
 James 82, 87, 144,
 166
 Robert 67
 Sarah 166
Blackwood, Sam'l 115
Blades, Eli 229
Blagrave, Ban't 177
 Harrison 177
 Henry 177
Blain, Alexander 121
 Alexander (Jr.) 121
 Alex. (Jr.) 121
 James 121
 Jno. 121
Blair, Alexander 67
 Andrew 67
 Henry 149
 James 67
 Jos. 199
 Samuel 32
Blake, Thomas 82
Blakeman, Moses 199
Blakey, George 131
Blan, Alexander 198
 Wm. 199
Bland, Charles 174
 David 217
 John 217
 John (Jr.) 217
 Jos. 89
 Osten 211
 Rachel 250
 Samuel 217
 William 217
Blankenbeker, Henry
 188
 Nichs. 188

Brendley, Jacob 98
Brenton, Henry 92, 228, 239
  James 92, 239
  John 229, 239
  Joseph 92
  Robert 92, 228
Brewer, Abraham 177
  Charles 217
  Daniel 177
  George 217
  John 106, 177
  Peter 211
  Samuel 175
  Thomas 217
  William 249
Brewner, Jacob 177
Briant, Alexander 211
  Anderson 199
  Benjamin 23
  Daniel 23
  Frank 211
  Zachariah 182
Brickey, Jarrot 177
Bridges, Absolom 177
  John 23, 177
  Wm. 166, 198
Bridgewaters, Leve 217
  Samuel 217
Briges, Isham 166
Briggs, Andrew 51
  Benj. 127
  Ebenezer 250
  Jno. 198
  John 217
  Samuel 121
  Thomson 211
  William 211, 250
Bright, Henry 115
  Jacob 115
  John 115
Brihmer, Jacob 211
Bringle, Christian 211
  George 250
Brinlee, Stephen 106
Brinsley, William 198
Brinson, David 157, 198
  Stout 149
  Tabulor 199
  Zebulin 144
  Zebulon 157
Brinton, Joseph 239
  Robt. 177
Briscoe, Edward 121, 250
  Jeremiah 250
  Parminus 217
  Walter 217
Brisscow, William 158
Britain, George 106
  James 106
  Levy 106
  Parks 106
Brite, Jacob 182
Britt, James 188
Briver, Samuel 224
Broadberry, David 4
Broaddrick, Wm. 188
Brock, Henry 31
  Wm. 263
Brockham, Will 217
Brockman, Thomas 144, 148
Brodhead, Daniel 60
Brook, George 67
  Toss 198
  William 67
Brooke, Ebinezer 31
Brookes, Joseph 82, 87

Brookey, John 32
Brookins, Samuel 175
Brooks, Abijaiah 199
  James 211
  Jas. 67
  Jessee 13
  John 67
  Miles 67
Broom, William 12
Brooner, George 77
Brothers, Absalom 198
  Cornelius 249
  Cornelius (Jr.) 250
  John 249
  Rbt. 198
Browder, Isham 77
Brown, Absolom 149
  Andrew 198
  Ann 249
  Anthony 249
  Arabe 149
  Barlett 149
  Bazil 250
  Benage 149
  Benjamin 250
  Beverley 148
  Charles 149, 157
  Chars. 182
  Coleman 250
  Daniel 23, 198, 199
  Dudley 259
  Elias 157
  Fradrick 149
  Garfield 115
  George 50, 144, 166, 182
  Henry 166
  Hugh 98
  Isaac 67
  James 44, 58, 61, 63, 166, 174, 177, 182, 211
  Jas. 27, 199
  Jeheue 13
  Jereboam 211
  Jerimh 188
  Jesse 50
  Jno. 63, 198, 199
  John 4, 50, 59, 62, 106, 108, 131, 149, 174, 177, 182, 188, 194, 211, 217
  Johnson 217
  Joseph 106, 115, 148, 217
  Lewis 67
  Matthew 149
  Morris 121
  Moses 106, 198
  Nathaniel 217
  Patrick 225
  Presley 44, 182
  Quilor 198
  Raphael 250
  Robert 13, 148, 211
  Robt. 182, 199
  Samuel 157, 217
  Scott 47, 182, 188
  Thomas 225
  Thos. 198
  Walter 217
  William 23, 148, 157
  William M. 67
  Wm. 188, 194, 198
Brownfield, Edw. 225
  James 249
  Rich. 225
  William 225

Brownlee, Alexander 108
Brownlow, John 61
Bruce, Alexander 44
  George 217
  James 217
  John 149
  Turner (Jr.) 217
  Vincent 182
  William 217
Brucks, Henry 166
  Lynch 166
  Robt. 166
Bruer, Vincent 182
Brumajim, James 198
Brumfield, Job 177
  Joel 67
  Wm. 177
Brumpton, Bryan 121
Bruner, Christon 166
  George 98, 166
  Jacob 98
  John 188
  Leonard 98
  Michael 98
  Peter 188
Brunk, Jacob 67, 121
Brunt, Peter 250
  Wm. 194
Brunts, James 250
  John 224
Bryan, David 177
  James 121, 174
  John 50
  Mary 4
  Morgan 239
  Samuel 2, 4
Bryant, Christo. 182
  Daniel 32
  Edward 131
  James 131
  Jesse 148
  John 115, 224
  John B. C. 149
  John G. 115
  Samuel 2
  Wm. 188
Brydon, Barbara 115
  Robert 50, 115
Bryent, John 149
Buchanan, Allexr. 182
  George 182
Buchannan, James 44, 182
  John 182
Bucher, Peter 175
Buck, Coonrod 199
  Wardner 77, 80
Buckhanen, James 23
Buckhannan, Jno. 132
Buckhannon, William 108
Buckman, Ignatius 250
Buckner, Aylett Exr. 67
  Aylette H. 66
  Henry W. 67
  Nicholas 98
  Philip 98
  Simon Bolivar (Gen.) 66
  Thos. 124
  William 65, 224
Buel, Timothy 4
Buford, Abram. 188
  James 188
  John 115, 188
Builderback, Jacob 229
Bukersraff, Benja. 141
Buky, Rudolphus 217
Bulavare, Esther 50

Bulger, Dan'l 188
Bulkhannon, Henry 198
Bull, Abraham 148, 239
  Bennett 177
  Thomas 211
Bullard, Joseph 13
  R. 50
  William 50
Buller, Isaac 23
Bullet, B. Clxr. 4
Bullett, Alexander 98
Bullitt, Alexr. S. 2
Bullock, Jno. 259
  John 250
Bulocks, (?)(heirs) 78
Bumbaugh, Thomas 67
Bumgardner, Christian 67
  Jacob 67
Bunch, Calloway 188
  Charles 188
  Clark 194
  George 106
  Henry 194
  James 106
  Joseph 174, 188
  Lenard 211
  Richd. 188
  Sabia 194
  Z. 175
Buncher, James 175
Bundy, Reuben 106
Bunham, John 50
Bunnell, Jeremiah 67
Buntain, Andw. 182
  John 182
Buntin, Andw. 47
Bunton, William 121
  Wm. 175
Buran, Ibey 239
  Phillip 239
  William 239
Burbridge, Rollen 199
  Rowland 50
  Thomas 31
Burch, Benjamin 121
  Benjamin (Jr.) 121
  Christopher 217
  John 177
Burcham, David 249
  Jno. 198
  Saml'. 198
Burchel, Daniel 174
Burchem, Samuel 193
Burcher, Jas. 199
Burchfield, Robert 50
Burden, Joseph 141
Burdit, Joseph 115
  Joshua 115
Burdon, Edward 23
  William 23
Burdyne, Betty 250
Burford, Daniel 182
Burgain, Denis 144
  Isaac 144
  Jacob 144
Burgin, Charles 166
  Danes 166
  Isaac 166
  Jacob 166
Burham, James 50
Burian, Jesse 92
Burk, Andrew 77
  Elihu 32
  Richard 175
  Thomas 217
Burkes, George 229
  John 82
Burket, Eliazer 217

Burket (cont.)
  William 217
Burkot, Abraham 217
Burks, Charles 174, 188
  Geo. 121
  Isham 224
  John 87, 174, 188
  Nicholas 224
  Samuel 224
  Thompton 175
  Tompson 188
  William 121
  Wm. 121
Burner, Abraham 67
Burnes, Arthur 4
  Charles 198
Burnet, John 211
  Moses 23
Burnett, Bond 263
  Jno. 224
  Wm. 67
Burney, James 188
  Willm. 211
Burns, Arthur 177
  Equiller 13
  Micheal 211
  Peter 13
  Thomas 228
Burnside, Robert 157
  Walter 121
Burnum, Henry 166
  John 166
Burrace, Booze 225
Burress, John 194
  John (Jr.) 194
Burris, Nath'l 182
  Robert 67
  Samuel 182
Burriss, Charles 157
  John 131
  Wm. 188
Burt, Moses 108
Burtchum, Benajah 188
Burtin, Allin 144
  Isaac 144
  Samuel 144
Burton, Abraham 148
  Allen 177, 199
  Allon 148
  Ambrose 115
  Eliz. 182
  Geo. 261
  George 157
  Isaac 148
  Jarrard 239
  John 31, 194
  John (Sr.) 194
  Martha Ann 239
  Mary 108
  Robert 148
  Saml. 166
  William 148
Bush, Christopher 225
  Henry 67
  John 2, 4, 67, 92
  Mathias 182
  Phillip 2
  Samuel 2, 175
  Thomas 67
  William 131, 225
Bushart, Jacob 217
Bushong, Henry 188
  Jacob 182
Buskirk, John 229
  Michael 229
Butcher, Gasper 131,
    139
  Henry 217

Butcher (cont.)
  Joseph (Jr.) 157
  Joseph (Sr.) 157
  Richard 157
  Samuel 108
  William 157
Butlar, Edward 177
  James 177
  Jessee 177
  John 177
  Joseph 177
Butler, Anthony 65
  Bazel 194
  Edw. 198
  Edward 12
  Enoch 67
  George 182
  Ignatious 198
  James 67, 115
  Jno. 199
  Joel 67
  John 182
  Joseph 77
  Nancy 157
  Shubel 67
  Simon 67
  Thomas 144
  Thos. 166, 198
  William 67
Butner, Edward 198
  Isaac 157
Butt, Edmond 199
Buttler, John 132
  William 131, 229
Byby, John 50
  Neal 50
Bye, John 217
Byers, Daniel 225
Byerstaff, John 131
Bymson, Joseph 182
Byor, Philip 198
Byrd, John 108
Byres, Joseph 32
Byrk, Richard 239
Byrn, James 50
Byrne, Jno. 47
Byrns, John 182
C(?), Willm. (Jr.) 5
Caffey, Benjamin 251
Cahoon, John 182
Caidwell, Jas. 199
Cail, Thomas 5
Cain, Bailey 13
  George 116
  John 116
  Matthew 218
  Patrick 218
Caits, Isaac 14
  Joshua 13
Calbert, Daniel 92
Caldwell, David 24, 251
  George (Jr.) 177
  George (Sr.) 177
  James 211
  Jno. 199, 200
  John 24, 116, 188,
    250, 259
  Kingcaid 199
  Philips 175
  Robert 116, 178, 182
  Samuel 132, 143
  William 250
  Wm. 199
Calhoon, George 212
Calhoun, John 77
Calk, William 144, 166
Callahan, Dennis 183
  James 82

Clerk, Thomas 132
Clifford, John 44
  Michel 32
Clifton, Baldin 250
  Burdit 250
  Howsan 250
  Samuel 212
Cline, Jno. 199
Clines, Nicholas 240
  Peter 240
Clinton, Archiable 115
Cloin, John 158
Clopton, David 67
  John 67
Close, George 225
  Henry 68
  John W. 68
Closes, Michael 200
Clover, Henry 99
  Jacob 82, 87
Clowd, William 5
Cloyd, James 109
  Robert 32
  William 122
Clure, McWillm. 211
Clury, John 116
Clutter, Simeon 229
Clymer, George 62, 63
  James 68
  Jesse 68
Clynes, John 93, 240
  Joseph 93
  Nicholas 93
  Peter 93
Coachman, Jonathan 51
Coats, George 68, 177
Coalter, John 177
Coats, Thos. 68
  Wilson 132
Cobourn, John 33
  Susannah 188
Cochonhom, Jacob 177
Cochran, Andrew 158
  James 158
  John 158, 177
  Samuel 158
  William 158
Cochren, James 212
Cock, Bowler 58
Cockanon, John 182
Cockeowing, Jno. 200
Cockran, Samuel 149
Cockron, Denis 150
Cocks, James 87
Codry, John 14
Cofer, Jacob 144
  Reuben 200
Coffee, Jas. 200
  Jesse 167
  John W. 261
Coffey, John 106
Coffman, Elean. 48
  Ellenor 182
  Isaac 177
Coffy, Ambrouse 194
Cogdell, John 68
  Joseph 68
  Thomas 68
  Wm. 68
Coger, Michael 32
  Nicholas 263
Cogg, Thomas 178
Coghill, James 109
Cogswell, Jedediah 199
  Jeramiah 149
Coiles, Peter 200
Coin, Andrew 218
Colby, Charles 5

Coldwater, John 87
Cole, Fennie 263
  George 177
  Jessee 177
  John 24
  Joseph 44, 177
  Rich'd 32
  Stephen 263
  William 178
Colelasher, Abraham 240
  Jacob 240
Coleman, Bathsheba 240
  Martin 225
  Page 32
  Philip 4
Colgin, Daniel 99, 240
Colier, James 167
  John 167
  Jonathan 182
Collard, Elijah 100, 212
  Joseph 212
Collet, Isaac 121
  John 240, 247
  Stephen 121
Collette, Isaac 177
Colliar, John 194
Collier, Alexander 116
  Anthony 116
  James 144
  John 116, 144
  Robert 116
Collingsworth, Edmond 218
Collins, (?) 129
  (?) (Mr.) 147
  Adam 67
  Dudley 200
  Elisha 32
  Joel 32, 106
  John 32
  Joseph 32, 33, 106
  Josiah 199
  Lewis 132
  Thomas 158
  William 132, 218, 229
  William E. 229
  Zebulon 218
Colliver, Joseph 200
Colly, Charles 167
Colman, Coonrod 4
  Jacob (Sr.) 99
Colson, John 109
  Wm. 32
Colsten, Henry 106
  John 51
Colter, Thos. 188
Colvan, Job 14
  John 14
Colvell, Joseph 194
Colvile, Joseph 197
Colvin, Joseph 188, 193
  Joseph Vance 44
  Luke 212
Colwell, John 177
  Robert 4
Colyer, David 14
  Moses 109
Combs, Daniel 200
  David 218
  Edward 218
  Enoch 218
  John 77, 218
  Nelson 218
  Thomas 218, 229
  William 263
  William (Jr.) 218

Combs (cont.)
  William (Sr.) 218
Comines, William 5
Commens, Gabriel 109
Commingore, Henry 177
  John 177
Commins, Matthew 177
Commons, Hugh 106
  Jno. 200
  Wm. 106
Comnton, Richard 132
Coms, George 32
Comstock, Isaac 106
Con, Josiah 167
Conder, George 177
  John 177
Condict, Timothy 99
Conelly, Arthur 32
Coner, John 5
Conlee, William 68
Connaway, John 24
Connay, John 212
Connel, James 218
Conneley, William 229
Connelly, John 32, 229
  Wm. 32
  Thompson 229
Connely, Arthur 200
  Timothy 132
Conner, Daniel 158, 218
  Isaa 132
  James 218
  John 32
  Livingston 68
  Richard 217
  Thos. 178
  William 132
  Wm. 33, 194, 197
Conners, James 24
Connine, Andrew 177
Connolly, Timothy 225
Connoway, Joseph 218
Conrin, Hannah 188
  Jerrerd 188
Constant, William 67
Conway, Hugh 92, 239
  Miles W. 43
Conyear, Isaac 199
  Matthew 199
Conyears, William 68
Conyghym, Thos. 199
Cook, Abraham 51
  Absalem 144
  David 109
  Henry 109
  Hosea 32
  James 14
  James (Jr.) 132
  James (Sr.) 132
  Jesse 32
  John 2, 5, 14, 109, 177
  Joseph (Jr.) 132
  Margaret 51
  Moses 92, 229
  Reuben 14
  Richard 199
  Robert 23
  Samuel 5
  Seth 51
  Silas 14
  Wiles 167
  William 51, 132
  Wm. 68
Cooks, Wilis 199
Cooley, Daniel 115
  Ebenezer 199
  Thadus 149
  Wm. 149

Crisman, Isaac 261
Crist, George 229
  Jacob 225
Cristean, Gilbert 51
Crittendon, John 32
Crockel, James 240
Crocket, Anthony 183
  Hamilton 182
  Joseph 32
  William 183
Crockett, Antoy. 48
  Hamn. 48
  Robt. 199
  Wm. 48
Croghan, Henry 24
  Willm. 87
  Wm. 62, 82
Croock, Osias 167
Crook, Absalom 167
  Jeremiah 5
Crooks, James 212
  Jno. 199
Croshon, Jacob 5
  Jeremiah 5
Cross, Philip 199
  Zachariah 132
Crosse, Michael 200
Crosswait, Jacob 32
  Samuel 32
Croucher, William 149
Crow, Eli 24
  Jacob 177
  John 5, 33
  William 122
Crowdus, Wm. 178
Crown, Robert 87
Cruchfield, Wm. 178
Crume, Daniel 250
  Moses 218
  Ralph 218
Crumes, Jesse 218
Crump, Archer 68
  Joshua 66, 68, 177
  Mary 194
  Richd. 194
  Romeo 68
  Wm. 175
Crusan, Benjamin 44
Cruse, Thos. 167
Crutcher, James 212
  John 51, 212
  Thos. 212
Crutchner, George 218
Crytigh, Francis 5
Culberson, Wm. 199
Culbertson, John 225
Culbeson, John 44
Culdwell, Robert 158
Cull, Hugh 240
Cullom, Edmd. N. 263
  Edward N. 261, 263
  Edwd. N. 262
  Wm. 263
Cullon, James 106
Culver, Jonathan 212
Cumley, David 150
Cummins, John 218
  Matthew 121
  Peter 250
  Thomas 251
  William 99
Cummons, John 106
Cumptin, Varneld 143
Cumpton, Richard 225
  Varnald 141
  Z. 175
  Zach. 188
Cumstock, William 225

Cumstock (cont.) 106
  Wm. 106
Cumton, Levy 132
  Varnell 132
Cuningham, Jas. 200
Cunningham, Francis 229
  Frank 218
  Hugh 32
  James 99
  John 5, 250
Cuntryman, Henry 211
  Jacob 211, 229
Cup, Christopher 177
  Henry 14
Curd, Edmund 5
  James 32
  John 32, 63, 132
  Newton 188
  Price 63
  William 63
Curle, Archd. 166
Curral, Dudly 194
Curray, James 59
Curren, James 24
Currens, James 183
Curry, Andrew 182
  Daniel 98
  James 182
  John 122, 182, 183
  Nathan 82
  Sarah 122
  Thomas 99
  William 182, 183, 218
  Wm. 175
Curtes, Nathaniel 106
Curtner, Cristopher 51
  John 51
Cus, Henry 14
Cutrite, Peter 200
Cutting, Francis 109
Dabney, Benjamin 261
Dacon, James 212
Dailey, Charles 99
  John 99
  Philip 99
Daily, Bend't 251
Dale, Abraham 218
  Abram 33
  George 33
  George (Jr.) 33
  Isaac 33
  Rawley 33
  Robert 33
  Thos. 200
  William 33
  William (Jr.) 33
  Wm. 68
Daley, John 212
Damaree, Cornelius 178
Damewood, Boston 178
Danald, Reuben 200
Dancy, Laken 44
Danel, Daniel 200
Daniel, Aaron 116
  Charles 2, 5
  Coleman 92, 239, 246, 247
  Colman 240
  James 106, 240
  Jas. 263
  Jno. 200
  John 93, 240
  Martin 93, 240
  Mary 99
  Peter 99
  Robert 240, 247
  Spencer 107
  Terry 107

Daniel (cont.)
  Thomas 150, 240
  Vivion 5
  Walker 77
  William 24, 98, 183
  Wm. 5, 106, 188
Daniels, McElexr. 212
  Nathan 144
DanielsMc, Elexr. 212
Danily, Caleb 188
Dann, Jeremiah 33
Dannellee, Caleb 174
Danolson, Robert 99
Dant, John B. 251
  Joseph 251
Darland, Garrot 178
Darlington, Abraham 122
Darnal, Cornelous 194
  Danl. 194
  Henry 194
Darnald, Jno. 200
  Olever 240
  Thos. 200
Darneby, Edward 183
Darringer, Jacob 5
Darrnald, Wm. 200
Datharge, Killes 167
Daugherty, Jas. 178
  John 122
  Henry 174
  Michael 218
  Wm. 127, 178
David, Charles 48, 183
Davids, George 6
Davidson, George 24
  Hezekiah 68
  James 178
  John 14, 24, 188, 251
  Josiah 183
  William 219
Davie, Benjamin 200
  Henry 201
Davis, Alexander 167
  Aron 200
  Arthur 24
  Asel 116
  Azariah 15, 122, 178
  Baxter 263
  Benj. 188, 263
  Benjamin 24, 141, 174, 200
  Benjman 77
  Charles 77, 188
  Clement 15
  David 15, 251
  Edward 14, 178
  Edward (Sr.) 178
  Elexander 144
  Elihu 68
  Enock 194
  Evin 99
  George 68, 183, 219
  Giles 219
  Hamnaniah 33
  Hananiah 15
  Harison 77
  Harrison 200
  Henry 218
  Hugh 218
  Isaac 15, 200, 218
  Israel 68
  Jacob 24, 178
  James 5, 15, 109, 122, 141, 174, 178, 188, 218, 247, 263
  James (Jr.) 77
  James (Overs) 188
  James (Sr.) 77

Davis (cont.)
Jamis 15
Jane 122
Jas. 200
Jas. (Jr.) 200, 201
Jas. (Sr.) 201
Jeremiah 15, 194
Jesse 87, 109, 218
Jessee¦ 178
Jno. 200
John 33, 68, 77, 87,
100, 109, 144, 150,
167, 174, 178, 183,
194, 212, 230, 251,
261
John (Sr.) 150
Joseph 15, 33, 178,
188, 200
Joshua 188, 212
Josiah 15
Lemark 194
Lemuel 183
Luke 200
Moses 219
Nathaniel 200
Patrick 33
Peter 178
Phillip 251
Richard 33, 77, 107
Robert 77, 251
Sam'l 15, 188
Samuel 44, 51, 109,
144, 150, 263
Solomon 167
Theodorus 183
Theodorus (Jr.) 183
Thomas 77, 122, 133,
183
Thos. 167, 200
Thos. T. 188
Travin 218
Warren 218
Wiley 24
William 33, 183
Wm. 61, 188, 200
Zachariah 167
Davison, George 109
Thomas 33
Daviss, Clem. (Jr.) 133
Clem (Sr.) 133
Wm. 175
Davore, John 68
Davy, Free 188
Owen 44
Thomas 44
Dawes, Joseph 225
Dawit, Peter 219
Dawney, William 14
Dawsey, John 68
Dawson, Christilon 33
George 251
John 68
Keziah 5
Thomas 68
Day, Aaron 5
John 99, 122, 178
Wm. 194
Deacon, James 24
Dean, Benjamin 251
Francis 261
Henry 183
James 33
John 107, 183
Joshua 261
Leaven 183
Michl. 261
Richard 183
Summers 183

Dean (cont.)
Thoms. 183
William 24, 183
Willm. 183
Dearengar, John 33
Debenport, William 183
Debon, Joseph 183
Joseph (Jr.) 183
Debond, Abraham 178
Debrel, Charles (Col.)
261
Debrell, Charles 144
Debrill, Charles 159
Deckar, Abraham 99
Decker, Nicholas 100
Decouse, William 33
Decoursey, Wm. 5
Dedman, Saml. 200
Samuel 33
Wm. 200
Dedmond, Richmond 33
Deen, Richard 225
Robert 159
Deesan, John 15
Deeson, John 14
Samuel 15
Defever, John 68
Defevers, John 225
Degby, William 5
Degroas, Charles 174
Dehart, Ecklin 150
John 5
Delaney, Eliab 183
Joseph 33
Delany, Josh. 183
Deleplane, Joshua 24
Delham, Frances 33
Deliplane, Benjamin 24
Dement, Benona 99
George 240
Demint, John 51
Joreab 51
Demmere, Peter 93
Samuel 93
Demmeree, Da (S.J.) 188
Davd. 188
Peter 188
Sam'l 188
Demoree, Abraham 241
John 183
Peter 240
Samuel 241
Demoss, Peter 225
Demott, Abraham 178
John 188
Laurence 178
Peter 188
Dempsey, Jeptha 15
John 15
William 15
Denbo, Solomon 93
Denboe, Solomon 230
Dene, Saml. 200
Denham, John 159
Denhit, Peter 33
Denison, Daniel 33
Dennan, Anthony 240
John 241
William 241
Denne, Jno. 200
Saml. 200
Denney, Alexander 150
Aron 33
Sam'l 188
Dennis, John 130
Samuel 251
Dennison, Ben (Sr.) 68
Benj'n (Jr.) 68

Dennison (cont.)
Isaac 68
Zacheriah 68
Zadock 68
Denniston, Robt. 188
Denny, James 99
John 183, 261
Robt. 183
Sam'l 261
Willm. 212
Denton, Israel 218
Thomas 116, 183
Depaw, Charles 122
Depu, William 251
Depuis, Wm. 178
Derimiah, John 225
Deskin, Daniel 200
Despourt, Christo. 183
Devenport, James 33
Dever, John 122, 150
Devers, Henry 212
Richd. 212
Thos. 212
Devin, James 109
William 109
Devine, John 183
Margaret 183
Roger 51, 175
Samuel 183
Devore, Price 219
Devour, Daniel 93
Deweese, David 107
Thomas 107
Dewit, Elisha 212
James 212
Zachariah 212
Dewitt, Barnet 195
Henry 195, 255
Lewis 5
Martin 195
Paul 194
Peter 194
Walter 5, 116
William 5
Dial, Thomas 133
Dibrell, Chs. 261
Dick, (?) 62
Abraham 200
Alexander 61
Dickason, (?) 133
Dicken, Charles 178
John 251
William 259
Dickens, Ephriam 225
Dickey, David 183
Ebenezer 159
George 150
John 150, 183
Joseph 178
Robert 150
Robt. 195
Samuel 33, 183
Dickin, Joseph 178
William 251
Dickinson, Archey 33
Dickson, Griffy 44
James 15
Digs, Thomas 183
Dillender, Joseph 132
Dilles, Henry 68
Dilling, John 230
Dillingham, Jas. 14
Michael 14
Vachel 14
Vachel (Sr.) 15
Dilliplain, Ben 44
Dillon, Michl. 87
Michael 83

279

Dunn (cont.)
Timothy 263
Veneer 212
William 51
Dunstall, Richard 159
Dunwoodaci, Wm. 68
Dupey, Bartholomew 33
John 33
Dupuy, Bartholomew 247
David 14
James 14
Joseph 15, 247
Durbin, Christopher 144, 167
Edward 144, 167
John 167
Joseph 167
Thos. 167
Duree, Albert 183
Durham, John 69
John (Jr.) 178
John (Sr.) 178
Sam'l 178
Durmit, Edwd. 183
Durrum, James 144
Durst, David 33
Dusdal, Jas. 200
Duvall, Samuel 24
Dyar, John 15
Dye, Avery Constable 178
Isaac 225
Job 225
Dyer, Abraham 150
John 195, 251
John (Jr.) 251
Mary 150
William 251, 259
Dyers, John 68
Dykes, Wm. 6
Eads, Isaa 133
John 133
Eaglin, Richd. 212
Willm. 212
Eaken, Robert 100
Eakins, Alesr. 230
John 230
Earl, John 60
Sam'l 15
Early, Joseph 44
Thomas 44
William 44
Earukson, Benjamin 100
East, James 150
Joseph 34, 122
Neal 122
North 150, 195, 261, 263
Easter, Adam 225
Easters, William 230
Easterday, Lewis 51
Eastes, William 93
Eastin, Achilles 6
Philip 34
Redwood 230
Richard 100
William 122
Eastis, John 133, 141
William 133
Eastland, Wm. 178
Eastwood, Abner 77, 174
John 225
Eaton, Isaac 159
John 107
Joseph 33, 93
George 33
Eberman, Jacob (Jr.) 201
Jacob (Sr.) 201
Michael 201

Eberman (cont.)
Wm. 201
Edes, John 24
Edgar, Isiah 69
James 67
John (Jr.) 69
John (Sr.) 69
Johnston 69
Samuel 69
William 133
Edgeman, Thos. K. (Maj.) 261
Edmondson, Philip 189
Wm. 6
Edmonson, John 251
Patty 251
Edrington, Benj. 189
Benjamin 52
John 52
Joseph 51
Wm. 189
Edsill, Benjamin 69
Edward, Cade 6
Wm. 6
Edwards, Benjamin 52
David 230
Fredk. 100
Isaac 44, 230
James 174, 189
John 51, 116
Mildred 52
Milley 116
Simeon 51
Uriah 52
William 24, 219
Egbert, Nicholas 6
Egbird, David 33
Egerton, Benjaman 174
Egman, Kimble 263
Egnew, Samuel 6
Eillis, Isaac 100
Elam, Josiah 33
Elder, Alexander 24
Andrew 34
Ignatius 251
James 251
John 24, 230
Joseph 251
Robert 24
William 24, 251
Eldridge, Job 219
Samuel 219
Elem, John 133
Elis, Joseph 52
Eliston, Thomas 251
Elkins, Joshua 15
Elledge, Isaac
Ellerson, Robert 241
Ellin, Wm. 201
Ellis, Dannel 183
Eleazor 52
Jesse 52
Isaac 230
Obediah 52
William 52, 193
Ellison, James 195
John 195
Joseph 167
Peter 34
Robert 33
Thomas 34
Thos. 167
Elliot, Alexander 116
Eleazor 52
Jas. 201
Ralph 201
William 225
Elliott, Edward 251

Elliott (cont.)
Edwerd 251
George 122
Jno. 201
Rich. 201
Robert 34
Stephen 251
Thomas 15, 251
William 122
Wm. 34
Ellitt, Thomas 230
Ellot, John 159
Elmore, George 24
Matthew 109
Thornton 69
Elms, Williams 88
Elrod, Thomas 44
Elwood, James 241
Emberson, Francis 263
Jesse 109
Samuel 109
Walter 263
Wm. 263
Embre, Talton 167
Joseph 167
Embree, John 109, 178, 189
Embry, Jessy 144
John 144
Joseph 144
Emmerson, Jesse 48, 183
Emmison, Hugh 59
Emmon, Drewry 69
England, David 167, 201
James 174, 189
Engleman, Jacob 174
Simon 175
Englhish, Stephen 159
English, Charles 109
Elisha 51
Fannie 109
Stephen 109
Enlows, Abtaham 219
Henry 219
John 219
Joseph 219
Joseph (Sr.) 219
Mordecai 219
Ennis, Archibald 69
James 69
Wm. (Jr.) 69
Wm. (Sr.) 69
Enyeart, Abraham 159
John 159
Epperson, Richard 69
Errevine, Jno. 89
Erven, William 183
Ervin, Joseph 241
Robert 241
Erwin, John 212
Esley, Stephen 33
Esrey, John 212
Estell, Boudy 159
Samuel 159
William 159
Esten, John 144
Estes, Asa 15
Estill, William 44
Estin, John 167
Estup, Alexander 219
Ethington, John 34
Evans, David 34, 219, 230
(Illegible) 262
James 230, 261
Jas. 262
John 123
Joseph 93

Floyd, Benjamin 116
  Charles 100
  David 116
  George 116
  Gideon 52
  Henry 212
  Henry (Jr.) 212
  John 116, 212
  Morris 178
  Nathaniel 212
  Robert 100
  Thomas (Dr.) 34
  William 100
Foby, James 183
  Richard 183
Foley, Daniel 201
  Peter 34
Folkes, John 219
Folley, James 77
  Richard 77
Follis, Isaac 178, 183
Foot, Thos. 167
Forbes, Sam'l 262
Forbis, Alexander 168
  Hugh 201
  James 69, 109
  Jonathan 110
  Robert 69, 116
Forbush, Robert 159
Ford, Ezekiah 241
  George 69
  Hezakiah 100
  Jesse 25
  John 25, 150
  Peter 150
  Phillip 24
  William 69, 122
Forde, Thomas 133
Foreman, David 127, 183
Forester, Gressum 34
Forgason, William (Jr.) 133
  William (Sr.) 133
Forgerson, Arther 241
  Kinder 241
Forgia, Alexander 201
  Hugh 201
  Jno. 201
Forguson, John 195
  Thos. 201
  William 100
Forgusson, Wm. 201
Forker, Robert 34
Forkner, John 34
  Joseph 34
Forman, Joseph 219
  Thomas 219
Forrester, Nath'l 183
  Samuel 183
Forrister, Thom. 183
  Willm. 183
Forsithe, Mathew 183
Forsyth, James 174
Fort, David 24
  Frederic 201
  Frederick 168
  Jesse 15
  Micajah 16
  Peter 201
  Spear 24
Foster, Anthony 212
  Fredrick 225
  Henry 225
  Jacob 6
  Luke 88
  Robert 212
  Samuel 34
Fought, George 225

Fouller, James 159
Fountain, William 241
Fourney, Nicholas 122
Foushe, Daniel 212
Fouts, Lawrence 141
Fowke, Geo. 195
Fowler, Benjn. 167, 212
  Charles 252
  Edward 6, 69
  Jacob 6
  James 195
  Jerimiah 168
  John 52, 195
  Joseph 144, 168
  Joshua 100
  Matthew 168
  Matthew D. 69
  Richd. 167
  Zacheriah 219
Fox, Arthur 43
  John 167
  Richard 34
  Saml. 168
Frad, Jno. 201
  John 219
Fraim, Wm. 195
Frain, Archibald 88
Frakes, John 219
  John (Sr.) 219
  Philip 219
Frakex, Joseph 195
Frame, Archibald 83
  John 16
  William 88
Franceway, Norrod 77
Francis, John 150, 261
  Henry 150
  Jno. 262
  Leonard 25
  Saml. 201
  Sam'l. 262
  Samuel 150
Franklin, Clabon 178
  Elijah 262
  James 34
  Jas. 262
  John 34, 150
  Wm. 262
Fransway, Norad 141
Frazer, David 34
  George 34, 133, 139
  James 34
  Joseph 34
  Martin 175
  Wm. 34
Frazier, Alexander 225
Freeland, Garret 116
  James 122
  John 122
  Thomas 122
Freeman, Aaron 107
  Benjn. 183
  Elisha 100, 116, 127
  Rosanna 183
  Samuel 159
  Thomas 69, 100
  Thos. 178
French, David 88
  Henry 178
  Ignatius 212
  James 122, 168, 252
  John 25, 127
  Joseph 212
  Josiah 25
  Levi 25
  Moses 25
  Raphel 212
  Sam'l 178

French (cont.)
  Samuel 25
  Simon 15
  William 25
Fresh, Frances 116
  Gasper 122
Friel, Thomas 77
Friend, Isaac 225
Friggs, Conrad 141
Fristoe, Daniel 15
Froman, Isaac 251
  Jacob 189, 219
  Jacob (Jr.) 189
  Paul 219
Frought, Powel 52
Frund, John 34
Frowman, Thomas 230
Fry, Bazel 133
  Edward 174
Fryatt, Rob't 16
Frye, Benj. 210
  Benjn. 216
Fugate, Josiah 201
  Randolph 201
  Townsin 189
Fugett, Townson 175
Fuland, Robt. 201
Fulkenson, Philip 178
Fulkerson, Jacob 174
Fullengwider, Henry 93
  Jacob 93
  Peter 93
Fullenwider, Jacob 245
Fuller, Henry 34
Fullerton, William 77
Fullin, William 109
Fulton, Hugh 34
Funk, Henry 219
  Martin 212
Funkehouser, Christr. 133
Funkhouser, Christr. 133
Fuqua, John 195
  Jos. 195
Fuqueay, Joseph 69
Furgason, Hamlet 25
  James 25
  Richard 25
  Thomas 25
Furguson, David 69
  James 69
  John 69
  Robert 69
  Willm. 183
Furlow, John 44
  Robert 45
Fursythe, Jacob 195
Fustad, Anthony 201
G(?), George Travis 178
Gaddie, Jesse 69
  John 69
  Silas 69
  Wm. 69
Gaddy, Elijah 144
  Elisha 159
  Tolbert 69
Gaff, John 168
Gage, Aaron 231
  Daniel 178
  John 230
Gaines, William 175, 191
  Wm. 187, 189
Gains, William 52
Gaither, Cornelius 252
  John 219
Galagher, Charles 178
  Patrick 178
Galahas, Patrick 151

Galaspey, William 150
Galbreth, Hugh 110
Gale, James 52
    Joseph 34
Galey, Samuel 35
Galliway, John 252
    Robert 252
Galtoway, John 219
Gamble, Wm. 231
Gambrel, James 133
Gammon, Richard 201
Gan, William 123
Gano, Daniel 52, 61
    Isaac E. 50, 52
    John 52
    Richard 52
Gardain, Henry 213
Gardiner, George 225
    John 225
Gardner, Alexr. 69
    Edmund 69
    Elisha 69
    John 69
    Thomas 230
    Wm. 69
Garner, Henry 260, 262
    James 230
    Richd. 213
    Thomas 100
    Vincent 262
Garnet, Benjamin 52
    George 52
    John 34
    Sarah 52
    Thomas 35
Garr, John 189
Garrard, (?) (Gov.) 193
    Benj. 263
    James (Gov.) 44, 193,
        261
Garrel, Jno. 201
Garrenhart, Michl. 100
Garretson, Arthur 16
    James 16
    Joseph 16
Garrett, Elie 6
    Isaac 94
    John 94
    Mary 175
    Maurice 94
    Nathan 94
    William 6, 34, 94
Garrison, Abraham 116
    Benj'n. 69
    George 69
    Jas. 69
    John 69
    Matthew 69
Garrott, Ambr. 189
    Ambris 174
    Ely 174
    Isaac 230
    John 231
    Morris 231
    Nathan 230
    William 231
Garshin, Thomas 94
Garton, Uriah 34
Garvan, Isaac 123
Garvin, David 69
    Valentine 69
Gary, John 25
Gash, Michal (Jr.) 178
    Michal (Sr.) 178
    Thomas 178
Gashwiller, Joseph 178
Gaskins, John 25
Gass, David 160

Gass (cont.)
    John 168
Gasuway, John 230
    Richard 230
Gasway, John 94
    Richard 94
Gatch, Fredrick 213
Gates, David 174, 183
    Elijah 178
    James 178
    William 77, 178
Gatewood, Andrew 34
    Augustus 34
    John 34
    Peter 34
Gatliff, Charles 107,
    110, 151
    Cornelius 107
    James 107
    Reace 107
Gattson, Wm. 201
Gauff, William 219
Gausney, Wm. 6
Gay, James 34
    John 34
    Thomas 123
Gayle, John 6
Gayston, Hugh 107
Geary, Jas. 201
Gee, John 127
Geen, Rob. 262
Gelispie, William 110
Gentry, David 144, 160
    Richard 144, 160
George, James 25
    John F. 25
Gerdan, John 107
German, William 6
Germon, Richard 62
Gest, Thomas 52
Gibbens, John 35
Gibbin, Megan 178
Gibbs, Benjamin 252
    Elizabeth 141
    Ezekel 151
    Ezekiel 116
    Hugh 141
    Jarimah 151
    Jeremiah 116
    Robert 141
    Sam'l 16, 141
    William 141
Gibbson, Gadt 133
Gibson, Daniel 69
    Henry 16, 48, 183
    Jas. 201
    John 69
    Jonathan 189
    Saml. (Jr.) 201
    Saml. (Sr.) 201
    Sarah 52
    Thomas 69, 178
    William 178
    Wm. 107
Giddings, George 69
Gier, Samuel 219
Gilbert, John 139
    Micah 159
Gilbot, John W. 178
Gilcomb, Joseph 151
Gilkey, David 252
    Edward 219
    James 16
    William 25
Gilkinson, Wm. 201
Gilky, John 213
    Willm. 213
Gill, John 110, 151

Gill (cont.)
    Richard 110, 151
    Richard (Jr.) 151
    Samuel 116
    Tho. 189
    William 225
    Wm. 69
Gillaspie, David 189
    Simon 201
Gillbert, John 189
Gillett, Jonathan 151
Gillgore, John 77
Gilliham, Clement 252
Gillihan, Wm. 16
    Hugh 178
Gilliland, Thomas 225
Gillmon, Joseph 133
Gilmore, James 123
    Jaramiah 195
    John 183
    Robert 100
    Samuel 123
Gimlins, Andrew 174, 189
Gimmerson, Abraham 241
Gist, Thomas 25
Givens, George 123
    James 123
    James (Jr.) 122
    John 25, 35, 123
    Joseph 25
    Robert (Jr.) 123
    Robt. (Jr.) 127
    Samuel 123, 127
Givins, Martha 178
Glaize, Nathanl. 231
Glase, Adam 213
Glasgow, John 150
    Obediah 183
Glass, Dudley 25
    Robert 241
    Thomas 34
    William 25
Glaves, Mathew 6
Gleen, Hugh 160
    Joseph 160
    Martin 160
    William 159
Glen, David 219
Glenn, John 225
    Joseph 225
    William 94, 231
Glover, Jos. 110
    Richard 133
    Uriah 219
    William 110
Glovien, James 6
Goan, Claborne 107
    Isiah 107
Goare, Isaac 52
Goban, Joseph 100
    William 230
Gobb, Samuel 213
Gobel, Benjn. 213
Gobin, John 83
Goderd, William 178
Godfrey, Jas. 69
    Jno. 201
Goff, Jessee 134
    Thomas 134
    William 134
    William (Sr.) 134
    Wm. (Jr.) 69
    Wm. (Sr.) 69
Gogens, John 144
Goggins, William 110
Golden, Wm. 195
Goldsby, James 127
Goldsmith, Saml. 219

GomeryMc, Basel 213
Gooch, Matt'w M. 25
Gooch, Thos. 201
Gooden, Patrick 195
Goodin, James 263
  Richd. 263
Gooding, Alexander 107
  John 107
  Thomas 107
Goodlow, Bivin 35
Goodman, Amos 69
  Stephen 69
Goodnight, Jacob 123
  John 183
Goodnite, Abram. 183
  Henry 183
Goodpasture, Abraham 201
  Conelus 210
  Isaac 201
  Jno. 201
  Solomon (Jr.) 201
  Solomon (Sr.) 201
Goodwell, Daniel 219
  James 219
Goodwin, Edward 83, 88
  Isaac 225
  Jesse 16
  Robert 16
  Robert (Sr.) 16
  Saml. (Jr.) 225
  Sam'l 16
  Samuel (Sr.) 225
  Thomas 225, 230
  William 83, 88
Goodwine, Abraham 219
  John 219
Goody, George 159
Goolow, William 159
Gordan, Betty 183
  William 183
Gorden, David 241
  Richard 159
  William 16
Gordon, Ambro. 189
  George 25
  Robert 150
  Samuel 151
Gore, Benjamin 201
  John 201
  William 52
Gorham (?) 133, 139
Goron, John 34
Goshon, Mark 189
Goudy, John 183
Gough, Charles 252
  John B. 252
Gour, Laurence 213
Gover, And. 264
Grabel, David 213
Grable, Joseph 219
Grace, Henry 16
  John 262
Gragg, David 231
  Saml. 201
Graham, Arthur 34
  Christopher 219
  Ferguson 35
  Francis 151
  James 123, 219
  Jas. 201
  John 116, 213
  Mary 151
  Sam'l 183
  Samuel 77, 183
  William 52
  Wm. 201
Grammer, John 133
  William 133

Grant, Adam 252
  Charley 16
  John 1, 2, 6, 178
  Squire 2, 6
Grason, Reuben 133
  William 133
Grass, Henry 225
Gratehouse, Isaac 241
Graves, Anthony 139
  Benj. 110
  Charles 252
  David 34
  Edmond 35
  Edmund 230
  Leonard 183
  Philip 219
  William 175
Gray, David 213
  Drakeford 219
  George 34
  Isaac 45
  James 100, 213
  John 16, 45, 151, 189
  Johnathan 34
  Jonas 225
  Joseph 201, 252
  Leaven 168
  Margret 16
  Mathew 45
  Presley 219
  Reuben 69
  Richard 151
  Richd. 175
  Rich'd 34
  Robert 100, 123, 178, 230
  Rob't 16
  Thos. 168
  William 100, 219
  Wm. 201
Grayham, David 252
  James 189
  Marcus 252
  Tho. 189
  Wm. 69
Grayson, Ben 224
  Ben. 211
  Benjamin 174
  Benjn. 213
  Jno. 201
  Thomas 16
  William 16
Greathouse, Herman 219
  John 34
  John (Jr.) 34
  Wm. 34
Greaves, Anthony 133
  Frederick 133
Green, Benjamin 151, 213
  Edmond 201
  Henry 189
  James 6, 133
  Jessee 133
  Joseph 25
  Leven 219
  Lewis 107
  Martin 160
  Massey 77
  Robert 116
  Stephen (Jr.) 159
  Stephen (Sr.) 159
  William 16, 174, 175
  Willis 114, 120, 128
  Wm. 174
Greenstreet, James 25
  Peter 69
  William 25
Greenup, Christo. 189

Greenup (cont.)
  Christopher 174
Greenwall, John 225
  Joseph (Jr.) 225
  Joseph (Sr.) 225
Greenwalt, Lewis 225
Greenwood, Philip 94, 241
Greer, Robert 16
  Stephen 34
Gregg, John 88
Gregory, John 230
  Richard 230
  Samuel 34
Greiders, Henry 174
Gremsley, James 6
Grider, Christo. 189
  Henry 189
  Jacob 189
  Tobias 189
Grier, James 25
  Jesse 25
  Jonathan 25
  Josiah 25
  William 25
Griffe, John 241
Griffen, Anthony 195
  Ebenezer 34
  Gordon 34
  John 35
  Ralph 34
  Richd. (Jr.) 195
  Richd. (Sr.) 195
  Terry 195
  Wilson 16
Griffeth, Able 77
Griffin, Barney 183
  Ebenezer 6
  Ninian 52
  Owens 16
  Ralph 241
  Thomas 6
  Wm. 35
Griffith, (?) 133
  Christopher 133
  Eli 16
  Elias 77
  Thomas 52
  Wells 16
Griffy, Samuel 252
Griggsby, Charles 230
Grigory, Andrew 94
  John 94
  Richard 94, 252
  Smith 252
Grigs, Julies 134
Grigsby, Charles 83, 88
  Nathaniel 219
  Natle (Jr.) 219
Grimes, Amous 183
  David 133
  Elias 100
  Francis 252
  Hugh 83
  James 52, 201
  John 52, 252
  Leedwell 58
  Stephen 48, 183
Grimsley, James 34
Grinnel, Arnel 213
  Jeremiah 213
  Joshua 213
Grinstaff, Jacob 107
Grinstead, Jesse 69
  Wm. 34
Grisham, James 241
  Uriah 107
  Wm. 107
Grissom, James 100

Grisson, John 77
  William 77
Grissum, Laurence 110
  Tobe 110
Gristy, Clements 213
Gritton, John 178
Grover, Issiah 178
Groves, Frederick 25
Grubbs, Higgason 144
Grundy, Elizabeth 252
  Gardum 252
  George 252
  John 252
  Robert 252
  Samuel 252
Grunwell, Charles 252
Grumes, Hugh 88
Guant, Mary 178
Gudgull, Andrew 201
Guell, George 201
Guffee, Alexander 133
  Ephraim 262
  Ephraim (Jr.) 262
Guffey, Henry 262
  John 151
  Jones 151
  Samuel 151
Gugil, Jacob 201
Guill, Thos. 201
Guinn, Jones Thomas 94
  Mathew 160
  Thomas I. 230
Gullett, Andrew 16
Gulley, Thomas 151
  Thomas (Jr.) 151
Gulliher, Patrick 16
Gullion, Henry 52
  Jeremiah 52
  Robert 183
  Robt. 48
Gum, Elijah 69
  Jacob 69
  Jesse 69
  Shepherd 225
  William 168
Guthree, William 178
Guthrie, Adam 63, 219
  James 100
  Matt'w 16
Guthry, Elizabeth 123
  Levy 168
  Robert 123
Gutridge, John 160
Gutry, Wm. 168
Guttrey, Benj. 34
Habbert, Thomas 220
Hacket, Peter 168
Hackett, Nellson 202
  Nelson 193
Hackings, Thos. 202
Hackley, James 213
Hadden, Saml. 195
  William 36
  Wm. 36
Haden, Henry 213
  Willm. 213
Haff, Luke 231
  Paul 35
Hagen, Clement 213
  Edward 213
  Ignacius 213
  Jacob 152
  Prosser 152
  Walter 219
Hager, James 253
Haggard, Benjamin 117
Haggin, John 189
Hahn, Peeter 213

Hahn (cont.)
  Peter 220
Haidon, Jacob 141
Hail, Hannah 178
Haile, Levy 231
Hains, Even 160
Hald, Caleb 253
  John 253
Hale, James 107
  Jesse 184
  John 184
  Palmer 184
Hall, Aaron 195
  Andrew 17
  Arthur 220
  David 144, 168
  Edward 134
  E. L. 83
  Elisha L. 88
  Henry (Jr.) 178
  Henry (Sr,) 178
  James 107, 134, 145
  John 70, 110, 216, 226
  John (Sr.) 226
  Joseph 110
  Leonard 117
  Loudy 25
  Mary 213
  Michael 70
  Palmer 184
  Squire 168
  Thomas 36
  William 17, 52, 168, 179, 241
  Wm. 195
Halliday, John 253
Halloway, James 35
  JOhn 195
Halmark, William 78
Ham, William 144, 160
Hambelton, James 123
Hambleton, John 117, 193
  Patk. 168
  Wm. 117, 168
Hamelton, Charles 151
Hamilton, Abner 202
  Andrew 25
  Andy 48
  Archibald 202
  Clements 253
  Edward 25
  Elliot 202
  Isham 253
  James 253
  Jno. 202
  John 25
  Leonard 253
  Saml. 202
  Samuel 35
  Thos. 110
Hamm, Drury 151
Hammelton, James 213
  John 160
Hammersley, James 6
Hammilton, Archd. 183
  Mary 184
Hammocks, Wm. 17
Hammon, Isral 151
  Philip 151, 195
Hammond, (heirs) 184
  Christopher 26
  Edwd. 184
  Gervin 184
  Gervin (Sr.) 219
  Hudson 184
  Jas. 184
  Job 219

Hammond (cont.)
  John 35
  Willm. 184
Hammons, Leroy 262
  Peter 17
  Woodson 262
Hammons, Jno. (Sr.) 262
  John (Jr.) 262
  Joseph 231
Hammor, Abraham 160
Hampton, Andrew 35
  James 53
  Michael 175
Hamton, Caty 134
  Thomas 134
Hance, William 45
Hancock, Ann 189
  Benj. 262
  Jas. 263
  Jesse 262
  Js. 262
  Simon 263
  Stephen 160
  William 160
  Wm. 262, 263
Hand, John 252
Handcock, Samuel 57
  Simon 52
Handly, Alexander 253
  James 253
  John 134, 139
Handon, William 225
  Jessy 189
  Wm. 189
Haneline, John 195
Haner, Christopher 110
  James 184
Haney, Henry 168
  Wm.. 168
Hank, Peter 202
Hanks, George 35
  John 195
  Joseph 213
  Peter (Sr.) 195
  Willm. 213
  Wm. 195
Hanlin, Partrick 189
Hanna, Adom 178
  James 178
  Stephen 179
  Thomas 179
Hannah, Alexander 110
Hansberry, John 231
Hansbrough, Moriah 123
Hansford, Henry 202
  Wm. 202
Hansley, Davis 202
  Johnathan 231
  Richardson 231
Hany, David 134
Happer, Robert 70
  Stephen 70
Harbenson, Archibald 201
  Robt. 201
Harber, Amos 117
  Elijah 117
Harbert, Elisha 36
  Jas. 262
  Mat. 262
Harbison, James 184
  John 178, 253
  Rachel 178
  Thos. 179
Harbour, Elisha 160
  Joseph 17
Harden, Abram 26
  Benjamine 134
  Daniel 226

Harden (cont.)
James 213
Newless 78
Sam'l 141
Hardester, Hezekiah 6
Uriah 6
Hardesty, Caleb 219
Hardie, Samuel 61
William 61
Hardin, Absolam 26
Absolom 253
Ann 252
Benjamin 25, 252
Big John 252
Ede 253
George 25
Henry 252
Jane 253
Joab 26
John 70, 252
John (Jr.) 252
John P. 252
Marck 253
Martin 252
Moses 253
Nicholas 184
Sam'l 16
Solomon 70
Thomas 70
Harding, John 252
Robert 253
Stephen 253
Thomas 252
Hardmon, David 231
Johnathan 231
Joseph 231
Solomon 231
Hardon, Jacob 141
Hardwick, Geo. 195
John 151, 193
Jno. (Jr.) 195
John (Sr.) 195
William 123
Hardy, Elijah 6
George 70
Isham 66
Ishom 70
Hare, Andrew 174
Hargas, John 226
Hargester, Thomas 36
Harget, Peter 36
Hargis, Thomas 225
Hargraves, Hezekiah 134
Robert 139
Robert (Sr.) 134
Willis 134, 139
Hargreaves, Robt. (Jr.)
134
Harket, Peter 144
Harle, W. 263
Harlen, Joshua 134
Harlin, George 123, 178
James 178
John 189
Harlow, Claben 174
Elijah 174
Lewis 70
Michael 175, 202
Randal 70
Samuel 175
Susana 195
Tho. 195
Thomas 175
Harman, Abraham 78
Isack 78
Israel 26
Harmon, Jacob 110
Jacob (Jr.) 117

Harmon (cont.)
Jno. 202
Michal 178
Robert 36
Thomas 35
Thoms. 226
Voluntine 110
William 35
Harned, Edward 213
Innes 213
Jonathan 213
Jonathan (Jr.) 213
Willm. 213
Harness, Hezekiah 70
Harnis, Thomas 70
Harok, Samson 168
Harper, Betty 202
Charles 195
Hanse 70
Isaac 70
James 70
Jas. 202
Jonathan 70
John 144, 195
Mary 35
Matthew 70
Samuel (Jr.) 70
Samuel (Sr.) 70
Silas 70
Thos. 202
Harrel, Caleb 213
Harrias, Wm. 168
Harriman, John 189
Harrington, John 26
Harris, (?) 69
Andrew 152
Bambo (Negro) 220
Benjn. 169
Christopher 144, 168
David 160
Daniel 241
George 242
Isaac 213
James 44, 144, 151,
189, 213, 220, 241
Jas. 262
Jas. (Jr.) 262
Jinkins 134
John 70, 134, 141,
151, 184, 241
Jonathan 242
Joseph 220
Nathaniel 220
Overton 189
Richd. 262
Richmd. 168
Sherwood 169
Sam'l 189
Samuel 151, 226
Sarah 220
Stephen 220
Susanna 220
thomas 58
Thomas 151
Thos. 213
William 134, 144, 242
Willm. 88
Wm. 202
Harrison, Cuthbert 213
George 213
Greenberry 220
Henry 6
Jeremiah 25
Jessee 134
Jnt. 83
John 174, 189, 231
John (Jr.) 174, 189
Joshua 220

Harrison (cont.)
M. 198, 209
Micajah 194, 195
Nicholas 7
Thomas 123, 252
Thos. G. 179
William 134, 139
Harriss, Mary 151
Harrod, Ann 178
James 174, 176
Harrow, Jas. 202
Saml, 201
Hart, Charles 184, 263
David 184
George 220
Himy 213
Israel 117
James 195
John 178, 184
John (Rev.) 62
Samuel 184
Wm. 195
Hartgrove, John 110
Harthorn, Jas. 202
Hartman, David 83, 88
Hartt, Josiah 225
Harvey, John 6, 123
William (Jr.) 160
William (Sr.) 160
Harwood, John 6
Hashfield, John 123
Haskings, Gregory farmer
202
Jas. 202
Jno. 202
Haskins, James C. 70
Hatfield, Edward 213
JOhn 213
Jonas 213
Thos. 213
Val. 262
Hathaway, David 194
Hatheway, Davd. 195
Hatherly, Lanerd 168
Hatherway, Johnathan 202
Philip 202
Hatten, Elizabeth 53
Jno. 195
Hatton, Dempsey 53
Henry 7
Hauks, Lewis 18
Haussman, Jno. D. 80
Haustings, Charles 213
Haven, John 45
Havord, George 127
Haw, Jacob 134
Hawk, John 6
Hawks, John 101
Hawkings, Clabon 241
Hawkins, Elisha 53
Ezekiel 107
James 36
Jas. 69
Jess. 107
John 70, 117, 219
John (Jr.) 107
John (Sr.) 107
Joseph 160
Nathen 160
Nickless 160
Thomas 219
Thos. 17, 107
Will 53
Hawklin, Samuel 70
Hawley, Benjm. 195
David 70
Hawrigan, Patrick 253
Hawthorn, James 53

Hay, Adam 78, 220
  Cristopher 53
  Felty 220
  John 117
  Michal 78
  Micheal 141
  William 117
Haycraft, Joshua 220
  Saml. 226
Hayden, William 53
Haydin, William 253
Haydon, Abner 35
  Baziel 252
  Benj. 35
  Bennet 252
  Charles 252
  Ezekiel 35
  James 35, 53
  John 35, 253
  Noah 184
  Stanislaus 252
  Wm. 35
  Wm. (Jr.) 35
Hayes, Bennet 213
Haynes, Andrew 107
  William 226
Hays, Andrew 134
  Charles (Jr.) 160
  Charles (Sr.) 160
  Hugh 110
  James 110
  Jeremiah 202
  Joseph 213
  William 252
  William Thomas 59
  Wm. 70
Haysler, Jas. 202
Hayslet, Wm. 202
Hayton, James 113
Haywood, John 220
Hazan, Edmund 6
Haze, William 151
Hazel, Caleb 70, 226
Hazle, Daniel 26
Hazlip, Robert 70
Hazzard, John 35
  Martin 35
Head, Benjamin 53
  Cuthbert 213
  Edward 253
  Henry 253
Headdrick, Joseph 189
Headen, Balemus 201
Heady, James 219
  Stilwell 219
  Thomas (Jr.) 219
  Thomas (Sr.) 219
Heagle, John 151
Heard, John B. 252
Heartherly, Lenard 145
Heat, Benjamin 36
Heath, John 45, 58
  Joseph 45
  Samuel 45
Heatherly, Nathan 70
Heaton, Jno. 202
Heavenhill, Oliver 220
Hedden, Abram 35
Hedes, Enoch 202
Hedge, Levy 195
  Mathias 195
Hedger, Elias 58
Hedley, George 45
Hedrick, Jacob 202
Heins, Joseph 45
Helen, Thomas 226
Helm, Joseph 110
Helmes, William 231

Helms, George 123
  Leonard 123
  Marquis 123
  Peter 202
Hemdrick, George 7
Hemphill, James 242
Hencely, David 151
Henderson, Alex. 35
  Binnett 247
  David 168
  James 26, 123, 151
  Jno. 202
  John 35, 151, 174,
    178, 189
  Joseph 35
  Micheal 151
  Richard 76, 160
  Richd. (heirs) 78
  Robert 45, 152, 168
  Samuel 35
Hendrick, George 7
Hendricks, Absalom 202
  Enoch 202
  George 202
  Jacob 202
  James 145, 168, 226
  Nimrod 202
  Noah 202
  Wm. 202
Hendrickson, John 160
  Leonard 253
Hendrix, Isaac 184
  John 184
  Thomas 134, 139
  Will. 184
Hendron, Jno. 202
  Nimrod 202
  Taylor 202H
Henin, Andrew 151
Hening, Daviel 202
  Sarah 202
Hennery, William 160
Hennes, Henry 152
Hennon, Abell 189
Henry, Ezekiel 26
  John 17
  Moses 202
  Robert 151
  Thomas 17, 26, 134,
    139, 175
  Watson 110
  William 17, 134
Hensley, Charles 134
  George 35, 241
  James 242
  Joseph 195
  Richerson 35
  Samuel 70, 241
  William 184
Henton, Thos. (Jr.) 202
  Thos. (Sr.) 202
Herald, Jacob 26
  James 213
  Moses (Sr.) 220
Herd, James 60
Herendon, John 168
  Oan 168
Heringford, John 194
Herman, Asahal 220
Hern, William 17
Herndon, Cornelius 134,
    139
  Elisha 134
  George 134, 139
  James 129, 134, 139
  Owen 145
Herod, Edward 144
  Richard 220

Herod (cont.)
  Richard 220
  William 219
Heroild, Chester 213
Herrald, Isaac 220
  James 220
  John 220
  Moses 220
  William 220
Herreford, Andrew 202
  Jas. 202
  Jno. 202
Herrill, Robert 134
Herring, Ruben 78
  Sarah 202
  Shadwick 201
  Wm. 202
Herrod, Edward 168
  John 219
  William 219
Hervey, John 144
  William 144
  William Henry 144
Hess, Henry 178
Hester, Jacob 45
  Johnson 45
  Martin 6
  Mathias 231
Hestings, William 35
Hews, David 202
  Jas. 202
Hickey, Simon 35
Hicklin, Thomas 53
Hickling, Hugh 231
Hickman, Ezekiel 252
  Mary 202
  Thos. 53
  Will 53
  Willm. (Jr.) 53
Hicks, Absolom 141
  Daniel 152
  Henry 17
  James 16, 213
  Mashack 262
  Richard 17
Hide, Ezekiel 17
Hieatt, Joseph 160
Hiett, Abner 152
  Fredrick 152
  John 152
Higgin, Jas. 202
  Jesson 202
  Jno. 202
  Moses 202
  Wm. 202
Higgins, Ellinor 184
  Gideon 189
  Henry 184, 220
  James 83
  Jesse 16
  Jonathan 94
  Peter 110
  William 183
  Wm. 195
Highbaugh, Geo. 70
  Henry 70
  Jno. 70
Highbough, George 226
Hightower, Oldham 17
Hiler, James 35
Hill, Able 231
  Atkinson 213
  Burril 178
  Clemuel 151
  David 26
  Elizabeth 201
  Ephraim 25, 70
  Firgus 231

Hill (cont.)
Gabriel 195
Hardy 101, 231
James 70, 168, 202
Joel 144, 168
John 36, 168, 253
John B. 213
Joseph 26, 45, 202
Nelson 70
Robert 26, 151, 178
Thomas 184, 253
William 220
Willm. 213
Wm. 35
Hillicost, George 123
Hilly, Francis 127
Hilton, Henry H. 253
William 253
Hind, Elizabeth 70
James 117
John 70
Lewis 70
Samuel 70
William 70
Hindman, James 253
Matthew 70
Hinds, Andrew 210
Jas. 202
Joseph (Capt.) 262
Jos. (Jr.) 262
Jos. (Sr.) 262
Levi 263
Sam'l 263
Samuel 261
Hine, Thomas 253
Hineman, Matthw. 83
Hines, John 152, 178
Samuel 110
Thos. 213
William 179
Hinton, George 151
John 220
Joseph 202
Samuel 213
Stephen 220
His, Elisha 36
Hitchens, James 253
Hite, Abraham (Sr.) 101
Isaac 101
Joseph 101
Thomas 123
Hoback, Anderson 213
Anderson (Jr.) 213
Isaac 213
John 226
Micheal 213
Volentine 213
Hobbs, Eli 220
Jacob 241
John 220
Joseph 219
Joshua 213, 220
Hoblet, Boston 48, 184
Hoboy, Andrew 184
Philip 184
Hobs, Christopher 107
James 107
Vincen 107
Wm. 107
Hockaday, Isaac 168
Hodge, Andw. 195
Hamilton 195
Sam'l 16, 17
Hodgen, Robert 226
Hodgens, John 69
Andrus 189
Geo. 195
James 107

Hodges (cont.)
Jasey 168
John 195
Robert 26
William 195
Hodgson, Phinehas 189
Hog, Aaron 184
Hoga, Jno. 202
Hogan, James 17, 36
James (Fayette) 189
John 189
Joseph 110
Thomas 16
Walter 16
William 175
Wm. 107, 189
Hoges, Wm. 197
Hogg, (?) 78
Aron 123
Hogges, Jessy 144
Hogland, Abraham 219
Amos 219
Henry 94
James 94, 219, 242
Jamima 94
Jamimah 242
Margaret 220
Moses 219, 242
Nancy 242
Richard 94
Hogshead, Will 184
Hoke, Henry 242
Holbrook, George 94
Hold, Zachariah 6
Holderman, (?) 70
Jacob 66, 70
Holeman, Daniel 35
Edward 35
Edward (Jr.) 35
George 35
Henry 35
John 226
Nicholas 35
Holiday, John 26
Holin, John 178
Holland, Henry 252
John 127
William 144
Wm. 70, 160
Holley, Francis 144
John 145
Hollin, John B. 178
Hollingshead, Frances 36
Hollis, William 83
Holloday, James 70
Holloway, Claten 174
George 78
John 174
Mary 189
Robert 53
Holly, (?) 169
Nathaniel 141
Richd. 168
Holman, George 242
Richard 183
Holmes, David 202
Robert 88
William 213
Holms, Andrew 231
John 253
Rosanna 184
Holoway, George 80
Holsclaw, Elijah 174
Jacob 174
Jacob (Jr.) 189
Holt, Daniel 53
John 101
Thomas 220

Holt (cont.)
Thomas B.
Holte, Danieal 134
Holterman, Jacob 152
Holtzclaw, James 219
Kelly H. 220
Homes, John 195
Robert 83
Hon., Jones 202
Honeyman, Stephen 213
Hood, Luk 202
William 134
Hook, Benedick 213
Hooke, Andrew 101
George 101
Henry 101
Hoon, Aaron 144
Christopher 144
Matthew 144
Hoop, Benjamin 226
Sarah 226
Hooper, Enoch 26
Hoopman, Jacob 123
Hooser, Isaac 263
Jacob 263
Sampson 263
Hope, Richard 178
Hopewell, John 178
Thos. 184
Hopkins, Edmond 78
Eldridge 151, 202
Francis 117, 201
Henry 201
James 78
John 151
Robt. 201
Samuel 78
Samuel (Gen.) 76
William 117, 220
Wm. 202
Hopper, Moses 144, 168
William 144
Wm. 168
Hopson, William 253
Hopton, Stephen 141
Hord, James (Jr.) 107
James (Sr.) 107
Samuel 107
Thomas 107
Horine, George 123, 184
Jacob 128
Michael 123
Horms, John 231
Horn, Aaron 144
Asron 168
Christopher 144, 168
Joseph 151
Matthew 144, 168
William 160
Hornback, Abm. 101
Corns. 101
Isaac 101
James 184
Jas. 262
Saml. 101
Hornbeck, Abram. 226
Horton, George 202
Robert 17
Thomas 242
Hosley, James 6
Hostetter, Isaac 202
Houchins, Benj'n. 70
Charles 70
Houghstedler, Jno. 134
John 139
Houk, George 70
Hounsley, Charles 110
House, Andrew 35

House (cont.)
  John 184
  Levy 184
Houseman, John D. 78
Housley, Thomas 77, 80
Houston, Andrew 160
  John 220
  William 219
Houstown, John 213
Houts, Christopher 178
How, John 53, 94, 231
  Joseph 201
  Saml. 201
Howard, Allen 35, 242
  Benjamin 145
  Benjn. 168
  Caty 252
  Charles 178, 253
  Clament 169
  Elihue 134
  Hannah 160
  Henry 168
  James 6, 219, 242
  John 134, 139, 219
  Joseph 219
  Leroy 35
  Mark 175
  Samuel 219
  Thos. 213
  William 17, 134, 160
Howdeshel, Jacob 110
Howe, John 248
Howel, Jelson 78
Howell, James 134
  John 226
Howhemmer, Henry 151
Howley, Dennis 48, 183
Hows, William 151
Hoy, Sarah 168
  William 144
Hubbard, Ephraim 213
  George 25
  Zebulon 25
Hubbert, Eusebus 160
  Joseph 160
Hubble, William 52
Hubbort, Durret 160
Hubbs, Jacob 101
  Samuel 101
Huchens, John 213
Huckleberry, Fredk. 88
  George 101
Hucklebury, Fredk. 83
  Jacob 231
Huckstep, John 36
Huddle, George 7
Hudgel, John 252
  Joseph 252
Hudgens, Anne 110
  Daniel 110
  Jacob 16
Hudgins, Moses 263
Hudson, Ezekiel 134
  Thomas 134
Huff, Abram 178
  Charles 184
  Lawrence 219
  Richard 184
  Thomas 184
  William 25, 184
Huffaker, Jacob 262
  Xopher 262
Huffman, Christia 26
  Frederick 110, 117
  Isaac 26
  John 189
  Peter 26
  Teter 175

Hufman, Aaron 213
  Peter 189
Hughe, Ephm. 48
Huges, James 78
  Roland 77
Hugh, Andrew 174
  William 175
Hughbanks, James 220
Hughes, Abijah 101
  Barnabas 178
  Benjamin 94, 231
  Charles 17
  Daneal 80
  David 193
  Jesse 94
  John 83, 88, 123, 178
  Morgan 94
  Robert 253
  Thomas 241
Hughet, Goldsmith White 107
Hughey, Ephream 183
Hughit, Russell 141
Hughs, Absolom 151
  David 134
  David (Jr.) 134
  Edward 189
  George 174
  James 134, 220
  Jessee 134
  John 141, 219
  Joseph 35
  Roland 141
  William 134, 175
  William (Jr.) 220
  William (Sr.) 220
  Wm. 35, 189
Huk, Absalom 16
Huke, Wm. 202
Huker, Michael 134
Hukes, Sherwood 78
Huks, Willis 17
Hukum, Wm. 107
Hulchison, Saml. 88
Hull, Isaac 45
Humble, Mic'l 189
  Paul 189
Humes, Elzapham 6
  George 6
  Joel 6
  John 6, 94
  John (Jr.) 6
Humphrey, George 231
  John 231
  Merry 35, 231
  William 220
Humphries, George 247
  John 70
Hudley, Anthony 253
  Josiah 253
Hungate, Charles 183, 184
  John 183, 184
Hunt, Richard 110
  Thanz 202
  Thos. 202
  Wilson 36
Hunter, Alexander 253
  Dorothy 17
  Edw. 263
  Henry 94, 231
  John 6, 26, 123, 213
  Joseph 83, 88
  Margaret 202
  Nancy 178
  Robert 184
  Samuel 94, 242
  Zachariah 179
Huntsman, John 151

Hupp, George 252
Hurly, James 195
Husband, Anney 80
  John 77, 80
Husk, Edward 184
  William 16
Huson, Jane 35
Huss, Benjamin 231
Huston, Archable 110
  Archibold 151
  Isaac 70
  Jesse 70
  Mary 123
  Robert 151
  Stephen 123
  Wm. 70
Hutchcraft, John 134
Hutcherson, Thos. 110
Hutching, Aaron 178
Hutchings, John 25
Hutchinson, Charles 152
  John 151
  Laurance 152
Hutson, John 107
  Tanley 35
Hutten, Robert 53
Hutton, Alexander 202
  Hendrick 35
  Hennery 160
  James 35, 184, 189
  Jas. 48
  Jos. 48
  Joseph 184
  Saml. 48
  Samuel 183, 184
Huver, George 184
Hyette, Joseph 116
  William 117
Hyfield, Jeremiah 6
Hynch, George 226
Hynes, Andrew 220
  Richard 35
Hynns, Isaac 226
Hyzer, Jacob 70
Iles, Thos 202
Imgrim, Archer 231
Indecut, Aron 35
  Barzella 35
  Joseph 35
  Moses 35
Ines, Alexander 70
Infield, Thomas 242
Ingland, Stephen 195
Ingle, John 231
  John (Jr.) 231
Ingleman, Joseph 78
Inglish, Charles 152
Ingram, Js. 263
  Sam'l 263
  Wm. 262
Ingrim, Isaac 152
  Uriah 202
Inlow, Abram. 226
  Isam 226
Inman, William 101, 141
Innes, Harry 53
  Harry (Judge) 174
Innis, John 117
Ireland, John 35
  Peter 71
  Wm. 71
Irmin, John 101
Irvin, Abraham 179
  John 179, 184
  Robert 179
  Samuel 175
Irvine, Sam'l 189
  Will 165, 173

Irvine, (cont.)
  Wm. 169
Isaac, Jehu 71
Isaacs, John 123
  Samuel 71
Isabel, James 226
Isball, Thomas 17
Isbell, Danniel 160
  Godfrey. 262
Isham, William 184
Isom, Charles 174
Ison, Charles 189
  James 189
Ivey, James 26
Jack, Frances 35
  John 35
  Sam'l. 48
  Samuel 184
Jackes, John 203
Jackman, John 117
  Thos. 262
  Wm. 262
Jackmon, Richard 110
Jackson, Andrew (Gen.)
  130
  Burwell 129, 134,
    139, 140
  Chris. 226
  Chriso. 226
  Christopher 123
  Christopher (Jr.) 123
  Ephriam 57
  Jesse 226
  John 53, 110, 133,
    213, 253
  Joseph 110
  Leroy 226
  Philip 36
  Thomas 123, 184
  William 101, 220, 253
Jacobs, Samuel 231
  William 242
Jacson, William 160
Jaffries, Henry 169
Jaggers, Levi 70
  Nathan 71
  Wm. 70
Jamason, William 36
James, Benjamin 203
  Daniel 35, 53
  George 110, 231
  James 26
  John 110
  Joseph 220
  Thomas 184
  Tobias 195
  William 78
Jameson, George 35
  Jas. 203
  John 35
  Jno. 202
  Samuel 17
  Thos. 203
Jamison, John (Jr.) 36
  Samuel 36
January, Ephriam 35
  James 36
  John 36
  Thomas 36
Jarboe, John 213
  Joseph 213
  T. Jesse 213
Jarbow, John B. 253
  Henry 253
Jarobus, Thos. 202
Jarrel, Walter 203
Jate, Stephen 169
Jayne, Mathias 226

Jee, Jesse 213
Jeeter, Henry 17
Jefferies, Joseph 213
  Moses 213
Jeffrees, Dan'l 189
  Thomas 175
  Wm. 189
Jeffrey, Joseph 202
Jeffreys, Henry 203
Jeffris, Henry 174
  William 175
Jefreson, John 78
Jemmeson, Joseph 160
Jenkins, Elijah 203
  Jno. 203
  Joseph 26
  Matthew 35
  Samuel 110
  Wm. 203
Jennings, Isreal 220
Jeremiah, Thomas 253
Jerrel, Jno. 202
Jett, James 48, 184
Jimmerson, James 179
Jinkins, Jonathan 179
  Shedrick 17
  William 179
  Wm. (Sr.) 179
Jinkinson, Joseph 220
Jinnings, Jonath. 189
  Dianna 189
Jinnins, Ozias 152
  William 179
Jobe, Isaac 26
Jobes, Daniel 152
Johns, Elihu 70
  John 36, 231
Johnson, Alexander 26
  Andrew 35, 242
  Benjn. 226
  Cave 35
  Elexander 213
  Ephraim 213
  Ezekiel 213
  Hennery 160
  Hugh 17
  Jacob 26
  James 26, 189, 220
  Jas. 263
  Jeddiah 213
  John 17, 26, 110, 141,
    143, 220, 242, 262
  Jno. 48, 226
  Joseph 35
  Leonard 213
  Nathan 141
  Noel 123
  Peeter 213
  Robert 213
  Thomas (Capt.) 260
  Thos. 213, 262
  William 26, 101
  Wm. 36
Johnston, Andrew 123, 203
  Andrew Thomas 7
  Benjamin 83
  Benjamin (Jr.) 88
  Benjn. 88
  Benjn. (Jr.) 83
  Charles 58
  David 53, 107, 203, 2
    231
  Gabriel I. 63
  Ga. Jones 88
  James 7, 70, 107, 231,
    261
  Jno. 203
  John 7, 45, 117, 184

Johnston (cont.)
  Jonah 70
  Jos. 107
  Nathen 134
  Richard 7
  Robert 184
  Sam'l 123
  Thomas 101, 152
  Thos. 107
  William 88, 101, 117,
    152, 231
  Wm. 83, 107, 195
Johson, David 78
Jolly, Nelson 226
Jomes, Irvine 169
Jones, Abigail 203
  Allen 179
  Ambrous 195
  Ames 160
  Andrew 26
  Arthur 123
  Balaam 253
  Barnabas 70
  Benjamin 26, 45, 202,
    203
  Cad 145, 169, 202
  Cade 17
  Charles 203
  Charles (Jr.) 160
  Charles (Sr.) 160
  Christopher 101
  David 135, 184, 220
  Edmund 107
  Eliz'th 17
  Elliotte 262
  Ellot 152
  Fieldon 184
  Francess 161
  Frank 202
  Gab'l 189
  George 70, 101, 152
  George M. 70
  Georgewall 169
  Irvin 145
  Isaac 242
  Jabok 184
  James 7, 36, 134,
    160, 169, 174,
    261, 262
  James (Sr.) 134
  Jas. 202
  Jas. Esq. 262
  Jesse 26
  John 7, 35, 107, 110,
    117, 161, 179, 213,
    262
  John (Jr.) 35
  Jos. 48
  Joseph 161, 184
  Joshua 53, 261, 262
  Martin 179
  Mason 184
  Moses 184
  Mosias 169
  Philip 70
  Richard 26
  Robert 70
  Rodger 70
  Saml. P. 213
  Samuel 45
  Stephen 107, 134
  Thomas 17, 70, 127,
    184
  Thompson M. 184
  Thos. 169, 203
  Thos. (Jr.) 202
  Thos. (Sr.) 202
  Waymon 107

291

Jones (cont.)
  William 117, 145,
    169, 226, 253
  Wm. 70, 262
  Wm. (Jr.) 195
  Wm. (Sr.) 195
Jonese, Felden 78
Jonson, David 80
Jonson, John 169
Joplin, John (Jr.) 127
Jordan, John 107
Jordon, George 220
  John 220
  Patrick 184
  Peter 184
Joseph, Negro 220
Josselling, John 123
  William 123
Joy, Comfort 26
  Cumfort 134
Joyes, Patrick 83, 88
Jrehes, Robert 231
Jrevine, Joseph 220
Judah, Jno. 203
  Winepush 203
Judy, John 194
Julin, Stephen 195, 203
Junkin, Anthony 101
  Lancelott 101
Junkins, Anthony 242
  Samsetot 242
Juram, Abraham 107
Jurdim, John 17
Kalfrus, Fredk. 189
Kalglasen, David 7
Kalin, Asa 226
Kamper, John 117
Kanaday, Benj. 189
Kaneda, Samuel 94
Karr, Absolom 232
  John 111
Kasinger, William 66
Kaster, Coonrod 7
  Paul 232
  William 232
  William (Sr.) 232
Katchum, Daniel 94, 242
Katon, Hezekiah 53
Kauffman, Christian 220
  Jacob 220
Kay, Aug. 89
  John 36
Kaye, Augustus 84
Kays, Jno. 203
Kean, Sam'l 123
  William 124
Kee, John 7
  William 117
Keeling, Benjamin 253,
    259
  James 71, 254
  Richd. 71
  Thomas 253
  William 254, 259
Keen, Frances 36
Keenan, Patrack 7
Keenar, Abraham 17
Keeton, Isaac 195, 264
  Wm. 195
Kehely, Jno. 203
Kehley, Daniel 203
Keisar, Fredk. 101
Keith, Alexander 141
  Elexander 214
  Henry 130, 141, 143
  Willm. 214
Keldar, John 36
Kelham, John 26

Kellam, Isaac 36
Kellar, Isaac 36
Kelleham, Patrick 226
Kelley, Joseph 7
Kelly, Daniel 184
  George 7
  Jacob 184
  John 184, 214
  Nathan 2, 7
  Robert 71
  Samuel 36, 169, 184
  Thos. 203
  Timothy 179
  William 214, 254
Kemp, Reuben 7
  Ruben 175
Kenady, John 195
  Merady 195
Kencade, Robt. 232
Kendal, Anthony 7
  Thomas 253
  William 254
Kendall, Danl. 89
  Davis 254
  Thomas 89
  William 101
Kendrick, William 254
Kenedy, Joseph 26
  William 17
Kenen, William 45
Keney, Peter 152, 175
Kennaday, David 152
  James 152
Kennady, Andrew 152
  John (Jr.) 152
  John (Sr.) 152
  Robert 220
  Samuel 232
  Thomas 152
  William 101
  Wm. 179
Kenneday, Michael 127
  Thos. 263
Kennedy, (?) 173
  Andrew 147, 165
  Charles 214
  Ezekiel 184
  John 214
  Joseph 161
  Thomas 2
  William 184, 220
Kennet, Charles 254
Kenney, Elenander 161
Kennison, Absalm. 89
  Absalom 84
  James 253
  John 84, 89
  Joseph 253
Kenny, Joseph 89
Kenton, Mary 179
Kergin, Joseph 152
Kerley, Benja. 264
  William 145
Kerlin, James 84
Kerling, Joseph 242
Kermikle, Peter 184
Kerns, Peter 220
Kerny, Dan'l 127
Kerr, James 17, 179
Kesinger, Isaac 71
  Joseph 71
  Peter 71
  Solomon 71
  Wm. 71
Kesler, Henry 184
Kester, John 214
  Paul 214
  Willm. 214

Kester (cont.)
  Willm. (Jr.) 214
Key, Mathew M. 175
  Thomas 135
Keykendall, Jacob 101
  Moses 101
Keyn, Patrick 184
Kidd, James 117
Kidwell, John 161
Kiervick, John 220
Kieth, Henry 226
Kiger, George 7, 45
  John 7, 45
Kilbreath, David 242
  Evan 124
  James 242
  John 195
Kilburn, Henry 111
Kilerause, Robert 254
Kilgore, Chs. 264
  David 26
  John 7
  William 26
Killems, Gilbert 107
Kilpatrick, Hugh 152
  Joseph 226
  Moses 226
Kilwell, Jno. 263
Kimbell, Jesse 78
Kimberlin, Abrm. 174
  Jacob 111, 254
Kimble, Jesse 141
Kimbly, Andrew 220
KimMc, William 214
Kinada, Benjn. 53
Kincade, Andrew 36
  Archibald 36
  David 36
  George 26
  Hapson 36
  John 36
  Samuel 26
  Wm. 36
Kincaid, Robert 152
  Samuel 220
  William 152
Kinchloe, Lewis 220
  Stephen 220
  Thomas 220
  William 220
Kindal, Steaven 7
Kinder, Geo. 90
  Peter 36
  Peter (Jr.) 242
  Peter (Sr.) 242
Kindle, Benjn. 214
  Ewell 232
  Thomas 231
  William 214
  Worden 214
King, Aaron 152
  Abner 220
  Abram 36
  Arthur 71
  Cornelius 214
  Edward 7
  Elijah 220
  George 214
  Henry 107
  Hiram 71
  James 17
  Jeremiah 203
  John 36, 111, 152,
    214, 220
  John E. 253
  John P. S. 152
  Joseph 203
  Peeter 214

292

King (cont.)
  Philip 179
  Robert 220
  Smith 220
  Thomas 179, 220
  William 220
  Wuthers 214
Kingcaid, David 203
  Jno. 203
Kinkade, James 184
  John 36
Kinkaid, Andw. 161
  David 161
  James 161
  John 161
Kinley, James 111
Kinnacannon, Andrew 63
Kinney, Daniel 184
  Joseph 84
  Richard 184
KinsayMc, Enoch 214
Kipheart, Abraham 242
  Charles 242
  George 242
  Jacob 242
  John 242
Kirby, Saml. 89
  Sam'l 84
Kirk, Alexander 203
  Henry 254
  James 253, 259
  Robert 61
Kirkendall, Jane 26
  Jesse 26
Kirkendolpher, Christo. 220
Kirkham, Robert 36, 220
  Sam'l 36
Kirkindol, Abner 141
  Adam 141
Kirkindoll, Jacob 184
Kirkland, John 184
  Thos. 179
Kirkpatrick, Alex 36
  James 123
  Robert 161
Kirtley, Beverly 194, 195
Kirts, Cunrod 220
  George 220
  Jacob 220
  Martin 220
Kirtus, John 220
Kiser, Frederick (Jr.) 242
  Frederick (Sr.) 242
  John 242
Kissinger, John 111
Kitter, Coonrod 226
Kivell, Benjamin 26
Kizer, Christopher 36
Knary, Christopher 124
Knight, Isack 78
  James 36
  John 17, 78, 141, 231
  Thos. 17
Knot, Basil 220
Knox, David 179
  Hugh 78, 141
  James 111
  Jas. 203
  John 161
  Moses 195
  Robert 161
Koil, Kyle 7
  Robert 7
Koisar, Fredk. 101

Korah, Nathan 220
Korger, Michell 7
Kukendell, Adam 78
Kulp, Jacob 184
Kurolin, James 89
Kuydendall, Joseph 17
Kuydendell, Simon 78
Kuykendall, Abner 78
  John 78
Kuykendell, Amos 78
Kykindall, Peter 232
Kyle, Robert 7
Kyles, Thomas 253
Kyser, Henry 214
Lacassagne, Michl. 89
  Ml. 84
Lace, Matthias 152
Lacewell, Henry 152
  John 185
Lacey, Alkanah 135
  Lilel 135
  Nathaniel 135
Lackey, Andrew 169
  James 169
  James (Sr.) 169
  Thos. 169
Lacy, Benjamin 18
  Edward 27
  Lenard 26
  Mary 27
  Moses 195
Laferty, Barnabas 101
Lafon, Nicholas 53
Lair, Wm. 264
Laird, Ezekiah 214
  John 214
Lamasters, Benjamin 203
  Coonrod 203
  Richard 203
Lamb, Frederick 124, 214
  Jesse 27
  Samuel 36
  Susanna 179
  Wm. 36
Lambert, Abraham 220
  James 84, 89, 242
Lamberton, Wm. 71
Lamkin, David 71
  Samuel 27
Lamkins, Jeremiah 71
Lamm, John 135
  Nathan 117
  William 175
Lamme, Wm. 189
Lampbert, John 184
Lampton, John 117
  William 117
Lanham, Thomas 145
Lankford, Larkin 184
  Thomas 135
Lanwell, Sam'l 189
Lancaster, Jno. 203
  Joseph 203
  Raphel 220
  Thomas 7
  William 27
Land, James 152
  Thomas 161
Landers, Abraham 78
  Jacob 78, 142
  John 78
Landons, Abraham 80
Lane, Jas. 203
  Jno. 203
  Robert 135
  Tho. 196
Langford, Benjamin 111
  Mary 111

Langford (cont.)
  Stephen 111
Langley, Thos. 214
Langsdon, Charles 189
Langsford, Nicholas 220
Langston, Isaac 203
  Jacob 194
  Jacob (Jr.) 203
  Jacob (Sr.) 203
Lapesley, John 117
Lapety, Benijah 242
Laphety, Barney 242
  John 242
Lapsley, Margaret 184
Larcher, Jos. 263
Lard, Hezkj. 71
  Hezekiah 89
  Jesse 71
  John 71
  Joseph 71
Lare, Andrew 111
  Matthias 111
Larrance, Isaac 189
  James 189
  Sam'l 189
Lasby, Benjn. 214
  Solomon 214
Lasefield, Ezekiel 117
Lasey, Jas. 203
  Wm. 203
Lasy, James 194
Lashbrook, John 189
  Wm. 189
Lasley, Robert 232
Lasswell, Peter 189
Laswell, William 242
Latham, James 214
  Richd. 214
Latimar, Jacob 179
  John 179
Latimer, Sam'l 179
  Sam'l (Sr.) 179
Lauerance, William 78
Lauerane, Adam 78
  John 78
Laughlin, John 107
  Thos. 107
Laughoy, William 7
Laurence, John 61
  Mary 111
Lavin, John 153
Lawler, James 184
Lawless, Benjn. 185
Lawrance, James 174, 179
  John 179
  Joseph 179
  Robert 179
Lawrence, Adam 142
  David 179
  George 142
  Isaac 45
  John 135
Laws, Jeremiah 179
  Thomas 179
Lawson, Aaron 152
  David 117
  Elihu 152
  John 242
Laysun, Hite 7
Lea, W. Frances 36
Leach, George 89
  Henry 152
  James 189
  Keturah 7
  William 27
Leamon, Robert 232
Leamone, John 232
Leanard, Charles 232

Leap, Isaac 84
Lear, George 153
Leatch, James 174
Leatherman, Christian
  84, 232
  Jacob 7, 89
  John 232
  Peter 84, 232
  Xn. 89
Leaton, John 221
  Joseph 221
  Zach. 221
Ledgerwood, James 184
  Jas. 48
Lee, Alexander 45
  Charles 226
  Christopher 7
  David 214
  Frederick 226
  George 161
  Gersham 53
  Henry 71
  James 7, 36, 196
  John 53, 214, 220,
    221
  Josiah 214
  Peter 221
  Phillip 254
  Richard 161
  Sammuel 184
  William 152, 161,
    175, 184, 214,
    226, 232
  William (Jr.) 184
  Willm. (Jr.) 214
Leech, George 84
  Henry 71
  John 71
  Joseph 71
Lemar, Samuel 135
Leeper, Andrew 111
  Hugh 111
  John 78
Leer, Coonrod 18
Leewright, Catherine 221
Legrange, Aaron 189
Lejeans, Goodwin 44
Lemar, Luke 135
  William 27, 135
Lemaster, Caty 242
  James 94, 242
  Richard 94
Lemmon, Robert 95
Lemmons, Abraham 71
Lemon, John 214
Lemons, David 203
Lenin, Charles 101
Lent, William 221
Lenty, Nicholas 221
Leonard, James 214
  Willi 184
  William 254
Lerew, Isaac 226
Lerue, Daniel 27
  Peter 27
Lesenby, William 36
Lesley, Alexander 220
Lessoherage, Jno. 203
Letcher, Benj. 189
  Eliz. 189
  John 174
  Stephen G. 53
Letherman, Peter 89
Levaw, Abraham 135
Leveradge, John 152
Levi, Solomon 111
Levingston, Thomas 152
Levington, John 264

Leviston, George 101
Levy, Solomon 153
Lewason, Robert 61
Lewis, (?) 60
  Aaron 145
  Alexander 174
  Alexr. 189
  Alex'r 18
  Bijah 214
  David 7
  Earl 27
  Fielding 60
  Gabriel 60, 61
  Hugh 26, 27
  James 27
  Jesse 53
  John 27, 36, 60,
    153, 214, 221
  Joseph 111, 189, 214
  Mary 71
  Nathenneel 161
  Nicholas 36
  N. William 135
  Richd. 189
  Samuel 18
  Thomas 27, 36, 153,
    175, 220
  William 36
  Wm. 169
Lewmus, Reuben 7
Leza, Henry 71
Liget, John 242
Ligett, Alexr. 7
Ligget, James 36
Liggon, Thos. 179
Light, Jacob 71, 184
Lightfoot, Jno. 48
  John 184
Likings, Isaac 203
Lillard, Edward 179
  Ephraim 179
  James 179
  Jno. (Jr.) 48
  John 179
  John (Jr.) 184
  Thomas 47, 176, 184
  Thos. 48
Linagar, Jesson 203
  Wm. 203
Linard, Jesse 7
Linch, Danniel 203
  David 161
  Edward 169
  William 152
Lincoln, Abraham 254
  Bathsheba 254
  Hannaniah 214
  Mordicae 254
Lindley, Zenos 7
Lindsay, Caleb 18
Lindsey, Anthony 53
  George 203, 220
  Neviel 78
  Nicholas 53
  Olliver 7
  Thomas 7
  Vachal 53
Lindsy, Lewis 71
Lineh, Charles 214
Linkey, James 117
  Robert 117
Linley, John 18
  Sarah 18
  Thos. 18
  William 18
Linn, Adam 18
  Patrick 169
  William 78, 84

Linney, Charles 264
  Henry 264
Linsey, John 36
  Mark 264
  Theodones 36
Lion, Thos. 203
Lips, Jacob 36
Lipsey, John 184
Lisle, Jno. 203
Liston, Edmund 232
  Joseph 254
Lists, George 189
Lite, Jacob 7
Litherland, John 101
Litsen, Susanna 254
Little, James 2, 7
  Jane 254
  John 179
  Nathaniel 203
  Thomas 179
Littlepage, Epps 152
Littler, John 124
Litton, Caleb 194
  Calib 203
Lively, Canon 71
  Guilham 242
  Mark 71
  William 232
Liviston, Henry 203
Lloyd, Thomas 53
Loan, Benjamin 221
Lobb, Eliz. 189
  Reuben 71
Lock, Benjn. 185
  Jacob 185
  James 184
  Jeradus, 185
  John 78
  Joseph 153, 184
  Rebeccah 95
  Richard 153
Locker, John 152
Lockert, Levy 195
Locket, James 36
Lockey, Jeremiah 232
Lockheart, James 18
Lockmon, Vinson 179
Lockridge, Jno. 203
Loe, James 107
  John 107
Logan, Benjamin 111, 232
  Charles 18, 130,
    135, 140
  Chas. 143
  David 18, 111, 124,
    142, 143, 169, 195
  Elliston 18
  Hugh 18, 127
  James 78, 124, 232
  John 45, 53, 106,
    107, 111
  John (Jr.) 53
  Jonathan 18, 130, 142
  Jonathen 124
  Jonethan 143
  Mathew 124
  Matt'w 18
  Nahtaniel 127
  Nathaniel 124
  Robert 254
  Thomas 184
  Thos. 48, 111
  Timothy 153
  William 111
  Wm. 203
Logdon, Wm. 226
Loggston, James 135
  Thomas (Jr.) 135

Loggston (cont.)
  Thomas (Sr.) 135
  William 135
Logsdon, Edwd. (Jr.) 169
  Edwd. (Sr.) 169
  Elisha 71
  Hiram 71
  James 71
  John 71, 169
  John (Sr.) 71
  John K. (Jr.) 71
  Joseph 71
  Samuel 71
  Thomas 71
  Thos. 169
  Thos. (Sr.) 169
  Wm. 71
Logsted, Edward 145
  Joseph 145
  Thomas 145
Long, Abraham 184
  Anderson 94, 242
  Benjamin 45
  George 184
  Jacob 184
  Jno. 263
  John 36, 53, 184,
    189, 254
  Samuel 185
  William 117, 179, 184
Longe, John 169
Longham, Elias 59
Longly, Thomas 45
Longstreth, Jonathan 145
Lonsdale, Isaac 214
  Wm. 203
Loomis, Reuben 7
Looney, Jonathan 179
Lorger, John 124
Lorin, John 145
Lorocon, John 169
Losson, James 45
Lot, William 36
Lout, Daniel 221
Love, Elizabeth 203
  Robert 117
Lovelass, Veacheal 152
Lovey, Peyron 125
Low, Edward 124
  John 26
  Joshua 27
  Lawrance 179
  Sam'l 124
  William 26
Lowden, Robert 94, 242
  Thomas 242
Lowe, Richard 214
Lowhorn, Thomas 152
Lowis, Aaron 169
Lowney, Thos. 214
Lowrey, Robert 232
Lowrin, John 7
Lowry, James 169
  John 36
  Mary 27
  Stephen 36
  Thomas (Jr.) 135
  Thomas (Sr.) 135
Loyallass, Reuben 18
Loyd, Thomas 145
Loyde, Saml. 169
Luallin, John 254
Lucas, Abraham 232
  Henry 254
  Ignatius 254
  Jesse 184
  John 36, 232
  Leah 184

Lucas (cont.)
  Richard 184
  William 101
Lucust, Abraham 220
  Abrah (Sr.) 221
  John 220
Lucy, Sercy 171
Ludewick, Christian 179
Luie, Abner 214
  Davod 214
  William 214
Lumpkins, John 111
  Philip 111
Lumley, Wm. 7
Lunicks, Charles 169
Lunkirt, Peter 179
Lunsford, George 94
Lushe, George V. 27
  James 27
  Robert 27
Lusk, Hugh 36
  William 175
Luske, George V. 27
  James 27
  Robert 27
Luster, Thos. 18
Lutterel, John 18
Luvet, David 203
  Ignatious 203
  Nancy 203
  Thos. 203
  Wm. 203
Luwherge, Jas. 203
Luzader, Isack 78
Lyan, David 184
  Ezekiel 185
  James 184
  John 185
  Joseph 185
Lykins, William 185
Lyn, Joseph 111
Lyndon, Danl. 226
  Jacob 226
Lynim, Andrew 117
Lynn, William 89
Lyon, James 226
  Samuel 184
Lyons, James (Sr.) 226
  John 152
Lysle, Henry 195
Lyster, John 179
  Peter 184
Macatee, Leonard 214
  Thos. 214
Macauley, James 84
Mack, Jeremiah 243
Mackey, Elenander 162
  James 124
  John 162
Maclary, Michael 170
MaCormack, John 185
Macy, Clement 72
Madison, George 23, 37,
    135, 140, 194, 198
  George (Gov.) 129
  Rowland 129, 135, 140
Maddick, Nathl. 170
Maddison, William
    Strother 58
Maddox, Absolom 232
  Dan 232
  Wilson 232
Madox, Thomas 79
Maeher, James M. 221
Mafarsen, Jesse 203
Maffet, Will 221
Magary, Daniel 203
  Robt. 203

Magee, Rafe 169
  Robt. 170
Magraw, John 124
Maguha, Wm. 204
Mahan, James 45, 107
  John 179
  Thos. 107
Main, Wm. 121
Mairtin, Nimrod 233
  Thomas 233
Major, John (Sr.) 53,
    54
  Thomas 54
Majors, James 54
Makentire, Thos. 226
Malin, Isaac (Jr.) 221
Malone, John 226
Maloney, Robert 179
Malot, John 170
Manham, Ephram 79
Mansfield, John 124,
    179
Mansker, George (Jr.)
    136
  George (Sr.) 136
Manskers, (?) 129
Manifee, Nimrod 118
  Wm. 118
Manion, James 145, 170
  Thomas 145
  Thos. 169
Mann, And'w 18
  Asa 255
  Charles 112
  George 18
  Jacob 19, 112
  John 255
  Moses 155
  William 117
Mannaz, Rich'd. 18
Manning, Ephariam 27
  John 254
  William 54
Mappin, Jas. (Jr.) 204
  Jas. (Sr.) 204
  Jno. 204
Marberry, Joel 203
  Lewis 213
Marchal, George 170
Marchall, John T. 124
Marchum 124
Marchbanks, George 27
  Johnston 27
Mardon, Jacob 71
Mariwether, Jas. 102
Markland, Jonathan 8
  Thomas 8
Marks, George 221
Markswell, George 95
Markwell, William 45
Marky, David 18
Marnahan, John 8
Marquis, Christopher 221
  James 221
  William 221
Marrs, Barnabas 190
  M. Henry 190
  Sam'l 190
Mars, William 135
Marshal, Charles 58
  Humphrey 37
  John 45, 136
  Sarah 118
  Thomas 45
  William 58, 59
Marshall, Charles 58,
    59
  David 8

295

Marshall (cont.)
Geo. 8
George 247
Hubbet 204
Isaac 84
Jno. 204
John 37, 221
Jonathan 8
Mark 221
Robert 61, 221
T. (Jr.) 46
Thomas 37
Thos. (Jr.) 37
William 53, 58, 59, 221
William (Jr.) 58
Willm. 59
Marshel, William 135
Marstan, John 54
Martain, Charles 135
Marten, Aron 243
Henry 37
John 37
Lewis 243
Peter 243
William 161, 243
Wm. 37
Marter, Oney 162
Martial, William 112
Martin, Ann 263
Anna 190
Alex. 38
Alexr. 37
Aquitta 226
Benj. 37, 263
Benjamin 64, 145
Edward 214
Elijah 54
Esael 45
Ezariah 196
George 89
Henry 196
James 38
James G. 185
Janaway 204
Jerimiah 37
John 8, 37, 111, 124, 221, 233, 263
John (Jr.) 232
Lewellin 190
Nathaniel 254
Reuben 27
Russel 204
Sarah 204, 233
Thomas 37, 54, 221
Will 221
William 179
Will'm 37
Wm. 107, 179
Martine, J. W. 71
Martiny, Earnest 37
Marton, James 170
Masae, Harris 162
Mason, George 221
James 54, 124, 142, 143
Joseph 142, 143
Pleasant 204
William 124, 161
Massae, David 162
Masse, Tho. 196
Massey, Catherine 203
Joshua 221
Massie, Harris 145
Masten, John 37, 243
Mastin, William 254
Masterson, Charles 214
Hugh 214

Masterson (cont.)
Hugh (Jr.) 214
Jerry 214
John 214
John (Jr.) 214
Zack 214
Mathew, William 8
Wm. 127
Mathews, Chitister 8
Guy 8
Joseph 162
Mathis, Andrew 28
Brister 112
Daniel 78
Morton 78
Matin, Saml. 226
Matney, Charles 264
Mattenly, James 233
Matterson, George 59
Matthews, Edward 95
John 153
Jos. 263
Paul 221
Wm. 226
Wm. (Jr.) 226
Mattingly, Baxter 214
Clements 254
Ignatius 254
John 254, 255
Joseph 214
Leonard 254
Luke 254
Phillip 214
Richd. 214
Robert 254
William 254
Mattix, Edwd. 263
Mattock, Ralph 118
Maulden, Ambrose 129
Morten 136, 140
Morton 129
Richard 136
West 136
Mauldin, Ambrose 142
James 142
Maulding, Morton 129
Maun, Beverly 185
Maurey, Eli 72
Maury, (?) 69
Maxberry, John 118
Sam'l 118
Samuel 118
Maxey, Ephraim 72
Ephriam 66, 72
Jessee 135
Philip 66, 72
Maxwell, Bazel 162
Bazeleel 153
David 154
Edward 27
Jno. 263
John 27, 135, 153
Thomas 162
William 135
May, (?) 60
Ambrose 18
Balaam 136
Chisham 18
David 221
Gabriel 221
George 62, 243
Henry 179
Humphrey 124
Jacob 112
Jesse 161
John 221
Nicholas 204
William 185, 221, 233

Mayberry, John 19
Mayes, Andrew 27
George 27
Mayfield, George 72, 118
Isaac 118
John 38
Micajah 102
Mayhall, Timothy 185
Timy. 49
William 185
Mayo, Joseph 214
Mays, Wm. 175
McAdow, David 19
McAfee, James 185
James (Jr.) 185
John 185
Robert 185
Sam'l 185
McAllister, Ancas 76
Eaneas 80
Eneas 78
McAndrew, Buneon 54
McAtee, Henry 255
Mcbee, Silas 135
Mcbey, Silase 78
McBrayer, Hugh 48
James 185
Jas. 49
Jno. 48
McBrayers, Hugh 185
John 185
McBride, James 37
Peter 203
Robert 233
Sam'l 37
Wm. 190
McCabe, Thomas 28
McCaddoms, Jas. 179
McCain, Robert 128
McCall, Benj. I. 66
John 58
William 54
McCallister, Aeneas 80
Enos 142
Sarah 153
McCamey, Robt. 185
McCampbell, Jno. 48
McCample, John 185
McCandler, Wm. 71
McCandlis, James 8
McCanley, Andrew 38
McCarkle, Alex. 263
McCarley, (?) 211
James 111
McCarmack, Hugh 117
McCarter, Robert 233
Mccarty, Jno. 204
McCarty, Jonathan 221
Thomas 102
McCary, John 71
McCasland, John 221
McCastland, Andw. 263
McCastlin, Margaret 185
Richard 185
McCastling, James 102
McCaul, Benj'n J. 72
McCauley, Jas. 89
McCay, Daniel 211
John 211
McChaney, Jas. 204
McCinley, James 233
McClain, Charles 136
David 233
Ephrim 136
George 72
James 185
John 71, 185
Thomas 102

296

McClaland, Jas. 8
Mcclanahan, Jas. 203
McClane, John 212
  Matthew 135
  Samuel 136
  Wm. 212
McClary, Sam'l 37, 185
  Samuel 37, 153
McClavel, Jane 111
McClaw, Thomas 185
McClay, (?) 211
McCleland, Daniel 84
  Danl. 247
  E. 247
  Joseph 233
McClellan, Danl. 89
McClelland, Alexander
  204
McClellen, Daniel 243
McClenden, Benja. 18
McClennen, William 221
McClerey, John 27
McClintic, John 102
  Samuel 102
  Wm. 204
McClung, Matthew 193
  William 221
McClunge, Mathew 196
McClure, Allexr. 185
  Daniel 102
  David 226
  George 102
  James 8, 111, 243
  Jean 203
  Joan 243
  John 37, 102, 111,
    243, 255
  Mary 102
  Moses 38
  Nathan 111
  Nathaniel 37
  Robt. 111
  Samuel 37
  Stale 185
  Staley 48
  Thomas 37, 38, 111
  William 102, 243
  Willm. 211
  Wm. 111, 211
Mcclure, Thos. 203, 204
McColester, George 111
McColgan, Edward 255
  James 255
McColgin, Jno. 226
McCollerster, James 161
McCollester, Dan 18
McCollom, James 8
  John 8
  John (Jr.) 8
McComas, Magt. 226
McComb, John 78
  William 78
McCimmin, Matt 37
McConnel, Alex. 37
  John 37
McConnell, James 37
  Mary 37
  Will'm 37
  Wm. (Jr.) 37
McCoombe, John 142
McCord, William 153
McCorkle, Elizabeth 37
McCorle, Samuel 233
McCormack, George 185
  James 162
  John 8
  Matt'w 27
  Peter 233

McCormack (cont.)
  Wm. 232
Mccorman, Jas. 204
  Wm. 204
McCormic, Peter 102
McCormick, Daniel 124
  Joseph 124
  William 124
McCortney, James 233
McCoun, James 185
  John 185
McCourtney, John 233
McCowan, Geo. (Sr.) 18
McCowen, George (Jr.) 18
  Sam'l 18
McCown, Wm. 18
McCoy, James 78
  Robert 8
  Thomas 27
McCracken, Senica 54
McCrackin, Cyrus 37
  John 37
McCreary, Andw. 54
McCubbin, James 71
  John 71
  Joseph 71
  Zacheriah 71
McCullah, Jno. 204
  William 162
McCullom, Thos. 264
McCullough, James 185,
  221
  Jas. 18
McCullum, James 221
  Jo 221
  John 221
Mccullum, Jno. 203
McCumsey, John 37
McCune, Andrew 38
  David 154
McCurdy, Thomas 135
McCutchen, Hugh 135
  James 135
  Jon'a (Jr.) 136
  Robert 135
  Samuel 135
McDaniel, (?) 211
  Aaron 145
  Alexr. 233
  Charity 71
  James 136, 145, 233
  James (Sr.) 233
  John 204
  Neal 153, 233
  Peter 102
  Ruben 204
  Thomas 136
  Wm. 37
Mcdaniel, Aaron 170
  David 170
  Franc. 170
  James 170
McDaniels, Elexr. 212
McDannal, Jno. 196
  Wm. 196
McDannel, James 185
  John 19
  William 185
McDannold, Angi 190
  Sam 190
McDennel, William 154
McDermid, Hugh 263
McDermit, Hugh 261
McDonald, Archyd 221
  John 221
  Redm 221
McDonley, Alexr. 8
McDoo, John 190

McDoogle, Charles 95
Mcdowel, Rbt. 203
McDowel, Wm. 175
McDowell, Alexander 118
  Charles 232
  Joseph 190
  Robt. 221
  Sam'l. 189
  Sam'l. (Jr.) 189
  Samuel 175
  Wm. 189, 228, 239
McDowl, Alexr. 102
Mcdows, Jas. 204
McDugle, Robert 8
  Rbt. 204
McElhenney, James 153
McElmurray, David 142
  Jean 142
McElmurry, David 19
McElway, Henry 153
McEneley, John 153
McEntire, Alexander 203
  Jno. 204
McEntosh, Anguish 204
  Jno. 204
McEwan, William 117
McEwen, David 117
McEwing, Wm. 142
McFadden, Jacob 142
  Sam'l. 142
McFaddin, Andrew 140
  Hugh 185
  Shepherd 142
  William 140
Mcfaddin, Andrew 135
  Jacob 19
  John 136
  Sam'l 19
  Samuel 135
  William 135
McFaddins, (?) 129
McFaddon, Hugh 154
McFarlan, Walter 153
McFarlands, Alexander
  (Maj.) 260
McFarlin, Abr. 226
Mcfarlin, Walter 18
McFatridge, William 185
McFawl, David 221
McFox, Joseph 8
McGahha, Arther 243
McGary, Hugh 185
McGaughey, Arthur 66
McGee, John 185, 221
  Patrick 221
McGerah, Robert 78
McGhaughey, A. 71
  Arthur 71
McGill, Alex. 37
  Hugh 127
  Jno. 127
  Wm. 127
McGinnis, Jno. (Jr.) 179
  Jno. (Sr.) 179
  John 221
  Robt. 136
  Sam'l. 179
  Thos. 179
  Wm. 179
McGinniss, John 232
Mcglocking, Jno. (Jr.)
  204
  Jno. (Sr.) 204
  Hugh 204
  Neal 204
McGomery, (?) 211
  Basel 213
McGoodwin, Daniel 136

298

Meguire, John 174
Larrance 190
Mehee, Lydda 190
Wm. 190
Meholm, William 153
Mellon, Isaac 233
James 71
Meloney, August 190
Melown, John 102
Melton, Joel 72
John 214
Moses (Jr.) 221
Moses (Sr.) 221
Richard 221
Memorn, Dominack 135
John 135
Memorne, Domnack 135
Menear, Abrm. 190
Menise, Deniel 153
John 153
Stephen 153
Mennefee, Richard 204
Menser, Dan'l. 19
Jones 27
Mercer, (?) 62
George 254
James 62
John 27
Jones 263
Nichs. 263
Tho. 190
William 27
Meridith, Samuel 62
Merifield, Alexander 95
John 95
Merit, Joseph 145
Meriweather, George 59
Nicholas 59
Meriwether, David 84
Nicholas 95, 243, 244
William (Jr.) 102
Wm. (Sr.) 84
Merret, Stephen 153
Merridith, William 255
Merrifeild, Thos. 214
Merriman, Zachah. 214
Merrimether, Wm. 89
Merrit, Thomas 71
Thos. 264
Merriwether, W.D. 89
Merry, Calvin 214
Colvan 18
Cornelieus 27
Owen T. 72
Merryfield, John 18
Mershon, Benj. 54
Titus 54
Meryfiel, Mary 243
Meryfield, Allen 243
Reece 243
Messick, John 8
Metcalf, John 95
Metear, William 196
Meyear, Henry (Jr.) 204
Henry (Sr.) 204
Mezeek, Charles 99
M'faddin, John 18
Shepard 19
Michel, John 54
Mickey, Daniel 45
Mickin, Mark 38
Mickleborough, Robt. 124
Midcalf, James 95
Thos. 95
William 95
Middleton, Handley 71
H. John 37
Milburn, Dudley 37

Milburn (cont.)
Joseph 254
Miles, Edward 214
Elisha 179
Eve. 37
Henry 214
Isaac 179
Isaac (Sr.) 179
Jesse 221
John 54, 179, 185, 190
Joseph 255
Mary 254
Richard 27
Samuel 37
Seth 214
Wilford 255
William 27
Zephaniah 179
Millar, John 162
Saml. 102
William 102
Milhollin, Jonathan 102
Millender, Caty 214
David 214
Miller, Abraham 117
Adam 226
Andrew 135, 140, 153
Andw. 263
Charles 214
Christr. 226
Conrod 232
Coyranes 27
Daniel 179
David 232
Earnest 226
Ebineser 214
Elizabeth 196
George 19, 118, 124, 136, 185, 204
Hennery 161
Henry 37, 49, 185, 190, 221, 226
Isaac 233
Jacob 64, 145, 170, 204, 214
James 2, 8, 27, 71
John 8, 124, 135, 196, 226, 255
John (Jr.) 8
Joseph 27
Martin 19
Mary 27
Nancy 153
Nicholas 226
Peter 226
Rbt. 204
Robert 72
Roland 66
Saml. 226
Sarah 124
Thomas 45
William 124
William (Jr.) 153
William (Sr.) 153
William B.C. 153
Wm. 226
Milligen, Will 214
Millon, Alexr. 232
Million, John 145, 170
Robt. 170
Travise 169
Mills, Edward 45
Elizabeth 214
Ethelbert 214
Ignatius 254
Jacob 8, 45
John 214

Mills (cont.)
Thomas 45
Milner, Daniel 107
John 111
Milton, Charles 161
Thos. 204
Minday, Samuel 135
Miner, Jacob 179
Josiah 174
Larkin 179
Thomas 175, 232
Mingo, Jos. 264
Minor, John (Jr.) 61
Thomas 243
Minter, Thomas 102
William 185
Mise, Isaac 145, 169
Jeremiah 161
Miser, John 233
Mitchel, John 61, 63, 118, 153, 161
Robert 37
William 153
Mitchell, Frederick 221
George 221
James 179, 185
Jno. (Jr.) 203
Jno. (Sr.) 204
Joe F. 49
John 37
Joseph F. 185
Rbt. 203
Robert 185
Robt. 179
Rosanna 37
Thos. 203
William 8
Mitcheson, Edward 27
William 27
Miyear, Joseph 204
Wm. 204
Mize, Isaac 8
Mobbly, Benjemen (Jr.) 161
Benjemen (Sr.) 161
Edward 161
Mobley, Benjamin 117, 153
Clement 154
Edward 118
James 118
Mock, Daniel 254
Jacob 254
Mockabee, Jno. 204
Mockbee, John 193, 194
Modecit, John 185
Modrel, John 221
Moffet, Wm. 203
Mola, Joseph 203
Moland, Jesse 49, 185
Molton, John 185
Mon, Sam'l John 190
Monday, Saml. 204
Moneste, John 27
Mong, Adam 102
Montjoy, Alvin 8
Monroe, Alexr. 8
George 232
Phillip 232
William 8, 232
Montaque, Thomas 54
Thos. 37
Montfort, Jas. 179
Peter 179
Montgomery, Allenr 243
Alex. 140
Alx. 136
Edw'd 255

Montgomery (cont.)
Elisha 255
George 233
Hugh 179
Isaac 194, 204
J. 263
James 135, 145, 169, 261
Jane :111
Jas. 204
John 27, 54, 124, 153, 243, 255
Jos. 204, 264
Joseph 54, 153
Patrick 196
Robert 27, 54, 142
Robt. 37, 118
Sam. 214
Saml. 53, 204
Samuel 118
Simpson 226
Thomas 154, 221
Thos. 111, 118, 203
Thos. (Jr.) 204
Thos. (Sr.) 204
Wm. 8, 54, 111, 118, 179
Montgumree, James 190
Sam 190
Mooney, Jacob 102
John 37
Joseph 8
Lawrence 99
Patrick 37
Sam'l. 8
Moor, David (Jr.) 162
John 136, 145
Robert 145
William 135
William (Sr.) 162
Moore, Abraham 243
Adam 19
Alexander 27, 153
Archibald 71
Archild 71
Moore, Arthur 153
Austin 185
Benj. 37
Benton 153
Charles 185
Chas. 49
Daniel 185
David 71
David (Sr.) 161
Edward 127
Eleanathen 54
Fr. Jas. 89
Geo. 127
George 72, 170
Isham 72
James 169
Jas. Francis 84
Jesse 221
John 37, 169, 170, 185, 221, 243, 254
John (Jr.) 169
John (Sr.) 169
John G. 102
Jos. 48
Joseph 37, 185, 204
Josiah 27
Lodwick 153
Mary 185
Moses 84
Nicholas 221
Obidiah 124
Quinten 37
Quinton 204

Moore (cont.)
Rbt. 203
Robt. 111
Robt. (Sr.) 170
Sam'l. 124
Shadrock 37
Simean 185
Thomas 185, 194
Thos. 204
William 18, 179, 185
Wm. 127, 190
Zebulon 185
Zebulon (Jr.) 185
Moores, Hennery 161
Moosby, David 190
Joseph 190
Robt. 190
Moppon, Curnelus 161
More, Benjamin 8
Moses 175
Samuel 8
Morehead, Armd 221
Charles 214
Morfet, Robert 37
Morgain, Mary 145
Morgan, (?) (Genl.) 60
Ahle 233
Charles 214
Daniel (Genl.) 60
David 84, 89
Elenor 226
Jeremiah 135
Jerimiah 140
Joseph 135
Lenard 233
Patrick 254
Philip 179
Ralph 204
Samuel 221
Simon 58
William 204
Morison, James 78
Morlen, Hugh 136
Lucy 196
Morrel, Thos. 203
Morris, David 45
Evans 38
Harry 243
Isaac 8
James 153
Jesse 118, 154
Jno. 263
John 136, 243
Joshua 243
Richard 185
Thomas 18, 19
William 243
Morrison, David 124
Hugh 254
Isaac 214
John 112
William 161
Morriss, Christo. 196
Jacob 196
John 204
Saml. 196
William 136
Morrow, Margaret 175
Rbt. 203
Richard 136
Samuel 161
William 19, 153, 243
Mortan, Richard 142, 143
Morten, Richd. 214
Saml. 214
Mortimer, Charles T. 57
Mortin, Lucy 196
Morton, Benjn. 169

Morton (cont.)
James 232
Richard 130
Thomas 221
Mosby, Thomas 8
Moseley, Samuel 107
Mosely, Thomas 135, 136, 140
Moses, Edward 204
Mosess, Moses 204
Moss, Andrew 107
David 179
Edward 161
Frederick 37
John 179
William 179
Wm. 37
Mosley, Robert 226
Mosterson, Thos. 214
Willm. 214
Willm. (Jr.) 214
Motesed, Nathaniel 111
Mothershead, Mary 8
Motly, John 196
Mounce, John 154
Mounee, Samuel 243
Mounts, Absolum 264
Jno. 203, 204
Moxley, Samuel 54
Mudd, Luke 254
Muhlenberg, (?) 130
Mulane, Jno. 204
Wm. 204
Mulany, Wm. 203
Mulberry, Jno. 203
Muldery, Hugh 38
Muldraugh, John 255
Mulen, Isaac (Sr.) 221
Mullens, Gabl. 169
Mullikin, Borton 221
James 221
Mullins, Wm. 264
Mumly, Jas. 204
Munday, Edmond 185
Mundle, John 102
Munford, Richard 66
Richard I. 66
Richd. 72
Rich'd 71
Thomas 71
Thomas B. 66
Monroe, Arthur 196
Munroy, Jno. 204
Munson, Allen 243
Isaac 37
Samuel 37
Samuel (Jr.) 37
Murchie, John 60
Murday, Samuel 135
Murphey, James 232
John 118
Peter 8
Murphy, Arthur 27
Cath'n 185
Daniel 179
Gabriel 221
George 27
Hays 254
James 102
John 53, 71
Ralph 203
Thomas 153
Zephamiah 117
Zepheniah 154
Murral, George 124
Murray, Benjamin 59
Charles 71
Phenie 204

Murray (cont.)
William 53, 59, 102
Murren, Michael 117
Murry, Charles 254
John 221
Murtin, Charles 204
Muse, George 8
Musker, Nowell 118
Musselman, Chrisly 37
Henry 204
Musset, John 196
Muster, John 54
Muter, George 174
Mutre, George 38
M'Waters, Benja. 19
Hugh 19
James 19
Myars, Jacob 190
Mich'l 190
Peter 190
Myers, Jacob 124, 174, 247, 254
Jos. 197
Joseph 196
Lewis 124
Michael 254
Mikle 175
Philip 136
William 254
Myles, John 179
Nagle, M. 175
Nailer, George 204
Nall, James 222
John (Jr.) 221
John (Sr.) 221
Nalle, John 255
Nanby, John 145
Nancarow, John 136, 140
Napper, John 38
Willm. 215
Nash, John 54
Marrill 112
Nation, Edward 179
George 185
Joseph 185
William 185
Wm. 175
Nave, Lanard 170
Naylor, George 124
Neal, Andrew 136
Barnard 127
Briant 214
Charles 38, 190
Geo. 127
George 38
John 38
John (Sr.) 136
Thomas 102, 136
William 54
Neald, William 233
Neale, Elias 84, 89
Nealy, Isaac 124
Neel, John 136, 221
Makall 9
Samuel 214
Spencer 221
William 9, 112, 221
Neeld, William 95
Neele, Abraham 185
Elias 185
Nathan 185
Robert 185
Neeley, Joseph 244
Neelly, Andw. 19
John 19
NeelMc, John 215
Neely, David 255

Neely (cont.)
James 28, 196, 255
John 255
Nees, Henry 226
Neff, Henry 128
Neighbours, John 255
Neil, Nico. 89
Nell, John 255
Nelson, Abraham 136
Benjamin 38
Robert 9
Saml. 204
Samuel 118
Thos. 205
William 118
Wm. 205
Nesler, Joseph 136, 140
Christo. 136
Neuman, Thos. 214
Nevell, William 38
Nevill, James 112
Neville, Samuel 263
New, James 185
Jethra 54
John 185
Newberry, Henry 54
Newboldt, Sarah 221
Newell, Samuel 261
Newkirk, Benja. 102
Elias 95, 102, 205
Peter 102
Tobias 102
Newland, Abram 170
Jacob 95
Newman, Henry 185, 233
Jacob 79, 233
John 28
John Posey 222
Simon 136, 140
Newton, Ignatius 255
John 72
John N. 255
Peter 118, 185
Tho. 196
Ney, Samuel 185
Nezbit, James 112
Nichelson, William 154
Nicholas, Abiel 255
Francis 264
George 179, 204, 205
Jno. 263
Js. 263
Stephen 264
Nichols, Wm. 107
Nicholson, Daniel 102
Richd. 107
Thomas 38
Nickels, John 194
Nickeson, John 162
Nickles, Deniel 154
Geo. 196
Joseph 196
Joshua 154
John 196
Robt. 196
Tho. 196
Valentine 221
Wm. 196
Nickolas, Thomas 95
Nickolson, James 118
Nickum, Micha. 190
Nield, Elias 244
Nilson, William 154
Nixon, Henry 38
Jonathan 102
Noah, George (Jr.) 112
George (Sr.) 112
Nobb, Widow 215

Noble, Darrell 118
David 162
Jno. 205
John 118
Mark 118
William 118
Noel, Barret 190
Basel 244
Caleb 54
Scott 190
William 179
Nokes, George 185
Nolain, Phil. 89
Noland, Abraham 142
Ephraim 102
Henry 145, 170
William 170
Nolen, Jesse 162
Noon, Jean 162
Norman, Thos. 264
William 244
Norrell, Lipscomb 175
Norris, Ezekiel 28
Henry 214
Jacob 205
Jno. 204
Phillip 214
Rodolph 214
Norriss, Ezekeial 136
Northcut, William 45
Nortin, Wm. 196
Norton, David 205
Jacob 263
Martha 263
Wm. 72
Notingham, Phillip 255
Nourse, William 179
Nowell, Drusilla 118
Garrett 118
Nowlin, Lewis 233, 255
Nuby, John 170
Nucom, William 154
Nugent, Robert 221
Willoughby 221
Null, Nicholas 136
Nut, Robert A. 72
Nutgrass, Gray 190
Nuttle, Elijah 38
Oaks, John 72
Oats, Roger 264
Obannon, James 124
Jno. 89
Oberturf, Martin 205
Ocaley, Benjamin 145
William 145
Odair, John 255
Odam, Willis 118
Odel, John 79
Oden, Thos. 205
O'Donald, John 226
O'Donally, Cornelius 9
Odon, Thos. 170
Oeve, Eleanander 162
Elizabeth 162
Isaac 162
Offill, Elzaphen 205
Jno. 205
Samuel 205
Ogdon, Benjamin 222
Ogg, Thomas 9
Oglesby, Wm. 190
OHair, Michael 196
Oiler, George 170
Okaly, Benjamin 170
Okely, Christopher 205
Edmond 205
Pleasent 205
Thos. 205

Okely (cont.)
Wm. 205
Oldham, John 72
Saml. 84, 89
William 89, 210
Wm. 84
Oldom, Jasey 170
Richd. 170
Oleor, George 145
Oliver, Andrew 154
Jno. 89
John 38, 84
Peter 45
Thomas 54
O'Neal, Bryant 244
Oneal, Hirham 136
James 255
Jonithen 136
Mitchel 136
Robert 38
William 38
Oneel, Bryant 112
Ooley, Peter 72
Ops, Jacob 89
Orchard, Alexander 170
James 72
John 170
Wm. 72, 170
Orear, William 145, 170
Organ, John 233
Ormsby, John 185
Stephen 215
W. John 215
Orol, Wm. 72
Orr, Alexander 28
Robert 28
Samuel 255
William 28
Orsburn, Usual 9
Osborn, William 103
Osbourn, Benjm. 226
Daniel 72
Ebenezer 226
Osburn, Johnathan 233
Michl. 233
Nicholas 222
Samuel 222
Wm. 205
Otto, John 79
Overall, John 222
Nathaniel 222
Thomson 222
William 222
Overlin, John 255
William 222
Overstreet, Js. 262
Overton, Richd. 175
Owans, Jeremiah 179
John 179
Thomas 179
Owefield, Elias 196
Owen, Abraham 95, 244, 248
Brackett 95, 233
Charles B. 72
David 95, 233
Jacob 103
John 95, 244
Joseph 72, 95
Peter 72
William 54, 215
Owens, Ezra 142
Ezirah 79
George 89
John 28, 264
Mordekiah 19
Ruben 79
William 28, 79, 222

Owens (cont.)
Wm. 264
Owing, John Cockey 200
Joshua 205
Owings, Ely 205
Nathan 205
Owley, Christopher 154
David 154
Henry 154
John 154
Michael 154
Peter 154
William 154
William (Jr.) 154
Ownbey, James 174
Ownby, James 190
Owsley, Anthony 118
Daniel 118
Henry 118
Thomas 154
Thomas (Jr.) 118, 154
Thomas (Sr.) 118
William 118, 196
Oxer, Michael 196
Simon 196
Oxford, Jno. 205
Samuel 136
P(?)ceafull, John 264
Packston, Samuel 9
Paddock, Ebenezar 222
Willm. 185
Paddon, Johnathan 233
Padfield, William 19
Page, James 28
Pain, Frank 215
Paine, Warfare 205
Painter, Joseph 136
Pairgmint, Sarah 215
Pairtree, John 190
Palmer, James 72
Palmore, Permenius 136
Pancake, Simon 180
Pane, Jonathan 255
Samuel 255
Panley, John 215
Pannell, Moses 96
Pannerbaker, Wiand 222
Will 222
Parepoynt, Frans. 226
Parham, Thos. 170
Paris, Ezekiel 264
Moses 162
Robert 244
Robt. 248
Parish, Benjamin 206
Benjm. 196
Parker, Alex 38
Edward 145. 205
Ezl. 206
Isaac 28
Isiah 185
James 38, 215
John 38, 222, 244
Richard 256
Richd. 215
Robert 256
Steven 9
Thomas 119, 136
Thos. 244
Parkhurst, Jno. 196
Parks, Andw. 85
Culberson 233
Joseph 103
Sam'l. 19
Soloman 264
Thomas 45
William 119, 180
Parmer, Legrand 72

Parmer (cont.)
Thomas 54
Parr, Aaron 185
Parres, Ezekiel 9
Parris, Robert 154
Parrish, Benjn. 190
Joseph 45, 206
Little Berry 72
Parsans, James 255
Parson, Jno. 205
Parsons, Ezl. 206
Partelow, Abraham 154
George 154
Parten, James 162
Partetow, Solomon 170
Pasley, James 162
Passmore, Augustean 96
Augustine 186
Paten, Elias 215
Elisha 215
Patent, Daniel 215
Pater, Elisha 215
Paterson, Joseph 38
Robert 61
Thos. 206
Paton, Daniel 193
Jacob 125, 162
Yelberton 162
Patrick, Benjn. 226
Lydia 222
Robert 244
Samuel 256
Patten, James 85
William 124
Patterson, Alexander 55
Alexr. 19
Charles 61
Chas. 87
J. 72
James 9, 103, 154
John 96, 154, 180, 244
Moses 38
Robert 38, 54
Thomas 79, 136, 154
William 79, 154
Pattie, John 38
Patton, Ebenezar 222
Ebenezer 234
James 79
Jas. 205
Jno. 206
Joseph 206
Phillip 154
Robt. 206
Samuel 180
Paul, Ann 222
Jacob 136
Jonathan 222
Michael 149, 196, 206
Paule, Andrew 233
Pawe, Jeremiah 222
Pawlin, Isaacker 179
Pawling, Henry 118
Paxton, Thomas 185
Thos. 49
Payn, Charles 255
Payne, Edward 38
Edward (Jr.) 38
Henry 38, 185
James 196
Jilson 196
Jilston 193
Jonathan 222
Joseph 107
McDaniel 54
Obediah 107
Phil. 264

Raglin, (?) 64
Ragon, Amos 127
Ragsdale, Drury 60
Railborn, Henry 196
Railbourn, David 196
    Geo. 196
Railes, Wm. 206
Railsback, John 190
Raines, Wm. 190
Rains, James 180
Raleigh, Henry 222
Raley, James 39
    John 259
Ralph, Morris 90
Ralston, Isaac 137
Ramey, Jno. 206
    Matthew 190
    Wm. 190
Ramley, John 103
Ramsey, Alex. 39
    George 39
    James 180
    Jonathan 28, 142
    Josiah 142
    Rbt. 206
    Saml. 206
    Seth 119
    Thomas 103
    Wm. 206
Randol, Henry 222
Randolph, Charles 163
    Thomas 222
Rankin, Adam 79, 180
Rankins, Adam 39
    David 39
    David (Jr.) 39
    Jeremiah 39
    Thomas 39
    William 39
Rannolds, Henry 155
Ranny, John 73
Ransdal, John 186
    Wharton 186
    Zachariah 186
Ransdall, Willi 186
Rapier, J. Richd. 215
Rardon, Ann 9
    Timothy 9
Rasco, William 20
Ratliff, John 155
    Richard 119
Rawlins, Ezekl. 85
Ray, Absolom 256
    Benjamin 256
    James 65, 186
    John 186, 256
    Joseph 256
    Nathaniel 256
    Richard 256
    William 96, 256
    Wm. 264
Rayburn, James 55
    Robert 125
    William 155
Rayly, Henry S. 256
    John 256
    John B. 256
Raymer, Abraham 129, 137,
    140
    Abraham (Sr.) 137
Razor, John 180
Reace, David 73
    Joshew 107
Read, Andrew 227
    James 264
    John 96, 264
    William 215
Reager, Burk 90

Reager (cont.)
    Jacob 90
Reake, Wiett 206
Reams, Neddy 73
    Robert 73
Reamy, Saml. 196
Rear, Alex. 39
Reas, Thomas 9
Rease, Jno. 206
Reatherford, Caty 112
    Eliz. 190
    John 112
Reaves, Nathaniel 256
    Thomas C. 73
Rector, Danl. 196
Redick, Joseph 9
    Thomas 9
Reding, Isaac 38
Redman, George 145
Redmond, Thomas 227
Redmund, John (Jr.) 222
    John (Sr.) 222
    Richard 222
    Thomas 222
Reece, David 20
    Elisha 29
    George 90
Reed, Alexander 155
    Archble 9
    Benjn. 190
    David 222
    Edward 137
    Elenander 163
    George 73, 180, 215
    Hambleton 45
    Heny. 85
    James 45, 119, 163
    Jno. (Jr.) 259
    John 96, 103, 119,
        125, 163, 190, 215,
        258, 259
    John (Jr.) 163
    John (Sr.) 163
    Joseph 29, 215
    Leonard 137
    Samuel 45
    William 9, 137
Reede, Asher 215
Reedenour, John 9
Reeder, Micajah 29
Reeds, Wm. 206
Rees, David 39
    George 85
    William 125
Reese, Charles 137
Reeves, Asea 45
    Eley 45
    James 20, 180
    John 20
    Joseph 206
    Martha 20
    Samuel 222
    William 20, 45
    William (Jr.) 20
Regar, Elizabeth 85
Reid, Alexr. 234
    Barnett 234
    Caleb 234
    David 234
    George 234
    Henry 90
    John 103
    John (Sr.) 103
    Jousha 234
    Lenard 145
    Leonard 171
    Phillip 215
    Wm. 196

Reiley, John 234
Reily, John 125
Relley, Thos. 206
Remer, David 206
Renfro, Olive 28
Renfrow, Joshua 28
Renix, James 127
    Wm. (Jr.) 128
Rennels, Richard 155
Rennex, Heney 125
    William 125
Rennicks, John 55
Rennolds, Thomas 155
Renshaw, Sam'l. 190
Rentfro, James 39, 54
Restine, John 222
Retherfor, John (Sr.)
    163
Retherford, John 125
    John (Jr.) 163
Reuby, Peter 186
Reves, Grief 145
Reyburn, Ralph 145, 206
    Wm. 206
Reynald, Andru 58
Reynalds, James 61
    Sd. 61
Reynerson, Joakin 180
    Reynes 180
Reynold, Charles 9
    Geo. 9
    John 125
    Jonah 9
Reynolds, Charles 125
    Chs. 73
    David 73
    Edward 73
    James 39
    Matthias 73
    Nathan 73
    Thomas 55
Reyny, Thomas 256
Reyon, John 55
Rhea, John 215
Rhoades, Henry 130
    John 73
Rhodes, Daniel (Sr.)
    142
    Danl. 227
    Dan'l. (Jr.) 142
    Frederick 39
    Henry 142, 143, 227
    Jacob 227
    Solomon 142
    William 85, 90
Riblen, Wm. 206
Rice, Andrew 190
    Benjamin 39
    Benjn. 190
    Bevel 45
    Charles 119
    David (Rev.) 190
    Edmund 85
    Edward 90
    Gab'l 190
    Gabriel 174
    Hierian 170
    Jas. 206
    Jesse 256
    Jessy 190
    John 137, 155, 190
    Joseph 155, 206
    Larkin 256
    Nathan 175, 190
    Nicholas 227
    Polley 190
    Richard 39
    Samuel 155

305

Rice (cont.)
  William 39, 96, 256
  William (Jr.) 96
  William B. 186
  William M. 186
Ricey, James O. 175
Richards, George 256
  John 45
  Josiah 206
  Juley 206
  Nathan 227
  Philimon 79
  Philomen 55
  Rheuben 45
  Robt. 206
  William 39, 55
  Wm. 206
Richardson, Isham 73
  James 103, 234
  Jesse 119
  Jonathan 206
  John 73, 180
  Joseph 125
  Margt. 180
  Nathl. 55
  Stepn. 85, 100
  Wm. 73, 119
Richay, Jane 175
Riche, Tabitha 73
Richerson, William 38
Richey, James 186
  John 215
  Stephen 186
  Thomas 234
  William 155, 234
Richie, James 39
  Samuel 39
  Thomas 85
Richmond, Willm. 186
Richmons, Wm. 49
Richason, Timothy 125
Rickets, Archie 39
  Peeter 215
  Robert 45
  Zachy 256
Ricketson, Timothy 215
Riddle, George 9
  Moses 125
  Wm. 206
Riden, Wm. 196
Ridge, William 256
Ridgel, Anne 112
Ridgway, Joseph 222
  Samuel 222
Ridman, George 171
Riffle, Jocab 9
Rifle, David 206
Riggs, Beththuel 163
  Bethwell 9
  Dan'l 20
  Greensberry 196
  Isaac 196
  Jas. 196
  Silace 196
  William 256
Right, (?) 147
  David 244
  Gideon 163
  John 163
  Obedick 244
  Sam'l 262
  William 125
Righthous, Thos. 49
Righthouse, Thomas 186
Rigs, John 39, 45
Riland, Nicholas 234
  Richard 222
Riney, Bazil 256

Riney (cont.)
  Clements 256
  Jonathan 256
Ringgo, Cornelius 206
  Henry 206
  Joseph 206
  Peter 206
  Saml. 206
  W. (Jr.) 206
Rip, Christopher 125
Ripidan, Frederick 180
Risley, David 96
  John 96
Ritchey, James 29
  John 29
  Robert 29
Ritchie, John 222
Rittenhouse, Jesse 90
Rizley, Daniel 186
Roach, Francis 28, 256
  Frank 174
  John 29
  Little Bery 175
  Littlebory 190
Roads, Robert 163
Rob, James 85
Robards, Edward 145
  Elisha 145
  Eliz. 190
  Frances 145
  George 190
  Jessy 190
  John 264
  Joseph 190
  Nathan 145
  Wm. S. 180
Robb, James 90
Roben, Vincent 96
Robens, Isaac 96
Roberds, John 9
  Lewis 180
  Nathan 171
  Wm. 171
Roberson, Andrew 9
  Stephen 175
Robert, John 96
  Thomas 137
  William 234, 235
  Wm. 248
Roberts, Abner 222
  Agness. 234
  Alexander 125
  Benjamin 96, 222, 234
  Edw. 196, 206
  Francess 163
  James 20, 55
  Jesse 112
  Jno. 206
  John 2, 20, 39, 55,
    60, 163, 175, 196
  Joseph 20, 241, 248
  Joshua 20
  Nathen 163
  Obediah 20, 142
  Phillip 206
  Thomas 20, 39
  Thos. 215
  Willm. 215
  William 38, 55, 96,
    222
Robertson, Abner 20
  Alexr. 186, 190
  David 163
  George 29, 215, 256
  Henry 186
  James 20, 103, 186,
    244
  James (Jr.) 163

Robertson (cont.)
  James (Sr.) 163
  Jas. 20
  Jeremiah 39
  Joel 9
  John 20, 163, 186,
    215, 222, 237
  Joseph 9, 186
  Margt. 190
  Mich 190
  Mills 55
  Owen 55
  Robert 186
  Samuel 55, 163, 256
  Sarah 190
  Steph. 190
  Thos. 163
  William 163, 186, 222
  Wm. 73
Robeson, Absolam 196
  Eleanor 73
  James 196
  John 73
Robins, Aaron 256
  James 234
  John 125, 256
  Mary 256
  Rachel 244
  Richd. 264
  Vincent 244
  Wm. 264
Robinson, Amos 28
  Ben. 206
  George 55
  Hannah 125
  Heny. 49
  Hugh 206
  James 155, 175
  Jno. 49, 206
  John 112
  Luke 125
  Mathew 155
  Oso 112
  William 125, 193
  Wm. 49, 104, 175,
    206, 262
Robson, Allen 73
Rochester, John 180, 190
Rock, James 125
  John 180
  Jno. 207
Roden, William 45
Rodes, Henry 130
  Robert 144, 145, 146
Rodger, Jean 20
Rodgers, Andrew 222
  Daniel 222
  Edwd. 20
  John 20, 180
  Larkin 20
  William 194
  William C. 28
Rodman, Hugh 234
Roe, Robert 73
Roger, Jas. 206
  Saml. 206
  Stephen 206
  Wm. 206
Rogers, Anthony 163
  Elijah 264
  George 262
  James 215
  Jno. 206
  John 103
  Joseph 207
  Mathew 215
  Mathew (Jr.) 215
  Patrick 206

Rogers, Thos. 207
  William 215
  Wm. 196
Roland, Henry 170
  Richd. 170
Rolen, Robt. 196
Rolison, Lauerance (Jr.)
  79
  Laurence (Sr.) 79
  William 79
Rolisson, Lawrence 142
Rolling, Reuben 29
Rollings, Assahel 103
Rollinger, Stephen 227
Rollins, Aaron 227, 244
  Edward 227
  James 180
  Joseph 186
Rolls, Nathaniel 206
  Marmaduke 119
Rolph, James 45
Rolston, George 45
  Wm. 73
Roman, Andrew 222
Romans, Isaac 73
  Jacob 73
Romine, Christy 234
  James 244
  John 103
Roney, Mary 190
  Roger 190
Rook, Patrick 207
Rorick, Reuben 227
Rose, Benja. 103
  Edward 222
  Henry 29
  John 99
  George 107
  Godbre 96
  Lewis 190
  Martin 96
  Matthew 96
Rosebrough, Jos. 206
  Wm. 206
Rosenborough, William
  193
Ross, Ambrus 155
  Daniel 125
  James 142, 222
  Jno. 206
  Jonathan 9
  John 45, 215, 234
  Jacob 215
  Lawrence 90
  Lazarus 222
  Shapley 90
  Thomas 155
  Zachariah 55
Rothert, (?) 129
  Otto A. 130
Rouds, David 206
Rounder, Joseph 90, 256
  Molly 256
  Peter 90
Rounsvill, Isaac 137
Rous, Wilson 45
Rousaville, Josiah 28
Rountree, Dudley 66, 73
  Turner R. 73
Rout, George 9, 256
  William 9
Routt, George 206
Row, Adam 256
  Marton 79
Rowan, Andrew 79, 103
  Willm. 215
Rowe, John 73
Rowen, Andrew 142

Rowland, David 39
  George 55
  John 39, 180
  Micajah 137
  Robert 180
Rowlet, William 55
Rowlett, Peter 73
  Phil 73
  Littleberry 73
Rowls, Hardy 119
Roxven, Francis 9
Royalty, Isham 180
  Thomas 180
Rubey, Petter 79
Ruble, Isaac 222
  Jacob 222
Ruby, Asa 215
  James 262
  Lawrence 222
  Thos. 262
Rucker, Ephriam 186
  James 38
Rud, Thomas 39
Ruddick, John 107
Rudy, William 29
Rue, Henry 206
  Matthew L. 264
  Richard 38, 244
Ruelile, Jacob 234
Rufner, Ruben 112
Ruhy, Edward 137
Runnals, Bartlett 73
  Wm. 73
Runnels, Daniels 107
Runner, Micheal 215
Rush, John 9, 171
  Peter 171
Russel, Charles 256
  Edward 155
  James 222
  John 186
  Joseph 112
Russell, James 28, 264
  John 28
  Obediah 29
  Nicholas 96
Russle, Abraham 137
  Daniel 222
  Handly 137
Russor, Joseph 45
Rutgess, Aarond 79
Ruth, John 186
Rutherford, Benjamine 137
  James 137
  Joseph 119
  Thomas 137
Rutor, Maximilly 28
Rutter, James 256
Ryan, James 264
  John 125
  Michael 222
Ryburn, John (Jr.) 79
  John (Sr.) 79
Rychey, John 215
Ryel, John 155
Ryker, Gerades 244
  John 96, 244
  Jorardus 96
  Samuel 96, 244
Ryle, Joseph 9
Ryley, John 247
Ryneason, Barnet 186
Ryon, George 206
  James 256
Sacre, James 55
Saddlers, George 29
Saduskie, Jacob 39
  James 39

Safford, Thomas 104
Safley, John 155
Saftly, Jno. 207
Sage, Alexander 186
  Henry 180
  John 180, 186
Sale, Anthy. 104
Salian, William 155
Salley, John 155
  Stephen 145, 163
Salling, Wm. 73
Sally, William 236
Salmon, John 186
  Nath'l 186
Salyears, Isaiah 107
Sammones, Nathan 49
Sammons, Jno. 49
Sample, Benjamin 39
  George 207
  John 39
  Samuel 39
Samples, David 245
  Sam'l 244
Sams, Joseph N. 29
Samuel, James 215
  Jiles 55
  Peter 55
  Reuben 55
  William 55, 56
Samuels, John 222
  Robert 223
  Willm. 215
Sandefur, Jas. 180
Sanders, Christ. 85
  Edward 73
  Henry 10
  James 40
  John 10, 39, 73
  Joseph 73
  Julias 29
  Katherine 39
  Samuel 73
  Wm. 197
  Zach. 264
Sandress, Joseph 215
Sands, James 223
  William 223
Sanduskie, (?) 260
Sandusky, Antho'y 257
  John 257
Sanford, Henry 196
  John 186
Sanklin, Andw. 207
Sanson, Elizabeth 207
Sapington, Hartly 171
Sapinton, Hanalas 145
  James 145, 171
  John 145
  John (Jr.) 145
Sapp, John 145
  John (Jr.) 171
  John (Sr.) 171
Sappington, John (Jr.) 171
  John (Sr.) 171
  Sylvens 40
Sarrency, Caml. 207
  David 207
  Jacob 207
Satterfield, James 29
Satterley, Jno. 49
  Saml. 49
Satterly, Samuel 186
Saunders. E. Jas. 90
  Frank 264
  James 56
  Jeffrey 20
  John 55, 155, 264
  Joseph 227

Saunders, (cont.)
  Martin 20
  Mary 227
  Nathaniel 55
  Nathl. (Jr.) 55
  Saml. 227
  Saml. (Jr.) 227
Savage, Nathaniel 58
Sawers, John 163
Saxton, Samuel 29
Scace, James 39
Scaggs, Jeremiah 216
  Mary 216
Scales, John 215
Scandland, Benj. 257
Scanland, Edmond 56
  Robert 55
Scantling, Alex'd 245
Scarlett, Jno. 29
Schooling, Josep. 191
Schoonover, David 227
Scipes, Joseph 236
  M. John 236
Scisney, Mary 227
Scoggins, Ethelred 20
Sconey, Henry 10
  Thomas 10
Scoonover, David 186
Scot, John 40
  Samuell 39
  William 45
Scott, Alexander 29
  Andrew 104
  Arter 237
  Arthur 222
  Benjamin 55
  Charles 39
  Daniel 216
  David 39, 171
  Elijah 40
  Elisha 40
  Gabriel 39
  George 39, 40, 191,
    257
  Hattie (Miss) 193
  Jacob 137
  James 39, 104, 175,
    191, 227, 245
  John 20, 29, 85, 91,
    113, 207, 236, 264
  Joseph 155, 175, 191
  Levi 40
  Matthew 155
  Obediah 10
  Richard 20
  Robert 39, 104
  Sam'l 20, 21, 191
  Sam'l (Jr.) 191
  Samuel 175
  Thomas 20, 39, 223
  William 32, 39, 40
  Willm. 216
  Wm. 40
Scotter, George 39
Scrogen, William 56
Scroggins, Humphrey 197
Seals, John 215
Seaman, Charles 247
  Jonah 247
Searcy, Bartlet 40
  Charles 145
  Edmond 40
  Richard 40
Seaton, Flenor 104
  Rodham 104
  William 257
Sebastian, Benjamin 104
  Samuel 236

Sebring, Rulef 180
Seburn, Jacob 171
Secret, William 45
See, Coonrod 40, 197
  George 55
  John 40, 197
Seeff, John 236
Self, John 73
  Sally 73
Selfe, John 163
Sellars, Isham 79
Seller, Mathew 29
Sellers, James 119
  John 119
  Joseph 119
  Nathaniel 119
  Thos. 107
Senate, Richard 186
Senior, Bryan 10
Sercy, Charles 171
  Lucy 171
  Richd. 171
  Richd. (Sr.) 171
Sergents, Thomas 9
Sersy, Esa 163
Servant, Wm. 128
Settle, Joseph 215
  Thomas 55
Settles, John 79
Sevan, Edward 223
  Jusrinan 223
Severns, Daniel B. 223
  John 223
Sewell, James 196
Shackelford, (?) 147
  Jno. 91
Shackleford, Sam'l 126
Shaddock, James 222
  John 186
Shadoin, John 73
Shadrock, John 119
Shafer, Jacob 215
Shain, Frank 216
  William 216
Shake, Christo. 103
  George 104
Shakelford, Zachariah
    113
Shakleford, Carter 163
Shakles, Richard 227
Shane, Edward 223
Shanklin, Richd. 104
Shanks, Zacheriah 223
Shannasa, Willm. 215
Shannen, John 137
  Joseph 137
Shannon, Alexr. 236,
    248
  Hugh 113
  John 245
  Saml. 57
  Samuel 57, 96, 235,
    236
  Thomas 126, 228, 237,
    238
  Thos. 248
  William 96
Sharp, Abraham 186
  Adam 20
  Anthony 236
  George 126
  James 10
  John 10, 104, 236,
    264
  Mat 264
  Max'l 140
  Maxwell 137
  Moses 207

Sharp (cont.)
  Richd. 10
  Robert 186
  Robt. 207
  Solomon 186
  Thomas 137
  Wm. 227, 264
Shastean, Jas. 207
  Jesson 207
Shatteen, Jesse 264
Shaver, David 236
  Peter 112
Shavers, George 207
Shaw, Bannans 227
  Jacob 236
  John 104, 215
  Matthias 180
  Samuel 40
  Thomas 180
  Thos. 112
  William 29
Shawhan, Darley 10
Shawver, Peter 207
Sheafer, Peter 180
Shearly, William 186
Shearro, Ann 191
Sheckelford, (?) 147
Sheeks, David 264
  Geo. 264
Sheels, Edward 163
Sheen, John 9
Sheets, Henry 56
  William 55
Shehan, Bostain 215
Shekelford, James (Jr.)
    155
  James (Sr.) 155
Shelby, (?) (Gov.) 76
  Amose 137
  Isaac 125
  Isaac (Gov.) 2, 130,
    249
  Moses 29, 142, 143
Shelladay, Andrew 191
  Edwd. 191
  George 191
  Hester 191
Shelley, Absalom 21
  David 20
  John 21
  Reuben 21
  William 21
Shelton, Sam'l 191
  Samuel 175
  Thos. 171
Shenault, (?) 147
  David 171
  Wm. 171
Shepard, James 137
Shephard, John 236
Shepherd, Adam 216
  Christ'r 245
  Davis 245
  James 245
  John 119
  Martha 245
  William 186
Sherald, Arrington 257
Sheriden, Martin 40,
    58
Sherrald, Elisha 257
Shesteen, Jesse 155
Shewbard, John 256
Shewmaker, John 175
  Lenard 107
Shields, James 186
  John 215, 222
  Wm. 191

Ship, Richard 257
Shipley, Edward 180
  George 180
Shipman, Nicholas 113
Shipmon, Stephen 113
Shirley, Daniel 73
  Samuel 73
Shiveley, Henry 85, 90
  Jacob 85, 90, 227
  John 45
  Michael 227
Shively, Christian 85
  Christr. 91
  Jno. 227
Shoats, Gabl. 264
Shoemaker, Even 186
  Jesse 186
  William 257
Shofner, Henry 186
Sholls, Henery 79
Shoohoon, Darley 10
  Shawhan 10
Shook, David 207
Shoptaw, Andrew 223
  John 223
  John (Sr.) 223
  William 223
Shores, Reuben 264
  Wm. 264
Short, Charles 236
  Joel 112, 155
  John 40, 55, 112
  Moses 73
  William 155, 236
Shots, John 223
Shotwell, Daniel 107
  John 45
Shouce, Christian 186
  Jacob 186
Shouse, Chas. 49
  Christian 39
  Henry 39
  Jacob 49
Shout, Edw. 207
Showd, John 137
Shrade, John 91
Shrayder, Jacob 104
Shread, John 256
  Peter 257
Shrewsberry, Drury 264
Shrout, Peter 207
Shulie, Christean 207
Shulse, Henry 207
  Joseph 207
Shumaker, Wm. 175
Shuman, George 191
Shumate, Margaret 223
  Nimd. 223
Shurd, Cornelius 10
Shurley, Catrenah 163
  Charles 163
Shurm, Nicholas 137
Shutt, Jacob 227
Shutts, Mathias 227
Shy, Jessy 191
  Robt. 191
  Sam'l 191
Sibert, Peter 257
Sibley, John 79
Sidebottom, Charles 113
  Jos. 40
  Peter 113
Sideburn, Charles 227
Sidner, Laurence 207
Siercey, John 39
Silkwood, Barzalla 222
  Berzilly 236
Sillers, Jerimiah 186

Sills, Adam 244
Silvers, John 257
  Joseph 119
  Samuel 257
Silvertooth, Mary 186
Simbrill, Francis 249,
  257, 259
Simmons, Moses 180
  Richard 223
  Thomas 186
  Thos. 49
  Verlinear 223
  William 223
Simnson, Levi 223
Simon, John 104
Simonds, John 171
Simonton, Robert 223
Simpson, Agnes 245
  Benjamin 29
  Charles 155
  Christo. 262
  George H. 74
  James 236
  Jas. 262
  Jno. 207
  John 39, 78, 79, 126,
    222, 257
  Joseph 194, 207, 245
  Joshua 264
  Js. 262
  Moses 264
  Reuben 264
  Robert 142, 186
  Sarah 125
  Soloman 245
  Thomas 29, 222, 257
  Thos. 262, 264
  William 29, 137
  Wm. 119, 262
Sims, John 73, 257
  Martin 264
Singhorse, George 207
Singleton, Benr. 223
  Christo. 191
  Christo. (Jr.) 191
  Christopher 174
  Edmond 39
  Geo. 262
  Jeconiah 39
  John 174
  Manoah 39
  Philip 245
  Rich'd 245
  Robt. 119
Sinkes, Charles 10
  Jacob 10
Sinclair, Job. 207
Sinclear, Nelly 97
Sinnett, John 40
Sire, Jno. 207
Skaggs, Archibald 227
  David 227
  Henry 227
  Henry (Jr.) 227
  James 73, 227
  Jno. 227
  John 73
  Matthew 73
  Moses 227
  Nancy 73
  Richard 73
  Sarah 73, 227
  Solomon 227
  Thos. 227
  Wm. 227
Shelton, William 180
Skidmore, John 245
  Joseph 207

Skidmore (cont.)
  Saml. 207
  Thos. 163
Skillet, John 137
Skinner, Jonathan 207
  Joseph 145, 171
Slack, Randolph 257
  Randolph (Jr.) 257
  William 257
Slade, Anne 112
  William 119
Slater, John 215
  John Toms 56
Slaton, John 223
  Tyre 155
Slaughter, (?) (Gov.) 66
  Cadw. 104
  Frank 215
  Frans. R. 104
  Frs. R. 98
  Gab'l 186, 192
  Gabriel 176, 181
  George 55, 90, 210
  James 191, 216
  Jesse 186
  John 104, 107
  Robert (Sr.) 186
  Robt. 191
  Thomas S. 65
  Thos. 215
Sleaton, James 155
Sled, Wm. 191
Sleet, John 119
Slevin, John 155
Sleyton, Jas. 264
Sloan, Alex 127
  John 126
  William 126
Slocum, John 137
Sloe, Joel 107
Slone, Bryant 223
  William 155
Sloon, John 125
Slover, John 79, 142
Slow, Thomas 45
Small, Henry 262
  John 155, 262
  Matt 262
  Thos. 262
  William 222
  Wm. 262
Smallwood, Been 207
Smart, James 29
Smelcer, Jacob 74
  Paulcer 186
Smelser, Paulser 20
Smiley, Geo. 262
  George 155, 125
  Hugh 155
  James 223
  Thos. 262
  William 222
Smilie, Robt. 245
Smith, (?) (Rev.) 145
  Aaron 190
  Adam 104, 174
  Americah 207
  Anthony 197
  Armistred 180
  Benj. 73
  Benjamin 257
  Benjamine 137
  Benj'n R. 29
  Bennet 163
  Carr 171
  Charles 216
  Christopher 174
  Daniel 74

Smith (cont.)
David 10, 21, 90,
  223, 245
Davd. 264
Dennis 223
Edward 186, 227
Edwd. 191
Elias G. 79
Elijah. 39, 107, 119
Eliz. 190
Elizabeth 40
Enoch 193, 194, 207
Gadian 107
George (Jr.) 180
George (Sr.) 180
Godfrey 180
Henry 10, 46, 73,
  103, 104, 207
Hugh 190
Jacob 97
James 10, 40, 45,
  125, 155, 171, 175,
  190, 215
James P. S. 155
Jas. 207
Jerimiah 186
Jesse 126
Jessy 190
Jinney 236
Jno. 207
Jno. (Black S.) 190
Jno. (Capt.) 190
Jno. (Colo.) 190
Jno.(Son of Jam.) 190
Jno. (Taylor) 190
John 2, 9, 20, 55,
  58, 74, 91, 104,
  125, 126, 142, 155,
  197, 216, 236, 244
John P. 2
Joseph 10, 40
Joshua 163
Laurence 216
Mary 223
Matthew 264
Michael 207
Moses 171
Nancy 74
Nattan 245
Nicholas 97, 257
Patrick 207
Peter 103, 207
Philip 104
Presley 257
Robert 29
Ruben 113
Rubin 155
Samuel 45
Scarlet 126
S. George 39
Stapton 257
Stephen 186
Susanna 245
Thomas 49, 79, 113,
  119, 126, 137, 142,
  145, 163, 186, 190,
  257
Thompson 186
Thos. 180
Walter 207
Weadon 155
William 10, 113, 125,
  126, 155, 163, 180,
  186, 223, 236, 257
Winstead 126
Wm. 10, 73, 85, 175,
  190, 197, 264
Wm. (Dect.) 190

Smith (cont.)
Zach. 190
Smither, Nicholas 245
  Robert 55
Smithers, Thos. 223
  William 55
Smithey, Thomas 40
  Wm. 39
  Wm. (Sr.) 40
Smithy, Thomas 186
Smock, Barna 180
  Charity 245
  Henry 180, 257
  Jacob 244
  John 191
Smoot, John 73
Smyth, Samuel 216
Snap, George 39
Snauter, Thos. 215
Snediger, Isaac 207
  Moses 207
Sneed, Tho. 191
  Wm. 107
Sneede, James 85
Snell, Charles 145
  John 40
Snelling, Hugh 257
  William 257
Snett, John 155
Snider, Harmon 126
  John 215
  Samuel 215
Snoddy, John 163
Snow, Elizabeth 163
Solomon, Negro 223
Somers, Elijah 207
  Jno. 207
Son, Abram 29
Sorter, Jacob 191
Sortor, Henry 180
  John 180
Soseby, Dnl. 207
  Thos. 207
South, Henry 257
  John 145, 171, 264
  Mary 145
  Saml. 171
  Weldon 171
  William 171
  Zadiciah 171
Southerland, Lanty 171
  Uriah 128
Southren, William 119
Southward, James 223
Sowder, Michl. 191
Spaldin, Benedict 257
Spalding, Thomas 186
Sparks, Daniel 104
  James 96
  Thomas 113
Sparrow, Henry 180
  Jas. B. 180
  Jas. B. (Sr.) 180
  John 180
  Mary 180
Spawlden, Wm. 40
Speaks, Rebecca 257
Spears, Jacob 126
  Moses 104
  Paul 104
  Robert 103
Speed, James 191
Spelding, C. Moses 236
Spelman, Charles 174
Spencer, Amasa 180
  George 126
  James 10
  Jesse 155

Spencer (cont.)
  John 10, 20, 236
  Michal 257
  Spear 236
  Spier 222
  Thomas 223
  Walter 236
  William 9, 10
Spilman, Benj. 191
  Charles 191
  Henry 222
Spilmon, George 171
Spimon, Thos. 180
Spingston, Peter 227
Splmon, James 180
Spoonemer, Philip 113
Sprat, William 119
Spriggs, Levin 215
Springate, William 125,
  186
Springer, Ann 257
  Benj. 10
  Edw. 40
  Isaac 257
  John 257
Springle, Henry 90
  Michl. 90
Springtow, Joseph 227
Sprinkle, George 80
  Jacob 79, 80, 130,
  142
  John 79, 80, 142
  Michal 80
  Michal (Jr.) 79
  Michal (Sr.) 79, 80
  Michael 130
  Micheal 142
  Michl. 85
Sprout, Jno. 207
Spruce, John 85
Spurgeon, Ezekiel 10
  Isaac 10
Spurlock, Jesse 44
  Wm. 107
Spurr, Jesse 186
Srawborn, Thos. 171
Sruesberry, Allen 155
Stacey, Jesse 264
  Peter 85
Stacy, Peter 91
Stafford, Benja. 104
  Henry 207
  William 194
  Wm. 207
Stagner, Barney 163
  Henry 20
Stags, Joseph 45
Stalcup, Hannah 257
Stalker, Thomas 145
Stalkup, Emmon 186
Stall, Joel 73
Stallard, Walter 223
Stallens, Samuel 215
Stamp, Frederick 137
Stamper, Joshua Cp. 145
Stan, Edward 171
Standeford, David 90
  James 104
Standerford, Geo. 10
Standiburn, Thomas 96
Standiford, David 244
  Ephraim 223
Standley, David 236
  Joseph 236
Standly, Abraham 137, 140
  David 137, 140
  John 137
  Joseph 97

Thomas (cont.)
Enos 257
Evan Jam's 227
Harding 257
Henry 180, 257
Isaac 216, 257
James 216
Jesse 164
Joel :208
John 30, 40, 107,
180, 186, 197
Joseph 186, 262
Lewis 257
Mark 86, 91
Masse 180
Owen 257
Ozwell 187
Saml. 207
Thilemon 40
William 40, 180, 237
Wm. 40
Thomkens, James 79
Thomplins, Archebal 197
Jas. 197
Thompson, Alex. 262
Alexander 126
Archibald 180
Closs 40
Closs (Jr.) 40
Daniel 74
David 180
Dvd. 208
Even 186
Francis 208
George 86, 186, 207
Henry 187
Isaac 57
James 21, 30, 119,
187, 197
Jno. 208
Joel 21
John 21, 29, 74, 180,
187, 237
Joseph 29, 79, 187,
208, 257
Js. 262
Laurence 40
Lawrance 186
Lawrence 180
Leon'd 186
Lewis 208
Nancy 57
Peter 21
Robert 30
Robert S. 66, 74
Rodger 187
Saml. 172
Samuel 57
Thos. 180, 208
Uriah 227
William 56, 57, 74,
104, 126, 180, 198,
209
Wm. 180
Thomson, Andrew 46, 183,
139
Anthony 223
Athanatius 216
James 223
John 137
Robert 216
William 208
Thorn, Daniel 79
Elizabeth 245
Peter 142
Thornbery, Tho. 191
Thornbury, Thomas 175
Thornsburg, Amos 180

Thornsburg (cont.)
Joel 180
Thornton, John 57
Wm. 207
Thos, Jno. 227
Thrailkeld, Wm. 175
Thrasher, John 10
John (Jr.) 10
Josiah 10
Stephen 10
Threldkeld, Daniel 186
John 186
Threlkeld, Thos. 175
Wm. 191
Thruston, Buck 91
Thukston, Thomas 187
Thurman, Elisha 29
Joshua 175
Philip 40
Thuston, Ezekiel 197
Tibbs, Foushee 126
Joseph 216
Tice, John 29
Tichener, Jacob 237
Tichenor, Daniel (Jr.)
223
Daniel (Sr.) 223
Joseph 223, 237
Tigart, John 137
Tilford, James 237
Tillee, James (Jr.) 138
James (Sr.) 137
John 137
Tillery, Wm. 40
Tillfair, Isaac 191
Timberlake, John 172
Richd. 172
Timmins, Tulliver 186
Timmons, George 79, 187
Sam'l 187
Stephen 186
Tinford, Wm. 264
Tingley, Benjeman 79
Tinnen, Lawrence 138
Tinsher, William 172
Tinsley, Archd. 56
James 227
Jonathan 56
Tipton, Thomas 156
Thos. 208
Wm. 191
Tirey, John 237
Tirpin, Edmond 191
Henry 191
Hugh 191
Jerimiah 191
Tho. 191
Titsworth, Ben 208
Jas. 208
Margaret 208
Titus, Joseph 164
Tivis, Robert 172
Thos. 172
Tobin, Robert 257
Tod, Joseph 172
Thos. 172
Todd, John 40, 191, 237
Levi 42
Robt. 63
Thomas 56, 126
Thomas (Judge) 174
Tolbert, Benjamin 155
Edmond 79
Isham 208
Tolin, Chas. 197
Toliver, Charles 61
Tolley, Cornelius 180
Tolly, Isham 187
John 29

Tolly (cont.)
William 180
Tomkins, Edward 119
Tommas, John 191
Tompson, Arthur 191
Closs 10
Isaac 208
Jediah 41
John 41, 191
Robert 40
Toney, Alexander 120
Jessy 191
Tope, Frederick 137
Torbet, James 40
Towns, Ola 145
Oza 145
Townsen, Joshua 172
Light 245
Oswald 172
Townsend, Samuel 216
Trabue, Daniel 40
Edward 40
Olamph 40
Tracey, Samuel 40
Nathaniel 237
Tracy, Sam'l 167
John 189
William 186
Trasey, Saml. 49
Wm. 49
Jno. 49
Trasy, Rasamus 216
Traux, William 223
Travis, Charles 41
Danniel 164
John S. 56
Trawven, William 137
Treadeway, John 197
Trent, Alexander 74
Bryan 227
Trible, Andrew 172
Trigg, William 56
Trimble, David 208
James 40
Jas. 208
John 40, 197
Robert 40
Trobridge, Job (Jr.) 74
Job (Sr.) 74
Trocksell, Adam 208
David 208
Frederic 208
Jno. 208
Tronsdel, John 40
Trotter, Charles 74
Christopher 208
David 40, 164
Dick 208
Wm. 74
Trousdail, John 164
Troutman, Jacob 223
Peter 197
Trowbridge, Sally 74
Troxall, Jacob 264
Peter 264
Xpher 264
Troxel, Fredk. 191
Truby, Christopher 113
Truet, George 46
Truman, Edward 223
Trumbow, George 120
Jacob 208
Jno. 208
Trump, Frederick 74
Trunum, Thomas 257
Trussle, Solomon 10
Tryon, Jeremiah 11
Noah 10

Vinson (cont.)
Wm. 172, 208
Vittiton, Saml. 216
Stephen 216
Vooden, Henry 11
William 11
Voorhees, Peter G. 56
Vorhis, Albert 180
Cornelius 180
Francis 181
Vories, Court 187
Jacob 187
Vorouse, Abrm. 191
Cornelius 191
James 191
Jno. (Blue) 191
Luke 191
Vowels, John 216
Vowls, Matthew 223
Waddel, Henry 156
Waddle, David 120
Wade, Dawson 265
Greenbury 258
John 258, 265
John (Jr.) 258
Joseph 91, 258, 265
Pleasant 107
Richd. 265
Wm. 265
Wadlington, James 30
John 30
Thomas 30
Thos. 21
Wagenon, John (Jr.) 79
John (Sr.) 79
Waggener, John 191
Wagle, Jacob 105
Wagoner, John 80
Waid, Dawson 209
Dawson (Jr.) 209
Jas. 209
Joseph 209
Richard 164
Waidright, (?) 104
Wakefield, Daniel 223
John 223
Matthew 224
Wakeland, Wm. C. 175
Walden, Ben 208
Williams 42
Walker, Alexander 113,
156, 181
Andrew 11
Ann 223
Asaph 146, 164
David 41
George 41
Henry 41, 216
James 146, 164, 172,
197
Jno. Jones 227
John 41, 79, 143
Js. 265
Peter 187
Philip 181, 258
Randal 41
Richard 156
Rich'd 21
Robert 181
Robt. 197
Samuel 41
Stephen 146, 164
Thomas 258
William 164, 258
Wm. 41
Walkers, Joel 107
Walkins, Saml. 91
Walkup, John 181

Wall, Francis 191
Gab'l 191
Jacob 191
Jacob (Jr.) 191
Micajah 138
Robt. 191
Wallace, Caleb 41
David 80
George 143
Jacob 22
Jas. 105
John 41, 224
Joseph 41
Michal 164
Olliver 209
Ro. 265
Timothy 21
Widow 80
William 142
Wm. 22
Wallece, Michael 156
Wallen, James 156
William 156
Waller, John 2, 11, 75,
258
Pleasant 22
Walles, Oliver 156
William 156
Wallice, David 138
Walling, George 30
Wallons, Thomas 46
Walls, Christophel 208
Thomas 11
Walter, Peter 208
Walters, Barnabas 227
Conrod 227
Jadiah 75
Jno. 227
Nancy 227
Walton, Jabe 46
Larkin C. 75
Matthew 258
Ward, Brinkly 138
Britten 138
Denny 113
George 138
James 138, 193, 197
Jas. 208
John 41, 138, 187
Joseph 41
Richard 91
Thomas 120
Washington 208
William 21, 80
Wm. 208
Wardrope, Wiatt 74
Younger 74
Ware, Dudley 156
Edmond 56
Isaac
William 56
Warfield, Caleb 75
Calep 208
Warford, David 105
John 105
Warmsley, Thos. 208
Wm. 208
Warner, George 187
Jacob 208
John 46
Warran, (?) 181
Warren, Burress 120
Charles 113
Jno. 208
John 113
Peter 49, 187
Thomas 164
Warnick, Jacob 208

Warrin, James 126
William 126
Warsing, Jacob 75
Wash, Benjamin 126
William 156
Washburn, George 237
Lewis 11, 175
Phillip 258
Washington, George (Gen.)
249
Waters, Barney 138
John 105
J. Richd. 91
Phillemon 258
Rd. Jones 86
Wathen, Jeremiah 216
Watherington, Edward 126
Wm. 126
Wathers, Benjamin 223
Watkins, Asolum 181
Benj. 265
Elijah 75
James 75, 227
John 41, 75
Saml. 227
Samuel 75, 86
Willis 156
Watley, Wiley 138
Wats, John 41
Watson, Eseriah 209
Henry 224
Jacob 209
James 224
Jas. 209
John 59
Joseph 164
Josiah 30
Richd. 216
Saml. 197, 209
Shemi 30
Thomas 59
Thos. 60
William 97, 224
Wm. 208
Watts, Gideon 174, 191
James 265
John 197
Peter 175, 191
Thomas 11
William 187
Wm. 175
Wayd, Jno. 49
Waymond, Edmund 238
Wayne, Ephriam 209
Weagel, Jacob 172
John 172
Weagle, Jacob 209
Weas, Philip 113
Weathers, James 258
John 114
Margaret 11
Weaver, Peter 11
Web, John 46
Webb, John 75
Martin 75
Sam'l 187
Webster, Richard 181
William 197
Weekley, Thomas 41
Weekly, John 258
Weeks, Benjamin 181
Weir, David 56
Weiseger, Daniel 60
Weisiger, Daniel 49
Welb, Esse 80
Welbourn, Edward 107
Welch, Edward 11
George 41

Welch (cont.)
James 128
John 46
Saml. 86
Samuel 105
Thos. 172, 209
William 11, 105
Weldon, John 21
Vachael 258
Wells, Abraham 224
David 173
Edward 224, 238
Haston 197
Henry 146
John 75, 164
John (Sr.) 197
Joseph 172
Lewis 75
Phil 75
Robert 173
Saml. 86, 91
Thomas 11, 75
William 80, 187
Wm. 75, 197
Welsh, Nicholas 227
William 224
Weltch, Thomas 146
Wentzell, Daniel 91
Danl. 86
Weond, Mathias 187
Werrell, William 11
William (Jr.) 11
West, Amose 140
Charles 41
Isaac 262
James 75
Jeremiah 181
John 61, 75, 187,
208
Johnnathan 146
Jonathan 172, 208
Joseph 164, 175
Joshua 187
Leonard 138
Nathaniel 237
Nathl. 172
Nicholas 216
Richard 129, 138, 146
Richd. 172
Solomon 262
Thomas 75, 146, 181
Thos. 172
William 187
Wm. 172
Westerfield, Jas. 181
Westerman, Charles 41
Westfall, Henry 105
Westner, George 208
Westremen, Charles 164
Wetherholt, Jacob 227
Weysiger, Daniel 56
Wharton, Richard 41
Whealdon, Joseph 156
Wheat, Coonrad 105
Jacob 105
Wheatley, Thos. 216
Wheatly, Leonard 258
Wheeler, Benjamin 97
Eschelus 156
John 30, 172
Jos. 264
Joseph 97
Wheeller, Benjemen 164
Wheldon, John 156
Wheler, Zadock 258
Whitaker, Abraham 97
Acquilla 97
Elisha 97

Whitaker (cont.)
Martha 97
Whitcliff, Charles 258
White, Agness 57
Ambrose 56
Andrew 216
Anthony Walton 62
Blecher 164
Charles 209
David 98, 172
Elizabeth 97
Equilli 165
George 120, 126, 146
Hugh 138
Jacob 11
James 41, 146, 172,
187, 224
James T. 30
Jas. 49
Jno. 209
Jno. (Jr.) 209
Jno. (Sr.) 209
John 21, 22, 41, 146,
165, 172
John (Jr.) 138, 146
Joseph 237
Peter 237
Peter (Jr.) 92
Randolph 181
Sam'l. 22
Solomon 143
William 41, 56, 105,
187, 227
Wm. 41, 49, 107
Whiteacre, Henry 41
John 41
Mark 41
Thomas 41
Whiteaker, Alex. 138
James 138
Whitecotton, James 258
Whitecraft, Jno. 208
Whitehead, Wm. 181
Whitehouse, James 181
Whiteker, Abram 237
Aqualla 237, 238
Charles 237
Elijah 237
Elisha 237
Isaac 237
Jessee 237
John 237
Levy 237
Martha 237
Whiteneck, Abraham 181
John 181
Whiteside, Thos. 181
Whitesides, Robert 156
Samuel 258
Wm. 41
Whitesitt, William 138
Whitler, John 187
Whitley, James 113
Thomas 120
William 113
Whitloe, Pleasant 172
Whitman, Chris. 75
Dan'l 75
John 75
Richd. 75
Thomas 75
William 66
Wm. 75
Whittaker, Aquilla 62
Whitting, Charles 113
Whitwell, Robert 181
Wimer, John 209
Wimset, Ignatius 216

Wiat, John 42
Wible, Adam 224
Wick, Moses 208
Wickersham, Sampson 187
Wickliffe, Martin H. 65
Widner, George 56
Wiett, Frank 208
Thos. 209
Wilburn, Thomas 156
Zacariah 165
Wilcocks, David 172
George 172
Wilcockson, Aron 49
Wilcox, Charles 142
David 194, 208
Edward 156
John 156, 248
Thomas 138
Wilcoxin, Aaron 187
Aron 41
Daniel 41
Wilder, Jos. (Jr.) 107
Jos. (Sr.) 107
Wiley, Aquilla 126
Benjamin 126, 128
Hugh G. 30
Jacob 223
James 156
John 11
Joseph 30
Luke 156
Stephen 223
William 126
William (Jr.) 156
William (Sr.) 156
Wilham, William 181
Wilhelm, Alexr. 227
Wilhoit, Nicho. 191
Wiliams, Daniel 146
Wilkason, John C. 145
Wilkerson, (?) 169
John 113
Presley 172
Wilkeson, Drury 197
Moses 197
Wilkies, Josept 46
Wilkines, John 126
Wilkins, (?) 70
John 80
Wilkinson, Benja. 105
David 208
Willcox, Ezra 216
William 216
Willer, Bottle 181
Willes, Matthew 224
Willet, George 216
James 216
Samuel 216
William 216
Willhite, John 41
Nicholas 175
William, Andrew 56
David 127, 187
Evan 91
John 237
Shadroch 146
Wright 258
Williams, Alford 41
Alfred 11
Aron 138
Arthur 30, 172
Bartholemew 30
Basil 97
Benjemen 164
Beverly 187
Caleb 165
Chas. 126
Danl. 197

Williams (cont.)
Dan'l 22
David 208
Edw. 197
Edward 146, 165, 216
Elijah 120
Ellison 11
Evan 216
Frederic 208
Hennery 164
Henry 146, 208
Isaac 146, 258
Jacob 172
James 11, 21, 41, 58,
74, 97, 138, 146,
164, 224
Jesse 30
Jessee (Jr.) 30
Jno. 208
John 11, 22, 30, 41,
46, 97, 105, 120,
138, 146, 164, 181,
197, 224
John D. 75
John (Sr.) 41
Joseph 191, 208
Laurence 46
Martin 97
Mary 41
Mason 197
Nancy W. 66
Nathaniel 208
Noah 216
Obediah 11
Parrot 224
Peter 97
Philip 146, 208
Phillip 164
Rolley 209
Rowland 138
Samuel 138, 224
Septimus 30
Shadrick 164, 172
Simpson 223
Stephen 22
Theophelas 97
Thomas 46, 138, 216,
227
Thomas (Jr.) 120
Thomas (Sr.) 120
Thos. 181, 208, 216
Vincin 156
William 146
Wm. 164, 172
Williamson, Ann 105
John 237
Richard 30
Willing, Thomas 258
Willingham, Isham 143
Thos. 143
Willis, Drury 156
Edward 187
John 127, 175, 187
Joseph 181
Joseph (Sr.) 187
Major 127
Sherrod 156
William 181
Willison, Rich'd 11
Wills, Jas. 197
Jno. 209
John 197
John S. 61
Wm. 197
Willson, Christy 75
Daniel 216
George 97
James 74, 138

Willson (cont.)
Jas. 208
Jeremiah 208
Jno. 74
John 75, 216
John (Jr.) 75
Joseph 208
Thos. 208
Uriah 208
Uriah (Sr.) 208
William 11
Willm. 216
Wm. 75, 209
Wilson, Agnis 258
Alexdr. 197
Amis 46
Andw. 197
Finelon 56
Francis 191
Geo. 86, 197
George 46, 91, 114
Hill 11
James 11, 21, 41, 164,
181, 224
Jas. 75
Jeremiah 74
John 21, 22, 56, 75,
146, 172, 181, 194,
224, 237
Joshua 56
Josiah 258
Marget 41
Mary 41
Matthew 113
Matt'w 22
Moses 197
Rich'd 21
Robert 224
Robert (Jr.) 224
Robt. 86
Sam'l 126
Samuel 46, 138, 187,
227
Thomas 41, 187
Thoms. 187
Thos. 21, 49
Uriah 194
Vance 224
Thomas 46
William 75, 224
Wm. 197
Wiltberger, J.W. 74
Winchester, Richd. 227
William 105
Winemillar, Jacob 80
Winfield, Jonah 216
Winingham, Thomas 80
Winkfield, William 138
Winkley, Joseph 86, 105
Winlock, Jo. 91
Joseph 237
Wm. 74
Winn, John 75
Winnentvandanter, (?)
238
Winningham, Isham 80
Winnint, (?) 238
Winscot, Joseph 172
Winscott, Isaac 156
Winset, Raphael 258
Stephen 258
Winsor, Christopher 11
Thomas 11
Winters, Samuel 227
Wisdom, John 164
Thomas 164
Thos. 42
Wise, Adam 224

Wise (cont.)
Amose 138
Caleb 224
Daniel 223, 238
Henry 223
Jacob 224
Richard 224
Valentine 227
Wisehart, George 224
Wiseman, John 216
Withers, John 247
Withrow, James 216
John 216
Wolf, Jacob 113
Peter 224
Wolfscail, George 164
Joseph 165
William 165
Wolfscale, Geo. 265
Wolsey, George 156
Womack, Alen 59
Allen 59
Woner, Peter 126
Woocey, John 138, 140
Wood, Abraham 46, 165
Andrew 46
David 22
Edward 113
Elijah 41
Francis 172
George T. 66, 75
G. T. 75
Henry 258
Isaac 191
Isaac W. 75
James 41
Jesse 66, 75
Jno. 208
John 46, 107, 113,
216, 237
Malcam 208
Rbt. 208
Robert 91
Thomas 41, 113
Thomas J. (Maj. Gen.)
66
William 46
William J. 74
Woodard, Michael 237
Saml. 208
Woodcock, Joseph 187
Wooden, Ruben 156
Woodin, Robert 105
Wooding, Barnet 44
Woodland, Absolam 197
Wm. 197
Woodrough, James 172
John 146, 172
David 146, 172
Woodruff, Jesse 193
Jessey 197
Woods, Adam 164
Andw. 164
Archabald 30
Archible 164
Barth'w 22
James 224
J. John 216
John 138, 164
Michael 175
Mich'l 191
Peter 164
Robert 30
Sam'l 187, 265
Sam'l (Jr.) 191
Samuel 156
William 164
Woodsides, Robert 30